Who Should Read This Book?

"Read" may be the wrong word. "Engage" would be better, because this is not so much a book as it is a classic text, and Jewish classics are not read so much as they are engaged. Included here are a classic text of Jewish prayer, spanning 2,000 years of Jewish experience with the world and with God; and ten thoughtful commentaries on that text, each one reaching back in a different way, again through 2,000 years of time. The question ought to be "Who should engage this book in personal dialogue?"

If you like to pray, or find prayer services baffling: Whether you are Orthodox, Conservative, Recontructionist, or Reform, you will find that *My People's Prayer Book* tells you what you need to know to pray.

- The Hebrew text here is the most authentic one we have, and the variations among the Jewish movements are described and explained. They are all treated as equally authentic.

- The translation is honest, altogether unique, and outfitted with notes comparing it to others' translations.

- Of special interest is a full description of the Halakhah (the "how to") of prayer and the philosophy behind it.

If you are a spiritual seeker or Jewishly curious: If you have wondered what Judaism is all about, the prayer book is the place to begin. It is the one and only book that Jews read each and every day. The commentaries explain how the prayers were born, and synopsize insights of founding Rabbis, medieval authorities, Chasidic masters, and modern theologians. The layout replicates the look of Jewish classics: a text surrounded by many marginal commentaries, allowing you to skip back and forth across centuries of insight.

If you are a teacher or a student: This is a perfect book for adult studies, or for youth groups, teenagers, and camps. Any single page provides comparative insight from the length and breadth of Jewish tradition, about the texts that have mattered most in the daily life of the Jewish people.

If you are a scholar: Though written in friendly prose, this book is composed by scholars: professors of Bible, Rabbinics, Medieval Studies, Liturgy, Theology, Linguistics, Jewish Law, Mysticism, and Modern Jewish Thought. No other work summarizes current wisdom on Jewish prayer, drawn from so many disciplines.

If you are not Jewish: You need not be Jewish to understand this book. It provides access for everyone to the Jewish wisdom tradition. It chronicles the ongoing Jewish-Christian dialogue and the roots of Christian prayer in Christianity's Jewish origins.

The *My People's Prayer Book: Traditional Prayers, Modern Commentaries* series

My People's Prayer Book

TRADITIONAL PRAYERS, MODERN COMMENTARIES

Vol. 5—*Birkhot Hashachar* (Morning Blessings)

EDITED BY RABBI LAWRENCE A. HOFFMAN

CONTRIBUTORS

MARC BRETTLER

ELLIOT N. DORFF

DAVID ELLENSON

ELLEN FRANKEL

JOEL M. HOFFMAN

LAWRENCE A. HOFFMAN

YOEL H. KAHN

LAWRENCE KUSHNER

DANIEL LANDES

NEHEMIA POLEN

Jewish Lights Publishing
Woodstock, Vermont

My People's Prayer Book: Traditional Prayers, Modern Commentaries
Vol. 5— *Birkhot Hashachar* (Morning Blessings)

© 2001 by Lawrence A. Hoffman

Library of Congress Cataloging-in-Publication Data
My people's prayer book : traditional prayers, modern commentaries / edited and with introductions by Lawrence A. Hoffman.
p.   cm.
Includes the traditional text of the siddur, English translation, and commentaries.
Contents: vol. 5. *Birkhot Hashachar* (Morning Blessings).
ISBN 1-879045-83-4 (hc)
1. Siddur. 2. Siddurim—Texts. 3. Judaism—Liturgy—Texts.
I. Hoffman, Lawrence A., 1942– . II. Siddur. English & Hebrew.
BM674.39.M96 1997
296.4'5—dc21   97-26836
                               CIP

First Edition

10 9 8 7 6 5 4 3 2 1

Manufactured in the United States of America

Published by Jewish Lights Publishing
A Division of LongHill Partners, Inc.
Sunset Farm Offices, Route 4, P.O. Box 237
Woodstock, VT 05091
Tel: (802) 457-4000   Fax: (802) 457-4004
www.jewishlights.com

Contents

CONTRIBUTORS

MARC BRETTLER . . . . *Our Biblical Heritage*

ELLIOT N. DORFF . . . . *Theological Reflections*

DAVID ELLENSON . . . . *How the Modern Prayer Book Evolved*

ELLEN FRANKEL . . . . *A Woman's Voice*

JOEL M. HOFFMAN . . . . *What the Prayers Really Say*

LAWRENCE A. HOFFMAN . . . . *History of the Liturgy*

YOEL H. KAHN . . . . *Ancient and Modern Variations*

LAWRENCE KUSHNER AND NEHEMIA POLEN . . *Chasidic and Mystical Perspectives*

DANIEL LANDES . . . . *The Halakhah of Prayer*

About My People's Prayer Book

My People's Prayer Book is designed to look like a traditional Jewish book. Ever since the dawn of modern printing, Jews have arranged their books so that instead of reading in a linear fashion from the first line of the first page to the last line of the last one, readers were encouraged to linger on a single page and to consult commentaries across the gamut of Jewish thought, all at one and the same time. Every page thus contained a cross-cut of the totality of Jewish tradition.

That intellectual leap across many minds and through the centuries was accomplished by printing a text in the middle of the page and surrounding it with commentaries. Readers could scan the first line or two of the various commentaries and then choose to continue the ones that interested them most, by turning the page— more or less the way newspaper readers get a sense of everything happening on a single day by glancing at all the headlines on page one, then following select stories as they are continued on separate pages further on.

Each new rubric (or liturgical section) is, therefore, introduced in traditional style: the Hebrew prayer with translation in the middle of the page, and the beginning lines of all the commentaries in the margins. Commentaries are continued on the next page or a few pages later (the page number is provided). Readers may dwell for a while on all the comments, deciding which ones to pursue at any given sitting. They may want to compare comments, reading first one and then another. Or having decided, after a while, that a particular commentator is of special interest, they may instinctively search out the opening lines of that commentator's work, as they appear in each introductory page, and then read them through to arrive at a summary understanding of what that particular person has to say.

Introduction to the Liturgy

The Shape of the Daily Service

Lawrence A. Hoffman

Liturgy can seem confusing, more like a shapeless mass of verbiage than a carefully constructed whole; a jumble of noise, not a symphony; a blotch of random colors, hardly a masterpiece of art. But prayer *is* an art form, and like the other arts, the first step toward appreciation is to recognize the pattern at work within it.

There are three daily services: morning *(Shacharit)*, afternoon *(Minchah)*, and evening *(Ma'ariv)* or *(Arvit)*. For convenience sake, the latter two are usually recited in tandem, one just before dark, and the other immediately after sunset. All three follow the same basic structure, but the morning service is the most complete. It is composed of seven consecutive units that build upon each other to create a definitive pattern. Though the words of each unit have been fluid for centuries, the structural integrity of the service has remained sacrosanct since the beginning.

Services are made of prayers, but not all prayers are alike. Some are biblical quotations, ranging in size from a single line to entire chapters, usually psalms. There are rabbinic citations also, chunks of Mishnah or Talmud that serve as Torah study within the service. Medieval poetry occurs here too, familiar things like *Adon Olam* or older staples (called *piyyutim*—sing., *piyyut*) marked less by rhyme and rhythm than by clever word plays and alphabetic acrostics. And there are long passages of prose, the work again of medieval spiritual masters, but couched in standard rabbinic style without regard for poetic rules.

Most of all, however, the Siddur is filled with blessings, a uniquely rabbinic vehicle for addressing God, and the primary liturgical expression of Jewish spirituality.

Blessings (known also as benedictions or, in Hebrew, *b'rakhot*—sing., *b'rakhah*) are so familiar that Jewish worshipers take them for granted. We are mostly aware of "short blessings," the one-line formulas that are customarily recited before eating, for instance, or before performing a commandment. But there are "long blessings" too, generally whole paragraphs or even sets of paragraphs on a given theme. These are best thought of as small theological essays on topics like deliverance, the sanctity of time, and the rebuilding of Jerusalem. They sometimes start with the words *Barukh atah Adonai...* ("Blessed are You, Adonai..."), and then they are easily spotted. But more frequently, they begin with no particular verbal formula and are hard to identify until their last line, which invariably does say, *Barukh atah Adonai...* ("Blessed are You, Adonai...") followed by a short synopsis of the blessing's theme ("...who sanctifies the Sabbath," "...who hears prayer," "...who redeems Israel," and so forth). This final summarizing sentence is called a *chatimah,* meaning a "seal," like the seal made from a signet ring that seals an envelope.

The bulk of the service as it was laid down in antiquity consists of strings of blessings, one after the other, or of biblical quotations bracketed by blessings that introduce and conclude them. By the tenth century, the creation of blessings had largely ceased, and eventually, Jewish law actually opposed the coining of new ones, on the grounds that post-talmudic Judaism was too spiritually unworthy to try to emulate the literary work of the giants of the Jewish past. Not all Jews agree with that assessment today, but, mostly, the traditional liturgy that forms our text here contains no blessings later than the tenth century.

One obvious exception is a blessing prescribed for women, contained in the liturgy discussed in this volume. As we shall see, the Morning Blessings contain a singular blessing by which men thank God for not making them women—an idea borrowed directly from Greco-Roman culture. By the thirteenth century (at the latest), women had developed their own alternative benedictions, one of which was passed down through the generations and is now part of the standard liturgy. Most liberal denominations have excised both of these gendered benedictions, but the traditional liturgy still contains them, and they are reproduced here. (See "On Gentiles, Slaves, and Women: The Blessings 'Who Did Not Make Me,'" pp. 17–34; and commentaries, pp. 119–142.)

The word we use to refer to all the literary units in the prayer book, without regard to whether they are blessings, psalms, poems, or something else, is "rubric." A rubric is any discrete building block of the service, sometimes a single prayer (this blessing rather than that, or this quotation, but not that poem) and sometimes a whole set of prayers that stands out in contradistinction to other sets. The Morning Blessings *(Birkhot Hashachar)* for instance (our topic here), is a large rubric, composed primarily of short blessings related to beginning the day and study passages that allow Jews to fulfill the commandment of *Talmud Torah* (Torah study) before embarking on their daily tasks. Within that very large rubric, there are smaller units that may also be called rubrics in their own right, like the blessings just mentioned for men and for women, a medieval poem *(Yigdal)* that summarizes the philosophy of Moses Maimonides (1135–1204), and the various passages from the Bible and rabbinic literature that are recited as Torah study. The word "rubric," therefore, is used loosely, as a convenient means to refer to a prayer or set of prayers, regardless of their literary form or where they come from.

At the liturgy's core are two large rubrics, to which Volumes 1 and 2 were devoted: the *Sh'ma* and Its Blessings and the *Amidah*—known also as the *T'fillah* or *Sh'moneh Esreh.* On certain days (Shabbat, holidays, Mondays, and Thursdays—market days in antiquity, when crowds were likely to gather in the cities) a third major rubric is added—the public reading of Torah (the subject of Volume 4). The *Sh'ma* and Its Blessings is essentially the Jewish creed, a statement of what Jews have traditionally affirmed about God, the cosmos, and our relationship to God and to history. The *Amidah* is largely petitionary. It is convenient to think of the *Sh'ma* as a Jewish conversation *about* God and the *Amidah* as a Jewish conversation *with* God. The Torah reading is a recapitulation of Sinai, an attempt to discover the will of God through sacred scripture and a rehearsal of our sacred story. Since the *Sh'ma* and Its Blessings begins the official service, it features a communal Call to Prayer at the beginning: our familiar *Bar'khu*. We should picture these units building upon each other in a crescendo-like manner, as follows:

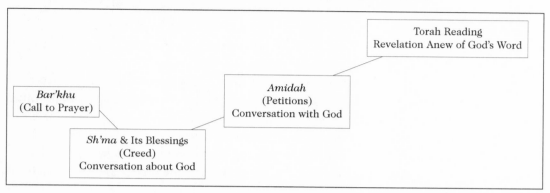

It is, however, hard for individuals who are normally distracted by everyday concerns to constitute a community given over wholeheartedly to prayer. Already in the second century, therefore, we hear of some Rabbis who assembled prior to the Call to Prayer in order to sing psalms of praise known as a *Hallel*, and even before that—at home, not the synagogue—it was customary to begin the day immediately upon awakening by reciting a series of daily blessings along with some study texts. By the ninth century, both units had become mandatory, and the early blessings and study (renamed together *Birkhot Hashachar*, that is, "Morning Blessings") had been moved from home to synagogue. The warm-up section of psalms, called *P'sukei D'zimrah*—meaning "Verses of Song"—was the subject of Volume 3, and the prior recital of daily blessings and study texts is our topic here (Volume 5). Since both of these rubrics now precede the main body of the service, gradually building up to it, the larger diagram can be charted like this:

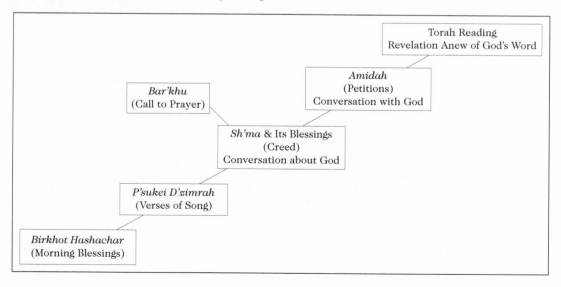

Two other expansions of this basic structure probably occurred in the first two centuries C.E., although our evidence for their being that early is less certain.

First, a Conclusion was added. It featured a final prayer called the *Kaddish,* which as yet had nothing to do with mourning, but merely closed the service, by looking ahead to the coming of God's ultimate reign of justice. Eventually, other prayers were added to the Conclusion, including *Alenu,* which had originally been composed as an introduction to the blowing of the shofar on Rosh Hashanah, but was moved here in the Middle Ages. Both the final *Kaddish* and *Alenu* will appear in a later volume of this series.

But the *Kaddish* was eventually inserted, in one form or another, throughout the service, as a form of "oral punctuation," so to speak. People had no written prayer books yet, so a "whole *Kaddish*" signaled a full stop, a half *Kaddish* indicated a minor change in rubric, and so forth. In this volume we will encounter a particularly interesting form of the *Kaddish*: the *Kaddish D'rabbanan*—literally, the "Rabbis' *Kaddish*"—which contains an explicit prayer for the well-being of students of Torah (see pp. 187–190).

Second, the Rabbis, who were keenly aware of the limits to human mortality, advised all Jews to come to terms daily with their frailty and ethical imperfection. To do so, they provided an opportunity for a silent confession following the *Amidah* but before the Torah reading. In time, this evolved into silent prayer in general, an opportunity for individuals to assemble their most private thoughts before God; and later still, sometime in the Middle Ages, it expanded on average weekdays into an entire set of supplicatory prayers called the *Tachanun* (the topic of a later volume in this series).

The daily service was thus passed down to us with shape and design. Beginning with (1) daily blessings that celebrate the new day and emphasize the study

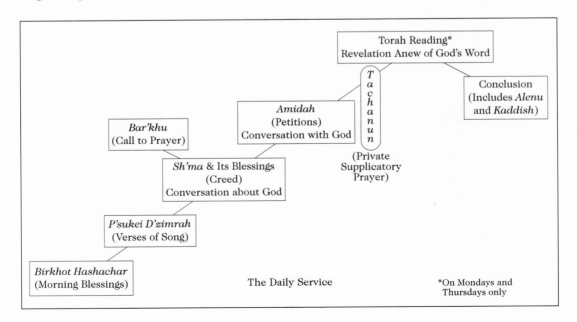

The Daily Service

of sacred texts *(Birkhot Hashachar)*, it then continues with (2) songs and psalms *(P'sukei D'zimrah)* to imbue a sense of spiritual readiness. There then follows the core of the liturgy: an official Call to Prayer *(Bar'khu)* to introduce (3) the recital of Jewish belief (the *Sh'ma* and Its Blessings) and (4) communal petitions (the *Amidah*). Individuals then pause to speak privately to God in (5) silent prayer (later expanded into the *Tachanun*), and then, on select days, they (6) read from Torah. The whole concludes with (7) a final *Kaddish* to which other prayers, most notably *Alenu,* were added later.

On Shabbat and holidays, this basic structure expands to admit special material relevant to the day in question and contracts to omit prayers that are inappropriate for the occasion. On Shabbat, for instance, the official blessings of petition in the *Amidah* are excluded, as Shabbat is felt to be so perfect in itself as to make petitioning unnecessary. But an entire service is added, a service called *Musaf* (literally, "Addition"), to correspond to the extra sacrifice that once characterized Shabbat worship in the Temple. Similarly, a prophetic reading called the *Haftarah* joins the Torah reading, and extra psalms and readings for the Sabbath are inserted here and there. The same is true for holidays when, in addition, numerous *piyyutim* are said, especially for the High Holy Days, when the sheer size of the liturgy seems to get out of hand. But even there, the basic structure remains intact, so that those who know its intrinsic shape can get beyond what looks like random verbiage to find the genius behind the liturgy's design.

Blessings and Study

The Jewish Way to Begin a Day

Lawrence A. Hoffman

HOME OR SYNAGOGUE PRAYER?

Today's synagogue is a place of prayer *(bet hat'fillah)*, of assembly *(bet hak'nesset)*, and of study *(bet hamidrash)*. But that traditional triad of functions arose much later than we imagine. Synagogues came into being in the first or second century B.C.E. as places for assembly and (to some extent) study too, but they did not emerge as places of prayer until much later.

Until the Temple was destroyed (70 C.E), Judaism's official public worship was sacrifice, not prayer. A regimen of prayer was beginning to take shape in rabbinic circles, and after the Temple's fall it matured into a full-fledged service, but the Rabbis shunned the synagogue as a gathering place for the masses, hardly where proper prayer might occur. Only by the second century C.E. (if not later still), did the Rabbis transfer their liturgy to the synagogue, and even after they did, the idea of personal prayer occurring elsewhere never died. So even after communal worship moved to the synagogue, the prayers with which Jews started their day—the Morning Blessings *(Birkhot Hashachar)*—continued at home.

In the ninth century, these early morning prayers too were moved to the synagogue. Rav Amram, the chief religious authority of Babylonia (present-day Iraq), assigned them there in a responsum to Jews in western Europe, and since that responsum—really a prayer book that we now call *Seder Rav Amram*—became authoritative for world Jewry, almost everyone has been saying *Birkhot Hashachar* publicly.

Amram's reasoning had mostly to do with ritual purity. The Morning Blessings were talmudic; they had been intended to accompany the ordinary acts of awakening (opening one's eyes, getting out of bed, and so forth). But Amram lived in a post-talmudic era, after Islam had come to power. Influenced both by rabbinic tradition itself and secondarily by the etiquette of prayer that marked the surrounding Islamic society, Amram insisted that prayer should not be said with unwashed hands. So Amram postponed the blessings to the synagogue service later in the morning, when people would have washed their hands. Later authorities added another reason for making the Morning Blessings public prayer rather than home devotion. Primarily, as

Judaism spread beyond the relative handful of Rabbis who had begun it, it became less probable that Jews would know what blessings to say. With the technology of printing still centuries away, worshipers had no prayer books that prescribed what to do. In synagogue, however, they could listen to the prayer leader read the blessings from a handwritten copy of the prayer book and answer "Amen." To this day, the Morning Blessings are generally said publicly, not in private.

People who know their origin, however, often say them at home anyway. Moses Maimonides (1135–1204) condemned Amram's decision to make them public, so Jews who say them upon awakening and only then leave for synagogue have precedent on their side. Thanks to Amram, the *Birkhot Hashachar* are printed in the traditional Siddur as part of the early morning service, but thanks to Maimonides, they are considered only quasi-public in nature (they can be said without a *minyan* for instance). Some *shul*-goers regularly arrive late, content in the knowledge that they have already said the Morning Blessings as part of waking up at home.

And prayer books vary a great deal in their organization of the material. Of the two main songs here, *Adon Olam* and *Yigdal*, the Vilna Gaon (1720–1797) seems to have said the former almost immediately upon awakening and omitted the latter altogether. The lengthy kabbalistic meditations around donning *tallit* and *t'fillin* are missing from the Spanish-Portuguese rite. Liberal services usually combine part of the *Birkhot Hashachar* with selections from the *P'sukei D'zimrah*—that is, the psalms and songs that immediately follow the Morning Blessings and directly precede the official Call to Prayer (see Volume 3, *P'sukei D'zimrah [Morning Psalms]*). What emerges is a mixture of the *Birkhot Hashachar* (Morning Blessings) and *P'sukei D'zimrah* (Morning Psalms), as a combined public warm-up before worship officially begins.

BLESSINGS AT THE CORE

Originally, then, the core of the *Birkhot Hashachar* was a set of blessings that accompanied each act of awakening. These are listed in the Talmud (primarily, Ber. 60b), and although there may once have existed more of them than we have now, the talmudic ones about which we have evidence cover such ordinary acts as opening our eyes, getting dressed, and using the bathroom. Others were equally mundane to the Rabbis who introduced them, but would seem extraordinary to us were we to invent them from scratch. Likening sleep to death, for instance, and holding that we are divinely endowed with body and soul, the Rabbis compared awakening to the final resurrection that we will enjoy after we die. So one blessing anticipates the soul's final reunification with the body after death.

Another blessing we might not come up with on our own is a blessing for Torah study. But the Rabbis thought it inconceivable to begin a day without studying Torah, so our current ritual has not one but three separate blessings over Torah (probably a list of alternatives once, but now a canonized set said together as part of waking up).

The *Birkhot Hashachar* contains passages for study too. It therefore has two core parts: blessings (including blessings for study) and portions of Torah that are studied. We will return to the study passages, but before the story gets more complicated, it is important to remember that the original form of the *Birkhot Hashachar* was simple: a set of blessings (including blessings over Torah) and study passages from Jewish texts.

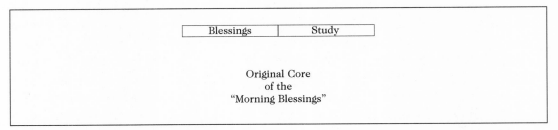

PREPARATION ADDED

This simple arrangement expanded in the Middle Ages. To begin with, a relatively lengthy preparation to the Morning Blessings emerged. By the second century C.E., blessings for putting on *tallit* and *t'fillin* were coined, and these were later outfitted with other readings, especially by kabbalists of the sixteenth century and beyond, who read esoteric significance into prayer garb. In addition, once the Morning Blessings were moved to the synagogue, *Mah Tovu* ("How wonderful are Your tents"), a prayer for entering the synagogue, was appended even prior to the prayers for *tallit* and *t'fillin*. Then two hymns were added: an anonymous poem called *Adon Olam* ("Eternal Lord") and *Yigdal* ("Exalted…be [the living God]"), a fourteenth-century philosophical composition. The Introduction to the Morning Blessings, alone, therefore, looked like this:

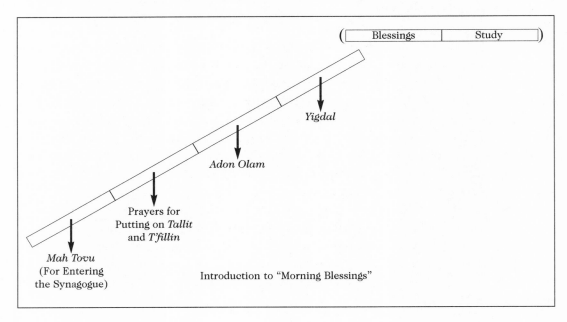

LEGAL THINKING APPLIED

The rest of the *Birkhot Hashachar* was originally just blessings followed by study passages. But various customs regarding what to say when and other issues arose because Jewish legal requirements that had evolved by the Middle Ages did not always fit the way the *Birkhot Hashachar* were being said.

One issue was what we can call the "Rule of Immediacy," which states that Blessings of Commandment are supposed to be followed immediately by the performance of the commandment over which those blessings are said. Amram *ended* his list of wake-up blessings with the blessings for study and then went immediately into study, so as to obey the rule. But others inherited a list where the study blessings were in the middle, not the end. With the study passages occurring only some time later, the Rule of Immediacy was being breached. Yet it made sense to say the study blessings early on, since the Rabbis believed in starting their day with study, not postponing it until other things had happened first.

That was the situation inherited by Jacob ben Asher, the author of the *Tur*, a particularly influential code of Jewish law dating from the fourteenth century. He said the study blessings early, immediately after the blessings for washing and using the bathroom. But the Rule of Immediacy required that he then study right away. So he divided the study passages in two: he placed a small set of sample study texts immediately afterward, then continued with the rest of the Morning Blessings (as well as other material that had built up through the centuries), and only then, at the end, did he say the remaining study texts. His order went from (1) introduction to (2) several of the blessings (ending with the study blessings) and then to (3) specially designated passages of study and the rest of the blessings. What had originally been a single set of blessings thus became two separate sets, divided by some study.

The study passages Jacob ben Asher chose came from three sources: Torah (the written Five Books of Moses), Mishnah (the earliest promulgated version of Oral Tradition—c. 200 C.E.), and Talmud (the Babylonian Talmud, or Bavli, codified sixth to seventh centuries C.E.). The reason for the mixture is given in the Talmud itself (Kid. 30a): "Rav Safra taught that people should divide their lives into thirds, a third for studying Bible, a third for studying Mishnah, and a third for studying Talmud. But how do we know how long we will live? Rav Safra meant we should divide our days." The inserted Torah study, therefore, included daily sections divided among all three: Bible, Mishnah, and Talmud.

The blessings had been carried originally in the Talmud—that is where the prayer book got them in the first place—and Jacob ben Asher's early study section from Talmud is none other than the remaining Morning Blessings. Just by listing them for recitation, our liturgical editor made them double up as a study passage in their own right, as well as a set of blessings. We have therefore labeled the inserted study section "Study and Blessings."

Originally, the rest of the study sections would have followed, but various medieval compositions were inserted first. Since the Torah blessings now led directly to the sample study texts, the Rule of Immediacy had been followed, and it didn't much matter what order the rest of the service took. Jacob ben Asher therefore prescribed (1) an Introduction; (2) Morning Blessings; and (3) Study and Blessings—all of which we have already looked at. He then continued with the rest of the order as we have it today: the medieval additions and the bulk of the study passages that had always been at the end of the service and that still remained there. Other things were added later as well. When all was said and done, the additions included (4) the *Akedah* and (5) the *Sh'ma*. All of that concluded with (6) the remaining study passages.

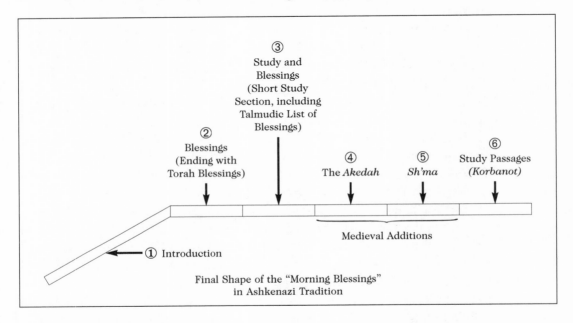

Final Shape of the "Morning Blessings"
in Ashkenazi Tradition

All three of these things—the *Akedah* (4), the *Sh'ma* (5), and the study passages (6)—share a common theme and represent yet a final motif of the *Birkhot Hashachar:* sacrifice and atonement.

SACRIFICE AND ATONEMENT

It is convenient to look first at the *Sh'ma* (5), if only because it is what the majority of us find the most familiar. The *Sh'ma* is officially prescribed only after the Call to Prayer (the *Bar'khu*) in the morning and evening services, where it is bracketed by blessings on the themes of creation, revelation, and redemption (see Volume 1, *The Sh'ma and Its Blessings*, chart, p. 20). That is why it is especially interesting to find an extra recitation here. Its accompanying blessings are omitted, and of the lengthy biblical citations that compose its entirety (Deut. 6:4–9 and 11:13–21; Num. 15:37–41), all we get here is the single most familiar line, from which it gets its name, Deuteronomy

6:4—*Sh'ma yisra'el...* ("Hear O Israel: Adonai is our God; Adonai is One"). But even the appearance of this single line is noteworthy. How do we explain it?

The usual explanation comes from the great researcher Jacob Mann, who wrote a famous article in 1925 claiming that it was inserted as a response to persecution. He theorized that the *Sh'ma* was added here (and other places as well) during times when anti-Jewish rulers forbade its recitation in the normal section of our liturgy. Rather than doing without it, Jews said it surreptitiously in places of the service where censors were unlikely to look.

Nowadays, that theory seems less credible than it did in 1925, though it is still repeated from time to time as if it were true. It has good medieval sources to back it up. The problem is that even those sources were composed many hundreds of years after the *Sh'ma* had been added to the Morning Blessings. Their authors were as perplexed as we are to find it there, especially because it had no talmudic mandate, so it looked redundant to the "real" *Sh'ma* that gets said shortly after, immediately following the *Bar'khu* (the Call to Prayer). Accepting the halakhic perspective that nothing in the service is unnecessary, they propounded the creative solution that this first and all-important line of the *Sh'ma,* the affirmation of monotheism, had been added when persecuting regimes prevented its being said in its proper place; and ever since (they imagined)—to memorialize the bad times—it had remained there. Mann just repeated these claims, when in fact they had come about not as a serious historical recollection, but as a fabricated pseudo-historical account to solve a halakhic difficulty.

Unfortunately, even though Mann's reconstruction is unlikely, we have no certain alternative that explains things any better. Another solution, from the *Tur* itself (O. Ch. 56), suggests that this extra *Sh'ma* is there to make sure that it gets recited on time. Rabbi Judah Hechasid (twelfth century) is said to have worried that he might get caught up saying so many extra morning prayers that by the time he got to the mandatory morning *Sh'ma,* it would be beyond the proper halakhic time for saying it. That too seems a somewhat strained interpretation, however, especially since no one else reports the same fear, and one wonders what all the prayers were that Judah, but no one else, was saying. In all likelihood, the extra *Sh'ma* was inherited by western Jewish communities who no longer knew why. Hating an ideological vacuum, they made up rationales for its necessity.

The possibility exists, however, that the extra *Sh'ma* is related to the overall theme of sacrifice and atonement—a twin idea that consumed the attention of Jews during the Middle Ages. We can see how that is so, if we look next at the other medieval additions: (4) the *Akedah* (the binding of Isaac—Gen. 22:1–19) and (6) the study passages that follow.

The study passages with which the Morning Blessings end are called *korbanot,* the Hebrew word for "sacrifices" (sing., *korban*). They are biblical and post-biblical descriptions of the Temple cult. In the interests of saving space and presenting a more manageable book, we have chosen not to include these passages here (in the standard Birnbaum Siddur, they take up seven Hebrew pages), especially as their highly technical nature makes them barely accessible to modern readers. Most liberal prayer books leave them out (see Ellenson, "Rabbi Ishmael says," pp. 174, 179–180). Nonetheless, the significance of these passages to the traditional Morning Blessings demands our attention, especially as that will help us understand the inclusion of the *Akedah* and, perhaps, the extra *Sh'ma* as well.

Animal sacrifice so disgusts most of us that it is very hard to appreciate how central it once was, not just for Jews but for all ancient peoples. It was as natural a response to them as uttering a profound "Thank God!" might be for us. From biblical times to the late Roman empire—well over a thousand years—sacrifice was virtually the only public worship anyone knew. It was the normal way God made pacts with people (e.g., Noah, when the flood stops; Abraham, to establish his covenant; Jacob at his dream of heavenly angels). Elijah confronts the false prophets of Baal over the issue of whose sacrifice will attract fire from heaven. Deuteronomy centralizes the cult in Jerusalem, and when the Jerusalem Temple fell, it was the absence of a place to offer sacrifices that most appalled the Israelites who survived the war. When Persia conquered Babylonia and allowed the exiles to return, a new and more glorious Temple was quickly planned, so that sacrifices might begin again.

The Torah was canonized by the same priests who rebuilt the Temple and who subsequently ruled Judean society as a theocracy. They presented biblical legislation and its complex rules of sacrifice as God-given. Most of the sacrificial instructions were placed in Leviticus, the central book of the Torah, which, by virtue of its placement, indicated just how central the sacrifices were to the entire Jewish system of legislation. In 167 B.C.E., revolt broke out under the Hasmonean family (whom we sometimes call the Maccabees, after the most famous member of the clan, Judah, nicknamed "Maccabee"). But the Hasmoneans too were priests, so the new regime was equally as sacrifice-centered as the old one had been. Until 70 C.E., when the Temple finally fell, it was sacrifice that was assumed to guarantee the public welfare of the Jewish commonwealth.

The cult went by several names, most notably *avodah*, meaning "work," as in "public work." That is where the word "liturgy" too comes from—the Greek *leitourgia*, meaning also "public work." In antiquity, virtually all peoples conceptualized sacrifice as the "work" that God wants back from us. Since sacrifice satisfies the divine will and placates divine wrath, it is the best public work imaginable, in that it guarantees communal well-being.

By emphasizing sacrifice, therefore, the Israelites, and then later (as they were renamed) the Jews, reflected the perception of all peoples in those days. Both Egypt and Sumer, the oldest civilizations whose descendants the Israelites had encountered had advanced cults with priestly castes who prepared the offerings. Canaanites, Assyrians, Babylonians, Persians, Greeks, and Romans all had sacrificial cults. They varied on what was offered and to whom, but not on the essential necessity of offering something.

How sacrifice began, as a formative chapter in human religion, we do not know, despite a dozen or so scholarly theories purporting to tell us. What we do know is that by the time Leviticus came into being (fifth century B.C.E.), the Jewish system was already in place.

Three principal types of sacrifice were available: the *olah* (burnt offering); the *minchah* (grain offering); and the *zevach sh'lamim* (a gift of greeting). The *olah*—cattle, sheep, or birds—was completely consumed on the altar; God was said to like its smell as a burnt offering. The *minchah* was composed of flour, olive oil, and incense, then prepared on a griddle or in an oven, and offered in part to God, in part to the priests for consumption. The *zevach sh'lamim* was a sacrifice of tribute to God reestablishing relationships over a sacred meal.

Beyond these main categories, there were others, particularly expiatory sacrifices (usually called *chatat* and *asham,* meaning "sin offering" and "guilt offering"). The details are endless, but what interests us is that by the time the Second Temple fell, it was the expiatory function of sacrifice that was missed most. Even sacrifices that biblical legislation had not primarily described as expiatory were remembered as such. The whole point of the Temple was seen in retrospect as the means by which society in general and individual Jews in particular had remained in God's good graces. To some extent, prayer became a substitute for the sacrificial system, since prayer was "the offering of our lips." The Talmud could not have been clearer on that score. "Demands for sacrifice are all very well and good as long the Temple stands," said the Rabbis, "but what will happen when the Temple no longer exists?" God replies, "I have already prepared for you an order of sacrifices *[korbanot]*. When you recite them before Me, I will account it as if you had actually performed the sacrifices before Me, and I will pardon you for all your sins" (Ta'an. 27b).

The word for "order" here is the Hebrew *seder*. It is a technical term akin to the Latin *ordo,* both of which mean not just "order" but "order of prayer." The Talmud itself, then, testifies to the liturgical recitation of sacrificial readings called *korbanot* as a stand-in for sacrifices that have become impossible. An order of *korbanot* was added here and there in our liturgy, most notably in the *Musaf* service, the "additional" service for Shabbat and holidays, corresponding to the additional sacrifice once offered at those times, and also in the *Birkhot Hashachar*.

So the early morning study passages are primarily sacrificial. They describe the biblical and rabbinic understanding of how animals would be prepared for slaughter and offered up on the altar that had once stood in the Temple court. Their point is neither idle recollection nor the practical retention of sacrificial knowledge in case Jews should ever rebuild the Temple. They are read because we cannot actually do what they say. They are themselves called "sacrifices" *(korbanot),* as if they were the real thing. And when we finish reading them, our liturgy concludes, "May it be your will, Adonai our God and our ancestors' God, that the Temple be quickly rebuilt in our days…. There we will serve You with reverence, as in days of old and the early years."

Modern Jews have dealt differently with these *korbanot*. Orthodox Jews say them while finding a variety of interpretations to them. Conservative Jews have variously omitted them, replaced them, or altered their intent by treating them as historical recollections only. Reform and Reconstructionist Jews generally omit them altogether. Before modern times, however, they were as unquestioned a part of the liturgy as the *Sh'ma* or the *Amidah;* the latter, in fact, included its own reference to the sacrificial system and a petition for its restoration (see Volume 2, *The Amidah,* pp. 154–157).

The centrality of atonement as a theological concept went hand in hand with a growing sense of human sinfulness. For reasons that we do not know, the first and second centuries C.E. emphasized the fact of human sin far more than earlier centuries had. Much of the New Testament is virtually given over to the theme of human sin; Josephus describes the sect of the Essenes who fled Jerusalem because it was a sinful city; the Rabbis, too, were increasingly preoccupied with the need for atonement and pardon. Each daily *Amidah* was originally followed by a confession. The introduction of *korbanot* was part and parcel of this larger issue: the religious guilt that the first and second century emphasized.

Additionally, there remained the uneasy suspicion that sacrifice, real sacrifice, was not wholly beyond us—if not our own, then sacrifice by others. In that regard, Abraham's attempt to kill Isaac at the *Akedah* received extraordinary attention.

The story of the *Akedah* is just one of many narratives in the Bible. For the Rabbis, however, it took on special significance, especially after it became the Torah reading for the second day of Rosh Hashanah. In the Land of Israel, where Rosh Hashanah was celebrated for only one day, the Torah reading was God's visit to Sarah, to proclaim her coming conception of Isaac (Genesis 21). When Babylonian Jews began keeping a second day, they chose the very next chapter, where their Torah scrolls were opened to anyway: Genesis 22. But Genesis 22 happens to be the *Akedah*. European Jews inherited the Babylonian liturgical calendar, so found themselves struggling with the *Akedah* every Rosh Hashanah.

But the haunting story of Isaac's near death was to capture European Jewish imagination from another source also. Babylonia is in the east: the Tigris-Euphrates Valley. In the west—the Christianized Roman empire, centered now in Constantinople, and extending down through the Land of Israel, which Romans called Palaestina (Palestine)—Christian commentators had explained that Isaac's ordeal prefigured Jesus' death on the cross, but was not as good, since Jesus actually died as a sacrifice, whereas Isaac was saved. Jews in second-century Palestine had responded to that claim, suggesting that Isaac too had really died and been resurrected, just as Jesus was said to be. European traditions thus inherited two streams of thought regarding the binding of Isaac: the calendrical emphasis from Babylonia and the Christian polemic from Palestine—both of which merged to become the ideological inheritance of Jews who lived at the intersection of Babylonian prayer traditions and western Christian culture. Europeans therefore had particular interest in seeing extra meaning within the story of Isaac's near death at his father's hand.

The whole point of the Christian claim was that Jesus had gone farther than Isaac. Isaac had been just a child, going along unwittingly with what Abraham did; besides, Jesus had really died for humanity's sins, whereas Isaac had been spared in the end. Rabbinic interpretation countered these Christian views by making Isaac a young man in his thirties at the time of the *Akedah*, roughly the age of Jesus when the Romans crucified him. In addition, the midrash even claimed that the angel who stayed Abraham's hand arrived too late. Isaac had really died that fateful day on Mount Moriah, but had been resurrected immediately.

Isaac thus became the quintessential Jewish human offering, a Jewish expiatory sacrifice equal to Jesus. Poetry, for the High Holy Days especially, pleaded with God to remember the sacrifice of Isaac and forgive Israel's sins. A special genre of synagogue poem called an *Akedah* elaborated endlessly on the merit that succeeding generations might enjoy because of Isaac's sacrifice. Abraham was lauded as the ideal man of faith because he had hearkened to God in so wholehearted a way.

And by the high Middle Ages, yet a further chapter in the story of Isaac's trial emerged. In 1096, the first crusaders set out from France to answer Pope Urban VI's call to take up the cross and conquer the Holy Land. While reconnoitering in the Rhineland, they unleashed their crusader zeal upon the largest and most learned Jewish population in northern Europe. Rhineland Jewry had been founded by Italian Jews who had transported Jewish culture over the Alps in the tenth century. By the eleventh century, they had founded academies that boasted scholars like Rabbenu Gershom, *M'or Hagolah* ("Light of the Diaspora"). Rashi went to school there, before returning to France. That German Jewish glory ended with the massacre of Rhineland Jewry.

Remarkably enough, German Jews now bewailed the loss of life by again, and differently, invoking Isaac. If we are to believe the poetry they wrote for the occasion, Jewish mothers and fathers actually killed their own children rather than let them fall into the hands of the Crusaders who would have tortured them, not just killed them. A prayer for every Sabbath, *Av harachamim* ("Father of mercy")—see Volume 4, *Seder K'riat Hatorah (The Torah Service)*, pp. 177–180—sought vengeance from "the one who demands blood." In addition, poets reverted to the biblical view of Isaac, who is saved from death, and pronounced their children Isaac's better, since they truly died, while Isaac had not; and more: they died as martyrs, *al kiddush hashem,* "for the sanctification of God's name." In post-Crusade Europe, dying for the sanctification of God's name was held up as an ideal. As Isaac's trial had become the Christian model for Jesus' crucifixion, so too it became the Jewish model for the medieval "Isaacs" who were slaughtered on the altars of the Crusades. As the sacrifices of old had atoned for Israel's sins, so now would their sacrificed children provide expiation.

The redemptive role of Isaac spread to Spain as well. While Rhineland Jews were being slaughtered, Spanish Jewry was enjoying a golden age with no hint whatever that it would eventually end. By the late fourteenth century, however, anti-Jewish riots broke out in Spain too, and in 1492 Spanish Jews were expelled from homes that they had occupied for centuries. They took into exile the Kabbalah, a mystical system that had been born in Provence, then matured in Spain, and was about to undergo yet a new metamorphosis in response to Spanish emigration to the Land of Israel. Much of kabbalistic thought was consumed with the need for redemption and the state of sin that was postponing it. Isaac Luria, the founder of the most famous school of sixteenth-century Kabbalah, wrote about the *Akedah,* "The earlier that one starts reading it the better, since the morning service evokes the grace of Abraham, that being the time of day when he left to tie up Isaac. That is, therefore, a good time to temper God's judgment."

We understand now why the *Akedah* entered our liturgy. It is a late medieval addition, allied in principle to the *korbanot:* a mythic recollection of Isaac's "sacrifice" in a further attempt to effect atonement.

And, in fact, the extra morning *Sh'ma* may also be about the same thing. Biblical passages rarely appear alone in our liturgy. They are introduced and concluded by rabbinic readings that give the reader cues as to how to read the passage in question. The *Sh'ma* here begins with a very telling paragraph, saying:

> We do not offer our supplications before You based on our righteousness.... But we are your people...the children of Abraham...to whom you took an oath on Mount Moriah; the descendants of Isaac, his only son, who was bound on the altar.... Therefore...we are happy, we who, early and late, by night and morning, twice a day, say: *Sh'ma yisra'el....*

Here are Abraham and Isaac again. We, as individuals, are without merit. But we inherit merit from our ancestors, including, most particularly, "Isaac...who was bound on the altar."

This is not a *recitation* of the *Sh'ma* so much as it is a *description* of ourselves reciting it. It is not an "extra" proclamation—it is no proclamation at all. It is, instead, the justification (given our sinfulness) of our saying it later (as the introductory paragraph says) "early and late, by night and morning, twice a day"—that is, after the *Bar'khu,* the "Call to Prayer." Here, the early morning liturgy just establishes our right to say the *Sh'ma* and, by extension, to stand before God in all our imperfect humanity.

The entire *Birkhot Hashachar* thus greets the new day through blessings and study of Torah, but also with *korbanot,* a recollection of the *Akedah,* and (despite our imperfections) an affirmation of our right as Jews to proclaim God one. The day is met not just physically, but metaphysically: we awaken as individuals, but quickly affirm ourselves as mattering because of our covenant with God.

On Gentiles, Slaves, and Women

The Blessings "Who Did Not Make Me"

A. HISTORICAL SURVEY

Yoel H. Kahn

The traditional prayer book includes a sequence of three blessings in which a man thanks God for not making him a gentile, a woman, or a slave. These blessings often make modern Jews uncomfortable, both for their negative formulation and because of their apparent disparagement of others. Actually, these blessings have been controversial for two thousand years! Since the instruction to recite them is included in the Babylonian Talmud, rabbinic authorities have duly insisted on doing so, but starting in the Talmud itself and continuing ever since, Jews have debated the proper formulation of the blessings, as well as who should recite them and when. The history of these blessings says a great deal about how Jews have regularly used the words of the liturgy to create and express identity.

Since the eighth century and perhaps earlier, these blessings have been a part of the daily liturgy. That is not, however, how they started. Printed editions of the Babylonian Talmud (Men. 43b) quote Rabbi Meir as saying: "A person must recite three blessings every day, and they are: [Praised are You...] who has made me an Israelite, who did not make me a woman, who did not make me an ignoramus."[1] The Talmud's version of the prayers is close but not identical to the version that we find in later prayer books. In the Talmud, the first term is phrased affirmatively, "who has made me an Israelite [yisra'el]" rather than negatively, "who has not made me a gentile." Many modern prayer books also prefer the affirmative, "made me an Israelite" (customarily translated as "made me a Jew"). Often a note points out that this substitution is consistent with the Talmud's language. When we look at manuscripts of the Talmud, however, dating from before the printing press, we find that they all say, "who did not make me a gentile." Those that have the reading "made me an Israelite" show clear evidence of having been censored and corrected. Printed editions of the Talmud do not preserve the original wording; rather (as we shall see in greater detail later) they reflect changes imposed by church censors starting in the fifteenth century.

The talmudic text contains another difference from the version that was to become standard in prayer books. Its third blessing is "who did not make me an ignoramus." But the prayer book has "who did not make me a slave." The Talmud itself explains this change with a story:

> Rav Acha bar Jacob heard his son reciting the blessing "[Praised are You...] who did not make me an ignoramus." [Rabbi Acha] said to [his son]: "Such arrogance!" [i.e., isn't that condescending?]. He [the son] responded: "What should I say instead?" [His father replied: "Say...] who has not made me a slave."

Based on this story, the sequence "gentile...woman...slave" became standard. However, not everyone accepted Rabbi Acha's change; in many early prayer book manuscripts, "not an ignoramus" appears, either instead of or in addition to "not a slave."

Where did the blessings come from in the first place? How did it all begin?

FROM SLOGAN TO PRAYER

These three blessings were not always part of the liturgy, and it is not even clear that they were meant to be. The Talmud is filled with inspirational comments, so the force of its statement may have been, "A pious person might want to do this daily" rather than any kind of fixed requirement. But where did this set of ideas originate? Traditional Jewish teaching is that they were the invention of the Rabbis or, perhaps, a rediscovered older practice going back even beyond them. The tradition cannot imagine that Jewish prayers originated from a non-Jewish source. But in fact, in this case at least, they did. Originally these were not prayers at all but slogans that affirmed the identity of the people who said them. Our Jewish text is a response to similar sayings that Jews living in late antiquity heard from their Greek neighbors.

A central tenet of ancient Greek culture was faith in the superiority of Greeks over others. Non-Hellenic groups were universally characterized as "barbarian." This assertion of Greek superiority, along with other ideas about Greek identity, were summed up in an aphorism that the fourth-century B.C.E. Greek biographer Diogenes Laertius attributed to none other than Socrates: "[Socrates] used to say there were three blessings for which he was grateful to fortune: first, that I was born a person and not a beast; next, that I was born a man and not a woman; third, a Greek and not a barbarian."

Variations on these themes are found in a variety of classical texts, almost all in the form "I am grateful for being *affirmative* and not *negative*." Jews in late antiquity were no doubt familiar with such widely circulating slogans, hearing them in the public bathhouse, the marketplace, and other shared cultural locations. The saying that Diogenes puts in the mouth of Socrates is not an exact replica of the Talmud's three blessings, but it is similar, and fortunately, the Talmud is not our only source for what rabbinic Jews were doing and saying. In the Genizah, the storeroom of the medieval Jewish community of Cairo, we have many documents with different liturgical traditions than those found in the Talmud or those that became canonized by the Geonim in the ninth and tenth centuries. In general, the Genizah preserves the liturgy and practices of the Land of Israel and its surrounding areas, including Egypt, in contrast to the Babylonian Talmud's emphasis on Babylonian practice. Of the Genizah's many different formulations of these blessings, virtually all have the form "made me *affirmative* and not *negative*." A typical example is, "Praised are You, Adonai our God, King of the universe, who made me a person and not a beast, a man and not a woman, an Israelite and not a gentile, one who circumcises [others] and [is] not uncircumcised [himself], free and not a slave."[2]

This example contains five paired identity-statements, but some scholars believe that the last two are later additions.[3] If this was the case, the "original" Palestinian Jewish formulation may have exactly mirrored the Greek version as recorded by Diogenes.

COMPARISON OF HELLENISTIC AND PALESTINIAN TEXTS

DIOGENES LAERTIUS, "THALES," I. 33	GENIZAH FRAGMENT, TS NS 121:5
[I] was grateful to fortune	Praised are You…who made me
that I was born a person and not a beast	a person and not a beast
I was born a man and not a woman	a man and not a woman
a Greek and not a barbarian.	an Israelite and not a gentile.

In contrast to the Babylonian Talmud's formulation of the blessing, which places "not a gentile" first in the sequence, the Genizah locates it third, perfectly mirroring the Greek version, "Greek and not a barbarian."[4] This suggests that the earliest Jewish form of the saying may have been a direct adaptation of the Hellenistic version. The first two oppositions ("a person and not a beast" and "a man and not a woman") made as much sense for Jews as for Greeks, so were adopted without change. The third, however ("a Greek and not a barbarian"), needed some editing. We can imagine Jews hearing this pro-Greek slogan and throwing it right back by thanking the God of Israel, instead of the Greek gods, for having made oneself a Jew, and not Greek. In late antiquity, the Hebrew word *goy* may have had the dual connotation of not just "gentile," but "Greek" in particular, so that the barb was even sharper, as both Jews and their Greek hearers knew that Jews were distinguishing themselves not just from non-Jews generally, but Greeks especially.

Further evidence for the popular familiarity of this saying comes from the New Testament. Both Jewish and Greek versions of these dichotomies circulated widely in the first century C.E., so Paul tried to trump them both by asserting the ultimate superiority of "baptism into Christ" (Gal. 3:28): "There is neither Jew nor Greek, there is neither slave nor free, there is neither male nor female; for you are all one in Christ Jesus." The respective superior positions, "Greek [and not a barbarian]" and "Jew [and not a Greek/gentile]" are themselves equally dissolved, according to Paul, in baptism. The erasure of the differences between Greek and Jew must have mattered especially in the early church, which was divided by the conflicting backgrounds of its members. The further opposition that both Greek and Jewish versions share, male versus female, is also erased here.

In the Genizah texts, we find a great variety of these blessings. Many include "who did not make me an ignoramus" but then add "who did not make me a slave." In this way, the older version was preserved along with the Talmud's instruction to correct the wording. The blessing "who made me a person and not a beast" or "who did not make me a beast," which does not appear in the Talmud at all, is also found in many Genizah fragments. These variations continued to be preserved for centuries by Jews in Italy, for instance, where the customs of the Land of Israel (as opposed to Babylonia) were taken especially seriously. Long after the language of the prayer book was largely standardized, these blessings continued to demonstrate alternative formulations. It was ultimately the printing press that was responsible for the replacement of local variations with the rabbinically approved "proper" versions.

CENSORSHIP AND RESISTANCE

In the thirteenth century, church leaders began charging that the Talmud blasphemes Christians. Among other things, they said the word *goy* meant "Christian," not just "gentile," or "non-Jew." These accusations were extended to prayer books, where (following the Greek prototype) the standard liturgy thanked God "for making me a Jew and not a *goy*." Jews responded by saying that just as the various rabbinic references to a person named "Jesus" were not the same "Jesus" as was venerated by the church, so the *goyim* mentioned in Jewish texts were not "Christians" but ancient "idolatrous peoples." This was sometimes the case, but when church authorities were not persuaded, some 12,000 Hebrew books were burned in Paris in February 1234. The word *goy* was considered suspect from that time onward. To avoid having more books burned, Jews offered to remove the objectionable passages. In 1263, Pope Clement IV permitted the return of Hebrew books to their owners following the expurgation of offensive passages and the submission of suspect volumes to an authorized reviewer. While this procedure was not formally used again until the sixteenth century, it became common by the late 1400s for Jews voluntarily to self-censor their own books as a precautionary measure.

The invention of printing magnified the church's concern with heretical works. In 1516, Pope Leo X ordered all books to be submitted to a censor prior to publication. This edict ultimately resulted in the first *Index of Forbidden Books*. The burgeoning institutionalization of control reached Hebrew books specifically under Pope Julius III (1554), and the principle that otherwise objectionable books could be printed and owned if their "obnoxious passages" had been expurgated was affirmed in the *Index of Trent* ten years later. On many occasions, the Inquisition carried out searches of synagogues and homes. But since cooperation with the Holy Office was preferable to the virtual loss of access to post-biblical Jewish literature, Jews went to great lengths to amend passages themselves and present their books for inspection.

Most extant medieval Italian prayer books, for example, were reviewed by church censors, but even before they could get their hands on them, Jewish owners had voluntarily removed the most offensive terms, at least, including "who did not make me a gentile." They explained that *goy* ("gentile") meant some long-gone historical population, not Christians. It was, therefore, usually replaced by a euphemism descriptive of antiquity: "who did not make a Kuthite," for instance, or "an Aramean"— two non-Jewish peoples identified in the Bible; or even, "not an Ishmaelite," a particularly politic choice, given the Christian hatred for Islam. Other prayer books changed the negative "who did not make me a gentile" into the affirmative "who made me an Israelite." Some manuscript copyists erased this blessing completely, usually leaving a large blank where it would normally appear.

Did Jews pray the new words in their books? Or did they recognize the euphemism and say the words that had been displaced? We do not know. Considering the experience and memories of their books being destroyed and their voluntary cooperation in the church's censorship effort, I doubt that Jews recited the prohibited words or expressions *aloud,* at least. Spies and informants were not uncommon. But many Jews deliberately indicated that something was missing from the page: they wrote vowels without consonants or (as just noted) left a space for the missing words. A more dangerous subterfuge was the substitution of a more insulting word in place of the censored one, but a word that would go uncontested because it was not in the lexicon of prohibited phrases. In the elaborately illustrated *Rothschild Machzor* (Florence, 1492), "not a gentile" is replaced by the Talmud's original recommendation "not an ignoramus." No learned Jew could have missed the intent of this emendation, but the substitution was overlooked by censors.

In an effort to assemble and preserve the Jewish literary heritage, the Jewish National and University Library in Jerusalem houses the Institute of Microfilmed Hebrew Manuscripts. The Institute has microfilms of tens of thousands of Hebrew manuscripts from libraries and collections around the world. Looking at these manuscripts, a reader can see visual evidence of the battle between Jews and their censors. Three fifteenth-century Italian prayer books, for instance, originally read, "who did not make me a gentile." Some time later, the word "gentile" was scratched out. The "corrected" version was submitted to the censor, who duly ruled the books acceptable for use. Later, in an amateur hand (quite unlike the beautiful calligraphy of the original text), someone added an obscure Hebrew expression: *balti m'daber* ("one that does not speak"). To my knowledge, this phrase does not appear anywhere else in Hebrew religious literature. What does it mean? Medieval philosophers distinguished human beings from animals on the grounds that only humans are *chai m'daber* ("a living thing that speaks"). *Balti m'daber* is a subtle euphemism for "animal" or "beast"—that is, "not yet human." These prayer books successfully replaced the objectionable "who did not make me a gentile" with a more offensive, but not self-evidently so, "who did not make me an animal."

Medieval prayer books were usually submitted to the censor and returned with objectionable phrases erased, but nothing substituted in their place. Accordingly, Jews had to insert a replacement into the erased line. In our case, the replacement was not an approved euphemism like "Kuthite," but a new phrase. It was coined to resonate with the old blessing "who did not make me a beast" but without raising red flags itself because it was not on the Christian inquisitors' index of "objectionable" Hebrew words. The time of these insertions is impossible to establish; they were, however, made by an amateur, not a professional scribe. When the Inquisition censored Hebrew prayer books by removing the blessing "who did not make me a gentile," these anonymous Jews retaliated with a new form of the ancient blessing, "who did not make me a [dumb] animal." In their minds, surely, "gentiles" were "speechless [animals]." If the intent of Christian censorship was to muzzle Jewish religious speech, this blessing became an act of spiritual resistance that reasserted the superiority of the Jew (as the real human) over gentile oppressors whose inquisitorial tactics rendered them less than human.

A BLESSING FOR WOMEN

While the controversy over the wording of "who did not make me a gentile" has largely been resolved for modern Jews, the question of whether men should say "who did not make me a woman" (and what, if anything, women should say in its place) is still being debated. Greeks and Jews of late antiquity may have disagreed on why men were superior to women, but they agreed on its truth. The Jewish rationale was that women are exempt from some *mitzvot*. Commentators therefore explained that men should express gratitude for the privilege of being able to fulfill them all.

For the first thousand years after these blessings entered Jewish tradition, there is no recorded evidence of what Jewish women said or did about this blessing. Only in the medieval code, the *Tur,* by Jacob ben Asher (Spain, 1269–c.1340), do we learn that "women customarily say, 'who made me according to His will,' and it is possible that they do this like one who accepts the justice of a bad [decree]." Later apologists defend this blessing, but Jacob ben Asher understands it simply as a statement of women's resignation to secondary status: their situation may not be desirable, but it is in accordance with God's will.

The impetus for reciting such a blessing may have come from an attempt to honor another talmudic statement, also taught in the name of Rabbi Meir, that one hundred blessings should be recited daily; given the difficulty of saying such a large number every day, women might need a blessing to take the place of the one that only men can say. Not every rabbinic authority, however, approved of adding a blessing not found in the Talmud. Some suggested that the blessing should not be recited at all. Still, under the influence of the *Shulchan Arukh,* this blessing for women prevailed (although some Orthodox authorities today do not permit its recitation using the introductory formula that invokes God's name).

Missing from the record are the voices of Jewish women. Rabbinic authorities say only that it is "the women's custom" to recite this blessing; they never say who wrote the blessing text or who instructed women to say it. A feminist historical perspective, however, suggests that women themselves initiated their own blessing. True, the content of this blessing and (especially) its interpretation by male authorities may be seen as contributing to the social and religious oppression of women, but its creation and entrance into the liturgy may also be viewed as an example of medieval Jewish women's agency and assertiveness. *In place of being rendered invisible, women inscribed themselves into the liturgy.* The widespread acknowledgment by men that women were saying this blessing indicates that Jewish women were praying in Hebrew and were invested in their own visibility in the prayer book. The evidence of Jewish women who were scribes, authors, or engaged in other literary activity in medieval and renaissance Europe demonstrates that women themselves may have authored or generated this blessing, which they then transmitted among each other.

Moreover, some women were patently not satisfied with saying "who made me according to His will." Three renaissance manuscripts, written for women in southern Europe during the fourteenth or fifteenth century, preserve more assertive alternatives. Many Jewish communities had their own vernacular, and the Jews of Provence spoke Shuadit, a Judeo-Provencal dialect. A prayer book copied as a gift for a Provencal woman contains the blessing "Praised...who made me a woman."[5] Against the rabbinic interpretation of "according to His will" as the action of one "who accepts the justice of a bad decree," this text posits being a woman as itself worthy of thanksgiving.

While we lack precise details of the date or authorship of the Shuadit prayer, we know more about the other two surviving prayer books. Both were copied by an Italian cantor and scribe, Abraham Farissol—in Ferrara, in 1478, and in Mantua, in 1480.[6] These two prayer books are even stronger: they say, "who made me a woman and not a man." While the blessing style of "made me *affirmative* and not *negative*" was still common, this blessing is beyond the pale of what any male rabbinic figure could have accepted. Close scrutiny of these manuscripts shows that one prayer book was written this way originally. The second was written first with only "made me a woman"; a later hand added "and not a man."

While only these three manuscripts have survived, other Jewish women must also have known about these proto-feminist liturgical formulations. Women had their own traditions that were not preserved in the official written record. Clearly, not all women experienced their lot as being inherently secondary, as characterized by rabbinic authors. Even this limited evidence demonstrates that the actual lives of Renaissance Jewish women are not entirely represented by the descriptions found in halakhic codes, responsa, or other sources written by rabbinic men.

The special blessing for women, then, reinforced the patriarchal religious and social order but was also a path to "resistance." Its history demonstrates how creative women inscribed themselves in the liturgy where they had previously been invisible. When later rabbinic figures overcame their initial resistance and embraced a particular version of the blessing that they could live with as well within the rabbinic world-view, some Jewish women—and their allies—composed and recited a definitive alternative. The blessing "who made me a woman and not a man" is to the original it replaces as the early "Jew and not a gentile" was to the Greek slogan it echoed. In recent years, observant women in Israel and abroad have been exploring yet other alternatives that they can use in their daily prayer.

ISRAEL AND THE NATIONS

Convinced that the relationship between the Jews and their neighbors had entered a new epoch, early modern Jews removed passages from the liturgy that they found incompatible with their new status or that they feared might be misunderstood. Modernizing Jews believed, in the words of prayer book editor Leopold Stein (1810–1882), that it was "appropriate to eliminate those passages in the prayer book that spoke of the separation between Israel and the nations. Such texts [were] inappropriate in an era of emancipation and civic equality between Jew and gentile."[7] Contrary to what we often imagine, premodern prayer books were not known for their accuracy. Establishing a precise and accurate text was the contribution of the eighteenth and nineteenth centuries. In that effort, no prayer was as disputed as "who did not make me a gentile."

As long as prayer books had no translations, the issue of "meaning" was moot. But the new practice of printing a vernacular translation on a facing page presented challenges. Some editors preserved the traditional Hebrew text while altering the meaning in the vernacular. Isaac Mannheimer, rabbi of Vienna (1793–1865), for instance, retained the Hebrew of "did not make me a gentile [goy]," but wrote "made me an Israelite" in the German. Other editors altered the Hebrew as well. Already by the late eighteenth century, the replacement of choice for "who did not make me a goy" was "who did not make me a nokhri ['foreigner' or 'stranger']."

This emendation was adopted early on by traditionalists like Isaac Satanow (1732–1804), a modern Hebrew writer and publisher in Berlin, who recommended it in his 1785 grammatical commentary on the prayer book, *V'ye'etar Yitzchak*. The most important influence, however, was Isaac Seligman Baer (1825–1897) a grammarian, scholar, and liturgist who further endorsed this change in his influential critical edition of the prayer book, *Seder Avodat Yisrael* (1863):

> This is a proper correction for even if our Rabbis of blessed memory customarily used *goy* to refer to a non-Jew...*nokhri* is the correct word if the intention is to refer to a person who is not of the seed of Israel; we are obligated to arrange our prayers in clear language.

Baer's influence, as well as the use of *nokhri* in the many editions of the traditional prayer book edited by his teacher Wolf Heidenheim (1757–1832), a definitive trendsetter in evolving Orthodox circles, made *nokhri* normative in most "modern Orthodox" and proto-Conservative prayer books. While the justification cited by Baer was entirely sincere, there was an additional goal. As Jacob Mecklenburg (the traditionalist rabbinic leader in Koenigsberg, 1785–1865) put it, making this change would silence "the mouths of our slanderers amongst the nations over this blessing."[8]

Increasingly, in the nineteenth century, evolutionary theory and colonialist politics conspired to develop the myth of European civilization having evolved from a presumed earlier state of "uncivilized savagery," still observable in faraway tribes being studied by anthropologists. Upwardly mobile Jews identified with Europe. They emphasized a common bond with their European neighbors while lauding the spiritual worthiness of the European world. Just as fifteenth-century Jews had fought to keep their books from censors, so nineteenth-century Jews identified with the Christian majority against its presumed idolatrous and uncivilized origins. The *nokhri* stood for ancient pre-Christians or far-off savages but, in either case, the antithesis of civilized Europeans.

But eliminating distinctions between Jew and non-Jew created another problem: if the distinctions between Jew and gentile were no longer meaningful, what rationale existed for separate Jewish identity? The answer seemed to be a reaffirmation of the election and special mission of Israel. Nineteenth-century non-Orthodox prayer books, therefore, simultaneously de-emphasized Jewish separateness while re-emphasizing the special calling of Israel. One result was a new blessing composed in England, in 1841, by layman D. W. Marks: "[W]ho has chosen us to be unto thee a peculiar [*sic*] people." Thirteen years later, in 1854, Reform rabbi Abraham Geiger composed his own blessing that emphasized election but, unlike Marks, made no particular mention of Israel: "Praised are You…who made me for his service." Liberals agreed about being called to a special mission, but for some, this summons was entirely individual—severed from intrinsic connection to Israel the People. The objectionable sexist blessing was easily assigned to the "Oriental" past and either overlooked or deleted. The differentiation of Jews from non-Jews was more complex. While the Orthodox were prepared to redefine the status of the non-Jew, Reformers were torn between their yearning to erase all differences and their faithfulness to a distinct Jewish mission and purpose.

AMERICA

In 1946, the American Conservative movement published its *Sabbath and Festival Prayerbook,* which reformulated the three blessings in a way that has since become common to American non-Orthodox practice: "Praised are You…who hast made me in Thine image…who hast made me free…who hast to made me an Israelite." Robert Gordis, chair of the committee that prepared the book, explained the origin of this innovation in an article written forty years after its introduction. The editorial committee had considered removing the blessings but felt that "deleting the three Preliminary Blessings was unsatisfactory because they contain significant religious values that should be preserved."

In reality, the committee was intent on maintaining not the *ideas* but the *structure* of the received liturgy—the three traditional blessings were replaced, not erased. Maintaining the structure while changing the language provides a pretense of continuity despite actual novelty. The new words provided a new idea; as Gordis himself explained, "who did not make me a slave" became "who made me free," a blessing for political freedom:

> One had only to adopt *she'asani yisra'el* ("who made me a Jew") for the first blessing and to formulate the second in the positive, *she'asani ben chorin* ("who made me free"). In its new form, the blessing "who made me free" expresses the basic conviction that freedom is not a gift conferred to human beings by governmental fiat and therefore liable to be restricted or removed at the pleasure of the ruler or the desire of the majority. Freedom is the inalienable right of every human being, deriving from his estate as a creature fashioned in the image of God.[9]

Earlier generations understood "who did not make me a slave" literally, just as ancient Greeks and rabbinic Jews surely did. Twentieth-century American Jews saw in it theological grounding for civil rights. Gordis's invocation of the language of American political discourse—later in the article he quotes the Declaration of Independence—is consistent with American Judaism's midcentury effort to fit into American civil religion.

Gordis credits Rabbi Max Gelb with proposing the replacement of "who did not make me a woman" with *she'asani b'tsalmo* ("who has made me in His image"). This change too, he acknowledges, introduces a new religious value, "the concept that each human being is endowed by God with an innate and inviolable dignity and responsibility."

While structurally, then, there is a one-to-one correspondence with the blessings they have replaced, the new blessings resonate with each other more than back to their predecessors. The rewording of the blessings—and the new meanings that their new language invokes—became customary for non-Orthodox liturgy in the latter half of the twentieth century.

◆ ◆ ◆

NOTES

1. Although the printed text attributes this passage to Rabbi Meir, the Palestinian Talmud, most manuscripts, and early sources quote this passage in the name of Rabbi Judah. Since the next comment on the Talmud is by Rabbi Meir, it is likely that at some point a copyist erroneously wrote his name in place of Rabbi Judah's. This error was recopied until it become so common that the passage is universally taught "in the name of Rabbi Meir" even if we know that originally it probably was attributed to a different tannaitic teacher.

2. Taylor-Schechter [T-S] NS 121:5. This elaborate formulation was preserved in later texts, too; see, for example, ms. HUC 442.

3. Compare Genizah fragments T-S 229:2, T-S 271:21; and Cambridge ms. Add. 3160:1: described in Jacob Mann, "Geniza Fragments of the Palestinian Order of Service," *HUCA* 2 (1925): 275. Cf. Naphtali Wieder, "On the Blessings 'Goy,' 'Eved,' 'Ishah,' 'B'hemah,' and 'Bor,'" *Sinai* 85 (1984): 108, n. 53.

4. Both Greek and Hebrew have been translated into English. Other translations of the Greek offer "dumb beast" in place of "barbarian," and in this case, "human being" and "person" are interchangeable.

5. George Jachnowitz, "…Who Made Me a Woman," *Commentary* 71:4 (April 1981): 63–64.

6. 1478 = JTSA ms. 8255; 1480 = JNUL ms. 8o5492.

7. David Ellenson, "The Mannheimer Prayerbooks and Modern Central European Communal Liturgies: A Representative Comparison of Mid-Nineteenth Century Works," in *Between Tradition and Culture: The Dialectics of Modern Jewish Religious Identity* (Atlanta: Scholars Press, 1994), p. 76.

8. Jacob Tzvi Mecklenburg, *Siddur Derekh Hachayim* (Tel Aviv: Sinai, 1954), p. 45.

9. Robert Gordis, "'In His Image': A New Blessing, an Old Truth," *Conservative Judaism* 40:1 (1987): 81–85.

On Gentiles, Slaves, and Women

The Blessings "Who Did Not Make Me"

B. HALAKHIC ANALYSIS

Daniel Landes

These three blessings of status have come under attack recently but have been equally the subject of debate for centuries. As they have survived to this day, we should keep an open mind as to what their purpose is.

They are first mentioned in the Tosefta (a parallel work to the Mishnah, containing opinions by the Tannaim (Rabbis prior to the year 200 C.E.):

> Rabbi Judah says: A person must say three blessings daily: "Blessed...who did not make me a gentile [goy]"; "Blessed...who did not make me an ignoramus [bor]"; "Blessed...who did not make me a woman [ishah]." "A gentile," because it says, "All nations are as nothing before Him; and they are counted to Him as less than nothing and vanity" (Isaiah 40:17). "An ignoramus," for an ignoramus does not fear sin. "A woman," for women are not obligated to perform commandments.[1]

The Tosefta compares the ignoramus to a king's servant who has never cooked before but who is asked to cook a dish for him. Lacking cooking skills, the servant insults the king with an unpalatable meal. Rabbenu Yonah (Spain, 1180–1263) explains, "One who never [bothered] learning Torah cannot perform God's commandments correctly." The Tosefta seems to be mandating gratitude for three privileges that accompany being commanded by Torah: the privilege of serving the true God; the privilege of having learned Torah to serve Him properly; and the privilege to observe as many commandments as possible.

The Talmud Yerushalmi (Ber. 9:1) repeats the Tosefta but without its concluding analogy. The Babylonian Talmud too (Men. 43b) takes up the issue, but in the context of a prior declaration by Rabbi Meir that "a person must say one hundred blessings every day." The discussion is worth citing:

> Rabbi Meir said: A person must say three blessings every day. These are: "Who has made me an Israelite" [i.e., in the positive, not the negative]; "Who did not make

me a woman"; "Who did not make me an ignoramus." Rav Acha bar Jacob heard his son say, "Who did not make me an ignoramus." He objected, "Such arrogance!" [i.e., isn't that condescending?]. He [the son] responded: "What should I say instead?" [His father replied: "Say] 'Who did not make me a slave.'" "But [the son demurred] a slave is the same as a woman!" [i.e., both are exempt from positive time-bound commandments]. "A slave is far inferior [*zil t'fei*]," replied the father.

The Babli thus replaces "ignoramus" with "slave," and that is what we say to this day.

Other issues emerge as well. The status blessings are contextualized alongside the unquestioned ruling that we say one hundred blessings daily. Rabbenu Gershom (*M'or Hagolah*, "Light of the Diaspora," 960–1026, Mainz) connects the two issues, stating that these three blessings are distinct from the other Morning Blessings in that (unlike normal blessings of petition or of commandment) they are not recited over something we need. Nonetheless they are part of the one hundred. This numbering is significant, for on Shabbat and holidays, where the blessings of the *Amidah* are reduced from nineteen to seven, it is difficult to reach one hundred. These three, therefore, are important just to get the tally, but also in their own right, as we shall see.

While the Babli gives no reason for the blessings, Rashi explains them in terms of the obligation to do *mitzvot*. Unlike the Tosefta and the Palestinian Talmud, which dismiss the gentile on the basis of being "nothing" in the sight of God, Rashi believes the point is that neither gentiles nor women are responsible to do all the *mitzvot*. Rashi recognizes women's halakhic responsibilities as enumerated in the Talmud, but he knows they are not obligated as fully as men and so can be bunched with gentiles, who are not obligated at all. This is crucial for Rashi's explanation of the ignoramus, who is unique in that even though he is ignorant, he is nonetheless completely commanded in *mitzvot*.

Let us return to the replacement of "ignoramus" with "slave" (see Maimonides, Laws of Acquisition, Ch. 4.). The slave referred to is the *eved k'na'ani* ("Canaanite slave"). Within a year of being acquired, a gentile slave must be sold to another gentile or must undergo conversion to the status of the *eved k'na'ani*. His conversion—through circumcision and *t'vilah*, that is, immersion in the *mikvah*—makes him Jewish but still in servitude. He is responsible for negative commandments and the perennial positive commandments, but—like women—not for time-bound positive commandments. It is precisely the slave's halakhic similarity to women that led the son in the talmudic story to question his father's substitution of "slave" for "ignoramus." If slaves are like women regarding *mitzvot* (he reasoned), isn't a separate blessing thanking God for "not making me a slave" redundant? The answer that the father gave was that fundamentally, slaves are "far inferior" to women.

We are left with several intertwined questions:

1. How is a slave "far inferior" to a woman? Is the application of *mitzvot* the defining characteristic, or are there others?

2. When they say that "a person" should say these blessings, all three rabbinic citations use the Hebrew word *adam* for "a person," and *adam* usually connotes both man and woman; what then does a woman say as her three blessings?

3. What is the significance of the fact that the Babli couches the last blessing in the positive—*she'asani yisra'el* "who made me a Jew"—instead of the negative—*shelo asani goy*, "who did not make me a gentile"?

Attending to the last question is a productive way to begin. The positive formulation is indeed a surprise, since it contradicts both the Tosefta and the Yerushalmi, which couch the blessing in the negative. Since the negative formula is the one that is found in the other two blessings, it is favored (despite the Babli) by most of the Rishonim (early halakhists, prior to the sixteenth century).[2] While we do find "who has made me an Israelite," *(she'asani yisra'el)* in the Rishonim (e.g., the printed Rosh to Ber. 62b), this has been seen by some scholars as elicited by Christian censors seeking to purge derogatory references about gentiles. By the sixteenth century, the perception that the positive statement was such a forced response prompted opposition to it by the Bach (*Bayit Chadash* on the *Tur*, Rabbi Joel Sirkes, 1561–1640, Poland). The Bach saw a further difficulty in the fact that "who has made me an Israelite" already implicitly includes the categories of "who has made me free" and "who has made me a man." Saying it would thus render the subsequent blessings redundant or, halakhically speaking, "blessings said in vain." And we cannot consolidate the three into one, because "it is our intention not to cut short but to expand our gratitude and to accompany every act of loving-kindness with its own blessing." The Bach therefore insisted on the negative formulation, according to the order of "gentile," "slave," and then "woman," so as to proceed higher and higher in status and thereby be certain that the status of each is not included in the prior blessing. The gentile is not commanded at all; the slave does not enjoy freedom of choice to assume new blessings; women may choose to perform most of the commandments.[3]

Is "who has made me an Israelite" then finished as a halakhic possibility? It would be better to say it is down, but not quite out, for a few reasons. First, a number of versions still have "woman" before "slave,"[4] in contrast to the Bach's precedence. Moreover, the final answer in the Babli to the question of whether the slave is the same as a woman was that the slave is *zil t'fei*. Earlier, we translated that as "far inferior." But Rabbenu Gershom derives the word *zil* from the root meaning "to go." He understands the response not at all as being "the slave is far inferior." Rather, the Talmud means that even though the slave technically shares the obligations of a woman, nonetheless, "go [and make] more [blessings]." Rashi too had offered this as a possible explanation. Evidently, then, the Bach's concern with making more unnecessary—and therefore forbidden—blessings is not universally held. We can add to this that "who has made me an Israelite" has been—and still is—used in various communities. In fact, in his commentary on the *Shulchan Arukh*, even the Gra (Elijah of Vilna, 1720–1797), who is so careful regarding wording, states that "who has made me an Israelite" is found in his manuscripts, with the evident conclusion that it may be employed. The halakhic upshot is that while "who did not make me a gentile" is the overwhelming preference, "who has made me an Israelite" enjoys both halakhic arguments and historical precedent.

We should now direct our attention to "who did not make me a woman." As we saw, the Tosefta and the Yerushalmi agreed that the reason for the blessing is that "women are not obligated in *mitzvot*." The Meiri (Menachem b. Solomon, 1249–1314, Perpignan, France) reads the Tosefta as "a woman is not obligated in *all mitzvot*"— meaning she is exempt from time-bound positive commandments only. The Raviah (Eliezer ben Joel Halevi, c. 1140–1225, Germany) reads the Yerushalmi in a similar way. The crucial word is "obligated." But what does "obligated" mean?

Halakhically, "obligation" *(chiyuv)* refers to the absolute requirement that a person perform a *mitzvah* (an act). But those who are not obligated nevertheless perform a *mitzvah* if they choose to do the act in question. The Halakhah shows an ever-increasing awareness of women's ability to decide voluntarily to perform commandments, for which they are not in advance obligated, but which, upon their doing them, indeed become a *mitzvah* for them. The slave, who is not free, cannot (by definition) decide voluntarily to adopt commandments. To be sure, other issues of status distinguish women from slaves. A slave, for instance, is said to lack *z'khut avot* ("ancestral merit"). Slaves are not fully trusted, since "one who increases slaves increases theft" (Avot 2:7). Further, unlike Jewish women, a Canaanite slave (the original referent of the term) is "still close to being a gentile" (Abudraham, p. 41). But the compelling difference is that while a slave "has *some* involvement in *mitzvot*," a woman is simply not automatically "obligated in *all mitzvot*," (P'risha, R. Joshua Hakohen Falk, 1555–1614, Poland). Still, she can enter the *mitzvah* framework as she chooses *mitzvot* and performs them.

What blessing does a woman make, then? The assumption of the codifiers is that she says "who did not make me a gentile" and "who did not make me a slave," though possibly adjusting the Hebrew for gender *(goyah* instead of *goy* and *shifchah* ["maidservant"] instead of *eved)*. Others rule that the liturgy is generic, and therefore no such gender adjustment is required.

In any event, women obviously do not say "who did not make me a woman" and, according to some authorities, should not even answer "Amen" if they hear a man recite that. But it will be recalled that the talmudic enactment of these blessings says *adam* ("a person") should say them (all three blessings), and *adam* ("person") is not gender-specific. So women ought to have *some* blessing to say as their alternative to "who did not make me a woman." Abudraham (thirteenth- to fourteenth-century Spain) therefore reports, "In place of 'who did not make me a woman,' women have been accustomed to say 'who has made me according to His will.'" We do not know who initiated this blessing, but regardless of its origin, it is evident that women in many communities chose to recite it. That means, halakhically, that it is understood to have emerged voluntarily from women.

While many authorities dismiss it because they deny the validity of blessings that are not written in the Talmud,[5] it has been accepted—if not endorsed—by most legal decisors, evidently out of the principle of *minhag yisra'el din* ("the custom of Israel is law"). Indeed, even the Gra (Elijah of Vilna, 1720–1797), who normally rejects such blessings even if they are customary, finds a prophetic source for this one in Jonah 1:14: "For You, O Lord, by Your will have brought this about"; this (he says, in his commentary on Jonah) is a *remez* (a "hint") of the validity of the woman's blessing "who has made me according to His will."

But what does the blessing mean? Before turning directly to it, Abudraham notes that women "have the fear of their husbands upon them and cannot fulfill even those commandments that they are commanded to do." This is why he characterizes the woman's blessing as a form of *tsiduk hadin* ("justification of judgment"), a term otherwise reserved for the acceptance we are to have for tragedy. He sees the blessing, apparently, as a woman's justification of such a judgment in her life.

Tsiduk hadin is a paradoxical concept, in that it assumes something terrible has occurred, but at the same time the victim justifies God's judgment. The bad is not denied, but it is not ascribed *negatively* to God. For instance, death is a bad thing. But the funeral liturgy (called *Tsiduk Hadin*) affirms, "The actions of the Rock [God] are perfect." One need not accept death without the normal outcry of dismay and sadness; but one accepts God as the perfect source for everything, including death. We can assume that Abudraham sees the same theological message in the blessing by women. The fact that women do not share, a priori, in the totality of *mitzvot* and that family responsibilities may prove so overwhelming that they cannot fulfill even those *mitzvot* that they are commanded to do, is a bad situation. One might even argue that we should struggle to change it. But it should not on that account be denied. "Who has made me according to His will" acknowledges the situation while accepting it as part of the perfect God's plan.

Abudraham's interpretation is radical. The *Tur* (fourteenth century) repeats the same explanation, in effect, but accepts it only provisionally, as an interpretation that is "possible" *(efshar)*. And there are other interpretations too: that even though women are exempt from some nine (or so) positive time-bound *mitzvot*, the ones for which they are responsible (including ones that are special [although not limited] to them) are quite sufficient. If so, no "justification of judgment" need occur, in which case the woman's blessing is positively intended in every regard. *Turei Zahav* (or the Taz; David ben Samuel Halevi, seventeenth-century commentator on the *Shulchan Arukh*) interprets "who did not make me a woman" to mean that a man feels no deprivation at lacking the *ma'alah* ("high quality") that a woman possesses; "who made me according to His image" then becomes a full-hearted thanksgiving for a quality given to women but not to men.

But there is a radical interpretation on the other side. Rabbi Aaron Soloveitchik (contemporary Orthodox authority and Rosh Yeshiva of Yeshivas Brisk, Chicago, and R.I.E.T.S. of Yeshiva University, New York) is astonished by "crass" attacks on both blessings by those who falsely see "who has made me according to His will" as indicating that it would be better not to have been created a woman. According to Reb Aaron (as he is affectionately known in the Orthodox world), the woman's blessing implies the highest level of being, in that women are created by nature to be "as the will" of the Holy One. The man's blessing implies "that He did not make me [entirely] in accordance with His will." It is the blessing by men, not by women, that amounts to a *tsiduk hadin*. He, not she, says in effect, *Barukh dayan ha'emet* ("Blessed is the true judge"), the classic "justification of judgment" that is said on hearing bad news, such as the death of a relative or teacher. Reb Aaron explains:

> The Holy One created man and woman with different natures. Man is created with an attack personality. From his origins, he is inclined by his anger and inner rage to bring his plans to fruition through wrath. Therefore, God increased for him positive time-bound *mitzvot*, so as to temper these inclinations and to sublimate them into good.

> But God created woman with inclinations toward doing good and feeling empathy. Thus her unique organ is the womb—*rechem*—Hebrew also for "empathy." This is God's nature also. And since a woman's inclinations resemble God's, only she can say, "Who made me according to His will" as she possesses an attribute which reflects God's.... A man who says "Who did not make me a woman," must realize that through service [to God], he must attain the loving-kindness, empathy, and good deeds that are already part of woman's nature.[6]

We can now review the halakhic options for those who approach these blessings with intent to say them, albeit with struggle.

1. "Who did not make me a gentile": Though a radical solution, this might be replaced with "who has made me an Israelite." That formulation raises the Bach's problem that it would prevent the recitation of the other two blessings that are contained implicitly within it and would result in not fulfilling the rabbinic edict to say all three blessings of status (and also, possibly, falling short of the mandated one hundred blessings a day). Nonetheless, if one argues that order and wording do not matter, because *zil t'fei* means "Go on and make as many blessings as possible," then the other two blessings could be said without concern.

   Most authorities, however, prefer the original wording. People who want to retain the traditional negative formulation but object to the use of "gentile" *(goy)* might (according to some) instead say "stranger" *(nokhri)* or "idolator" *(akum—* because of the Rabbis' universal opposition to idolatry).[7] Both formulae occur in various rites (see *Mishnah B'rurah* 47); one's intent, however, upon reciting these blessings, must take into account the dominant explanation: performance of *mitzvot*. Even gentiles are covenanted by the seven Noahide laws of fundamental morality and belief in God, for instance.

2. "Who did not make me a slave": Nowadays, when slavery is only a theoretical construct, this blessing should cause no problem to anyone. But here too, one should say the blessing with the issue of *mitzvot* in mind, remembering, that is, that a Canaanite slave (to whom the blessing properly refers) had *mitzvot*.

3. "Who did not make me a woman": Women are fully covenanted, albeit with fewer obligatory positive commandments. *Machatzit Hashekel* to the *Shulchan Arukh* (by Samuel Halevi Kellin, eighteenth century) considers the possibility of saying *she'asani ish* ("who has made me a man"). The only liability here is that it differs in form from the other two blessings, which are in the negative. But given the argument for the first blessing being recited positively, it would seem that the third one could theoretically be reformulated that way, even though, unlike "who did not make me a gentile," there is no textual precedent. Here too, the reality of a woman having some, even if not all, *mitzvot* should be kept in mind.

4. "Who made me according to His will": If these blessings are said aloud in the synagogue, as opposed to privately at home, then "who made me according to His will" should be recited audibly as a positive affirmation of women's nature (following the Taz).[8] Thus we did in an Orthodox synagogue I led, and it was warmly approved by many visiting scholars. Finally, one has the option of teaching the thought behind these twin blessings to emphasize the closeness of classic feminine virtues to the divine ideal and the need for both women and men to aspire to them.

◆ ◆ ◆

NOTES

1. Tos. Ber. Lieberman ed. 6:18.

2. Including *Rif*, Ber. Ch. 9; Maimonides (Laws of Prayer 7:6); an old version of the Rosh to Ber. 9:23 (in *Divrei Chamudot*); Abudraham, *Tur*, O. Ch. 46; and *Shulchan Arukh*, O. Ch. 46:4.

3. Cf. Bach, *Divrei Chamudot*, and *Lechem Mishnah* (Abraham b. Moses di Boton, 1545–1588, Salonika) to Maimonides, Laws of Prayer 7:6. The latter despairs over Maimonides' listing of *ishah* before *eved*. R. Yosef Kapach's (Yemen, Jerusalem, d. 2000) edition and commentary of Maimonides, however, has *ishah* last.

4. B. Men., where *eved* is substituted for *bor*; also Maimonides printed Laws of Prayer and the original Tosefta and Yerushalmi.

5. For example, *Arukh Hashulchan*, O. Ch. 6.

6. Novellae on Maimonides' *Book of Love*, Laws of Prayer 7:6.

7. *Barukh She'Amar* of R. Baruch HaLevi Epstein, early twentieth century, St. Petersburg; attributed to the Chafetz Chayim, Rabbi Israel Meir HaKohen Kagan of Radum, Poland, also early twentieth century, as the form of blessing that he used.

8. See R. Ovadiah Yosef (contemporary Israeli authority and former Chief Sephardi Rabbi), *Yechaveh Da'at* 4:15, for discussion of men responding to women's blessings in synagogue.

The Halakhah of Waking Up

Daniel Landes

BOTH A "BEFORE" AND AN "AFTER"

Birkhot Hashachar is more than a laundry list of blessings. The Talmud prescribes them for the natural acts of rising, beginning with an acknowledgment of a divinely given soul that is removed at death but returned in the future. Other blessings accompany acts such as hearing the rooster crow, dressing, rising, and walking; still others reflect on spiritual ideals, and end by acknowledging God, who "rewards his people Israel with great kindness."

The blessings over *tsitsit* and *t'fillin* are *birkhot mitzvah* ("blessings over performing a *mitzvah* [a commandment]"). The rest are *birkhot hodaah* ("blessings of praise"), referring to things we enjoy that are specific to the morning. The Morning Blessings thus respond to the lost process of enjoying our morning world. It is more than a mere introduction to the prayers that follow. It is its own celebration of "before"—before we move on to the rest of the morning service.

But it is also an "after," in that the Talmud connects it ritually with going to sleep the night before. The bedtime *Sh'ma* concludes with thanksgiving for the gift of sleep and requests a peaceful sleep; a portion in Torah; and a life free from sin, trial, and shame. It is really a petition to survive the night terrors, in order to serve God the next day. The Talmud's discussion of the Morning Blessings anticipates the triumphant "afterward" that the worshiper had in mind the night before. The Morning Blessings give thanks for the mundane enjoyments of the new day.

It is also, however, a "before" to the *Shacharit* (morning) service. This conception follows from the blessing over handwashing, the one blessing here (aside from *tsitsit* and *t'fillin*) with the formula "who has sanctified...and commanded us." The commandment is necessary, says the Rosh (Rabbenu Asher, 1250–1328, Germany and Spain), because "hands are active during sleep and have probably touched one of the foul places of the body." They require washing "before one recites the *Sh'ma* and *Amidah*" (Commentary to Ber. 9:23; Responsum 4:1). Washing is the "before" that allows these other prayers to be said.

The Rashba (Rabbi Shlomo ben Adret, Barcelona, 1235–1310) takes a different approach (Responsum I:191): "In the morning, we become new creations, as it is written: 'They are new every morning' (Lam. 3:23). We therefore sanctify ourselves by washing, like the priest who sanctified his hands from the laver prior to his divine service, for our service is prayer."

We can now delineate three viewpoints regarding handwashing. First, talmudically, it is part of the successful passage from night and sleep. Maimonides agreed. He reworked the talmudic order of blessings, believing that "these eighteen blessings…should be said whenever the appropriate moment arises" (Laws of Prayer 7:7). For the Talmud, Maimonides, and Tosafot, then, the *Birkhot Hashachar* are blessings of obligation regarding the enjoyment of a new day after the previous night's sleep.

Second, we have the functional approach of the Rosh, for whom handwashing renders hands clean from nighttime activity. Washing represents a necessary "before" for the *Sh'ma* and *Amidah*. Third is the breakthrough approach of Rashba, for whom handwashing and the rest of the Morning Blessings are a discrete unit representing both "after" and "before." They are an "after" in that they mark the triumph of life over death inherent in every morning. The Rashba thus reads the first prayer of the day, *Elohai n'shamah* ("My God, the soul…"), not only as a reference to the return of the soul to the body in an afterlife, but as resurrection in the here and now. All the Morning Blessings celebrate this miracle. We wash specifically with a cup because that is how the priests washed in the Temple, and we thereby promise to serve God in this world as pure priests of the Temple.

The resurrection theory of the Rashba, which was further elaborated upon by the Zohar, has in turn further defined the evening ritual of going to sleep. If sleep is like death, the evening *Sh'ma* ought to require a confession—as we see from the *Seder Hayom* (a kabbalistic-halakhic work on prayer by Moshe Makiri, sixteenth-century Safed):

> Sleep is one-sixtieth of death, and before one departs this world it is fitting to accept the yoke of heaven (say the *Sh'ma*) and to love and fear God (say the *V'ahavta*). Therefore, it is customary and proper to recite the deathbed confession, for we do not know our time, and we have seen many who have gone to sleep and not risen.

The Rashba diverts the night ritual from concern with death to our embrace of it. The Zohar adds that the morning washing stems from the loss of our "divine spirit" at night. Regaining it is resurrection (*Bet Yosef,* Joseph Caro, sixteenth century, Land of Israel, O. Ch. 4; and *Shulchan Arukh D'Rav* of R. Shneur Zalman of Liady, eighteenth-century founder of Chabad Chasidism, O. Ch. 4a). Having gone through death, one arises triumphant in the morning and celebrates new life through the Morning Blessings.

It was Joseph Caro who integrated all the views into a single viable set of practices. While we say the blessings over handwashing specifically before prayer, and may say *Birkhot Hashachar* in the synagogue (following the Rosh) and use a cup (following the Rashba), we also pour the water on our hands three times to remove the "impurity" of death, which, says the Zohar, is left on our hands by sleep. In the modern morning ritual, therefore, we find all the approaches reflected. It is part of a cycle of life and death (Talmud and Maimonides), an "after" to the death aspects of sleep (Zohar), but a "before" to the *Sh'ma* and *Amidah,* and to a day of serving God through prayer and good deeds (Rashba).

STRUCTURAL PARALLELS WITH *SHACHARIT*

The Morning Blessings are a "before" of the morning service as a whole *(Shacharit)* in other ways too. First, it is structurally parallel to *Shacharit*. Maimonides, for instance, lists eighteen blessings in it—the same as the original *Amidah*. In addition, four constituent parts of *Shacharit* correspond to four parts of the Morning Blessings. *Shacharit* moves from (1) *P'sukei D'zimrah*, to (2) the *Sh'ma* and Its Blessings, to (3) the *Amidah*, to (4) the reading of Torah. So, too, the Morning Blessings go from (1) the blessings of arising, to (2) the *Sh'ma*, to (3) study passages on the sacrifices, to (4) the exegetical principles of Rabbi Ishmael by which Torah is interpreted.

1. The *P'sukei D'zimrah* of *Shacharit* equals the blessings of *Birkhot Hashachar*. Both deepen our feeling of dependence on God as we appreciate our world.
2. The *Sh'ma* and Its Blessings of *Shacharit* equals the *Sh'ma* in the Morning Blessings.
3. The *Amidah* of *Shacharit* equals the sacrificial readings in the Morning Blessings, since the *Amidah* is considered to have taken the place of sacrifices when the Temple was destroyed.
4. The reading of Torah *(K'riat Hatorah)* in *Shacharit* equals the exegetical principles of Rabbi Ishmael, since the written law presupposes the rules of oral interpretation.

Moreover (5), the *Shacharit* service (as we have it) contains a section called *Tachanun* ("supplications" for God's mercy). And the Morning Blessings were eventually outfitted with the account of the *Akedah* (the binding of Isaac), which is taken traditionally as an evocation of God's mercy.

The full parallel of these two "services" (with the exception of the *Tachanun*) looks like this:

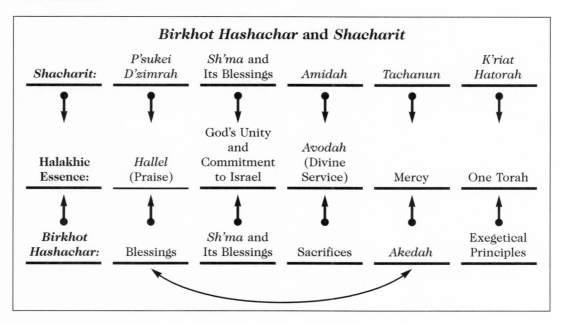

Birkhot Hashachar and *Shacharit*

Shacharit:	P'sukei D'zimrah	Sh'ma and Its Blessings	Amidah	Tachanun	K'riat Hatorah
Halakhic Essence:	Hallel (Praise)	God's Unity and Commitment to Israel	Avodah (Divine Service)	Mercy	One Torah
Birkhot Hashachar:	Blessings	Sh'ma and Its Blessings	Sacrifices	Akedah	Exegetical Principles

But *Birkhot Hashachar* is essentially private, intended for home recital before coming to services. Maimonides objects to their common recitation as part of the synagogue service (Laws of Prayer 7:9); following the Talmud, he insists that they be said according to the corresponding actions that they celebrate. But Maimonides lost the fight. The *Shulchan Arukh* (O. Ch. 46:2) assigns the *Birkhot Hashachar* to the synagogue once and for all, because "ignorant people…do not know" these prayers and require a communal recitation. Nonetheless, it remains preferable to say *Birkhot Hashachar* privately, preferably before the prayer leader begins them in the service (*Arukh Hashulchan,* O. Ch. 6:13).

MORNING SERVICE AS CIRCLE OF IDENTITY

We can now look at the way the daily morning service moves back and forth between the two poles of Jewish identity: private individuality and membership in Jewish community.

Even after they were moved to the synagogue, the Morning Blessings retained their original sense of private worship. The *P'sukei D'zimrah* (the next major rubric) is more public, but is still a "warm-up" for the *really* public worship after the Call to Prayer *(Bar'khu)*. The *Sh'ma* and Its Blessings, which follow, however, must certainly be communal prayer, since *Bar'khu* inaugurates it. But traditionally, the *Sh'ma* itself is recited individually, eyes covered with our hand. Here, then, we have community prayer with a temporary stepping back by the individual. Next is the *Amidah*—first silently as personal prayer within community, and then repeated by the prayer leader as the community prayer par excellence. At its height, during the *K'dushah,* the community expands to include even the angels.

The *Amidah* is followed by the *Tachanun,* which is radically private, even to the point of demanding that individuals feign a prostrate position before God, making supplications. The reading of Torah, however, is radically public, a re-evocation of Sinai with God as lawgiver and all Israel present. In the final major prayer, the *Alenu,* Israel is publicly present as the chosen eschatological community. The next day, the circle of identity begins again.

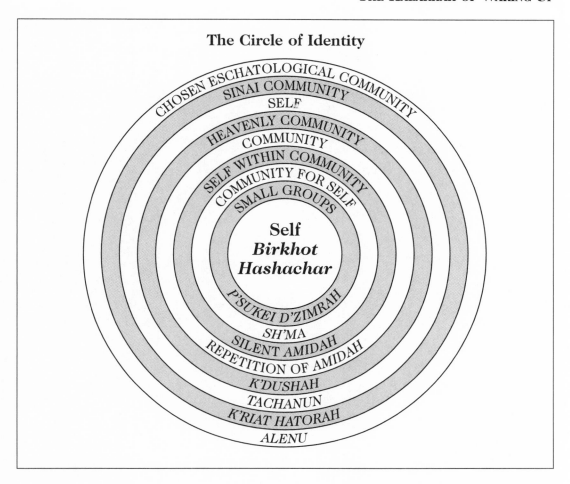

The Circle of Identity

THE STAIRCASE OF HALAKHIC RESURRECTION

We have seen the understanding of *Birkhot Hashachar* as resurrection, this being an "after" to the death experience of sleep and a triumphant "before" to *Shacharit*. The halakhic imperatives associated with specific prayers continue this motif throughout the rest of *Shacharit*.

We start with the nighttime *Sh'ma (K'riat Sh'ma al Hamitah)* and its confrontation with death through the accompanying deathbed confession, so as to achieve atonement as the day ends. As we saw, the following morning features the opening act of handwashing, symbolizing the resurrection of body and soul. *P'sukei D'zimrah* encapsulates a Daily *Hallel,* psalms that offer praise for God's miraculous daily renewal of creation (see Volume 3, *P'sukei D'zimrah [Morning Psalms]*). The *Sh'ma* focuses on declaring the unity of God, through word and intention. The *Amidah* is defined halakhically as *bakashah,* "petition" which brings our this-worldly concerns under God's providential care. *Tachanun* is exemplified by *n'filat apa'im* (prostration), emphasizing further our fragile dependence on God. The reading of Torah reiterates our acceptance of Torah as the commanding force in our lives and leads us to *Alenu,* in which we charge ourselves with the divine task of pursuing God's goals in this world: to repair the world under God's reign.

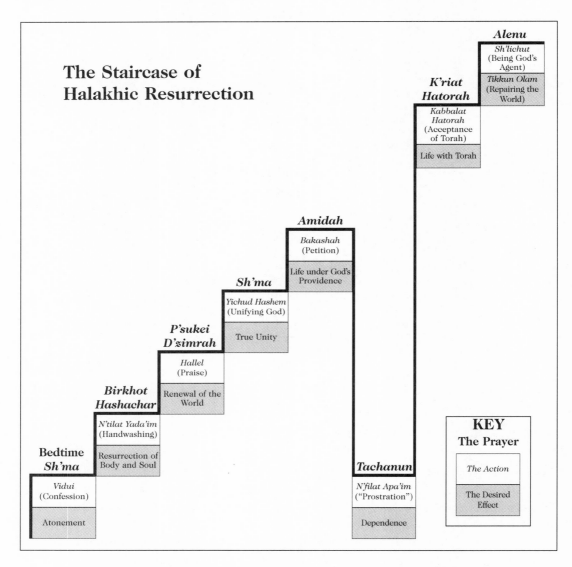

Thus, the progression from facing death and seeking atonement proceeds to the daily miracle of resurrection and from there to renewal of the world, proclamation of the unity of God, the integration of our own fragile lives under God's care, the reception of God's Torah, and, finally, accepting our role in resurrecting the world as it should be. More than a mere ancillary requirement of daily prayer, *Birkhot Hashachar* initiates a staircase of halakhic transformation of reality.

LAWS UPON ARISING

The *Birkhot Hashachar* are intimately tied to the way we greet each new day. Discussion of the liturgy is impossible without recording the activities that accompany it.

1. Upon arising, say *Modeh ani...* (women: *Modah ani...*).

מוֹדָה אֲנִי לְפָנֶיךָ, מֶלֶךְ חַי וְקַיָּם, שֶׁהֶחֱזַרְתָּ בִּי נִשְׁמָתִי
בְּחֶמְלָה; רַבָּה אֱמוּנָתֶךָ.

("I gratefully acknowledge You, living and enduring ruler, for returning my soul to me; great is Your faithfulness.")

2. Upon need, attend the lavatory.
3. Upon leaving the lavatory, wash hands with a cup, making sure that you have walked no more than four *amot* (sing., *amah*) away from bed. (*Amah* is a measure, amounting roughly to a forearm: the distance from the elbow to the tip of the little finger.) To simplify matters, the confines of a home are considered four *amot*.

    a. The water must be clear, clean, and abundant enough to cover your hands three times.

    b. Pour from a cup, not by placing hands under the tap.

    c. The vessel must be clean. Do not use a spout.

    d. Hands should be bare; remove all rings and the like. (A necessary bandage may remain—you may pour around it. If it must remain dry, wipe hands vigorously with clean towel in lieu of using water.)

    e. Take the full cup with the right hand, switch it to the left and pour onto the right hand. Then switch the cup to the right hand and pour onto the left. Continue until each hand has been poured over three times; some people pour over each hand successively three times.

    f. Pour over the entire hand. If water is scarce, pour at least onto the last knuckle.

    g. Upon completion of washing, raise hands slightly.

    h. As you dry hands, recite the blessing, *al n'tilat yada'im* ("about washing our hands").

    i. The above procedure is the same for washing before meals, with the exception that the general custom then is to wash hands only twice. (Many Chasidim wash three times at meals and four times in the morning.)

4. Then recite *asher yatsar* ("who formed"—the blessing after relieving oneself), and immediately *Elohai n'shamah* ("My God, the soul You have put within me..."), which refers to the restoration of body and soul. Follow with the full range of blessings, assuming one is dressed modestly. Otherwise, wait to recite them at the synagogue.

5. Alternatively, if one follows Maimonides, say the following blessings with the proper acts to which they relate:

a. On arising: *Elohai n'shamah* ("My God, the soul You have put within me…").

b. On hearing the rooster crow: *hanoten lasekhvi* ("who gives the cunning rooster its ability to distinguish…").

c. While donning clothes: *malbish arumim* ("who clothes the naked").

d. While covering the head: *oter yisra'el b'tifarah* ("who crowns Israel with glory").

e. While placing a hand over the eyes: *poke'ach ivrim* ("who opens the eyes of the blind").

f. While sitting up on the bed: *matir asurim* ("who frees the captive").

g. While placing feet on the ground: *roka ha'arets* ("who spreads out the land on the water").

h. While standing up: *zokef k'fufim* ("who raises up the hunched over").

i. While washing hands *al n'tilat yada'im* ("about washing our hands").

j. While washing the face: *hama'avir shenah* ("who removes sleep") through *gomel chasadim tovim* ("who rewards…with great kindness").

k. Upon leaving the lavatory: *asher yatsar* ("who has formed").

l. While putting on a belt: *ozer yisra'el* ("who girds Israel").

m. While putting on shoes: *she'asah li kol tsorki* ("who has provided me with all my needs").

n. While beginning to walk: *hameikhin mitsadei gaver* ("who makes firm man's steps").

For Maimonides, these blessings are said in the order performed and only if the appropriate actions are actually performed. If one, for example, goes barefoot, then one omits *she'asah li kol tsorki*. The general custom, however, is to say all the blessings at one time. If we do not perform the relevant actions, we are to visualize the acts involved, relying upon the fact that the blessings are part of general praise for God.

6. The status blessings ("who did not make me") are said daily.

7. In general, *Birkhot Hashachar* may be said as early as dawn. Earlier risers may recite all the blessings, except *hanoten lasekhvi*, which must wait until cockcrow or the break of dawn (since *sekhvi* means not just a rooster but the human mind too and so represents our own ability to discern daylight).

If one has neglected to say the blessings until after *Shacharit*, one may say them then, with the exception of *n'tilat yada'im* ("washing our hands"), which must accompany handwashing.

Introduction to the Commentaries

How to Look for Meaning in the Prayers

Lawrence A. Hoffman

THE ART OF JEWISH READING

I remember the day I looked at a manuscript of a prayer book that no one could identify. It had been smuggled out of Russia, then the Soviet Union, and was obviously the liturgy for Rosh Hashanah, but who had written it? And when? It was handwritten, so the style told us much, but in addition, someone had written marginal notes in another handwriting, and yet a third person had written comments to the comments— a third unknown scholar of years gone by whose name we wanted to rescue from oblivion.

Standing before the massive volume, I reflected on the sheer joy of studying a traditional Jewish text. I had seen printed versions before, but never a handwritten instance. What a wonderful habit we Jews developed once upon a time: writing a text in the middle of the page and then filling up the margins with commentaries. Every page becomes a cross-cut through Jewish history. Jewish Bibles come that way; so do the Talmud, the Mishnah, and the codes. We never read just the text. We always read it through the prism of the way other people have read it.

To be a Jewish reader, then, is to join the ranks of the millions of readers who came before us, leaving their comments in the margins, the way animals leave tracks in the woods. Go deep into the forest, and you will come across deer runs, for example: paths to water sources, carved out by hundreds of thousands of deer over time. The deer do not just inhabit the forest; they are part of the forest; they change the forest's contours as they live there, just as the forest changes them, by offering shelter, food, and water. There is no virgin forest, really; it is an ecosystem, a balance between the vegetation and the animals who live there.

So, too, there are no virgin texts. They too are ecosystems, sustaining millions of readers over time. When we read our classic texts, we tread the paths of prior readers, in search of spiritual nourishment. *My People's Prayer Book* is therefore not just the Siddur text; it is the text as read by prominent readers from among the people. You are invited to share our path, and even to break new ground yourself, passing on to others your own marginal notes, should you wish.

For the Hebrew text of this volume, we have used the standard Hebrew of the Siddur as provided by the venerable Philip Birnbaum. Back in 1949, Birnbaum labored over a Siddur that would contain the traditional liturgy in a modern scientific format. He combined the standard Ashkenazi rite with some modifications that had crept in and become popular in America. More than any other text, it is Birnbaum's that has met the test of time and that best represents the traditional liturgy most North Americans know best.

That text was then translated by Joel M. Hoffman, in consultation with Marc Brettler. The translation strives to reproduce not only the content of the original Hebrew, but also its tone, register, and style, so as to bring to modern readers the same experience (to the greatest extent possible) that the original authors would have conveyed with their words. In terms of content, we assume that by and large, words have meaning only to the extent that they contribute to sentences and concepts—as, for example, "by and large," which has nothing to do with "by" or "large."

We try to reproduce a tone and register similar to the original text: formal, but not archaic; prose or poetry, depending on the Hebrew. Where the Hebrew uses obscure words, we try to do the same, and where it uses common idiom, we try to use equally common idiom. Parallel structure and other similar literary devices found in the Hebrew are replicated as much as possible in the English translation. We have not doctored the text to make it more palatable to modern consciousness. Blatant sexisms are retained, for instance, wherever we think the author intended them. We depend upon our commentaries to bridge the gap between the translation of the original and our modern sensibilities.

The heart and soul of *Minhag Ami* is its choice of commentaries that surround the prayerbook text. Translator Joel M. Hoffman explains his choice of words, provides alternatives, and compares his own translation with others. Marc Brettler comments particularly on the way the Bible is embedded in the Siddur. Ellen Frankel ("A Woman's Voice") and Elliot N. Dorff provide theological reflections on what the prayers might mean, should mean, could mean, cannot mean, or have to mean (even if we wish they didn't). Daniel Landes gives us the Halakhah of prayer, the rules and traditions by which this sacred liturgical drama has traditionally been carried out: the Halakhah of waking up, for instance, and a halakhic analysis of the controversial blessings that begin "Who did not make me." Yoel H. Kahn has added a historical survey of the same "Who did not make me" benedictions. Lawrence Kushner and Nehemia Polen supply a kabbalistic commentary, adding wisdom from the world of Chasidic masters, and David Ellenson surveys liberal prayer books of the last two hundred years to see how their writers agonized over attempts to update this book of Jewish books for modern times. My own contribution is a summary of what we know about the historical development of the liturgy: when prayers were written and what they meant in the context of their day.

Some of the commentaries require greater elaboration here, however. The contributors cite a specific body of literature or have made some choices that readers should know about in advance.

Translator Joel M. Hoffman had to make a judicious selection of translations to compare with his own. For an Orthodox version, he relied on Philip Birnbaum's classic (1949) *Daily Prayer Book: Hasiddur Hashalem* ("Birnbaum"), but looked also at *Siddur Kol Ya'akov* ("Artscroll," 1984). American Reform was represented by the *Gates of Prayer* ("GOP," 1975) and revisions since; Conservative Jews will find their *Siddur Sim Shalom* ("SSS," 1985) and Reconstructionists will see their *Kol Haneshamah* ("KH," 1994) cited. He compared British liturgy too: *Forms of Prayer* ("FOP," 1977) from the Reform Synagogues of Great Britain; and both *Service of the Heart* ("SOH," 1967) and *Siddur Lev Chadash* ("SLC," 1995) from the Union of Liberal and Progressive Synagogues. For biblical citations, including the *Sh'ma*, he consulted the Jewish Publication Society Bible *("JPS")* but compared it with the *New Revised Standard* Bible of 1989 *("NRSV")*, and *The Five Books of Moses,* by Everett Fox ("Fox," 1995).

My own historical commentary had to deal with the fact that the Birnbaum Siddur is only for Ashkenazi Jews, more specifically, the Ashkenazi version common in eastern Europe, often under the influence of Elijah ben Solomon of Vilna, known as the Vilna Gaon (1720–1797). To balance the picture, I cite Sefardi practice also.

But the word "Sefardi" has two distinct meanings. Nowadays, it usually describes Jews whose liturgy was influenced by Chasidism and the specific brand of Kabbalah initiated by Isaac Luria (the "Ari"), in sixteenth-century Palestine. Master liturgist and scholar of texts E. Daniel Goldschmidt compiled a scientific edition of this variant, and I used that to represent "Sefardi practice." But "Sefardi" can also mean the old Spanish-Portuguese custom carried by Jews from Spain in 1492 and then brought to the Netherlands, whence it moved to England (among other places) and eventually to America as well. When I want to draw attention to this Spanish-Portuguese custom, I call it that, using as my guide the standard work published in England at the turn of the century by Moses Gaster, *The Book of Prayer and Order of Service According to the Custom of the Spanish and Portuguese Jews*. I try also to cite *Seder Rav Amram* and *Siddur Saadiah*, the first two Jewish prayer books of which we are aware, from ninth- and tenth-century Babylon. And from the same era, roughly, I use the Genizah Fragments, manuscripts telling us how Jews prayed in the Land of Israel prior to the Crusades.

David Ellenson was asked to fill in the gap caused by the fact that even the standard Ashkenazi and Sefardi versions hardly represent the majority of Jews today. As Jews have evolved, so have our modern movements, each with its own version of what our forebears once considered normative. The last two hundred years have witnessed the composition of countless Jewish prayer books, and Ellenson surveys the most prominent of these for instances where the traditional text evoked debate.

For historical reasons, many are Reform, beginning with the *Hamburg Temple Prayer Book*s of 1819 and 1841, the very first efforts to make the content of the classical liturgy comport with modern ideas. His survey of the nineteenth century also included *Seder T'filah D'var Yom B'Yomo* (1854; republished, 1870) by Rabbi Abraham Geiger, the preeminent leader of German Reform.

For early American liturgies, he turned to Rabbis Isaac Mayer Wise and David Einhorn. Wise's *Minhag America* (1857) was the most popular prayer book of its day, and Einhorn's *Olath Tamid* (1856) became the prototype for the *Union Prayer Book ("UPB"),* which was adopted in 1895 as the official liturgy for North American Reform Jews. In 1975, *Gates of Prayer ("GOP")* replaced the *UPB,* and in 1996 the latest in a series of gender-inclusive editions of *GOP* appeared. All three of these official movement books are cited here.

Among the non-American prayer books of the late 1900s, Ellenson made extensive use of *Ha'avodah Shebalev ("HS"),* adopted by the Israeli Progressive Movement in 1982; the 1998 Israeli Conservative Movement's *Siddur Va'ani T'fillati ("SVT");* and *Siddur Lev Chadash ("SLC"),* published by the Union of Progressive and Liberal Synagogues in London in 1995.

These prayer books are supplemented by several North American Conservative and Reconstructionist volumes. The former include various prayer books produced since 1958 by the Rabbinical Assembly of the Conservative Movement, but especially the 1985 *Siddur Sim Shalom.* Since Conservative worship is in Hebrew, however, and since the Hebrew is generally unchanged, while the vernacular equivalent is usually a literal translation of it, Ellenson has less to say about Conservative prayer books than he does of Reform volumes, where both Hebrew and English tend to vary widely. The Reconstructionist Movement, which, like Reform, has tended toward considerable liturgical creativity, is represented primarily by *Kol Haneshamah,* published in 1996, but from time to time he discusses earlier work, especially by Mordecai Kaplan, the founder of the movement.

Ellenson gives priority to denominationally associated prayer books because they have been most widely disseminated, but he does include some others, notably *The Book of Blessings,* authored in 1996 by Jewish feminist Marcia Falk. He uses more liberal prayer books than Orthodox ones, because liberal books were changed more, as their authors tried to remain true to their liturgical heritage, without doing an injustice to modern ideas about God, the universe, and human nature. Orthodox volumes are cited here, but references to them are limited.

The halakhic commentary was included not just to explain how prayers should be said. Even without that abiding practical concern, it would have found its way here because Halakhah (Jewish law) is essential to Judaism. Frequently misunderstood as mere legalism, it is actually more akin to Jewish poetry, in that it is the height of Jewish writing, the pinnacle of Jewish concern, sheer joy to create or to ponder. It describes, explains, and debates Jewish responsibility, yet is saturated with spiritual importance. Jewish movements can be differentiated by their approach to Halakhah, but Halakhah matters to them all.

A short overview of its history and some of its vocabulary will be helpful in advance.

The topic of Halakhah is the proper performance of the commandments, said to number 613, and divided into positive and negative ones, numbering 248 and 365, respectively. Strictly speaking, commandments derived directly from Torah (mid'ora'ita) are of a higher order than those rooted only in rabbinic ordinance (called mid'rabbanan), but all are binding.

The earliest stratum of Halakhah is found primarily in the Mishnah, a code of Jewish practice promulgated about 200 C.E. The Mishnah is the foundation for further rabbinic discussion in Palestine and Babylonia, which culminated in the two Talmuds, one from each center, and called the Palestinian Talmud (or the Yerushalmi), and the Babylonian Talmud (or the Babli). While dates for both are uncertain, the former is customarily dated to about 400 C.E., and the latter between 550 and 650.

With the canonization of the Babli, Jewish law developed largely from commentary to the Talmuds and from responsa, applications of talmudic and other precedents to actual cases. These are still the norm today, but they were initiated by authorities in Babylonia called Geonim (sing. Gaon) from about 750 to shortly after 1000. By the turn of the millennium, other schools had developed in North Africa particularly, but also in western Europe. Authorities in these centers are usually called Rishonim ("first" or "early" [ones]) until the sixteenth century, when they become known as Acharonim ("last" or "later" [ones]).

The first law code is geonic (from about 750), but it was the Rishonim who really inaugurated the trend toward codifying, giving us many works, including three major ones that are widely cited here: The *Mishneh Torah*, by Maimonides (Moses ben Maimon, 1035–1104), born in Spain, but active most of his life in Egypt; the *Tur*, by Jacob ben Asher (1275–1340), son of another giant, Asher ben Yechiel, who had moved to Spain from Germany, allowing Ashkenazi and Sefardi practice to intertwine in his son's magnum opus; and the *Shulchan Arukh*, by Joseph Caro (1488–1575), who is technically the first generation of the Acharonim, but who wrote influential commentaries on both the *Mishneh Torah* and the *Tur* before composing what would become the most widely used legal corpus ever.

This halakhic commentary draws on all of the above, as well as numerous other authorities, including especially the following: Jacob Emden (1697–1779), a German rabbi, kabbalist, and halakhic authority who bequeathed us his own Siddur and commentary; Elijah ben Solomon of Vilna (1720–1797), better known as the Gra or the Vilna Gaon, the most outstanding halakhic authority in eighteenth-century Lithuania and an intellectual leader who pioneered the modern, but traditional, study of classical texts; *Mishnah B'rurah*, a decisive commentary on part of the *Shulchan Arukh*, composed by Israel Meir HaKohen Kagan (1838–1933) of Poland; *Arukh Hashulchan*, a summary of halakhic opinion that spans the various codes and their interpreters, published in parts from 1883 to 1907 by Yechiel Michael Epstein (1829–1098) of Belorussia and Lithuania; Avraham Karelitz (1878–1953), better known as the Chazon Ish, a modern master of Halakhah who began as an authority in Vilna, but who moved to Israel, and advised the early Israeli government on halakhic matters; and Rabbi Joseph Soloveitchik (1903–1993), who moved from Lithuania to

Berlin to Boston, where he became known as "the Rov", leaving a lasting impression on today's generation of halakhists.

Other commentators too tend to favor some sources over others. But by and large their comments require no detailed introduction here.

We have gone out of our way to provide a panoply of scholars, all students of the prayerbook text, and all committed to a life of prayer, but representative of left, right, and center in the Jewish world. They represent all of us, all of *Am Yisrael,* all of those God had in mind when God said to Ezekiel (34:30), "They shall know that I, Adonai their God, am with them, and they, the House of Israel, are My people." Unabashedly scholarly and religious at one and the same time, *Minhag Ami,* "A Way of Prayer for My People," will be deemed a success if it provides the spiritual insight required to fulfill yet another prophecy (Isa. 52:6), that through our prayers,

> My people *[ami]* may know My name
> That they may know, therefore, in that day,
> That I, the One who speaks,
> Behold! Here I am.

1 Preparation for Prayer

A. ENTERING THE SYNAGOGUE: *MAH TOVU*

[Upon entering the synagogue:]

¹How wonderful are Your tents, Jacob, Your abodes, Israel! ²I, by Your great love, enter Your house, and bow down reverently before Your holy shrine. ³Adonai, I love Your house of dwelling, the abode of Your glory. ⁴I will humbly bow down low before Adonai, my Maker. ⁵I offer my prayer to You, Adonai, at this time of favor; God, in Your great mercy; answer me with Your saving truth.

[Upon entering the synagogue:]

¹מַה טֹּבוּ אֹהָלֶיךָ יַעֲקֹב, מִשְׁכְּנֹתֶיךָ יִשְׂרָאֵל. ²וַאֲנִי בְּרֹב חַסְדְּךָ אָבוֹא בֵיתֶךָ, אֶשְׁתַּחֲוֶה אֶל הֵיכַל קָדְשְׁךָ בְּיִרְאָתֶךָ. ³יְיָ, אָהַבְתִּי מְעוֹן בֵּיתֶךָ, וּמְקוֹם מִשְׁכַּן כְּבוֹדֶךָ. ⁴וַאֲנִי אֶשְׁתַּחֲוֶה וְאֶכְרָעָה, אֶבְרְכָה לִפְנֵי יְיָ עֹשִׂי. ⁵וַאֲנִי תְפִלָּתִי לְךָ, יְיָ, עֵת רָצוֹן; אֱלֹהִים, בְּרָב־חַסְדֶּךָ, עֲנֵנִי בֶּאֱמֶת יִשְׁעֶךָ.

BRETTLER (BIBLE)

[1] *"How wonderful are Your tents"* From the third prophecy of Balaam (Num. 24:5), and an introduction to a mosaic of Bible verses taken to refer to the synagogue. In its biblical context, "tents" and "abodes" denote the Israelite encampment. In the singular, they refer specifically to the Tabernacle (the *mishkan*) in the wilderness and thus serve as an appropriate reference for a prayer upon entering the synagogue.

[2] *"I [va'ani] by Your great love, enter"* From Psalm 5:8, a lament asking God to let the worshiper pray at the Temple. The word "I" pre-dominates, as it comes first in the sentence. Stylistically, three of the five verses here begin with *va'ani*, emphasizing intense personalism.   *(p. 52)*

DORFF (THEOLOGY)

[1] *"How wonderful are Your tents"* It is hard to enter a space where we meet other people, let alone where we meet God. Our opening prayer thus piles on synonyms for places of worship ("tents," "abodes," "house," "holy shrine," "house of dwelling,") to makes us feel   *(p. 52)*

ELLENSON (MODERN LITURGIES)

[1] *"How wonderful are Your tents"* As a prayer for private recitation upon entering the synagogue, this has been a staple element in virtually all liberal prayer books for the last two centuries, which usually provide both Hebrew and vernacular texts. David   *(p. 53)*

FRANKEL (A WOMAN'S VOICE)

[1] *"How wonderful are Your tents"* How peculiar that we Jews begin our morning prayers by reciting the blessing forced from the mouth of the pagan prophet Balaam by divine fiat! For when the Moabite king Balak commanded Balaam to curse the Israelites who were threatening to overrun his territory, Balaam found himself compelled to bless them instead. Perhaps we are to take this as an object lesson, surrendering ourselves to praise God whether we will it or not.   *(p. 53)*

A. ENTERING THE SYNAGOGUE: *MAH TOVU*

[Upon entering the synagogue:]

[1] How wonderful are Your tents, Jacob, Your abodes, Israel! [2] I, by Your great love, enter Your house, and bow down reverently before Your holy shrine. [3] Adonai, I love Your house of dwelling, the abode of Your glory. [4] I will humbly bow down low before Adonai, my Maker.

J. HOFFMAN (TRANSLATION)

[1] *"How wonderful"* The Hebrew word *mah,* though literally "what," is commonly used the way we use "how" in English, and so it can start an exclamation (as here), not just a question. ("What good are Your tents?" is obviously wrong.)

As for "wonderful": Others, "goodly" or "good." "Great" is tempting, too. The Hebrew word means "good," but since it sounds poetic in Hebrew, it calls for a more powerful English equivalent.

2 *"I, by Your great love"* We purposely put "I" first in this and two following lines, as in the Hebrew. But the Hebrew lines are taken out of context. In their original context, the "I" is included for contrast. In this case (taken from Ps. 5:8), the context is: "An [evil] man is abhorrent to God, but I, by Your great love…." Out of context, the "I" in Hebrew could mean "I am the one who…."

2 *"Reverently"* More literally, "revering You" or "with reverence for You."

[Upon entering the synagogue:]

¹מַה טֹּבוּ אֹהָלֶיךָ יַעֲקֹב, מִשְׁכְּנֹתֶיךָ יִשְׂרָאֵל. ²וַאֲנִי בְּרֹב חַסְדְּךָ אָבוֹא בֵיתֶךָ, אֶשְׁתַּחֲוֶה אֶל הֵיכַל קָדְשְׁךָ בְּיִרְאָתֶךָ. ³יְיָ, אָהַבְתִּי מְעוֹן בֵּיתֶךָ, וּמְקוֹם מִשְׁכַּן כְּבוֹדֶךָ. ⁴וַאֲנִי אֶשְׁתַּחֲוֶה וְאֶכְרָעָה, אֶבְרְכָה לִפְנֵי יְיָ עֹשִׂי.

3 *"House of dwelling"* The point seems to be to create a parallel between the first line (which is the beginning of Balaam's famous blessing to Israel) and the Temple. So here we have *bayit*, a reference to the Temple, in parallel with "tent," but also (above) *heikhal kodsh'kha* ("holy shrine"), a similar term, and *et ratson*, a reference to proper sacrificial times (later generalized to times of prayer too).

Below, we find *mishkan [k'vodekha]* ("abode [of Your glory]") in parallel with "abode," above. Admittedly, *(p. 54)*

L. HOFFMAN (HISTORY)

IN ITSELF, THE BIRKHOT HASHACHAR IS PREPARATORY TO THE REST OF THE MORNING SERVICE. IT BEGINS, HOWEVER, WITH ITS OWN INTERNAL PREPARATION, CONSISTING OF: MAH TOVU (A PRAYER FOR ENTERING THE SYNAGOGUE); PRAYERS FOR PUTTING ON TALLIT AND T'FILLIN; AND TWO MORNING POEMS, ADON OLAM AND YIGDAL.

"How wonderful are Your tents" Fine irony accompanies the prayer that is said upon arriving at synagogue: a line from the biblical story of Baalam (Num. 24:5), an idolatrous prophet hired by King Balak, Israel's enemy, to curse the Israelites *(p. 54)*

KUSHNER & POLEN (CHASIDISM)

1 *"How wonderful [mah tovu] are Your tents, Jacob"* Karen Kushner once offered the following observation. These are the words of the non-Jewish prophet Balaam, while overlookinging encamped tribes of Israel spread out below him. In its biblical context (Num. 24:5), Balaam must be speaking what amounts to a poem of praise, as if to say, "All the Jews are together, and the scene is wonderful to behold." Now we see why *Mah Tovu* occurs at the very beginning of the morning liturgy. We should understand its imagery in light of what is physically happening in the sanctuary at the time of its recitation. Everyone is putting on his or her *tallit*. And this ritual customarily begins by draping *(p. 54)*

⁵I offer my prayer to You, Adonai, at this time of favor, God, in Your great mercy: answer me with Your saving truth.

⁵וַאֲנִי תְפִלָּתִי לְךָ, יְיָ, עֵת רָצוֹן; אֱלֹהִים, בְּרָב־חַסְדֶּךָ, עֲנֵנִי בֶּאֱמֶת יִשְׁעֶךָ.

BRETTLER (BIBLE)

³*"Adonai, I love Your house of dwelling"* Psalm 26:8, another lament, requesting God's help based on the worshiper's past piety, namely, he loved going to the Temple.

⁴*"I will humbly bow down low"* A modification of Psalm 95:6, but with tense and person changed to fit the context.

⁵*"I offer my prayer"* A final lament (Ps. 69:14) that transitions the worshiper from the setting of prayer (Temple/synagogue) and ancillary rituals (bowing) to the core issue: prayer and its efficacy. It also echoes God's "love" *(chesed)* of verse 2.

◆

DORFF (THEOLOGY)

at home. Still, it is not *our* home, but God's, a frightening possibility, perhaps. So the possessive pronouns are given in the second person, "Your," not the third person, "His," to indicate that even God can be addressed familiarly.

The many houses of worship listed here suggest also that the accidental features of this specific "house" for prayer matter less than what takes place there. And what is that? "I enter Your house" that "I love." There "I will bow down low before Adonai, my Maker." I will also "offer my prayer," hoping that it is "at this time of favor," and that "[You will] answer me with Your saving truth." The verbs, then, describe the *process* of prayer, and its purpose—to acknowledge God's dominion, to praise God for the gifts in our lives, and to pray for deliverance from the many things and conditions that limit us. We trust that our prayers at a "time of favor" will help us do what is necessary to experience God's deliverance.

Judaism prefers communal worship because, as the Rabbis see it (Ber. 53a; R.H. 32b; Meg. 27b), "A numerous people is the glory of the king" (Prov. 14:28)—meaning that since public prayer gives more honor to God, it will likely be more effective than private prayer. The Talmud, therefore, interprets a "time of favor," as a "time of public worship" (Ber. 8a), and most prayers refer to worshipers in the plural, as part of a community. Here, however, all the verbs are in the first person singular: *I* will "enter Your house" that "*I* love"; *I* "will bow down low" and "offer *my* prayer to You" there; and *I* hope that You "answer *me* with Your saving truth." Our first morning prayer thus teaches us that we begin our communal journey as individuals. As Martin Buber held, we must recognize our own unique "I" before entering into a relationship with a "Thou"—whether with God or with other human beings.

ELLENSON (MODERN LITURGIES)

Einhorn *(Olath Tamid)* offered it in German only. Geiger, *UPB,* Mordecai Kaplan (1963 edition of the Reconstructionist *Daily Prayer Book*), the Dutch *Tov L'hodot,* and the British Liberal *Siddur Lev Chadash* supply an additional introductory paragraph, "At the dawn I seek You," a Sephardi poem by eleventh-century Solomon Ibn Gabirol.

FRANKEL (A WOMAN'S VOICE)

In this prayer, we assume a posture of humility as we prepare to enter the physical and spiritual dwelling-place of God's *k'dushah* ("holiness"). No fewer than six synonyms for "place" are found within this short paragraph: *ohel* ("tent"), reminiscent of the *ohel mo'ed,* the Tent of Meeting that housed the ark in the desert; *mishkan* ("dwelling-place"), the term used for the portable Tabernacle; *bayit* ("house"), an intimate domestic space sheltering families from the elements; *heikhal* ("palace"), the abode of a king; *m'on* ("refuge"), where wild beasts seek safety from predators; and *makom* ("place"), one of the many names of God, omnipresent in our lives and experience. We begin our formal worship by orienting ourselves in space, for if we are disoriented, we will fail to direct our prayers with appropriate *kavvanah* ("direction") and miss the mark.

We get not only spatial markers to prepare our entry into the place of prayer, but emotional compass points as well. Into this special place we are to bring with us *yirah* ("reverence") and *ahavah* ("love"), as well as humility (through bowing) and blessing (in returning to God what we receive). In assuming these different postures, each placing us in a different relationship to God—as subject, peer, and benefactor—we prepare ourselves to enter the full experience of prayer, wherever it takes us.
And yet, despite all this preparation, we also acknowledge that our success in this venture will depend on more than our will or willfulness. We end our prelude—as we began it—with an appeal for *chesed* ("unconditional love"). For no matter how hard we try to adopt an appropriate attitude to prayer, no matter how ready we think we are to express our gratitude and praise, we will always fall short because we lack *emet yishekha,* that "redemptive truth" that only God can risk.

J. HOFFMAN (TRANSLATION)

"house of dwelling" doesn't mean much more than house. But we lack sufficient words for "house" in English ("residence," "berth," "pad," etc., all miss the mark).

[3] *"Abode of Your glory"* More literally, "place of the abode of Your glory."

[4] *"Humbly bow down low"* Three words in Hebrew each meaning "bow" are used in a row here. The last comes from the root that also means "bless," and so an alternative here is "bow down low and offer blessing."

[5] *"I offer my prayer to You"* See Volume 4, *Seder K'riat Hatorah (The Torah Service)*, p. 69.

◆

L. HOFFMAN (HISTORY)

on the eve of battle. On a cliff overlooking the Israelite camp, however, he is unable to curse them. Instead, he says, "How wonderful are Your tents, Jacob...." The Rabbis understand "tents" to mean "synagogues," prompting them to reinterpret Balaam's messages: How wonderful are our synagogues!

[2] *"I, by Your great love"* Manuscripts tell fascinating tales. A scribe of *Machzor Vitry*, the primary French medieval prayer manual, accentuates this sentence, by writing it in especially large script. Since it contains ten Hebrew words, Jews used it to establish the presence of a *minyan* (a quorum of ten) for prayer. Believing (as many do, even now) that pointing to people attracts the "evil eye," they had each individual recite one of the words of the sentence. When the last word was reached, they knew ten people had gathered.

◆

KUSHNER & POLEN (CHASIDISM)

the entire prayer shawl over one's head. But, since everyone is busy with his or her own private ritual, people rarely have an opportunity to survey the entire scene. To someone watching it (from above) however, all those Jews would appear to have literally made their own personal tents! "How wonderful are Your tents, Jacob!"

◆ ◆ ◆

B. PUTTING ON THE *TALLIT*

[Before putting on the tallit:]

1 O my soul, bless Adonai! 2 Adonai my God, You are very great, robed in glory and majesty. 3 You wrap light like a garment, spread out heaven like a curtain. 4 I hereby wrap myself in a *tallit* with tassels in order to fulfill the commandment of my Creator, as written in the Torah: 5 They shall make themselves a tassel on the corners of their clothes in every generation. 6 And as I cover myself with a *tallit* in this world, so may my soul be worthy of wearing a beautiful *tallit* in the world-to-come, in the Garden of Eden. Amen.

[While putting on the tallit:]

7 Blessed are You, Adonai our God, Ruler of the world, who sanctified us with His commandments and commanded us to wrap ourselves with a tasseled garment.

8 How precious is Your love, God, that mankind can take refuge in the shadow of Your wings. 9 They will eat from the abundance of Your house, and You will have them drink from Your stream of delight. 10 For with You is the source of life; in Your light do we see light. 11 Extend Your love to those who know You, and Your righteousness to the upright of heart.

12 May it be Your will, Adonai our God and our ancestors' God, that this commandment of tassels be considered as though I've fulfilled it in every aspect, detail, and purpose, and the 613 commandments that are related to it. Amen.

[Before putting on the tallit:]

¹בָּרְכִי נַפְשִׁי אֶת יְיָ; ²יְיָ אֱלֹהַי, גָּדַלְתָּ מְּאֹד, הוֹד וְהָדָר לָבָשְׁתָּ. ³עֹטֶה אוֹר כַּשַּׂלְמָה, נוֹטֶה שָׁמַיִם כַּירִיעָה.

⁴הִנְנִי מִתְעַטֵּף בְּטַלִּית שֶׁל צִיצִת כְּדֵי לְקַיֵּם מִצְוַת בּוֹרְאִי, כַּכָּתוּב בַּתּוֹרָה: ⁵וְעָשׂוּ לָהֶם צִיצִת עַל כַּנְפֵי בִגְדֵיהֶם לְדֹרֹתָם. ⁶וּכְשֵׁם שֶׁאֲנִי מִתְכַּסֶּה בְּטַלִּית בָּעוֹלָם הַזֶּה, כֵּן תִּזְכֶּה נִשְׁמָתִי לְהִתְלַבֵּשׁ בְּטַלִּית נָאָה לָעוֹלָם הַבָּא בְּגַן עֵדֶן. אָמֵן.

[While putting on the tallit:]

⁷בָּרוּךְ אַתָּה, יְיָ אֱלֹהֵינוּ, מֶלֶךְ הָעוֹלָם, אֲשֶׁר קִדְּשָׁנוּ בְּמִצְוֹתָיו וְצִוָּנוּ לְהִתְעַטֵּף בַּצִּיצִת.

⁸מַה יָּקָר חַסְדְּךָ, אֱלֹהִים, וּבְנֵי אָדָם בְּצֵל כְּנָפֶיךָ יֶחֱסָיוּן. ⁹יִרְוְיֻן מִדֶּשֶׁן בֵּיתֶךָ, וְנַחַל עֲדָנֶיךָ תַשְׁקֵם. ¹⁰כִּי עִמְּךָ מְקוֹר חַיִּים, בְּאוֹרְךָ נִרְאֶה אוֹר. ¹¹מְשֹׁךְ חַסְדְּךָ לְיֹדְעֶיךָ, וְצִדְקָתְךָ לְיִשְׁרֵי לֵב.

¹²יְהִי רָצוֹן מִלְּפָנֶיךָ, יְיָ אֱלֹהֵינוּ וֵאלֹהֵי אֲבוֹתֵינוּ, שֶׁתְּהֵא חֲשׁוּבָה מִצְוַת צִיצַת זוֹ כְּאִלּוּ קִיַּמְתִּיהָ בְּכָל פְּרָטֶיהָ וְדִקְדּוּקֶיהָ וְכַוָּנוֹתֶיהָ וְתַרְיַ"ג מִצְוֹת הַתְּלוּיִם בָּהּ. אָמֵן סֶלָה.

BRETTLER (BIBLE)

[1] *"O my soul, bless Adonai!"* Psalm 104:1–2, part of a highly mythological psalm that contradicts the standard creation narratives in Genesis 1–3. It pictures God "wrapped in a robe of light" while spreading out the heavens, establishing the earth, making springs gush forth, and so on. Its recitation while donning the *tallit* suggests a remarkable case of *imitatio dei:* putting on the *tallit* becomes equivalent to God's act of creation.

[4] *"I hereby wrap myself...as written in the Torah"* Quoting Numbers 15:38, from the third paragraph of the *Sh'ma.* On the biblical function of tassels (*tsitsit*), see Volume 1, *The Sh'ma and Its Blessings*, p. 112.

(p. 59)

DORFF (THEOLOGY)

[4] *"I hereby wrap myself in a* tallit *with tassels"* At its most basic level, the *tallit* is simply a four-cornered garment to which the tassels demanded by the Torah can be attached. The liturgy, though, extends its meaning in several directions. By quoting Psalm 104:1–2, *(p. 59)*

ELLENSON (MODERN LITURGY)

[1] *"O my soul, bless Adonai!"* Although *tsitsit* (ritual fringes) and a *tallit* (prayer shawl) have biblical and rabbinic precedent, previous generations of Reform Jews rejected them. Consequently, they usually omitted this meditation. Abraham Geiger included the blessing for the *tallit* in his moderate 1854 prayer book, which he intended as an inclusive offering for German liberal Jews in general; but he removed the meditations prior to it, because they were of mystical origin. And he decided not even to print the blessing in his more radical 1870 liturgy.

In the latter half of the twentieth century, Reform became more congenially disposed to ritual-mystical elements in Jewish tradition, with the result that its North American *(p. 60)*

B. PUTTING ON THE *TALLIT*

[Before putting on the tallit:]

[1] O my soul, bless Adonai! [2] Adonai my God, You are very great, robed in glory and majesty. [3] You wrap light like a garment, spread out heaven like a curtain. [4] I hereby wrap myself in a *tallit* with tassels in order to fulfill the commandment of my Creator, as written in the Torah: [5] They shall make themselves a tassel on the corners of their clothes in every generation.

FRANKEL (A WOMAN'S VOICE)

[4] *"I hereby wrap myself in a* tallit *"* Until a few decades ago, this piece of liturgy spoke to only half the congregation—men. Even now, most women do not don a *tallit,* and even those who do probably recite only the one-line blessing, *v'tsivanu l'hitatef batsitsit,* "who has commanded us to wrap ourselves with a tasseled garment," that constitutes the minimum prayer for putting on a *tallit.* It is a pity that women are not familiar with the paragraph before and the *(p. 62)*

J. HOFFMAN (TRANSLATION)

[1] *"O my soul"* We usually try to avoid the archaic "O" (and so we prefer "Israel," above, to "O Israel," etc.), but here it would be hard to do without some indication that the speaker's soul is being addressed.

[2] *"Robed [in glory]"* Literally, "wearing," but (following Birnbaum) we feel a more poetic word is in order.

[3] *"Wrap light like a garment"* Birnbaum gives us "wrap yourself in light..."—probably the ultimate   (p. 63)

[Before putting on the tallit:]

[1] בָּרְכִי נַפְשִׁי אֶת יְיָ; [2] יְיָ אֱלֹהַי, גָּדַלְתָּ מְאֹד, הוֹד וְהָדָר לָבָשְׁתָּ. [3] עֹטֶה אוֹר כַּשַּׂלְמָה, נוֹטֶה שָׁמַיִם כַּיְרִיעָה. [4] הִנְנִי מִתְעַטֵּף בְּטַלִּית שֶׁל צִיצִת כְּדֵי לְקַיֵּם מִצְוַת בּוֹרְאִי, כַּכָּתוּב בַּתּוֹרָה: [5] וְעָשׂוּ לָהֶם צִיצִת עַל כַּנְפֵי בִגְדֵיהֶם לְדֹרֹתָם.

L. HOFFMAN (HISTORY)

[4] *"I hereby wrap myself in a tallit"* The rationale for wearing a *tallit* comes from Numbers 15:39, "You shall see the *tsitsit* ["tassels"] and remember all the commandments of God and do them." We do not know what clothes originally held *tsitsit,* but by the second or third century, it was common for the Rabbis, at least, to attach them to a very large garment that enwrapped the whole body. Wrapping oneself had become a significant ritual expected   (p. 63)

KUSHNER & POLEN (CHASIDISM)

[4] *"I hereby wrap myself in a* tallit*"* Though not included in the standard prayer book, we have an outstanding *tallit* meditation written by Israel Meir HaKohen Kagan (1838–1933), known also as the Chafetz Chayim (*Mishnah B'rurah* 4, commenting on the *Shulchan Arukh,* O. Ch. 8). There we read that "at the moment of actual enwrapping the *tallit,* you cover your head until the *tallit* reaches your mouth and then you throw the four corners [around your neck and] over your left shoulder [effectively making the *tallit* into a sack covering your head] for a few seconds...." Some even go so far as to say that this act itself   (p. 64)

LANDES (HALAKHAH)

[1] *"O my soul, bless Adonai!"* Our first obligation of the day is not to ourselves, but to God. We therefore begin with prayer. We avoid the following before saying our morning prayers:

1. We do not begin personal work-related acts (Tos. Ber. 5b; *Arukh Hashulchan,* O. Ch. 89:20), although the Halakhah is more liberal with community-oriented acts such as collecting *ts'dakah*/charity or preparing for Shabbat if performing these later would be very inconvenient (*Sha'arei T'shuva,* 89:47).

2. We do not set out on a journey unless the delay for prayer would cause us to miss our   (p. 65)

6 And as I cover myself with a *tallit* in this world, so may my soul be worthy of wearing a beautiful *tallit* in the world-to-come, in the Garden of Eden. Amen.

[While putting on the tallit:]

7 Blessed are You, Adonai our God, Ruler of the world, who sanctified us with His commandments and commanded us to wrap ourselves with a tasseled garment.

8 How precious is Your love, God, that mankind can take refuge in the shadow of Your wings. 9 They will eat from the abundance of Your house, and You will have them drink from Your stream of delight. 10 For with You is the source of life; in Your light do we see light. 11 Extend Your love to those who know You, and Your righteousness to the upright of heart.

12 May it be Your will, Adonai our God and our ancestors' God, that this commandment of tassels be considered as though I've fulfilled it in every aspect, detail, and purpose, and the 613 commandments that are related to it. Amen.

⁶וּכְשֵׁם שֶׁאֲנִי מִתְכַּסֶּה בְטַלִּית בָּעוֹלָם הַזֶּה, כֵּן תִּזְכֶּה נִשְׁמָתִי לְהִתְלַבֵּשׁ בְּטַלִּית נָאָה לָעוֹלָם הַבָּא בְּגַן עֵדֶן. אָמֵן.

[While putting on the tallit:]

⁷בָּרוּךְ אַתָּה, יְיָ אֱלֹהֵינוּ, מֶלֶךְ הָעוֹלָם, אֲשֶׁר קִדְּשָׁנוּ בְּמִצְוֹתָיו וְצִוָּנוּ לְהִתְעַטֵּף בַּצִּיצִת.

⁸מַה יָּקָר חַסְדְּךָ, אֱלֹהִים, וּבְנֵי אָדָם בְּצֵל כְּנָפֶיךָ יֶחֱסָיוּן. ⁹יִרְוְיֻן מִדֶּשֶׁן בֵּיתֶךָ, וְנַחַל עֲדָנֶיךָ תַשְׁקֵם. ¹⁰כִּי עִמְּךָ מְקוֹר חַיִּים, בְּאוֹרְךָ נִרְאֶה אוֹר. ¹¹מְשֹׁךְ חַסְדְּךָ לְיֹדְעֶיךָ, וְצִדְקָתְךָ לְיִשְׁרֵי לֵב.

¹²יְהִי רָצוֹן מִלְפָנֶיךָ, יְיָ אֱלֹהֵינוּ וֵאלֹהֵי אֲבוֹתֵינוּ, שֶׁתְּהֵא חֲשׁוּבָה מִצְוַת צִיצִת זוֹ כְּאִלּוּ קִיַּמְתִּיהָ בְּכָל פְּרָטֶיהָ וְדִקְדּוּקֶיהָ וְכַוָּנוֹתֶיהָ וְתַרְיַ"ג מִצְוֹת הַתְּלוּיִם בָּהּ. אָמֵן סֶלָה.

BRETTLER (BIBLE)

[7] *"Blessed are You…ruler of the world* [Barukh atah Adonai…melekh ha'olam]" The standard rabbinic blessing *(b'rakhah)* formula, which incorporates several biblical elements, but in its totality is post-biblical. "Blessed are You" *(Barukh atah Adonai)* comes from late biblical texts, Psalm 119:12 and 1 Chronicles 29:10. "Ruler of the world" *(melekh ha'olam)* is often used of God (e.g., Ps. 146:10 and in a different grammatical form, Ps. 29:10). Biblically, however, *olam* is always temporal, meaning that God rules eternally. Rabbinically, it is both temporal ("eternity") and geographical ("the world").

[7] *"Sanctified us with His commandments"* That Jews are sanctified through commandments comes from the Holiness Collection in Leviticus 17–26 (see, e.g., 19:2ff.), and elsewhere (e.g., Exod. 22:30).

[8] *"How precious is Your love"* Psalm 36:8–10.

DORFF (THEOLOGY)

which depicts God as robing Himself in glory, majesty, and light, the liturgy suggests that by wrapping ourselves in the *tallit* we can become like God, letting God's mantle of glory, majesty, and light enter our lives. Second, the liturgy (in at least some versions) asks that "Just as I wrap myself in a *tallit* in this world, so may my soul wrap itself in a beautiful *tallit* in the world to come and in the Garden of Eden." Donning a *tallit* is thus linked to our hope for a life after death enwrapped in pleasantness. Third, in having us read Psalm 36:8–11 here, the liturgy likens wrapping our shoulders under the *tallit* to being taken under the wings of our gracious God.

The tassels *(tsitsit)* symbolize two Jewish convictions. Each one is made from four strands of thread that are pulled through a small hole at each the edges of the *tallit*, resulting in eight strands hanging from each edge. One of the four threads, the *shamash*, is longer than the others so that it can be wrapped around the others to make the tassel. One double knot using all eight strands (the four threads doubled over through the eyelet) is first tied near the edge of the garment; then four other double knots are tied to make the tassel. The *shamash* is wrapped around the other seven strands—first seven, then eight, then eleven, and (finally) thirteen times. Hebrew letters have numerical equivalents in the order of the alphabet: *alef* = 1, *bet* = 2, and so on. Fifteen (7 + 8) is the numerical equivalent of the first two letters of God's name *(yod heh)*, and eleven is the numerical equivalent of the second two letters of God's name *(vav heh)*. Thirteen is the numerical equivalent of the Hebrew word *echad*, "one." So the tassels symbolize the central theological affirmation of Judaism: God is one. In addition, the Hebrew word for tassels, *tsitsit*, has a numerical equivalent of six hundred, which together with the eight threads and five knots make 613, the number of commandments the tradition counts in the Torah. Thus the tassels also indicate that we are to obey God's commandments, indeed, that we are to wrap ourselves and our lives in the holiness they bring, as the blessing for putting on the *tallit* says.

———◆———

ELLENSON (MODERN LITURGY)

Gates of Prayer, the Dutch *Tov L'hodot*, and the Israeli *Ha'avodah Shebalev* all include this passage.

Reconstructionist Judaism has always applauded Jewish ritual as folkways that are integral to Judaism as a religious civilization. Still, the ultrarationalistic Mordecai Kaplan found the psalmist's description of a personal creator God who dons "light like a garment" ideologically objectionable. The 1963 Reconstructionist *Daily Prayer Book* therefore wrote its own meditation for *tallit* and *t'fillin* that identifies these rituals with the Jewish ethical obligation to work for the social amelioration of the world.

The same forces that caused contemporary Reform to readmit this meditation have impacted Reconstructionism also. The influence of Jewish renewal figures such as Zalman Schachter-Shalomi, Arthur Green, and Arthur Waskow upon Reconstructionism has led the movement to reincorporate personal God imagery as well as nonrationalistic and even mystical dimensions of Jewish tradition to a degree that would have been unthinkable for Kaplan. Consequently, its current *Kol Haneshamah* has forthrightly restored this passage, positively affirming its inspiring description of "how God, robed in splendor, wrapped in light, created the world."

Finally, this phrase, which was absent from older Conservative prayer books, reappears in the American *Siddur Sim Shalom*. The Israeli Conservative liturgy *(Siddur Va'ani T'fillati)*, however, replaces it with precise directions on how to don the *tallit* and an explanation of why it is worn only in the morning. As a sign of its newly found impulse toward gender equality and its historical commitment to Halakhah, *SVT* contends that the Jewish legal tradition not only *allows* women to wear the *tallit*, but even *obligates* them "to observe all the commandments, including the commandment of the *tsitsit*."

[4] *"I hereby wrap myself in a* tallit…*"* While numerous liberal Siddurim have restored the ritual of *tallit* to their rites, only the Conservative *Siddur Sim Shalom* and the Dutch Reform *Tov L'hodot* include this particular mystical meditation, and even they omit the last lines that refer to being robed in "a beautiful *tallit* in the world-to-come, in the Garden of Eden." Undoubtedly, modern editors find such a blatant description of the afterlife problematic.

[7] *"Blessed are You, Adonai our God, Ruler of the world"* Classical talmudic law stipulates that the formula for a blessing must mention God's name and sovereignty. Consequently, Jewish blessings have included the words "Adonai our God, Ruler of the world." Furthermore, they have begun with the words "Blessed are You" as a sign that

God is envisioned personally, but also as a being who is "bless-ed" in essence, irrespective of any act on the part of humans. From this latter perspective, to say "Blessed" is to acknowledge the metaphysical majesty of God. A number of contemporary Jews, however, most prominently Marcia Falk, have expressed serious reservations about what they perceive as the personal theology of "hierarchical opposition" that animates this formula. For these reasons, Falk has replaced the traditional formula with a new one that posits "a theology of immanence that will both affirm the sanctity of the world and shatter the idolatrous reign of the lord/God/king." Her novel blessing formula often begins with "Let us bless the Source of Life." She thus rejects the traditional notion of a personal creator God who reigns in majestic splendor over His subjects. Her substitution of "Let us bless" for "Blessed" affirms the divinity that inheres immanently in all life, as well as the active role human beings must play for the world to be sanctified.

Her novel prayer formula finds frequent expression in her *Book of Blessings,* but is found also at this point in *Kol Haneshamah,* thereby testifying to the influence that Falk (as well as other feminists) have had upon present-day Reconstructionist liturgy. In their accompanying commentary, the authors of *KH* observe that "many contemporary Jews are reciting *berakhot*/blessings in ways that reflect their theological outlooks and ethical concerns." Consequently, *KH* allows the worshiper several options: (1) either *Barukh* (feminine: *B'rukhah*) "Blessed are You Yah," or "Let us bless," in place of "Blessed are You"; (2) *"Shekhinah"* or "Source of Life," in lieu of "our God"; and (3) "Life of all the worlds" or "Spirit of the world," instead of "Ruler of the world." In speaking of these options, the Reconstructionist commentary indicates that "at any place where a blessing occurs in the liturgy, [these phrasal] elements can be combined to create alternative formulas for *berakhot.*" All this testifies to the innovative and radical nature of Reconstructionist prayer, as well as the openness that marks the Reconstructionst approach to Jewish tradition.

[7] *"Commanded us to wrap ourselves" Gates of Prayer* refuses to translate "commanded us" literally and opts instead for "teaches us." This translation follows from the Reform Movement's multilayered stand on Jewish ritual. On the one hand, the very inclusion of the blessing for the *tallit* indicates that present-day North American Reform Judaism is reestablishing a meaningful relationship with ritual. However, ritual pluralism remains its hallmark, so that engaging in it is a matter of personal choice, not obligation, as it would be for traditional Jews. *GOP* therefore stipulates that the blessing is included only "for those who wear the *tallit,*" and the muted translation "teaches" avoids the notion that ritual is commanded and, therefore, obligatory for all Jews.

[8] *"How precious is Your love" Ha'avodah Shebalev* (Israeli Reform), *Siddur Sim Shalom* (American Conservative), and *Tov L'hodot* (Dutch Reform) all restore this reading from Psalm 36:8–11 to their prayer rites, once more reflecting a turn toward tradition that seems to inform all sectors of contemporary non-Orthodox Judaism.

[12] *"May it be Your will…and the 613 commandments"* No liberal liturgy includes

these lines in their prayer service. The idea that wearing *tsitsit* is equal to fulfilling all 613 commandments is deemed too hyperbolic for non-Orthodox prayerbook authors, especially since they are likely to view the traditional numerical total as spurious in any event. It is only one estimate that tradition has passed down, and it includes commandments that are possible only in the Land of Israel, and only in a messianic age—including the entire sacrificial cult. Liberal authors hardly expect or even want Jews to fulfill them all.

FRANKEL (A WOMAN'S VOICE)

psalm after this blessing, for these two liturgical supplements draw their imagery from what has traditionally been the sphere of women's experience. God is described as "robed" *(lavashta)* in light as though wearing a "garment," *simlah* (the modern Hebrew word for "dress"). God spreads out the heavens like a curtain. As we wrap the *tallit* around our physical bodies, we pray that our souls will be dressed in a beautiful spiritual *tallit* in the world-to-come. God is depicted as a divine seamstress, weaving garments for those who dwell in heaven and on earth, in this world and in paradise.

Psalm 36, following the blessing for putting on the *tallit,* introduces several metaphors, all of which have traditionally been associated with women. God's kindness is compared to "wings" *(k'nafekha)* under whose shadow God's children take refuge. The *Shekhinah,* God's feminine aspect, is typically depicted as a winged presence sheltering Israel from harm. God is then described as one who nourishes us with choice "food" *(deshen)* and gives us drink from a stream of delights. The Hebrew root of this last term, *adanekha,* is the same word as "Eden" and means sensual pleasure. Indeed, when God tells Sarah that she is to give birth to a son at ninety years of age, she protests: "Am I to have enjoyment—*edna*—with my husband so old?" God here promises us that these miraculous garments of prayer will afford us spiritual pleasure.

The psalm next speaks about God's "fountain of life" *(m'kor chayim),* a phrase that has been adopted by Jewish feminists as a divine name with particular feminine resonance. More than any other image, water—in the form of wells, springs, and other sources—has been associated with women: Rebekah and Rachel meet their lovers at the village well; Miriam's life-giving well sustains the Israelites through the wilderness. So too God's loving-kindness *(chesed)* promises to nourish and enlighten us as we journey toward the Source of Being, sheltered under the divine wings.

J. HOFFMAN (TRANSLATION)

intention, but not what the Hebrew (from Ps. 104:2) says. *JPS* prefers "wrapped in a robe of light." *NRSV* gives us "Wrapped in light as with a garment."

⁴*"[I] hereby"* A formulaic word in English, mirroring the Hebrew *hin'ni*.

⁴*"Tallit"* The original meaning of this word was just "garment." But in context here we feel that "garment" is insufficient.

⁴*"Tassels"* Hebrew, *tsitsit*. Usually translated as "fringes." Surprisingly, this word in Hebrew is singular. See Volume 1, *The Sh'ma and Its Blessings*, p. 114.

⁶*"So may my soul be worthy"* For "soul," the Hebrew reads *n'shamah*. In the line directly above, a variant of *nefesh* was used for "soul"— that is, *nafshi, "my* soul." But that line merely joins together biblical citations, and *bar'khi nafshi* happens to be the quotation in Psalms 103 and 104. By contrast, *n'shamah* is specifically chosen here for its kabbalistic intent. (See L. Hoffman, "I hereby *[hin'ni]* wrap myself in a *tallit,"* p. 64.)

As for "be worthy": Others prefer "merit" or "deserve." The notion here is probably, "May my soul win the prize of wearing a *tallit* in the world-to-come." "Get to wear..." would be nice if it weren't the wrong register.

⁷*"A tasseled garment"* Hebrew, "tassels."

⁹*"Eat [from the abundance]"* More literally, "be sated." The English "sate," however, is not only rare but also negatively suggestive of "overeating," whereas the Hebrew connotes "eating and eating and eating" in a positive sense, the same sense in which one's "glass overflows" with goodness.

¹⁰*"In Your light"* Or perhaps, "through Your light." It's not immediately clear what the difference would be, probably because it's not immediately clear how we would see light either "in" or "through" God's light.

———◆———

L. HOFFMAN (HISTORY)

of judges before trials, teachers before discourses, and Rabbis preparing for prayer.

Some wore the *tallit* all day; others did not. It was, in any event, not worn at night, since the idea was to see the *tsitsit,* and without daylight, they could not be seen. Jews in the Land of Israel omitted from the evening service the last paragraph of the *Sh'ma* (Num. 15:37–41), since its point is the wearing—and, by extension, seeing—of *tsitsit.*

Eventually, Jews invented a *tallit katan* (a "little *tallit"*) as an undergarment to which to attach *tsitsit,* in cultures where Jews wanted to wear them all day long but, also, to look like everyone else. In a parallel (but unrelated) development, the absolute ban against wearing a *tallit* at night was relaxed, and post-seventeenth-century service leaders were often encouraged to wear a symbolic *tallit* while leading all services, "because of the honor due the congregation."

Reform Jews originally dispensed with the *tallit* as a vestige of old worship wear that, they thought, no longer had any meaning. Still, service leaders sometimes wore one or, if not an actual *tallit* with *tsitsit*, then at least a stole called an *atarah*. But gradually, by the late twentieth century, Reform Jews began reincorporating a *tallit* in their worship. At roughly the same time, some Orthodox Jews began making it a point to wear their *tallit katan* with the fringes displayed externally as a sign of keeping the commandment.

4 *"I hereby* [hin'ni] *wrap myself in a* tallit*"* The first person singular (rather than the plural), along with the telltale opening word *hin'ni* suggests this is a kabbalistic *kavvanah,* a meditation that supplies a "hidden" message of the prayer it introduces. Kabbalists believed that prayers have not just obvious meanings, but esoteric ones as well. (See "with this do I prepare," Volume 3, *P'sukei D'zimrah (Morning Prayers),* pp. 53, 66 [The Hebrew *Bhareni* there is equivalent to *hin'ni* here].) In this case, as with the prayers that follow for putting on *t'fillin,* the esoteric meaning is explicitly given. Wearing a *tallit* in our earthly life is rewarded by our soul being garbed in one for its stay in the world-to-come. (For *t'fillin,* see below, "By putting on *t'fillin* I hereby intend" and "Pour good oil on the seven branches of the menorah.")

The word for "soul" is *n'shamah*—in kabbalistic terms, the highest of the three parts of the soul. The lowest part, the *nefesh,* is akin to our animal-like instinctive nature. The middle part, the *ru'ach,* mediates between the upper soul (the *n'shamah*) and the *nefesh.* Only the *n'shamah* is the distinctively human endowment that understands Torah and ultimately merits eternal life.

KUSHNER & POLEN (CHASIDISM)

constitutes fulfillment of the commandment "to enwrap oneself with *tsitsit* [tassels]." Others say that this making a sack of one's *tallit* is done in the "manner of Arabs [protecting themselves from wind-driven sand]." Commenting on the above, Gedalyah Fleer, a Bratslaver Chasid in Jerusalem, suggests that when the *tallit* is made into such a sack over your head, it is an especially appropriate time to pray for the well-being of others, a time uniquely suited to the channeling of grace and healing.

LANDES (HALAKHAH)

only transport, but this does not exempt us from saying our prayers on board or upon arrival (*Magen Avraham*, O. Ch. 89:10).

3. We do not eat before we pray. The Talmud (Ber. 10b) considers eating before prayer the height of egoism, as if one is setting his or her interests before God's.

However, drinking water and even eating can be acceptable under certain circumstances, if not done not out of egoism but out of genuine physical need, or in order to aid concentration during prayer.

The restriction on eating before prayer is even more significant on Shabbat and holidays, when we say *Kiddush*, because of the additional restrictions and prohibition on eating anything before *Kiddush*.

If we must eat before prayer, we try, if possible, to say the Morning Blessings (*Birkhot Hashachar*) before eating. However, if this is difficult, health considerations come first. The sick may eat before prayer. Any out-of-the-ordinary weakness that can be remedied by eating may be considered an "illness" in this regard (*Magen Avraham*, O. Ch. 89:10). According to Maimonides, anyone who finds it difficult to concentrate on words of prayer before drinking or eating may do so, although one should eat no more than what one requires for concentration (Maimonides, Laws of Blessings, 4:10).

One may take medicines before prayer, and drink or eat with the medicine, if required (*Bet Yosef*, O. Ch. 89:2). This holds true even if the treatment can be taken at a later time.

Arukh Hashulchan includes caffeine addicts in the category of the "ill."

Most authorities permit drinking water before blessings or prayers, since drinking a glass of water is not an act of egoism (self-indulgence). Those who permit water would also permit coffee and tea, which are basically water. However, the addition of milk and sugar, which, unlike coffee and tea, contain nutrition, is the object of some controversy (*Arukh Hashulchan*, O. Ch. 89:4).

While older children should be educated to avoid eating before prayer, the tradition of not eating before prayer does not usually apply to children.

In certain communities (notably in North America), however, Shabbat morning prayers are held at a late hour, and services often do not end until midday or later. In such communities, two criteria should be considered: the ability of the average adult to concentrate on prayer without food or drink, and the concept of *oneg Shabbat* ("enjoyment of Shabbat"). Since we may not fast on Shabbat, even for half a day, not eating all morning is problematic (*Shulchan Arukh*, O. Ch. 288:1).

Some Chasidic communities ignore the ban on eating before prayer. They do not generally observe the laws concerning the required times for beginning prayers either, since they precede prayer with a variety of mystical preparatory meditations.

[7] *"To wrap ourselves with a tassled garment* [tsitsit]*"* The following laws apply to *tsitsit*:

1. While the toraitic *mitzvah* is to put *tsitsit* ("fringes") on a four-cornered garment, the Rabbis stipulate that a four-cornered garment be worn so that *tsitsit* can be attached.

2. Two garments are worn, the *tallit katan* (a poncho-like "small *tallit* under the shirt) and the *tallit gadol* (the large ceremonial garment worn during prayer). Since the purpose of *tsitsit* is to "remind you...of all of the commandments," it is clear that the *tallit katan* is the primary means of doing the *mitzvah*.

3. The *tsitsit* of both garments should be inspected (though not on Shabbat, when tying is forbidden) prior to wearing them.

4. The blessing is recited before putting them on.

5. One fulfills the *mitzvah* of wearing *tsitsit* even if the fringes of the *tallit katan* are tucked into one's trousers. The *mitzvah* of "You shall see them" is fulfilled by the fact that one feels them. "Seeing" is not meant literally; it refers to the fact that the positive commandment of *tsitsit* holds only during daylight.

6. It is nonetheless customary to wear the *tallit katan* at night, especially if one has not changed clothes. It is a pious Chasidic custom to wear them to bed.

7. If one puts them on with unwashed hands or before dawn, one waits to say the blessing until after washing or after dawn has broken.

8. Before putting on the *tallit gadol,* one recites the blessing and then wraps oneself in the *tallit.* One then covers the head with the *tallit* for a recognizable moment.

9. The Gra (Elijah of Vilna, 1720–1797) forbade the custom of some to wrap their head with the *tallit gadol* as a turban for the moment of concentration.

10. One must adjust one's *tallit* so that two of the fringes are in front and two in back. Thus one should not wear the *tallit* as a shawl.

11. If a *tallit* falls off completely, even for a moment, one must repeat the blessing. If one takes it off purposely with the intent to put it back on momentarily, no new blessing is needed.

12. One may recite the blessings over a borrowed *tallit* that belongs to the synagogue.

13. If one confused the blessing over the *tallit katan*—al mitzvat tsitsit ("concerning the *mitzvah* of *tsitsit*")—with that of the *tallit gadol*—l'hitateif batsitsit ("to wrap oneself in *tsitsit*")—or vice versa, one has still fulfilled the commandment (R'ma, O. Ch. 8:6).

◆ ◆ ◆

C. PUTTING ON *T'FILLIN*

[Before putting on t'fillin:]

[1] By putting on *t'fillin*, I hereby intend to fulfill the commandment of my Creator, who commanded us to put on *t'fillin,* as written in the Torah: [2] Bind them to your hand as a sign and set them between your eyes as a symbol. [3] They comprise the following four passages: "Hear...," "If you carefully heed...," "Sanctify...," "And when He brings you...," which contain His unity and oneness, blessed be His name throughout the world, that we should remember the miracles and wonders that He did with us when He brought us out from Egypt, for He has power and dominion, both heavenly and earthly, to do with them as He wishes. [4] And He has commanded us to put *t'fillin* on our arm in remembrance of His outstretched arm, and which is next to the heart, to subjugate our heart's desires and thoughts to His service, blessed be His name, and on our head, next to our brain, in order that the soul in my brain along with my other senses and powers be subjugated to His service, blessed be His name. [5] And because the *t'fillin* commandment flows through me with blessing, may I continue to have long life, holiness flowing through me with blessing, and holy thoughts, without any sinful thoughts whatsoever. [6] May our evil inclination not tempt or provoke us, but leave us to worship God as our hearts desire. Amen.

[Before putting on t'fillin:]

¹הִנְנִי מְכַוֵּן בְּהַנָּחַת תְּפִלִּין לְקַיֵּם מִצְוַת בּוֹרְאִי שֶׁצִּוָּנוּ לְהָנִיחַ תְּפִלִּין, כַּכָּתוּב בַּתּוֹרָה: ²וּקְשַׁרְתָּם לְאוֹת עַל יָדֶךָ, וְהָיוּ לְטֹטָפֹת בֵּין עֵינֶיךָ. ³וְהֵם אַרְבַּע פָּרָשִׁיּוֹת אֵלּוּ: שְׁמַע, וְהָיָה אִם שָׁמֹעַ, קַדֶּשׁ, וְהָיָה כִּי יְבִיאֲךָ, שֶׁיֵּשׁ בָּהֶם יִחוּדוֹ וְאַחְדּוּתוֹ יִתְבָּרַךְ שְׁמוֹ בָּעוֹלָם; וְשֶׁנִּזְכֹּר נִסִּים וְנִפְלָאוֹת שֶׁעָשָׂה עִמָּנוּ בְּהוֹצִיאוֹ אוֹתָנוּ מִמִּצְרָיִם, וַאֲשֶׁר לוֹ הַכֹּחַ וְהַמֶּמְשָׁלָה בָּעֶלְיוֹנִים וּבַתַּחְתּוֹנִים לַעֲשׂוֹת בָּהֶם כִּרְצוֹנוֹ. ⁴וְצִוָּנוּ לְהָנִיחַ עַל הַיָּד לְזִכְרוֹן זְרוֹעוֹ הַנְּטוּיָה; וְשֶׁהִיא נֶגֶד הַלֵּב, לְשַׁעְבֵּד בָּזֶה תַּאֲוֹת וּמַחְשְׁבוֹת לִבֵּנוּ לַעֲבוֹדָתוֹ, יִתְבָּרַךְ שְׁמוֹ; וְעַל הָרֹאשׁ נֶגֶד הַמֹּחַ, שֶׁהַנְּשָׁמָה שֶׁבְּמֹחִי עִם שְׁאָר חוּשַׁי וְכֹחוֹתַי כֻּלָּם יִהְיוּ מְשֻׁעְבָּדִים לַעֲבוֹדָתוֹ, יִתְבָּרַךְ שְׁמוֹ. ⁵וּמִשֶּׁפַע מִצְוַת תְּפִלִּין יִתְמַשֵּׁךְ עָלַי לִהְיוֹת לִי חַיִּים אֲרֻכִים וְשֶׁפַע קֹדֶשׁ וּמַחֲשָׁבוֹת קְדוֹשׁוֹת, בְּלִי הִרְהוֹר חֵטְא וְעָוֹן כְּלָל, ⁶וְשֶׁלֹּא יְפַתֵּנוּ וְלֹא יִתְגָּרֶה בָּנוּ יֵצֶר הָרָע, וְיַנִּיחֵנוּ לַעֲבוֹד אֶת יְיָ כַּאֲשֶׁר עִם לְבָבֵנוּ. אָמֵן.

67

[While putting t'fillin on arm, say:]

⁷Blessed are You, Adonai our God, Ruler of the world, who sanctified us with His commandments and commanded us to put on *t'fillin.*

[While putting t'fillin on head, say:]

⁸Blessed are You, Adonai our God, Ruler of the world, who sanctified us with His commandments and commanded us about the *mitzvah* of *t'fillin.* ⁹Blessed is the One the glory of whose kingdom is renowned forever.

¹⁰Share Your wisdom with me, God on high, and from Your knowledge help me know. ¹¹With Your love do great things for me, and with Your power cut off my enemies and adversaries. ¹²Pour good oil on the seven branches of the menorah, to extend the flow of Your goodness upon Your creatures, opening Your hand, and satisfying every living thing with favor.

[While winding the strap around the middle finger, three times, say:]

¹³I will betroth you to Me forever. ¹⁴I will betroth you to Me in righteousness, in justice, in kindness, and in mercy. ¹⁵I will betroth you to Me in faithfulness, and you will know Adonai. ¹⁶May it be Your will, Adonai our God and our ancestors' God, that this commandment of putting on *t'fillin* be considered as though I've fulfilled it in every aspect, detail, and purpose, and the 613 commandments that are related to it. Amen, Selah.

[While putting t'fillin on arm, say:]

⁷בָּרוּךְ אַתָּה, יְיָ אֱלֹהֵינוּ, מֶלֶךְ הָעוֹלָם, אֲשֶׁר קִדְּשָׁנוּ בְּמִצְוֹתָיו וְצִוָּנוּ לְהָנִיחַ תְּפִלִּין.

[While putting t'fillin on head, say:]

⁸בָּרוּךְ אַתָּה, יְיָ אֱלֹהֵינוּ, מֶלֶךְ הָעוֹלָם, אֲשֶׁר קִדְּשָׁנוּ בְּמִצְוֹתָיו וְצִוָּנוּ עַל מִצְוַת תְּפִלִּין. ⁹בָּרוּךְ שֵׁם כְּבוֹד מַלְכוּתוֹ לְעוֹלָם וָעֶד.

¹⁰וּמֵחָכְמָתְךָ, אֵל עֶלְיוֹן, תַּאֲצִיל עָלַי, וּמִבִּינָתְךָ תְּבִינֵנִי; ¹¹וּבְחַסְדְּךָ תַּגְדִּיל עָלַי, וּבִגְבוּרָתְךָ תַּצְמִית אֹיְבַי וְקָמַי; ¹²וְשֶׁמֶן הַטּוֹב תָּרִיק עַל שִׁבְעָה קְנֵי הַמְּנוֹרָה לְהַשְׁפִּיעַ טוּבְךָ לִבְרִיּוֹתֶיךָ. פּוֹתֵחַ אֶת יָדֶךָ, וּמַשְׂבִּיעַ לְכָל חַי רָצוֹן.

[While winding the strap around the middle finger, three times, say:]

¹³וְאֵרַשְׂתִּיךְ לִי לְעוֹלָם, ¹⁴וְאֵרַשְׂתִּיךְ לִי בְּצֶדֶק וּבְמִשְׁפָּט וּבְחֶסֶד וּבְרַחֲמִים. ¹⁵וְאֵרַשְׂתִּיךְ לִי בֶּאֱמוּנָה, וְיָדַעַתְּ אֶת יְיָ. ¹⁶וִיהִי רָצוֹן מִלְּפָנֶיךָ, יְיָ אֱלֹהֵינוּ וֵאלֹהֵי אֲבוֹתֵינוּ, שֶׁתְּהֵא חֲשׁוּבָה מִצְוַת הֲנָחַת תְּפִלִּין זוֹ כְּאִלּוּ קִיַּמְתִּיהָ בְּכָל פְּרָטֶיהָ וְדִקְדּוּקֶיהָ וְכַוָּנוֹתֶיהָ וְתַרְיַ"ג מִצְוֹת הַתְּלוּיִים בָּהּ. אָמֵן סֶלָה.

BRETTLER (BIBLE)

[1] *"As written in the Torah"* Deuteronomy 6:8, one of several passages that mention a sign on your arm and between your eyes (cf. Exod. 13:9, 16; Deut. 11:18). The Rabbis understand this as "phylacteries" *(t'fillin),* a term never used in the Bible, but related etymologically to *t'fillah,* "prayer." In the original biblical context, these texts may denote a protective amulet. But they may just be metaphoric allusions to remembering God as if God were inscribed on one's person.

[3] *"Four passages"* These four biblical passages have been found also in *t'fillin* discovered at Qumran, though their order is variable, and several *t'fillin* have additional texts, such as the Decalogue. *(p. 74)*

DORFF (THEOLOGY)

[1] *"By putting on* t'fillin, *I hereby intend to fulfill the commandment of my Creator."* This added meditation identifies putting on *t'fillin* as a "commandment of my Creator," indicating that the first and ultimate reason for wearing *t'fillin* is that God has commanded it. *(p. 74)*

ELLENSON (MODERN LITURGIES)

[1] *"By putting on* t'fillin*"* In accord with the present-day trend toward greater ritual practice in non-Orthodox Judaism, *Gates of Prayer, Kol Haneshamah* (Reconstructionist), *Ha'avodah Shebalev* (Israeli Reform), *Tov L'hodot* (Dutch Reform), *(p. 75)*

FRANKEL (A WOMAN'S VOICE)

[1] *"By putting on* t'fillin*"* The relationship of women to *t'fillin* has long been the subject of rabbinic controversy. According to the Mishnah and Talmud (Ber. 20a), women are exempt from this time-bound *mitzvah;* however, they may obligate themselves to observe it. Maimonides (twelfth century) ruled that because women are not so commanded, they may not recite the blessing over *t'fillin* because the phrase *v'tsivanu,* "Who has commanded us," does not apply to them. *(p. 77)*

C. PUTTING ON T'FILLIN

[Before putting on t'fillin:]

[1] By putting on *t'fillin.* I hereby intend to fulfill the commandment of my Creator, who commanded us to put on *t'fillin,* as written in the Torah: [2] Bind them to your hand as a sign and set them between your eyes as a symbol. [3] They comprise the following four passages: "Hear...," "If you carefully heed...," "Sanctify...," "And when He brings you...," which

J. HOFFMAN (TRANSLATION)

[1] *"[I] hereby"* See above, "[I] hereby."

[2] *"A symbol"* Hebrew, *totafot,* a word whose original meaning has been lost.

[3] *"They comprise"* The *t'fillin.*

[3] *"His [unity]"* God's.

[3] *"Unity and oneness"* Technical kabbalistic terms for which we have no equivalent in English.

[3] *"Throughout"* Or, perhaps, just "in."

[4] *"Put* t'fillin *on."* The Hebrew just

says "put on," using the verb usually associated with *t'fillin*.

[4] *"Our arm"* Literally, "the hand," *(hayad)* but Hebrew often omits possessive pronouns where English requires them. It is tempting to translate "hand" here, because immediately following we have another word for "arm" *(zaro'a)*, but the Hebrew word includes both the hand and the arm, and in fact, the *t'fillin* go on the arm.

[4] *"And which [is next to the heart]"* Presumably, the Hebrew (p. 78)

¹הִנְנִי מְכַוֵּן בַּהֲנָחַת תְּפִלִּין לְקַיֵּם מִצְוַת בּוֹרְאִי שֶׁצִּוָּנוּ לְהָנִיחַ תְּפִלִּין, כַּכָּתוּב בַּתּוֹרָה: ²וּקְשַׁרְתָּם לְאוֹת עַל יָדֶךָ, וְהָיוּ לְטֹטָפֹת בֵּין עֵינֶיךָ. ³וְהֵם אַרְבַּע פָּרָשִׁיּוֹת אֵלּוֹ: שְׁמַע, וְהָיָה אִם שָׁמֹעַ, קַדֶּשׁ, וְהָיָה כִּי יְבִאֲךָ, שֶׁיֵּשׁ בָּהֶם יִחוּדוֹ וְאַחְדוּתוֹ יִתְבָּרַךְ שְׁמוֹ בָּעוֹלָם:

L. HOFFMAN (HISTORY)

[1] *"By putting on* t'fillin, *I hereby intend"* A kabbalistic meditation in two parts, surrounding the actual blessings for *t'fillin*. This one is datable to the medieval kabbalist Isaiah Horowitz (1565[?]–1630). Like the parallel for putting on a *tallit* (see also, "I hereby *[hin'ni]* wrap myself in a *tallit*," above), this meditation too begins with *hin'ni*, "I hereby." In addition, the following verb is *m'khaven*, implying the essential idea that as we perform a *mitzvah*—in this case, putting on *t'fillin*— (p. 80)

KUSHNER & POLEN (CHASIDISM)

[1] *"By putting on* t'fillin" Rabbi Yechiel Yehoshua ben Yerachmiel Tzvi of Biala (*Siddur Chelkat Yehoshua,* 55) offers a spiritual explanation for the commandment to wrap *t'fillin* on our arms. Doing so, he suggests, literally guards us against sin. The imprint of the leather strap wrapped around our arms commonly remains on our skin for hours after the strap has been removed. This impression remains as a tangible (literally, in-our-flesh) reminder preventing our left hand from committing sin. (This, of course, might be an expression of Western culture's identification of the left side with evil. In French, the word for *left* is (p. 81)

LANDES (HALAKHAH)

[1] *"I hereby intend to fulfill the commandment…to put on* t'fillin" As the proof-text for the commandment reads: "these words which I command you today, will be upon your heart…" (Deut. 6:6), the *mitzvah* must be performed with *kavvanah,* that is, with heartfelt thoughtfulness. The paragraph here is a kabbalistic *kavvanah.* The *Shulchan Arukh* (O. Ch. 25:5) prescribes, more generally, "While putting on *t'fillin,* a person should meditate on the fact that God commanded us to put on these four *parashiyot* ["biblical paragraphs"], which contain the unity of His name and the Exodus from Egypt; we put them on the arm opposite the heart and on the head before the brain, to remember the miracles and (p. 81)

contain His unity and oneness, blessed be His name throughout the world, that we should remember the miracles and wonders that He did with us when He brought us out from Egypt, for He has power and dominion, both heavenly and earthly, to do with them as He wishes. 4 And He has commanded us to put *t'fillin* on our arm in rememberance of His outstretched arm, and which is next to the heart, to subjugate our heart's desires and thoughts to His service, blessed be His name, and on our head, next to our brain, in order that the soul in my brain along with my other senses and powers be subjugated to His service, blessed be His name. 5 And because the *t'fillin* commandment flows through me with blessing, may I continue to have long life, holiness flowing through me with blessing, and holy thoughts, without any sinful thoughts whatsoever. 6 May our evil inclination not tempt or provoke us, but leave us to worship God as our hearts desire. Amen.

וְשֶׁנִּזְכֹּר נִסִּים וְנִפְלָאוֹת שֶׁעָשָׂה עִמָּנוּ בְּהוֹצִיאוֹ אוֹתָנוּ מִמִּצְרַיִם, וַאֲשֶׁר לוֹ הַכֹּחַ וְהַמֶּמְשָׁלָה בָּעֶלְיוֹנִים וּבַתַּחְתּוֹנִים לַעֲשׂוֹת בָּהֶם כִּרְצוֹנוֹ. 4 וְצִוָּנוּ לְהָנִיחַ עַל הַיָּד לְזִכְרוֹן זְרוֹעוֹ הַנְּטוּיָה; וְשֶׁהִיא נֶגֶד הַלֵּב, לְשַׁעְבֵּד בָּזֶה תַּאֲוֹת וּמַחְשְׁבוֹת לִבֵּנוּ לַעֲבוֹדָתוֹ, יִתְבָּרַךְ שְׁמוֹ; וְעַל הָרֹאשׁ נֶגֶד הַמֹּחַ, שֶׁהַנְּשָׁמָה שֶׁבְּמֹחִי עִם שְׁאָר חוּשַׁי וְכֹחוֹתַי כֻּלָּם יִהְיוּ מְשֻׁעְבָּדִים לַעֲבוֹדָתוֹ, יִתְבָּרַךְ שְׁמוֹ. 5 וּמִשֶּׁפַע מִצְוַת תְּפִלִּין יִתְמַשֵּׁךְ עָלַי לִהְיוֹת לִי חַיִּים אֲרֻכִּים וְשֶׁפַע קֹדֶשׁ וּמַחֲשָׁבוֹת קְדוֹשׁוֹת, בְּלִי הִרְהוּר חֵטְא וְעָוֹן כְּלָל, 6 וְשֶׁלֹּא יְפַתֵּנוּ וְלֹא יִתְגָּרֶה בָּנוּ יֵצֶר הָרָע, וְיַנִּיחֵנוּ לַעֲבוֹד אֶת יְיָ כַּאֲשֶׁר עִם לְבָבֵנוּ. אָמֵן.

[While putting t'fillin on arm, say:]

7 Blessed are You, Adonai our God, Ruler of the world, who sanctified us with His commandments and commanded us to put on *t'fillin*.

[While putting t'fillin on head, say:]

8 Blessed are You, Adonai our God, Ruler of the world, who sanctified us with His commandments and commanded us about the *mitzvah* of *t'fillin*. **9** Blessed is the One the glory of whose kingdom is renowned forever.

10 Share Your wisdom with me, God on high, and from Your knowledge help me know. **11** With Your love do great things for me, and with Your power cut off my enemies and adversaries. **12** Pour good oil on the seven branches of the menorah, to extend the flow of Your goodness upon Your creatures, opening Your hand, and satisfying every living thing with favor.

[While winding the strap around the middle finger, three times, say:]

13 I will betroth you to Me forever. **14** I will betroth you to Me in righteousness, in justice, in kindness, and in mercy. **15** I will betroth you to Me in faithfulness, and you will know Adonai. **16** May it be Your will, Adonai our God and our ancestors' God, that this commandment of putting on *t'fillin* be considered as though I've fulfilled it in every aspect, detail, and purpose, and the 613 commandments that are related to it. Amen.

[While putting t'fillin on arm, say:]

‏**7** בָּרוּךְ אַתָּה, יְיָ אֱלֹהֵינוּ, מֶלֶךְ הָעוֹלָם, אֲשֶׁר קִדְּשָׁנוּ בְּמִצְוֹתָיו וְצִוָּנוּ לְהָנִיחַ תְּפִלִּין.

[While putting t'fillin on head, say:]

‏**8** בָּרוּךְ אַתָּה, יְיָ אֱלֹהֵינוּ, מֶלֶךְ הָעוֹלָם, אֲשֶׁר קִדְּשָׁנוּ בְּמִצְוֹתָיו וְצִוָּנוּ עַל מִצְוַת תְּפִלִּין. **9** בָּרוּךְ שֵׁם כְּבוֹד מַלְכוּתוֹ לְעוֹלָם וָעֶד.

‏**10** וּמֵחָכְמָתְךָ, אֵל עֶלְיוֹן, תַּאֲצִיל עָלַי, וּמִבִּינָתְךָ תְּבִינֵנִי; **11** וּבְחַסְדְּךָ תַּגְדִּיל עָלַי, וּבִגְבוּרָתְךָ תַּצְמִית אֹיְבַי וְקָמַי; **12** וְשֶׁמֶן הַטּוֹב תָּרִיק עַל שִׁבְעָה קְנֵי הַמְּנוֹרָה לְהַשְׁפִּיעַ טוּבְךָ לִבְרִיּוֹתֶיךָ. פּוֹתֵחַ אֶת יָדֶךָ, וּמַשְׂבִּיעַ לְכָל חַי רָצוֹן.

[While winding the strap around the middle finger, three times, say:]

‏**13** וְאֵרַשְׂתִּיךְ לִי לְעוֹלָם, **14** וְאֵרַשְׂתִּיךְ לִי בְּצֶדֶק וּבְמִשְׁפָּט וּבְחֶסֶד וּבְרַחֲמִים. **15** וְאֵרַשְׂתִּיךְ לִי בֶּאֱמוּנָה, וְיָדַעַתְּ אֶת יְיָ. **16** וִיהִי רָצוֹן מִלְּפָנֶיךָ, יְיָ אֱלֹהֵינוּ וֵאלֹהֵי אֲבוֹתֵינוּ, שֶׁתְּהֵא חֲשׁוּבָה מִצְוַת הֲנָחַת תְּפִלִּין זוֹ כְּאִלּוּ קִיַּמְתִּיהָ בְּכָל פְּרָטֶיהָ וְדִקְדּוּקֶיהָ וְכַוָּנוֹתֶיהָ וְתַרְיַ"ג מִצְוֹת הַתְּלוּיִם בָּהּ. אָמֵן סֶלָה.

BRETTLER (BIBLE)

[4] *"Commanded us to put* t'fillin *on"* Exodus 13:16 explicitly connects *t'fillin* to the Exodus: "It shall serve as a sign on your hand and a symbol *[totafot]* between your eyes that Adonai took us out of Egypt with a strong hand." But the following references to the "soul" and the "evil inclination" are post-biblical notions.

[4] *"Blessed be His name"* Based on a late psalm, 72:19.

[10–12] *"Share Your wisdom…opening Your hand"* A request for blessing from God's head (wisdom) and hand, reflecting the physical placement of the *t'fillin*. "You open Your hand" is Psalm 145:16.

[13] *"I will betroth you"* Hosea 2:21–22, depicting Israel as God's wife, being cast aside for promiscuity, but ultimately to be reconciled through a new marriage that will last forever. "Betroth" denotes the first stage of the biblical (and later rabbinic) marriage, where (biblically) the groom's father pays the bride's father a bride-price that commits the bride to the groom exclusive of other males. "Righteousness," "justice," and "faithfulness" probably refer to God's beneficence, but they may denote Israel's newfound faithfulness to God.

◆

DORFF (THEOLOGY)

But our author offers other rationales as well. This tension between obeying the commandments simply because God commanded them and doing so for extraneous reasons as well has been an ongoing feature of Judaism from the very beginning. The Torah, the Talmud, and both medieval and modern Jewish thinkers say we must obey God's commands whether or not we see any reason to them, but a tradition from the Torah itself suggests reasons for commandments also. Moses Maimonides (1135–1204) went furthest in this latter direction, by claiming that all the commandments are designed for human physical and philosophical betterment and that, with the exception of a single commandment (the burning of a red cow as a means of ritual purification for people who have been in touch with a corpse—see Num. 19), he could discern specific rationales behind every commandment from the Torah. Those who objected to this line of reasoning worried that people would think the commandments binding only if they fulfilled the stated objective, so that if the objective was not met, the commandment would no longer be followed. This paragraph clearly supplies human rationales, but is careful to declare the commandment binding as a divine command, regardless.

The first benefit of *t'fillin* mentioned here is that they teach us the unity and uniqueness of God, presumably by including as one of the four paragraphs the section from Deuteronomy 6, beginning, "Here O Israel: Adonai is our God; Adonai is One." Second, the *t'fillin* on our arm remind us of the strong arm by which God took us out of Egypt. Third, we place one box opposite the heart to declare our heart's subjugation to God. Fourth, the box on our forehead signifies the fact that our mind and senses are subject to God's service.

I suggest also that we place one box on our bicep, symbol of our physical strength, and another on our forehead, symbol of our mental faculties. We wrap the *t'fillin* strap around our arm seven times and then around our hand to form the word *shaddai,* "almighty." Thus the *t'fillin* symbolize how seven days a week we should devote both physical and mental capacities to God. Moreover, as we wrap the strap around our fingers, we recite the verses from Hosea ("I will betroth you to Me...") as if we were putting on rings of betrothal. We serve God not like a slave to a master, but like one lover to another.

◆

ELLENSON (MODERN LITURGIES)

and *Siddur Sim Shalom* (American Conservative) all include this meditation, though in abbreviated form. It was composed by Rabbi Isaiah Horowitz (1565[?]–1630), author of the famed mystical work *Shnei Luchot Hab'rit.* In his commentary on the traditional prayer book, Philip Birnbaum observes that the meditation "contains the thought that by wearing the *t'fillin* on the head and near the heart we are made conscious of our duty to employ our thoughts and emotions in the service of God." The authors of the non-Orthodox prayer books cited above must affirm this understanding. They include the meditation to promote a proper sense of devotion.

Earlier generations of Reform Jews dispensed with the *mitzvah* of *t'fillin.* The 1975 decision to restore the meditation and subsequent blessings for *t'fillin* bespeaks the American Reform's openness to ritual that *GOP* heralded. But *GOP* stops short of other liberal Siddurim that include this meditation, in that it does not translate the first Hebrew line, which asserts that by wearing *t'fillin,* "I hereby intend to fulfill the commandment of my Creator." Instead, it says simply, "In the Torah, it is written." *GOP* thus adopts a tactic used by liberal prayerbook composers for two centuries. It preserves the traditional Hebrew to create a certain affect as well as to promote communal unity, but employs the vernacular to mute what the Hebrew means. The nontranslation of the Hebrew reflects the discomfort *GOP* feels with the notion of "commandedness" when attached to a ritual practice such as *t'fillin.* Their decision here is consistent with the decision above, to translate "commanded us" (in relationship to the *tallit*) as "teaches us." (See above, "Commanded us to wrap ourselves.")

In the Reconstructionist *Kol Haneshamah* a traditional mystical *kavvanah* (meditation of intent) is inserted prior to the words "By putting on *t'fillin,*" but is rendered loosely in an inspirational English to assert that the ritual act is being performed "for the union of the blessed Holy One with all that is divine within the world, in awe and reverence for the task of bringing into harmony and perfect oneness all the ways that God is manifest in speech and deed, and in the name of all the people Israel." The line indicates the present-day centrality of Jewish mysticism in a movement that began (in part) as a rationalist rejection of mystical tradition.

The Israeli Conservative *Siddur Va'ani T'fillati* (unlike its American counterpart *Siddur Sim Shalom*) excludes this meditation. However, gender-inclusiveness as a hallmark of the Israeli Masorti (Conservative) rite is nowhere more evident than in the detailed instructions that *SVT* offers here on how to put on *t'fillin*. A lengthy set of textual instructions is accompanied by illustrations, including a picture of a woman wearing a *kippah* and *t'fillin*. This picture delivers a powerful message of the Masorti Movement's internalization of the feminist contention that patriarchal traditions posit the male as normative and relegate the female to the status of "other." The picture of a woman putting on *t'fillin* refutes the women's being "other." Indeed, it presents the entire Siddur as egalitarian—perhaps the most noteworthy single element in it.

[3] *"He has power and dominion, both heavenly and earthly, to do with them as He wishes."* Of all the non-Orthodox prayer books that include the Horowitz meditation, only the Dutch *Tov L'hodot* includes these lines from the prayer. The description of a supernatural wonder-working deity with absolute dominion over the universe was deemed theologically problematic by the authors of the others, who elected to omit them.

[5] *"And because the* t'fillin *commandment flows through me with blessing"* Here is a fully mystical line, complete with kabbalistic allusions that defy translation. It is therefore omitted from all current liberal rites except the Reconstructionist *Kol Haneshamah,* which characteristically embraces it with the following translation: "And through the flow of divine strength which I partake of through the *mitzvah* of *t'fillin,* may I be granted long life, and abundant holiness, and knowledge of the sacred." One can only imagine how the arch-rationalist founder of the movement Mordecai Kaplan would have regarded this insertion! Nevertheless, it reflects the profound influence of Jewish renewal elements within Reconstructionist Judaism today.

[5] *"Without any sinful thoughts whatsoever"* All liberal liturgies omit these lines. We are not sure why, but Mark Twain (of all people) may have reflected their view. Twain had considered the petition in the Lord's Prayer (the prayer recommended by Jesus to his disciples, according to the Gospels of Matthew and Luke) that asked, "Deliver us from temptation." In Twain's view, that request was morally perverse, since if we are never tempted to sin, we have nothing to say "No" to—in which case, how can we consider ourselves moral? This prayer asks for the equivalent of freedom from "temptation," so our prayerbook authors may have shared Twain's sophisticated moral viewpoint: asking to be free from "any sinful reflection whatever" amounts to doing away with the very essence of human morality—standing up to temptation and saying "No."

[8] *"Commanded us about the* mitzvah *of* t'fillin*"* All liberal volumes contain this blessing, but as with the *tallit, Gates of Prayer* translates "commanded us" here as "teaches us" (see above, "Commanded us to wrap ourselves"). Abraham Geiger included this blessing in his inclusive 1854 Siddur, but omitted it in his more radical 1870 edition.

[10] *"Share Your wisdom with me, God on high"* This kabbalistic meditation is found in none of the non-Orthodox Siddurim, even those that include the rite of *t'fillin.* However, *Kol Haneshamah* substitutes another mystical *kavvanah* (introductory meditation, rooted in kabbalistic thought) that speaks of the "union of the Blessed Holy One and the *Shekhinah*"—in kabbalistic terms, the male and female aspects of God. It features Leviticus 19:18, "You shall love your neighbor as yourself." *Siddur Sim Shalom* also inserts elements of this meditation, but it introduces Leviticus 19 with the declaration, "I hereby accept the obligation of fulfilling my Creator's *mitzvah* in the Torah"; and it omits any mention of unifying the "Blessed Holy One" with the "*Shekhinah*." The idea of introducing morning prayer with the idea of loving our neighbor is well attested in kabbalistic sources from the seventeenth century on. The Conservative Movement thus accepts this ethical impulse and, true to its ideology, links it to the centrality of doing *mitzvot.* However, it balks at accepting the mystical rationale behind the introductory meditation: achieving a mystical union of the male and female aspects of God.

[16] *"May it be Your will, Adonai our God"* We saw above (see "May it be Your will…and the 613 commandments") that all non-Orthodox prayer books omit the traditional meditation following the donning of *tsitsit* on the grounds that it is hyperbolic. Similarly, they exclude this devotion that reflects upon the commandment of *t'fillin.*

◆

FRANKEL (A WOMAN'S VOICE)

(He also ruled that a self-imposed obligation was of lesser value than an obligation prescribed externally.) Moses Isserles (sixteenth century) objected even to women's voluntarily assuming this *mitzvah,* though he granted that the Halakhah permits them to do so.

However, the majority view is more tolerant. The Talmud claims that David's daughter Michal used to put on *t'fillin* (R.H. 33a). So too, we are told, did Rashi's daughters. Rashi's own grandson, Rabbenu Tam, ruled that women who choose to wear *t'fillin* may recite the blessing, and Rashi's teacher, Isaac Halevi, not only permits, but requires them to do so.

[13] *"I will betroth you"* This section contains some of the most intimate anthropomorphic language found anywhere in the prayer book. The central metaphor

is "betrothal," taken from Hosea (2:21–22): "I will betroth you to Me forever…I will betroth you to Me in righteous." In its original biblical context, God explicitly speaks to Israel as his bride. But when these verses are transplanted to the prayer book as a *kavvanah,* a spiritual intention, what happens? Who is the bride here; who the husband? Does the male worshiper forsake his gender identity to become God's bride? Or does God assume a feminine identity to become his betrothed? And what about the female worshiper? Or lesbians and gays? What "gender-bending" must we undergo in order to betroth God through the act of donning *t'fillin*?

Rather than befuddle ourselves here in the fog of anthropomorphism, it is more fruitful to understand this metaphor as referring to the mystery of human-divine union, which transcends gender and even matter itself. When we bind ourselves with the cords of *t'fillin,* we cross a threshold into a new status of being, God's prayer-partner-in-love. To paraphrase Maimonides, we have no choice but to speak in gendered language, but God is not so limited.

◆

J. HOFFMAN (TRANSLATION)

pronoun (which is feminine singular) refers to the single *t'fillin shel yad;* but because that referent was not mentioned here, the singular pronoun sounds odd in Hebrew.

[4] *"Next to"* More commonly, "opposite," but the location is clearly not "opposite the heart" the way "opposite" is used in English. The Hebrew *k'neged* means "opposite", but also "equivalent to." The idea is that the *t'fillin* are next to the heart and have something in common with it.

[4] *"Subjugate"* In the Hebrew, the subject of "subjugate our heart's desires and thoughts [to divine ends]" is either the *t'fillin* or God. Artscroll properly translates it, as we do, leaving the subject ambiguous. Birnbaum, however, translates, "intimates that we ought to subject…"—a theological move from actual subjugation to intimation that we ourselves ought to subjugate "our heart's desires."

[4] *"Heart's desires and thoughts"* In English, one does not normally speak of the heart as having thoughts, but (see Volume 1, *The Sh'ma and Its Blessings,* pp. 100, 102) Hebrew assigns a different metaphoric role to the *lev,* the "heart." Elsewhere, therefore, we translate *lev* not as "heart," but as "mind" (where English locates our thoughts). Here, however, we must say "heart" because of where the arm *t'fillin* go: specifically next to the heart, not on the head, where we assume the "mind" is.

[4] *"Soul in my brain"* What's "my soul" doing in "my brain"? This is a technical kabbalistic reference to the *n'shamah* (the higher soul—see L. Hoffman, "I hereby [*hin'ni*] wrap myself in a *tallit,*" p. 64). "Brain" here is a reference to the place in the "s'firotic" world where the "soul" resides. Normally, kabbalistic references are woven

seamlessly into "regular" Hebrew, so that the Hebrew can be read at two levels, but here the "regular" meaning ("soul" or even "breath"—another option) is a stretch. Birnbaum translates, "mind," to obviate the problem, but this is the only place where *n'shamah* is so translated.

[5] *"Flows through me with blessing"* Hebrew, *shefa*, a word usually followed by a plural noun and used to mean "myriad [of]." But here it is following a singular noun, "the commandment of *t'fillin*." Again, what we have is a technical kabbalistic allusion to the flow of blessing occasioned by the performance of the commandment. So we translate "flow through me with blessing," here and immediately following.

[5] *"Sinful"* Two words in Hebrew, *chet* and *avon*, are used here.

[10] *"Wisdom"* This whole paragraph can be read on two levels, only one of which is translated. It is a simple Hebrew passage, but also a kabbalistically coded message, using technical terms like this one. Because English lacks all of these technical terms, we do not translate the kabbalistic level at which this word, as the entire paragraph, might be read. (See L. Hoffman, "Pour good oil on the seven branches of the menorah," p. 80.)

[10] *"Help me know"* Or just "teach me." We choose "help me know" to duplicate the root "know" in English ("know," "knowledge") to mimic the Hebrew.

[12] *"Extend the flow of"* Again, a kabbalistic term. See above, "Flows through me with blessing."

[12] *"Satisfying"* The Hebrew is *masbi'a*, which sounds like *mashpi'a*, used immediately above for "extend [the flow of your goodness]." Identity or near identity of words, even from radically different contexts, adds to poetic effect and augments the rhetorical plausibility of claims that language makes. We can see a similar phenomenon in modern-day America regarding rhymes. Slogans and sayings that rhyme are taken more seriously than those that do not—for example, "a stitch in time saves nine." Most people don't even know that it means "stitching a garment with a few stitches before it's too late will save more stitches later on" and, more generally, "taking care of things immediately is more efficient than not." But even people who don't understand it agree that it's profound—because it rhymes.

[13] *"You"* The Hebrew (taken from Hosea) makes it clear that the speaker is talking to a woman.

[14] *"In righteousness"* Or "through righteousness."

L. HOFFMAN (HISTORY)

we are to concentrate on its esoteric significance. Here, that significance is expressly named: the *t'fillin* in question are black boxes attached by straps to the head and arm. The boxes have four compartments, each one filled with a biblical excerpt. The esoteric point is not the cognitive content of the four excerpts but the fact that, numerically, they represent the four letters of the ineffable divine name; together, they form a *yichud,* a unification of the name, by which kabbalists meant the union of the male and female aspects of God and, deeper still, the coming together of the shattered universe in which we live.

[12] *"Pour good oil on the seven branches of the menorah"* As the kabbalists saw it, God and the universe are one, albeit fractured in the process of creation and requiring reunification. Until then, they are represented in their fractured state by ten separate elements (or "spheres," called *s'firot*; sing., *s'firah*). The separate spheres are said to have been flung loose from one another during the momentary act of creation. The first three are stages of divine thought, and the last seven are the seeds for the created universe that God's thought generates. The seven-branch menorah stands for the lower seven spheres that are showered by a plenitude of blessing called *shefa*. That blessing is said to "trickle down," as it were, through the stages of divine thought, two of which (the only two we can know) are called *chokhmah* ("intelligence") and *binah* ("wisdom"). The spheres are said to be arrayed in two columns, characterized by *chesed* and *g'vurah,* standing for God's twin attributes of love/mercy and might/justice, respectively. All these terms appear in our paragraph, which reads like ordinary Hebrew, but connotes to the cognoscenti the esoteric secret on which they are to concentrate while putting on their *t'fillin*—namely, through the unification of the name that the four *t'fillin* boxes represent, blessing will shower down upon us via *chokhmatkha* (Your *chokhmah*—"Your [God's] intelligence"); *binatkha* (Your *binah*—"Your wisdom"); *chasd'khah* (Your *chesed*—"Your mercy"); and *g'vurat'khah* (Your *g'vurah*—"Your might"). The image of good oil flowing through a menorah is, therefore, a kabbalistic metaphor for blessing "lubricating" the world.

The Kabbalah builds on the Talmud here, for the word *shemen* ("oil") is read by the Talmud (Shab. 153a) as *shem* ("name"), meaning the name of God implicit in the four boxes of the *t'fillin.*

[13-15] *"I will betroth you"* These words from Hosea were added here by Isaac Luria, to symbolize the role of *t'fillin* in bringing about a divine union between the masculine and feminine sides of God (a *yichud,* in kabbalistic terms). The three statements of "I will betroth you" are said as the hand strap is wound three times around the middle finger—as a sort of wedding ring.

KUSHNER & POLEN (CHASIDISM)

gauch; in Latin, it is *sinistra*. But the symbolism is nevertheless powerful.) As we commence our morning prayers, we stand before God with that potentially dangerous left side now literally bridled, its energy thoroughly harnessed and ready to serve the Creator.

Others have found in the placement of the arm's box on the same level with the heart an association with the passage in the Talmud (PT Ber. 9a) where God says, "Give me your heart."

And likewise, the placement of the box in the center of the forehead seems to physically allude to the third eye, classically the organ of spiritual vision. In this way, setting *t'fillin* "on our hand as a sign…and between our eyes as a symbol" (Deut. 6:8: see Volume 1, *The Sh'ma and Its Blessings,* p. 83) every day gives us power to marshal both our external and internal forces for God's service. By harnessing our physical power, directing our consciousness, and focusing our spiritual vision, we commence each weekday focused on God as the ultimate force and power in the universe. And just as we, Israel, bind ourselves to the divine presence, so may the Holy One bind Godself to the community of Israel.

Indeed, we learn in Berakhot 6a that God too wears *t'fillin*. But inside God's *t'fillin*, instead of passages proclaiming God's uniqueness, are the words: "Who is like Your people Israel, a unique people in the world!"

———◆———

LANDES (HALAKHAH)

wonders that God did for us. They testify to God's unity, and to the fact that He has the strength and dominion above and below to do with them as He wishes. We subjugate to God our soul, which is in the mind, and our heart, which is the seat of desires and thoughts."

[1] *"Commanded us to put on* t'fillin*"* We put on *t'fillin* after the *tallit* (*Shulchan Arukh,* O. Ch. 35:1), following the principle (Shab. 21b), "We perform commandments in ascending, rather than descending, order of sanctity" *(ma'alin bakodesh ve'ein moridin).* *T'fillin* are holier than the *tallit* because they contain God's name, so we put them on second.

According to Gra (Elijah of Vilna, 1720–1797), "first, we cover ourselves (superficially) in a garment that is a commandment, and then we bind ourselves to God with the *t'fillin*" (*Bi'ur Halakhah,* O. Ch. 25).

All authorities rule that *t'fillin* should be put on at home (*Shulchan Arukh* and R'ma, O. Ch. 25:2). If one observes this custom, one puts on the *tallit katan* first, followed by *t'fillin,* so that one arrives at the synagogue "clothed in *tsitsit* and crowned in *t'fillin,*" and then puts on the *tallit gadol* (*Shulchan Arukh,* ibid.). However, the vast majority of worshipers who put on *t'fillin* only at the synagogue put them on after the *tallit gadol.*

Deuteronomy 6:5–9 instructs us, "These words, which I command you today, will be on your heart…. Tie them as a sign on your arms and let them be (reminders) between your eyes." From here, we derive the commandment to wear *t'fillin* via the doctrine of *halakhah l'moshe misinai* ("tradition transmitted to Moses at Sinai"): that is, Moses received both the written and the oral Torah. The latter explains the former. Among the characteristics of *t'fillin* listed by the Talmud (Men. 32a–35b) as *halakhah l'moshe misinai* are:

1. The required excerpts from Torah are sewn into black boxes.
2. The boxes must be square, with the Hebrew letter *shin* (the initial letter of God's name, *Shaddai*) etched on the box.
3. The excerpts must be written on parchment and in ink.
4. The straps must have knots (according to Rashi, shaped like the Hebrew letter *yod*), the first letter of the four-letter name of God.
5. Maimonides rules (Laws of *T'fillin,* 1:3) that if even one of these aspects is left out, the *t'fillin* are not acceptable.

The four excerpts *(parashiyot),* written on four separate parchments (Maimonides, Laws of *T'fillin,* 1:1) are: Exodus 13:1–10; Exodus 13:11–16; Deuteronomy 6:4–9; and Deuteronomy 11:13–21.

The *t'fillin shel yad* (hand *t'fillin*) are put on first and worn on the "puffy flesh above the elbow" of the left hand, turned toward the heart, in fulfillment of the passage "These words, which I command you today, will be on your heart." The *t'fillin shel rosh* (head *t'fillin*) are put on last and are worn above the forehead, "where a baby's skull goes soft." The "box" should be centered exactly between the eyes, in fulfillment of the passage "Let them be [reminders] between your eyes"(Deut. 6:8), as should the knot behind the head.

T'fillin are worn on the left hand, based on a word play in Torah. *Yad'kha* ("your arm") is read as *yad kehah* ("weak arm"). Exclusively left-handed people (who write with their left hand) wear *t'fillin* on their right arm, as that is their weak arm. Since all *mitzvot* are performed with the right hand, we would expect *t'fillin* to be put on with the *right* hand. In actual fact, that occurs, as the *act* of the commandment (putting them on the left arm) is performed by the right.

[9] *"Blessed is the One the glory of whose kingdom is renowned forever"* There is some doubt regarding how many blessings to say, since the first blessing ("…to put on *t'fillin*") should apply to both the hand and head *t'fillin.* This is indeed the Sefardi custom to this day. Ashkenazi communities, however, say both, adding the declaration "blessed be the name…" to acknowledge the sanctity of the name we have uttered in the event that we have said an unnecessary blessing. Additionally, some people, after saying the first blessing, move the hand *t'fillin* out of place and then return it, thus deliberately creating an "interruption," so that we can legitimately say a separate blessing over the head *t'fillin.* The Ashkenazi communities adopted this custom despite almost all authorities who ruled otherwise, but the custom overcame the Halakhah in

this case. Nevertheless, *Arukh Hashulchan* rules that one may say only one blessing, if one chooses to do so.

Blessings over commandments are said standing.

———————— ◆ ◆ ◆ ————————

D. Exodus 13:1–16

Then Adonai said to Moses, [2] Consecrate every first-born to Me. [3] The first issue of any womb in Israel, of man or of beast, is Mine. [4] And Moses said to the nation: [5] Remember this day when you left Egypt, the house of slaves, because it was with strength of hand that Adonai brought you out of there. [6] No leavened bread shall be eaten. [7] Today you are leaving, in the month of Aviv. [8] And when Adonai brings you to the land of the Canaanite, the Hittite, the Amorite, the Hivvite, and the Jebusite, which He swore to your ancestors that He would give to you, a land flowing with milk and honey, you shall perform this service in this month: [9] For seven days you shall eat matzah, and the seventh day shall be a holiday for Adonai. [10] Matzah shall be eaten throughout the seven days, and no leavened bread shall be visible to you, and no leaven shall be visible to you, anywhere within your borders. [11] On that day you shall tell your child: [12] This is on account of what Adonai did for me when I left Egypt. It shall serve as a symbol on your hand and as a remembrance between your eyes, so that Adonai's Torah shall be on your tongue, because Adonai freed you from Egypt with a strong hand. [13] Keep this law at its proper time year by year. [14] And when Adonai brings you into the land of the Canaanite, as He swore to you and your ancestors that He would, and when He gives it to you, transfer every first issue of the womb to Adonai, and among all the first issues among the young animals that you have, transfer the males to Adonai. [15] And you shall redeem every firstling donkey with a lamb; if you do not redeem it, you must break its neck. [16] Redeem every first-born son among your

וַיְדַבֵּר יְיָ אֶל מֹשֶׁה לֵּאמֹר: [2]קַדֶּשׁ־לִי כָל בְּכוֹר, [3]פֶּטֶר כָּל רֶחֶם בִּבְנֵי יִשְׂרָאֵל, בָּאָדָם וּבַבְּהֵמָה, לִי הוּא. [4]וַיֹּאמֶר מֹשֶׁה אֶל הָעָם: [5]זָכוֹר אֶת הַיּוֹם הַזֶּה אֲשֶׁר יְצָאתֶם מִמִּצְרַיִם, מִבֵּית עֲבָדִים, כִּי בְּחֹזֶק יָד הוֹצִיא יְיָ אֶתְכֶם מִזֶּה; [6]וְלֹא יֵאָכֵל חָמֵץ. [7]הַיּוֹם אַתֶּם יֹצְאִים, בְּחֹדֶשׁ הָאָבִיב. [8]וְהָיָה כִי יְבִיאֲךָ יְיָ אֶל אֶרֶץ הַכְּנַעֲנִי, וְהַחִתִּי וְהָאֱמֹרִי וְהַחִוִּי וְהַיְבוּסִי, אֲשֶׁר נִשְׁבַּע לַאֲבֹתֶיךָ לָתֶת לָךְ, אֶרֶץ זָבַת חָלָב וּדְבָשׁ, וְעָבַדְתָּ אֶת הָעֲבֹדָה הַזֹּאת בַּחֹדֶשׁ הַזֶּה. [9]שִׁבְעַת־יָמִים תֹּאכַל מַצֹּת, וּבַיּוֹם הַשְּׁבִיעִי חַג לַיְיָ. [10]מַצּוֹת יֵאָכֵל אֵת שִׁבְעַת הַיָּמִים, וְלֹא יֵרָאֶה לְךָ חָמֵץ וְלֹא יֵרָאֶה לְךָ שְׂאֹר בְּכָל גְּבֻלֶךָ. [11]וְהִגַּדְתָּ לְבִנְךָ בַּיּוֹם הַהוּא לֵאמֹר: [12]בַּעֲבוּר זֶה עָשָׂה יְיָ לִי בְּצֵאתִי מִמִּצְרָיִם. וְהָיָה לְךָ לְאוֹת עַל יָדְךָ, וּלְזִכָּרוֹן בֵּין עֵינֶיךָ, לְמַעַן תִּהְיֶה תּוֹרַת יְיָ בְּפִיךָ, כִּי בְּיָד חֲזָקָה הוֹצִאֲךָ יְיָ מִמִּצְרָיִם. [13]וְשָׁמַרְתָּ אֶת הַחֻקָּה הַזֹּאת לְמוֹעֲדָה מִיָּמִים יָמִימָה. [14]וְהָיָה, כִּי יְבִאֲךָ יְיָ אֶל אֶרֶץ הַכְּנַעֲנִי, כַּאֲשֶׁר נִשְׁבַּע לְךָ וְלַאֲבֹתֶיךָ, וּנְתָנָהּ לָךְ. וְהַעֲבַרְתָּ כָל פֶּטֶר רֶחֶם לַיְיָ; וְכָל פֶּטֶר שֶׁגֶר בְּהֵמָה אֲשֶׁר יִהְיֶה לְךָ, הַזְּכָרִים, לַיְיָ. [15]וְכָל פֶּטֶר חֲמֹר תִּפְדֶּה בְשֶׂה,

children. [17] Tomorrow when your child asks you, "What is this for?" answer him: It was with strength of hand that Adonai brought us out of Egypt, out of the house of slaves. [18] And when Pharaoh refused to let us go, Adonai killed every first-born in the land of Egypt, from the first-born of man to the first-born of beast, and therefore I sacrifice every first male issue of the womb, and I redeem the first-born among my children. [19] It shall be a sign on your hand, and a symbol between your eyes, for it was with a strong hand that Adonai brought us out of Egypt.

[16]וְכָל בְּכוֹר אָדָם בְּבָנֶיךָ תִּפְדֶּה. [17]וְהָיָה, כִּי יִשְׁאָלְךָ בִנְךָ מָחָר לֵאמֹר מַה זֹּאת, וְאָמַרְתָּ אֵלָיו: בְּחֹזֶק יָד הוֹצִיאָנוּ יְיָ מִמִּצְרַיִם, מִבֵּית עֲבָדִים. [18]וַיְהִי כִּי הִקְשָׁה פַרְעֹה לְשַׁלְּחֵנוּ, וַיַּהֲרֹג יְיָ כָּל בְּכוֹר בְּאֶרֶץ מִצְרַיִם, מִבְּכֹר אָדָם וְעַד בְּכוֹר בְּהֵמָה, עַל כֵּן אֲנִי זֹבֵחַ לַייָ כָּל פֶּטֶר רֶחֶם, הַזְּכָרִים, וְכָל בְּכוֹר בָּנַי אֶפְדֶּה. [19]וְהָיָה לְאוֹת עַל יָדְכָה, וּלְטוֹטָפֹת בֵּין עֵינֶיךָ, כִּי בְּחֹזֶק יָד הוֹצִיאָנוּ יְיָ מִמִּצְרַיִם.

וְאִם לֹא תִפְדֶּה וַעֲרַפְתּוֹ;

BRETTLER (BIBLE)

[1] *"Adonai said to Moses"* Exodus 13:1–10; 11–16: included here because they are the last two biblical sections on the *t'fillin*. (The first two sections are recited later in the service, as part of the *Sh'ma*, so need not be included here.) Exodus 13:1–10 focuses on the legal implications of the Exodus: the dedication of the first-born (v. 1), a "service" in the appropriate month (v. 5), eating matzah (v. 6), banishing leavened food (v. 7), reciting something to one's children (v. 8), and donning *t'fillin* (v. 9). In the Bible, historical events are important not for their own sake, but for what they imply.

Exodus 13:11–16 discusses the need to *(p. 89)*

DORFF (THEOLOGY)

[1] *"Adonai said to Moses"* The *t'fillin* boxes contain the four passages where Torah commands us to put them on: Deuteronomy 6:4–9; Deuteronomy 11:13–21; Exodus 13:1–10; and Exodus 13:11–16. The two Deuteronomy passages are recited later as part of the *Sh'ma*, but *(p. 89)*

ELLENSON (MODERN LITURGIES)

[2] *"Consecrate every first-born to Me"* The Reform Movement has classically rejected the rite of redeeming the first-born males *(pidyon haben)*. As Mark Washofsky has explained in his outstanding work on a Reform approach to Jewish law, *Jewish* *(p. 90)*

FRANKEL (A WOMAN'S VOICE)

[1] *"Adonai said to Moses"* Although this biblical passage (Exod. 13:1–16) was obviously placed here because of its double allusion to *t'fillin,* it may also have served to reinforce the patriarchal ideal of first-born privilege. Within this passage, parallels are drawn among three "species" of first-born males: Egyptians, Israelites, and sacrificial animals. What binds them together is the relationship of substitution: Egyptians in place of Israelite slaves, firstlings of the flock in place of first-born Israelite sons. In both cases, God

D. EXODUS 13:1–16

[1] Then Adonai said to Moses, [2] Consecrate every first-born to Me. [3] The first issue of any womb in Israel, of man or of beast, is Mine. [4] And Moses said to the nation: [5] Remember this day when you left Egypt, the house of slaves, because it was with strength of hand that Adonai brought you out of there. [6] No leavened bread shall be eaten. [7] Today you are leaving, in the month of Aviv. [8] And when

spares the Israelite in exchange for his faithful obedience. Of this high-stakes barter, "on that day you shall tell your child."

Missing from the passage is reference to first-born females. According to the midrash, Egyptian first-born daughters were slain together with sons in the tenth plague (Exod. Rab. 18:3), but no mention is made of them here. No traditional ceremony exists for girls to parallel *pidyon haben* ("redemption of first-born males"). And although the Torah requires female animals for certain sacrifices (individual sin offerings) and permits them for others (peace offerings), this passage excludes all such references.

J. HOFFMAN (TRANSLATION)

[1] *"Then Adonai said to Moses"* This familiar phrase *(va'y'daber adonai el moshe leimor)* is often translated, "God spoke unto Moses, saying." But that translation, though common, seems

וַיְדַבֵּר יְיָ אֶל מֹשֶׁה לֵּאמֹר: [2]קַדֶּשׁ־לִי כָל בְּכוֹר, [3]פֶּטֶר כָּל רֶחֶם בִּבְנֵי יִשְׂרָאֵל, בָּאָדָם וּבַבְּהֵמָה, לִי הוּא. [4]וַיֹּאמֶר מֹשֶׁה אֶל הָעָם: [5]זָכוֹר אֶת הַיּוֹם הַזֶּה אֲשֶׁר יְצָאתֶם מִמִּצְרַיִם, מִבֵּית עֲבָדִים, כִּי בְּחֹזֶק יָד הוֹצִיא יְיָ אֶתְכֶם מִזֶּה; [6]וְלֹא יֵאָכֵל חָמֵץ. [7]הַיּוֹם אַתֶּם יֹצְאִים, בְּחֹדֶשׁ הָאָבִיב. [8]וְהָיָה כִי יְבִיאֲךָ יְיָ אֶל אֶרֶץ

stilted if not ungrammatical. In particular, the last word, *leimor,* which literally means "to say" and which is usually translated as "saying," really functions biblically exactly as our modern-day quotation marks do, and so is best left untranslated. The Bible had no punctuation marks, and so uses *leimor* to introduce direct speech.

[3] *"First issue"* Hebrew, *peter,* used here and elsewhere in conjunction with "womb." This may have been an ancient expression or may have simply been used to denote the first-born of

both animals and people. To us, "first-born" connotes only people, so we resort to "first issue."

[5] *"House of slaves"* More commonly, "bondage" or "slavery." But the Hebrew is clearly "slaves," perhaps implying an actual house where slaves lived and which the redeemed Israelites now have been able to escape. That reading is substantiated by the last word in the sentence, *mizeh,* meaning "from it" (literally). Nahum Sarna *(JPS Torah Commentary to Exodus)* concurs, noting archaeological finds of actual slave houses in Thebes, where laborers lived while constructing royal tombs in the Valley of the Kings.

[6] *"Leavened bread"* Hebrew, *chametz.* In all likelihood, the original term referred only to sour-dough-style bread that has risen, and not pita bread or other foods currently included in the category of *chametz,* though by rabbinic times it had come to mean all those foods that cannot be eaten on Passover.

[7] *"Aviv"* By rabbinic times, *aviv* also meant "spring," and so the phrase connoted "this spring month" as well.

[9] *"Matzah"* The English word "matzah" is a collective noun, so can refer to more than one piece. The Hebrew word is not collective and so usually (as here) appears in the plural.

[9] *"Holiday for Adonai"* Presumably, we celebrate the holiday "in honor of Adonai," but the Hebrew *(p. 90)*

Adonai brings you to the land of the Canaanite, the Hittite, the Amorite, the Hivvite, and the Jebusite, which He swore to your ancestors that He would give to you, a land flowing with milk and honey, you shall perform this service in this month: [9]For seven days you shall eat matzah, and the seventh day shall be a holiday for Adonai. [10]Matzah shall be eaten throughout the seven days, and no leavened bread shall be visible to you, and no leaven shall be visible to you, anywhere within your borders. [11]On that day you shall tell your child: [12]This is on account of what Adonai did for me when I left Egypt. It shall serve as a symbol on your hand and as a remembrance between your eyes, so that Adonai's Torah shall be on your tongue, because Adonai freed you from Egypt with a strong hand. [13]Keep this law at its proper time year by year. [14]And when Adonai brings you into the land of the Canaanite, as He swore to you and your ancestors that He would, and when He gives it to you, transfer every first issue of the womb to Adonai, and among all the first issues among the young animals that you have, transfer the males to Adonai. [15]And you shall redeem every firstling donkey with a lamb; if you do not redeem it, you must break its neck. [16]Redeem every first-born son among your children. [17]Tomorrow when your child asks you, "What is this for?"

הַכְּנַעֲנִי, וְהַחִתִּי וְהָאֱמֹרִי וְהַחִוִּי וְהַיְבוּסִי, אֲשֶׁר נִשְׁבַּע לַאֲבֹתֶיךָ לָתֶת לָךְ, אֶרֶץ זָבַת חָלָב וּדְבָשׁ, וְעָבַדְתָּ אֶת הָעֲבֹדָה הַזֹּאת בַּחֹדֶשׁ הַזֶּה. [9]שִׁבְעַת־יָמִים תֹּאכַל מַצֹּת, וּבַיּוֹם הַשְּׁבִיעִי חַג לַיְיָ. [10]מַצּוֹת יֵאָכֵל אֵת שִׁבְעַת הַיָּמִים, וְלֹא יֵרָאֶה לְךָ חָמֵץ וְלֹא יֵרָאֶה לְךָ שְׂאֹר בְּכָל גְּבֻלֶךָ. [11]וְהִגַּדְתָּ לְבִנְךָ בַּיּוֹם הַהוּא לֵאמֹר: [12]בַּעֲבוּר זֶה עָשָׂה יְיָ לִי בְּצֵאתִי מִמִּצְרָיִם. וְהָיָה לְךָ לְאוֹת עַל יָדְךָ, וּלְזִכָּרוֹן בֵּין עֵינֶיךָ, לְמַעַן תִּהְיֶה תּוֹרַת יְיָ בְּפִיךָ, כִּי בְּיָד חֲזָקָה הוֹצִאֲךָ יְיָ מִמִּצְרָיִם. [13]וְשָׁמַרְתָּ אֶת הַחֻקָּה הַזֹּאת לְמוֹעֲדָהּ מִיָּמִים יָמִימָה. [14]וְהָיָה, כִּי יְבִאֲךָ יְיָ אֶל אֶרֶץ הַכְּנַעֲנִי, כַּאֲשֶׁר נִשְׁבַּע לְךָ וְלַאֲבֹתֶיךָ, וּנְתָנָהּ לָךְ. וְהַעֲבַרְתָּ כָל פֶּטֶר רֶחֶם לַיְיָ; וְכָל פֶּטֶר שֶׁגֶר בְּהֵמָה אֲשֶׁר יִהְיֶה לְךָ, הַזְּכָרִים, לַיְיָ. [15]וְכָל פֶּטֶר חֲמֹר תִּפְדֶּה בְשֶׂה, וְאִם לֹא תִפְדֶּה וַעֲרַפְתּוֹ; [16]וְכֹל בְּכוֹר אָדָם בְּבָנֶיךָ תִּפְדֶּה. [17]וְהָיָה, כִּי יִשְׁאָלְךָ בִנְךָ מָחָר לֵאמֹר מַה זֹּאת, וְאָמַרְתָּ אֵלָיו: בְּחֹזֶק יָד הוֹצִיאָנוּ יְיָ מִמִּצְרַיִם, מִבֵּית עֲבָדִים. [18]וַיְהִי כִּי הִקְשָׁה פַרְעֹה לְשַׁלְּחֵנוּ, וַיַּהֲרֹג יְיָ כָל בְּכוֹר בְּאֶרֶץ מִצְרַיִם, מִבְּכוֹר אָדָם וְעַד בְּכוֹר בְּהֵמָה, עַל כֵּן אֲנִי זֹבֵחַ לַיְיָ כָּל פֶּטֶר רֶחֶם, הַזְּכָרִים, וְכָל בְּכוֹר בָּנַי אֶפְדֶּה. [19]וְהָיָה

answer him: It was with strength of hand that Adonai brought us out of Egypt, out of the house of slaves. [18]And when Pharaoh refused to let us go, Adonai killed every first-born in the land of Egypt, from the first-born of man to the first-born of beast, and therefore I sacrifice every first male issue of the womb, and I redeem the first-born among my children. [19]It shall be a sign on your hand, and a symbol between your eyes, for it was with a strong hand that Adonai brought us out of Egypt.

לְאוֹת עַל יָדְכָה, וּלְטוֹטָפֹת בֵּין עֵינֶיךָ, כִּי בְּחֹזֶק יָד הוֹצִיאָנוּ יְיָ מִמִּצְרָיִם.

BRETTLER (BIBLE)

redeem the Jewish first-born who are dedicated to God because they were spared in the tenth plague. Some biblical texts suggest that first-born Israelite boys were once actually offered as a human sacrifice (e.g., Exod. 22:28); this text would then be a theological rationale for banning that practice.

DORFF (THEOLOGY)

the two passages from Exodus 13 do not appear there, so are provided here instead. Some prayer books include the entire passage from Exodus so as to provide the context in which the command is given there: it comes in the thick of the drama of the Exodus, not just (as in Deuteronomy) as an act of remembrance for later generations.

Exodus explains the commandment, first, as a reminder that God redeemed us from Egypt "with a mighty hand"; and second, as a reminder of the commandment to redeem our first-born males in memory of the first-born Israelites who did not perish alongside the first-born of Egypt in the tenth plague. Deuteronomy 6 makes *t'fillin* a reminder of God's unity and of the love and fidelity that we should have for God; and Deuteronomy 11 makes them a symbol of God's commandments and of the reward and punishment that their fulfillment or disobedience entail.

ELLENSON (MODERN LITURGIES)

Living, the Reform Movement no longer recognizes "a hereditary priesthood"; nor does it believe "that the first-born son ought to occupy a status that is different from other sons and daughters." Hence this line is omitted from Reform as well as Reconstructionist prayer books. Even the Conservative Movement, however, which still practices the rite, excludes this reading from Exodus 13:1–16, the biblical source for the ritual in question, perhaps because its argument (we owe God our first-born because they were not killed alongside the Egyptian first-born) is not theologically palatable.

———◆———

J. HOFFMAN (TRANSLATION)

(and so our English) is ambiguous, as if open to the unlikely possibility that God is on holiday.

[10] *"Shall be eaten"* Curiously, the Hebrew verb is singular, in spite of the plural subject that precedes it.

[12] *"This is on account of what Adonai did for me"* This is the most likely interpretation of confusing Hebrew. Another possibility is: "It is because of this that Adonai did [good things?] for me."

[12] *"Remembrance"* Birnbaum, interpreting this phrase to refer to *t'fillin,* translates "remembrance" as "frontlets," but elsewhere (in the *Sh'ma,* for example), the word translated as "frontlets" is *totafot* whereas here we have *zikaron. Totafot* does, however, appear later (Exod. 13:16), so it is traditional to believe that *t'fillin* are meant here as well.

[13] *"Year by year"* Literally, "from day to day."

[14] *"Transfer…transfer"* In Hebrew the repetition of this verb is merely implied, but it is clearly needed in English.

[15] *"Firstling"* The Hebrew is the same *peter* we've been translating as "first issue."

[16] *"Among your children"* In parallel with "among the young animals" above. The animals are offered back to God; our own children are redeemed.

[17] *"Tomorrow"* A literal translation of the Hebrew. The most likely interpretation is "in days to come," but at times, in Hebrew and in English, "tomorrow" is used to imply a future time in general, and so we opt for a literal translation.

[17] *"What is this for?"* Hebrew, *mah zot.* In light of this seemingly bizarre practice, including breaking the neck of an unredeemed donkey, perhaps something stronger is in order: "What in the name of God are you doing!?"

[18] *"Refused"* This same verb is used for "harden" when God hardens Pharaoh's heart; the language reminds the reader of that story.

[19] *"Sign on your hand"* Judging from the Hebrew, this passage may have been added to the surrounding text much after the original had been written. The word for "your hand" *(yad'kha)* is spelled with a final *heh,* as in the Dead Sea Scrolls (which are centuries later than the rest of the Torah) and unlike the spelling that was common when the rest of this text was written. Of 162 biblical appearances of this word, this is the only time it is spelled with a *heh.*

[19] *"A symbol"* Others, "frontlets." See Volume 1, *The Sh'ma and Its Blessings,* p. 103.

◆ ◆ ◆

E. ADON OLAM

1 Eternal Lord who reigned supreme,
  Before all beings were created,
When everything was made according to
    His will,
Then He was called "King."

2 And when all shall cease to be,
He alone will reign supreme.
3 He was, He is,
And He will be crowned in glory.

4 He is One. 5 There is no second
To compare to Him or consort with Him.
6 Without beginning, without end,
Power and dominion are His.

7 He is my God, my living redeemer,
My stronghold in troubled times.
8 He is my sign and my banner,
My cup when I call on Him.

9 In His hand I trust my soul
When I sleep and when I wake.
10 And with my soul, my body too,
Adonai is mine. I shall not fear.

¹אֲדוֹן עוֹלָם אֲשֶׁר מָלַךְ
בְּטֶרֶם כָּל יְצִיר נִבְרָא.
לְעֵת נַעֲשָׂה בְחֶפְצוֹ כֹּל
אֲזַי מֶלֶךְ שְׁמוֹ נִקְרָא.

²וְאַחֲרֵי כִּכְלוֹת הַכֹּל
לְבַדּוֹ יִמְלֹךְ נוֹרָא.
³וְהוּא הָיָה וְהוּא הֹוֶה
וְהוּא יִהְיֶה בְּתִפְאָרָה.

⁴וְהוּא אֶחָד ⁵וְאֵין שֵׁנִי
לְהַמְשִׁיל לוֹ לְהַחְבִּירָה.
⁶בְּלִי רֵאשִׁית בְּלִי תַכְלִית
וְלוֹ הָעֹז וְהַמִּשְׂרָה.

⁷וְהוּא אֵלִי וְחַי גּוֹאֲלִי
וְצוּר חֶבְלִי בְּעֵת צָרָה.
⁸וְהוּא נִסִּי וּמָנוֹס לִי
מְנָת כּוֹסִי בְּיוֹם אֶקְרָא.

⁹בְּיָדוֹ אַפְקִיד רוּחִי
בְּעֵת אִישַׁן וְאָעִירָה.
¹⁰וְעִם רוּחִי גְּוִיָּתִי
יְיָ לִי וְלֹא אִירָא.

BRETTLER (BIBLE)

[1] *"Eternal Lord"* (Adon Olam) and "Exalted" *(Yigdal)* Two poems with meter and end-rhyme—features that biblical poetry lacks. Yet they adopt the biblical poetic device of parallelism, where each line is divided into two parts that are connected in meaning or structure (syntax).

Adon Olam presents a more radical view of God's kingship than the Bible (as in Ps. 93, for instance). It began even before creation, when God was already declared king, perhaps by the angels. When creation finally occurs, God's reign continues and lasts even after the world ends. The Bible too knows God's eternal reign (e.g., Ps. 10:16) and emphasizes it in

(p. 96)

DORFF (THEOLOGY)

[1] *"Eternal Lord* [Adon Olam]"* Many will be surprised to find *Adon Olam* and *Yigdal* at the beginning of the service, for we generally sing them at the very end. They have both been favorite hymns ever since their composition in the Middle Ages, and they truthfully *(p. 97)*

ELLENSON (MODERN LITURGIES)

[1] *"Eternal Lord"* In the nineteenth century, Reform liturgists customarily included this hymn here. Abraham Geiger and Isaac Mayer Wise offered it in both Hebrew and translation; David Einhorn produced a vernacular rendering only. Twentieth-century non-Orthodox editors have not followed their lead, however, possibly because they reserve the time-honored hymn for a closing song at the end of services. The exception, *Siddur Sim Shalom* (Conservative), follows tradition and includes it at this point.

E. ADON OLAM

[1] Eternal Lord who reigned supreme,
Before all beings were created,
When everything was made according to his will,
Then He was called "King."

[2] And when all shall cease to be,
He alone will reign supreme.

FRANKEL (A WOMAN'S VOICE)

[1] *"Eternal Lord"* There is a fascinating tension in this hymn between the contrasting divine aspects of immanence and transcendence. On the one hand, God is described in the first half of the poem as the eternal king, whose dominion predates the creation of the universe and whose rule will outlast it. Encompassing all, God is infinite and incomparable, the very essence of being.

And yet God is also remarkably intimate. In the second half of this prayer, the distant Lord of Creation becomes *eli,* "my God," and *go'ali,* "my redeemer." God is close enough to be summoned as soon as I call, to be carried as my personal "banner," *nisi;* to fill the "cup," *cosi,* in my hand; to serve as "my private hideaway," *manos li,* when I flee in fear from my enemies. That is why I can lie down each night with perfect trust that I will awaken each morning, my soul restored to what otherwise would have become my corpse, *g'viyati.* This awesome "Eternal Lord" who made everything, who rules supreme, this very same being I am able

¹אֲדוֹן עוֹלָם אֲשֶׁר מָלַךְ
בְּטֶרֶם כָּל יְצִיר נִבְרָא.
לְעֵת נַעֲשָׂה בְחֶפְצוֹ כֹּל
אֲזַי מֶלֶךְ שְׁמוֹ נִקְרָא.

²וְאַחֲרֵי כִּכְלוֹת הַכֹּל
לְבַדּוֹ יִמְלוֹךְ נוֹרָא.

to invoke by name: Adonai. How could I possibly be afraid?

J. HOFFMAN (TRANSLATION)

¹ *"Eternal Lord"* Adon Olam is a masterful work of poetry, taking advantage of lyric language, poetic imagery, and strict meter and rhyme. Our translation makes no attempt to mimic the meter or rhyme, and, unfortunately, contains only hints of the lyric language. We have thus captured the meaning, but not the import of this well-known *(p. 97)*

L. HOFFMAN (HISTORY)

¹ *"Eternal Lord* [Adon Olam] *"* Perhaps the best known poem in the Siddur, *Adon Olam* has attracted hundreds of melodies. In most rites, it accompanies another preparatory poem here, *Yigdal,* but its popularity has led to its recitation also as a common concluding melody. It is popularly attributed to the eleventh-century Spanish poet, Solomon ibn Gabirol, but without substantiating evidence.

The poem juxtaposes God's transcendence and immanence. Beginning with the former, we learn that God is a universal deity who preceded creation; will last beyond it; and rules all that is, eternally (even, apparently, before and after it comes into being). But just when the poem overwhelms us with God's grandeur, it changes course to proclaim God's intimate involvement with each and every one of us: for God is "my [!] God." Even as we sleep, we may safely entrust our soul in God's keeping, for "Adonai is mine; I shall not fear."

This final assurance has led some scholars to believe that *Adon Olam* was intended as a bedtime prayer. That may be so, but it might just as well have been a note of morning gratitude for awakening from sleep, and in any event, it does not really matter. Either way, the certainty of our own personal entanglement in a divine purpose mysteriously beyond our ken is what counts. How else shall we face death— as we all will? Here is the greatest Jewish promise of all: even the most *(p. 98)*

³ He was, He is,
And He will be crowned in glory.

⁴ He is One. ⁵ There is no second
To compare to Him or consort with
   Him.
⁶ Without beginning, without end,
Power and dominion are His.

⁷ He is my God, my living redeemer,
My stronghold in troubled times.
⁸ He is my sign and my banner,
My cup when I call on Him.

⁹ In His hand I trust my soul
When I sleep and when I wake.
¹⁰ And with my soul, my body too,
Adonai is mine. I shall not fear.

³וְהוּא הָיָה וְהוּא הֹוֶה
וְהוּא יִהְיֶה בְּתִפְאָרָה.

⁴וְהוּא אֶחָד ⁵וְאֵין שֵׁנִי
לְהַמְשִׁיל לוֹ לְהַחְבִּירָה.
⁶בְּלִי רֵאשִׁית בְּלִי תַכְלִית
וְלוֹ הָעֹז וְהַמִּשְׂרָה.

⁷וְהוּא אֵלִי וְחַי גּוֹאֲלִי
וְצוּר חֶבְלִי בְּעֵת צָרָה.
⁸וְהוּא נִסִּי וּמָנוֹס לִי
מְנָת כּוֹסִי בְּיוֹם אֶקְרָא.

⁹בְּיָדוֹ אַפְקִיד רוּחִי
בְּעֵת אִישַׁן וְאָעִירָה.
¹⁰וְעִם רוּחִי גְּוִיָּתִי
יְיָ לִי וְלֹא אִירָא.

BRETTLER (BIBLE)

contexts of catastrophic eschatologies (e.g., Isa. 24:23; Zech. 14), but never does the Bible explicitly extend God's kingship beyond the end of the world.

⁶ *"Without beginning"* Statements of God's uniqueness arose during the Babylonian exile as expressions of radical monotheism (e.g., "There is none other" [Isa. 45:5, 14, 18, 21]). That God is without beginning or end reflects the same exilic sentiment ("I am first, and I am last" [Isa. 44:6; 48:12]).

⁷ *"My living redeemer"* Paraphrasing Job 19:25, "I know that my redeemer lives."

⁸ *"He is my sign [v'hu nisi]"* A word play on the enigmatic image of Exod. 17:15, where an altar is named "*adonai nisi.*"

⁸ *"My cup [m'nat kosi]"* Biblically, God's cup is more likely filled with poison, but the reference here is to Psalm 16:5, "Adonai is my allotted share and portion."

⁹ *"In His hand I trust my soul [ruach]"* *Ruach*, biblically, denotes "life-force"; sleep is

a small death. Daniel 12:2 calls the dead "those who sleep in the earth." Awakening here may mean the afterlife, which rabbinic Judaism paints positively. By contrast, the biblical afterworld, *sh'ol,* is so unpleasant that psalmists regularly ask to be rescued from it.

— ◆ —

DORFF (THEOLOGY)

fit equally well in either place, for they articulate Judaism's foundational beliefs about God. Many of the melodies to these prayers are fast and even jaunty, in part because we sing them at the end of the service as a kind of farewell—as a child we looked forward to them because they meant that the service was over!—but also because both prayers retain the same number of syllables per line. *Adon Olam* in particular, with its easy, eight-syllable lines and its repetitive rhyme scheme, fits an amazing number of melodies.

Yet the themes of both poems are serious. *Adon Olam* proclaims God's eternal sovereignty: God ruled even before the universe was created and will continue to rule after it ends. God is one, and incomparable. "He is my God, my living redeemer, My stronghold in times of distress"; "He is my guide and my refuge" whom I trust to guard my spirit when I sleep and when I wake; "with my spirit and my body [I declare] the Lord is with me, I shall not fear." These are far-reaching doctrines about God's omnipotence and providence, serious assertions of a person of faith.

— ◆ —

J. HOFFMAN (TRANSLATION)

prayer. Because most of the original words were chosen for poetic purposes and not for their meaning alone, we see little point is providing detailed notes about the meaning of the Hebrew words, and so we only provide notes where our translation fails to capture part of the meaning.

[8] *"My sign and my banner"* The words for both "sign" and "banner" come from the root for "miracle," and so allude to miracles as well.

[8] *"My cup"* An allusion to "my cup overflows."

[9] *"Soul"* Or "spirit."
[10] *"Adonai is mine"* Or "Adonai is with me."

— ◆ —

L. HOFFMAN (HISTORY)

minuscule and shattered of lives matter to the infinite intelligence of the universe whom we name God; since "Adonai is mine; I shall not fear."

◆ ◆ ◆

F. YIGDAL

1 Exalted and praised be the living God.
2 He exists: His existence is timeless.

3 He is One: there is no oneness like His
oneness.

4 He is hidden: His oneness is endless.

5 He has no body: He is not a body.

6 We cannot fathom His holiness.

7 He preceded all that was created.

8 He was the first. 9 His beginning was
beginning-less.

10 He is the eternal Lord; every creature
Declares His greatness and dominion.

11 He gave His abundant prophecy to
The men of His choice and His glory.

12 Never again has there arisen in Israel
A prophet like Moses who beheld His
image.

13 God gave His Torah of truth to His people
Through His prophet, His faithful prophet.

14 God will never exchange or emend
His law for any other.

15 He watches us, and knows our secrets,
Foreseeing the end of every thing at its
inception.

16 He rewards good people according to
their acts,
And gives evil to the evil according to their
wickedness.

17 At the end of time He will send us our
messiah
To save all who wait for His final
redemption.

18 In His great mercy, God will revive the
dead.

19 Blessed be His glorious name for ever and
ever!

יִגְדַּל אֱלֹהִים חַי וְיִשְׁתַּבַּח [1]

נִמְצָא וְאֵין עֵת אֶל מְצִיאוּתוֹ. [2]

אֶחָד וְאֵין יָחִיד כְּיִחוּדוֹ [3]

נֶעְלָם וְגַם אֵין סוֹף לְאַחְדּוּתוֹ. [4]

אֵין לוֹ דְּמוּת הַגּוּף וְאֵינוֹ גוּף [5]

לֹא נַעֲרוֹךְ אֵלָיו קְדֻשָּׁתוֹ. [6]

קַדְמוֹן לְכָל דָּבָר אֲשֶׁר נִבְרָא [7]

רִאשׁוֹן וְאֵין רֵאשִׁית לְרֵאשִׁיתוֹ. [8] [9]

הִנּוֹ אֲדוֹן עוֹלָם וְכָל נוֹצָר [10]
יוֹרֶה גְדֻלָּתוֹ וּמַלְכוּתוֹ.

שֶׁפַע נְבוּאָתוֹ נְתָנוֹ אֶל [11]
אַנְשֵׁי סְגֻלָּתוֹ וְתִפְאַרְתּוֹ.

לֹא קָם בְּיִשְׂרָאֵל כְּמֹשֶׁה עוֹד [12]
נָבִיא וּמַבִּיט אֶת תְּמוּנָתוֹ.

תּוֹרַת אֱמֶת נָתַן לְעַמּוֹ אֵל [13]
עַל יַד נְבִיאוֹ נֶאֱמַן בֵּיתוֹ.

לֹא יַחֲלִיף הָאֵל וְלֹא יָמִיר [14]
דָתוֹ לְעוֹלָמִים לְזוּלָתוֹ.

צוֹפֶה וְיוֹדֵעַ סְתָרֵינוּ [15]
מַבִּיט לְסוֹף דָּבָר בְּקַדְמָתוֹ.

גּוֹמֵל לְאִישׁ חֶסֶד כְּמִפְעָלוֹ [16]
נוֹתֵן לְרָשָׁע רָע כְּרִשְׁעָתוֹ.

יִשְׁלַח לְקֵץ יָמִין מְשִׁיחֵנוּ [17]
לִפְדּוֹת מְחַכֵּי קֵץ יְשׁוּעָתוֹ.

מֵתִים יְחַיֶּה אֵל בְּרֹב חַסְדּוֹ [18]

בָּרוּךְ עֲדֵי עַד שֵׁם תְּהִלָּתוֹ. [19]

BRETTLER (BIBLE)

[1] *"The living God"* A living God was presupposed by the Bible, as by other ancient peoples, who required a creator deity to explain the world's existence. Some Israelites apparently concluded that once the world was created, no deity was needed to maintain it. The psalmist answers them by charging that only the "fool" could believe "there is no God" (Pss. 14:1; 53:2).

[3] *"One"* The Bible differs on what God's oneness means. In Exodus 15:11, "Who is like You among the gods…" (an early poem), God is incomparable, but not the only deity. After the exile, more radical monotheism became normative, albeit tempered by advanced angelology. *(p. 103)*

DORFF (THEOLOGY)

[1] *"Exalted and praised [Yigdal]"* *Yigdal* formulates Maimonides' Thirteen Principles of Faith in poetic form with a single rhyme throughout thirteen lines, each with sixteen syllables. It declares:

1. God's eternal existence, unity, and uniqueness; *(p. 104)*

ELLENSON (MODERN LITURGIES)

[1] *"Exalted [Yigdal]"* Geiger included this Maimonidean hymn in his inclusive 1854 prayer book, but removed it in the 1870 edition. No other Reform or Reconstructionist Siddur has placed *Yigdal* here either. Maimonides'

doctrine of God, the first part of the poem, could hardly be at issue, since Maimonides was generally looked to by the reformers as a great rationalist, who preached God's noncorporeality. But here, he went too far, including, for instance, the necessity of believing in bodily resurrection. The Conservative *Siddur Sim Shalom* retains the hymn here, following its general bow to traditional practice liturgically.

F. YIGDAL

[1] Exalted and praised be the living God.
[2] He exists: His existence is timeless.
[3] He is One: there is no oneness like His oneness.
[4] He is hidden: His oneness is endless.
[5] He has no body: He is not a body.
[6] We cannot fathom His holiness.

J. HOFFMAN (TRANSLATION)

[1] *"Exalted and praised"* Like *Adon Olam*, above, *Yigdal* is a poetic masterpiece, and so again we provide a translation that captures the literal meaning alone, and notes that expound on that literal meaning. Unfortunately, in this case (unlike with *Adon Olam*) our simplistic translation makes the poem seem almost silly, while the Hebrew version, quite to the contrary, expresses Maimonides' thirteen principles of faith beautifully. *(p. 105)*

L. HOFFMAN (HISTORY)

[1] *"Exalted [Yigdal]"* In many ways, Moses Maimonides (1135–1204) was the most influential and the most controversial Jewish philosopher ever. Among other things, he denied God's corporeality (having no body, God is utterly unlike anything we can imagine). Contrary to tradition, he also entertained the Aristotelian notion that matter (like God) may be eternal (a position he denied, even while claiming there could be no proof either way).

In 1200, Maimonides completed his major philosophical work, *Guide for the Perplexed,* using traditional format with supporting biblical verses that masked its radicalism. He had already constructed his credentials as a master jurist, by writing, among other things, a code of Jewish law (the *Mishneh Torah*), and a commentary to the Mishnah (the earliest corpus of rabbinic law, c. 200 C.E.). In this commentary, he formulated his principles of Jewish faith.

The philosophical controversies that surrounded Maimonides while he lived only worsened afterward, as detractors charged him with misrepresenting Jewish law and fomenting heresy. A supporter, Daniel ben Judah of Rome (fourteenth century), composed this poetic version of Maimonides' principles, which were added to the Siddur not merely as a prayer, but as a political polemic.

[12] *"Never again has there arisen"* The Torah itself closes with this affirmation of Moses' uniqueness (Deut. 34:10), but the claim took on new significance in Maimonides' day, for Maimonides lived in Egypt where the faith of the ruling Islamic authorities claimed precisely that Mohammed, not Moses, was the final and greatest prophet.

[18] *"God will revive the dead"* Perhaps the most controversial of Maimonides' Thirteen Principles of Faith, not because it was novel (on the contrary, resurrection was a cardinal matter of rabbinic faith), but because Maimonides was suspected of denying it. His code of Jewish law had emphasized immortality of the soul, not resurrection of the body. In 1191, he therefore composed a treatise on resurrection, reaffirming his faith in it. Even thereafter, however, he was accused of denying the principle as a necessary outcome of the halakhic system. As we see, he had already included resurrection among his Thirteen Principles, but doubts about his belief persisted well beyond his lifetime.

It is probably fair to say that, at the very least, resurrection was *(p. 106)*

[1] יִגְדַּל אֱלֹהִים חַי וְיִשְׁתַּבַּח

[2] נִמְצָא וְאֵין עֵת אֶל מְצִיאוּתוֹ.

[3] אֶחָד וְאֵין יָחִיד כְּיִחוּדוֹ

[4] נֶעְלָם וְגַם אֵין סוֹף לְאַחְדוּתוֹ.

[5] אֵין לוֹ דְמוּת הַגּוּף וְאֵינוֹ גוּף

[6] לֹא נַעֲרוֹךְ אֵלָיו קְדֻשָּׁתוֹ.

7 He preceded all that was created.

8 He was the first. 9His beginning was
   beginning-less.

10He is the eternal Lord; every
   creature

Declares His greatness and dominion.

11He gave His abundant prophecy to

The men of His choice and His glory.

12Never again has there arisen in
   Israel

A prophet like Moses who beheld His
   image.

13God gave His Torah of truth to His
   people

Through His prophet, His faithful
   prophet.

14God will never exchange or emend

His law for any other.

15He watches us, and knows our
   secrets,

Foreseeing the end of every thing at
   its inception.

16He rewards good people according
   to their acts,

And gives evil to the evil according to
   their wickedness.

17At the end of time He will send us
   our messiah

To save all who wait for His final
   redemption.

18In His great mercy, God will revive
   the dead.

19Blessed be His glorious name for
   ever and ever!

קַדְמוֹן לְכָל דָּבָר אֲשֶׁר נִבְרָא 7

רִאשׁוֹן 9וְאֵין רֵאשִׁית לְרֵאשִׁיתוֹ. 8

הִנּוֹ אֲדוֹן עוֹלָם וְכָל נוֹצָר 10

יוֹרֶה גְדֻלָּתוֹ וּמַלְכוּתוֹ.

שֶׁפַע נְבוּאָתוֹ נְתָנוֹ אֶל 11

אַנְשֵׁי סְגֻלָּתוֹ וְתִפְאַרְתּוֹ.

לֹא קָם בְּיִשְׂרָאֵל כְּמֹשֶׁה עוֹד 12

נָבִיא וּמַבִּיט אֶת תְּמוּנָתוֹ.

תּוֹרַת אֱמֶת נָתַן לְעַמּוֹ אֵל 13

עַל יַד נְבִיאוֹ נֶאֱמַן בֵּיתוֹ.

לֹא יַחֲלִיף הָאֵל וְלֹא יָמִיר 14

דָּתוֹ לְעוֹלָמִים לְזוּלָתוֹ.

צוֹפֶה וְיוֹדֵעַ סְתָרֵינוּ 15

מַבִּיט לְסוֹף דָּבָר בְּקַדְמָתוֹ.

גּוֹמֵל לְאִישׁ חֶסֶד כְּמִפְעָלוֹ 16

נוֹתֵן לְרָשָׁע רָע כְּרִשְׁעָתוֹ.

יִשְׁלַח לְקֵץ יָמִין מְשִׁיחֵנוּ 17

לִפְדּוֹת מְחַכֵּי קֵץ יְשׁוּעָתוֹ.

מֵתִים יְחַיֶּה אֵל בְּרֹב חַסְדּוֹ 18

בָּרוּךְ עֲדֵי עַד שֵׁם תְּהִלָּתוֹ. 19

BRETTLER (BIBLE)

[5] *"No body"* Most biblical texts depict God with hands, eyes, legs, and other body parts. God even wears clothes and sits on a throne (Isa. 6:1; Dan. 7:9). But a minority view denies God's corporeality, for example, in Ezekiel 1:26, God is only *"like* a person" *(k'mareh adam),* and Deuteronomy in particular emphasizes that God could not actually be seen at Sinai—in contrast with Exodus 24:10, "They saw the God of Israel, and under his feet...."

[10] *"Every creature declares"* In most biblical texts, God is a national deity for Jews alone. Deuteronomy 4:19 has God distribute astral bodies for other nations to worship. Some prophets, however, assume that in the ideal future, all people will worship God. Isaiah 66:23, a post-exilic text, predicts, "Every new moon, and every Sabbath, every person will prostrate themselves before Me, says Adonai." *Yigdal* takes this as an obligation in the here and now, not just at the end of days.

[11] *"His abundant prophecy"* Prophecy is central to the Bible, as to other Near Eastern cultures, which preferred, however, to discern the will of their deities through other methods. Deuteronomy 18:16 traces prophecy to Sinai, when it was given to Israel because the people feared the unmediated voice of God.

[12] *"Never again has there arisen"* Deuteronomy 18:15, 18 promises other prophets of the same stature of Moses, but generally, Moses' absolute incomparability is stressed in the Bible, especially at the end of Deuteronomy (34:10), which is cited here along with an allusion to Numbers 12:8, where Moses stands out as unique because he beheld God directly.

[13] *"God gave His Torah of truth"* From Deuteronomy 4:44, "the Torah that Moses placed before all Israel," and Nehemiah 9:13, "torahs of truth" *(torot emet).* Biblically, "Torah" denotes any set of laws, not specifically the Five Books of Moses. So Deuteronomy 4:44 means some specific teachings, not *the* Torah as we know it. This sense of Torah as multiple teachings allows Nehemiah 9:13 to speak meaningfully in the plural. When the very late Psalm 119:142, however, says "Your Torah is true," it may already have a single Torah in mind, as we do.

[14] *"God will never...emend"* The idea of a single changeless Torah is post-biblical. But it is based on Deuteronomy's contention that the law may not be amended (Deut. 4:2; 13:1) and the parallel notion that God, unlike humans, does not change his mind (1 Sam. 15:29).

[15] *"Our secrets...the end of every thing"* God's omniscience in the sense of knowing our innermost thoughts is biblical. But God is not seen biblically as knowing the future. When Abraham is prevented at the last moment from slaughtering Isaac, the messenger of God admits, "For *now* [presumably not before] I know that you fear God" (Gen. 22:12)—a clear indication that God does not know things in advance.

[16] *"Rewards good people"* The idea of corporate reward and punishment is central to Deuteronomy, but personal reward and punishment is found particularly in the Psalms. Psalm 1 opens deliberately with illustrations of the righteous flourishing, and the wicked insubstantial chaff. Proverbs offers a similar theology, as does Ezekiel 18, which contends with Deuteronomy, saying, "The person who sins—he alone will die" (v. 4); "A son...shall not die for the iniquity of the father.... If the son has done what is right...he shall live" (vv. 14, 17, 19). By contrast, Job illustrates a case where straightforward personal retribution fails.

[17] *"Our messiah"* Messianism is biblical, usually referring to a future Davidic king, as in Isaiah. 11:1, "A shoot shall grow out of the stump of Jesse [David's father]." The word "messiah" comes from *mashi'ach,* "the anointed one," a name reflecting anointing with oil, a coronation ritual. Oddly enough, however, the Bible never actually calls the anticipated king "messiah," and even though prophets like Isaiah, Jeremiah, and Ezekiel assume that he will arrive, Deutero-Isaiah (the anonymous author of Isa. 40–66) assigns the messianic promise to all Israel (Isa. 55:3). Other texts, such as Isaiah. 2:1–5, depict an ideal future in which God has a messianic role in a messianic age, but no personal messiah.

[18] *"Revive the dead"* The resurrection of the dead is found biblically only in Daniel 12:2, a late biblical tale told in response to the persecutions by Antiochus IV, which prompted the Hasmonean (or Maccabean) revolt in 167 B.C.E. In earlier biblical thought, the deceased went eternally to *sh'ol,* the underworld. In the dry-bones chapter of Ezekiel (37:1–14), resurrection symbolizes national restoration. Nowhere outside of Daniel does the Bible intimate that individuals will be resurrected.

◆

DORFF (THEOLOGY)

2. the gift of prophecy to Moses in a Torah that will never be amended (by, for example, Jesus or Mohammed);
3. God's knowledge of all our thoughts and deeds and God's reward for good and punishment for evil;
4. God's promises (a) to send a messiah at the end of historical time and (b) to revive the dead.

Maimonides first describes these doctrines in his commentary to Mishnah Sanhedrin 10:1, and he returns to them more fully in his later works: his code, the *Mishneh Torah* (primarily in the first and last sections), and his philosophical masterpiece, *Guide for the Perplexed.*

Despite Maimonides' philosophical and legal preeminence, each of his doctrinal views have found detracters, not just supporters. His very list of thirteen beliefs was attacked by philosophers like Simeon ben Zemaeh Duran (1361–1444), who suggested just three foundational principles. As a result, even though Maimonides' list is enshrined poetically here, as well as in a prose version after the weekday morning service (in some prayer books), it never became the official definition of what Jews *must* believe.

For that matter, no other list did either. This is in sharp contrast to Christianity, where even born and baptized Christians do not consider themselves Christian if they do not believe in Jesus as the messiah; and people who do not accept the specific creeds of a given Christian denomination would not classify themselves as one of its members. By contrast, Jewish identity is not a function of theological belief; it instead depends upon one of two things: birth to a Jewish mother (or father, in Reform Judaism) or conversion to Judaism.

That is not to say, though, that Judaism lacks belief. Quite the contrary. Even though being a Jew begins with birth or conversion, *serious* Jewish identity requires living in response to Jewish beliefs and prescriptions for action, called commandments. Both are open to considerable interpretation, but neither may be ignored. The closest we have to an official creed is the core of the liturgy: the *Sh'ma* and Its Blessings, and the *Amidah* (see Volume 1, *The Sh'ma and Its Blessings,* and Volume 2, *The Amidah*). The Jewish prayer book, the Siddur, is thus the quintessential handbook of Jewish theology. Maimonides' list is a later attempt to explicate those beliefs, but the open style of the Siddur, with beliefs asserted but subject to interpretation and amendment through added sections of prose and poetry, turned out to be the truly lasting format for expressing Jewish belief.

——◆——

J. HOFFMAN (TRANSLATION)

[2] *"Is timeless"* Birnbaum's "transcends time" is nice.

[4] *"Hidden"* Or "unknowable."

[12] *"His image"* God's Image.

[15] *"Foreseeing"* Literally, "seeing"

[15] *"Its inception"* Or, perhaps, "His inception."

[17] *"End of time"* The word for "end" is the same one used immediately below for "final."

——◆——

L. HOFFMAN (HISTORY)

relatively unimportant in Maimonides' system. He held that a messiah would come and establish world peace. Messianic times, however, would be altogether like the natural world that we know. Bodies would indeed be brought back to life and joined with their souls then, but these reconstituted bodies would die again. Ultimately, the intellect alone has eternal life, when it engages in pure contemplation of God.

◆ ◆ ◆

2 | Preliminary Blessings

[1] Blessed are You, Adonai our God, Ruler of the world, who sanctified us with His commandments and commanded us about washing our hands.

[2] Blessed are You, Adonai our God, Ruler of the world, who formed humans with wisdom and created a system of ducts and conduits in them. [3] It is well-known before Your throne of glory that if one of these should burst or one of these get blocked, it would be impossible to survive and stand before You. [4] Blessed are You, Adonai, who heals all creatures, doing wonders.

[5] Blessed are You, Adonai our God, Ruler of the world, who sanctified us with His commandments and commanded us to engage in words of Torah. [6] So, Adonai our God, make the words of Your Torah sweet to us and to the house of Israel, Your people, that we and our descendants, and the descendants of Your people, the house of Israel, that we all should know Your name and study Your Torah for its own sake. [7] Blessed are You, Adonai, who teaches Torah to His people Israel. [8] Blessed are You, Adonai our God, Ruler of the world, who chose us from all peoples, and gave us His Torah. [9] Blessed are You, Adonai, who gives the Torah.

¹בָּרוּךְ אַתָּה, יְיָ אֱלֹהֵינוּ, מֶלֶךְ הָעוֹלָם, אֲשֶׁר קִדְּשָׁנוּ בְּמִצְוֹתָיו וְצִוָּנוּ עַל נְטִילַת יָדַיִם.

²בָּרוּךְ אַתָּה, יְיָ אֱלֹהֵינוּ, מֶלֶךְ הָעוֹלָם, אֲשֶׁר יָצַר אֶת הָאָדָם בְּחָכְמָה, וּבָרָא בוֹ נְקָבִים נְקָבִים, חֲלוּלִים חֲלוּלִים. ³גָּלוּי וְיָדוּעַ לִפְנֵי כִסֵּא כְבוֹדֶךָ, שֶׁאִם יִפָּתֵחַ אֶחָד מֵהֶם אוֹ יִסָּתֵם אֶחָד מֵהֶם אִי אֶפְשָׁר לְהִתְקַיֵּם וְלַעֲמוֹד לְפָנֶיךָ. ⁴בָּרוּךְ אַתָּה, יְיָ, רוֹפֵא כָל בָּשָׂר וּמַפְלִיא לַעֲשׂוֹת.

⁵בָּרוּךְ אַתָּה, יְיָ אֱלֹהֵינוּ, מֶלֶךְ הָעוֹלָם, אֲשֶׁר קִדְּשָׁנוּ בְּמִצְוֹתָיו וְצִוָּנוּ לַעֲסוֹק בְּדִבְרֵי תוֹרָה. ⁶וְהַעֲרֶב נָא, יְיָ אֱלֹהֵינוּ, אֶת דִּבְרֵי תוֹרָתְךָ בְּפִינוּ, וּבְפִי עַמְּךָ בֵּית יִשְׂרָאֵל, וְנִהְיֶה אֲנַחְנוּ וְצֶאֱצָאֵינוּ, וְצֶאֱצָאֵי עַמְּךָ בֵּית יִשְׂרָאֵל, כֻּלָּנוּ יוֹדְעֵי שְׁמֶךָ וְלוֹמְדֵי תוֹרָתֶךָ לִשְׁמָהּ. ⁷בָּרוּךְ אַתָּה, יְיָ, הַמְלַמֵּד תּוֹרָה לְעַמּוֹ יִשְׂרָאֵל.

⁸בָּרוּךְ אַתָּה יְיָ אֱלֹהֵינוּ, מֶלֶךְ הָעוֹלָם, אֲשֶׁר בָּחַר בָּנוּ מִכָּל הָעַמִּים, וְנָתַן לָנוּ אֶת תּוֹרָתוֹ. ⁹בָּרוּךְ אַתָּה, יְיָ, נוֹתֵן הַתּוֹרָה.

BRETTLER (BIBLE)

[1] *"Washing our hands"* Washing hands and feet was a priestly obligation entailed by the need to be ritually pure before ministering at the Temple (Exod. 30:19, 21).

[5] *"Engage in words of Torah"* With the exception of Deuteronomy, the Torah is not self-conscious of itself as a book, so does not command its own study. Deuteronomy, however, emphasizes obedience to God's words (e.g., 7:12) and presumes familiarity with the law; it mandates a reading of at least part of the law once every seven years (31:9–13). Before the exile, that familiarity was the prerogative of the priestly *(p. 110)*

DORFF (THEOLOGY)

[2] *"Who formed humans with wisdom"* Though a prayer intended for recitation whenever we emerge from the bathroom after using the toilet, it appears here because the liturgy assumes we have done so shortly after waking up. The prayer (Ber. 11a and 60b, where it is attributed to *(p. 111)*

ELLENSON (MODERN LITURGIES)

[1] *"Commanded us about washing our hands"* Siddur Va'ani T'fillati and Siddur Sim Shalom include this benediction, but move it to the very beginning of the Morning Blessings rubric, so that it can be said upon washing one's hands after *(p. 112)*

FRANKEL (A WOMAN'S VOICE)

[1] *"About washing our hands"* This blessing inaugurates a series of benedictions taken from Berakhot 11a and 60b. And what a strange juxtaposition it is—thanking God simultaneously for teaching us Torah and for giving us internal plumbing that works! Could any two spheres be further apart? And yet in this odd pairing we find the genius of Jewish prayer: on the one hand, if our tubes and valves fail to function, how difficult it is to focus our minds on *(p. 113)*

[1] Blessed are You, Adonai our God, Ruler of the world, who sanctified us with His commandments and commanded us about washing our hands.

[2] Blessed are You, Adonai our God, Ruler of the world, who formed humans with wisdom and created a system of ducts and conduits in them. [3] It is well-known before Your throne of glory that if one of these should burst or one of these get blocked, it would be

J. HOFFMAN (TRANSLATION)

[1] *"About"* To command us "about" is a common translation of an equally common rabbinic idiom, "who has commanded us *al*." Halakhically, a distinction is made between this *al* form of a blessing over a commandment and an equally common alternative, "who has commanded us to" *(l')*. We honor the rabbinic use of *al*, therefore, with the unique translation (strange as it may sound) of "about [the commandment…]." *(p. 113)*

L. HOFFMAN (HISTORY)

BLESSINGS FOR ACTIVITIES CONSIDERED ESSENTIAL IMMEDIATELY UPON ARISING: STUDY, PRECEDED BY WASHING AND USING THE BATHROOM.

[1] *"About washing our hands"* Originally, the Morning Blessings were said personally upon awakening, as were various other blessings that once accompanied the individual's private process of awakening, getting dressed, and so on. Only with *Seder Rav Amram,* our first comprehensive *(p. 114)*

בָּרוּךְ אַתָּה, יְיָ אֱלֹהֵינוּ, מֶלֶךְ הָעוֹלָם, אֲשֶׁר קִדְּשָׁנוּ בְּמִצְוֹתָיו וְצִוָּנוּ עַל נְטִילַת יָדָיִם.

בָּרוּךְ אַתָּה, יְיָ אֱלֹהֵינוּ, מֶלֶךְ הָעוֹלָם, אֲשֶׁר יָצַר אֶת הָאָדָם בְּחָכְמָה, וּבָרָא בוֹ נְקָבִים נְקָבִים, חֲלוּלִים חֲלוּלִים. גָּלוּי וְיָדוּעַ לִפְנֵי כִסֵּא כְבוֹדֶךָ, שֶׁאִם יִפָּתֵחַ אֶחָד מֵהֶם אוֹ יִסָּתֵם אֶחָד מֵהֶם אִי אֶפְשָׁר לְהִתְקַיֵּם

KUSHNER & POLEN (CHASIDISM)

[2] *"Who formed"* In addition to the obvious, and healthy, acknowledgment of the mystery of the physical body's organic processes, Jewish spiritual tradition also finds in this benediction the theme of our interaction with the outside world. In other words, it's more than merely organs that are open and closed; it's also a matter of what is inside and outside. We are encouraged to contemplate not only the body's internal rhythms, but how what is inside the body gets outside *(p. 115)*

LANDES (HALAKHAH)

[1] *"Blessed…about washing our hands"* These blessings were originally intended for private recitation at home. They were composed in Hebrew, so raising the question of whether they may be said in English by people who do not understand Hebrew.

The general rule is that blessings may be said in any language we understand (Maimonides, Laws of Prayer, 16). The source for this ruling is the one certain Torah-authorized blessing over enjoyment, the *Birkat Hamazon* ("Grace after Meals"), which comes from Deuteronomy 8:10, "You will eat, and be satisfied, and bless A-donai your God for the good land He gave you." The Talmud (Sot. 33a) interprets this to mean "Bless God in any language in which you are able to bless Him."

Medieval and modern opinions vary. The Rosh (Asher ben Yechiel, Germany and Spain, 1250–1327) rules that the Hebrew blessings of people who do not understand Hebrew are not valid; they *must* repeat the blessing in a language that they understand (Commentary to Ber. 7:6). According to his reasoning, we cannot bless God if we do not know what we are saying. By contrast, Meiri (R. Menachem ben David Hameiri, Italy, 1249–1315) believes that one's obligation is fulfilled by saying a blessing in Hebrew even if it is not understood, although this would not hold true for any other language (Commentary to Ber. 40b). *(p. 117)* impossible to survive and stand before You. ⁴Blessed are You, Adonai, who heals all creatures, doing wonders.

⁵Blessed are You, Adonai our God, Ruler of the world, who sanctified us with His commandments and commanded us to engage in words of Torah. ⁶So, Adonai our God, make the words of Your Torah sweet to us and to the house of Israel, Your people, that we and our descendants, and the descendants of Your people, the house of Israel, that we all should know Your name and study Your Torah for its own sake. ⁷Blessed are You, Adonai, who teaches Torah to His people Israel. ⁸Blessed are You, Adonai our God, Ruler of the world, who chose us from all peoples, and gave us His Torah. ⁹Blessed are You, Adonai, who gives the Torah.

וְלַעֲמֹוד לְפָנֶיךָ. ⁴בָּרוּךְ אַתָּה, יְיָ, רוֹפֵא כָל בָּשָׂר וּמַפְלִיא לַעֲשֹוֹת.

⁵בָּרוּךְ אַתָּה, יְיָ אֱלֹהֵינוּ, מֶלֶךְ הָעוֹלָם, אֲשֶׁר קִדְּשָׁנוּ בְּמִצְוֹתָיו וְצִוָּנוּ לַעֲסוֹק בְּדִבְרֵי תוֹרָה. ⁶וְהַעֲרֶב־נָא, יְיָ אֱלֹהֵינוּ, אֶת דִּבְרֵי תוֹרָתְךָ בְּפִינוּ, וּבְפִי עַמְּךָ בֵּית יִשְׂרָאֵל, וְנִהְיֶה אֲנַחְנוּ וְצֶאֱצָאֵינוּ, וְצֶאֱצָאֵי עַמְּךָ בֵּית יִשְׂרָאֵל, כֻּלָּנוּ יוֹדְעֵי שְׁמֶךָ וְלוֹמְדֵי תוֹרָתֶךָ לִשְׁמָהּ. ⁷בָּרוּךְ אַתָּה, יְיָ, הַמְלַמֵּד תּוֹרָה לְעַמּוֹ יִשְׂרָאֵל. ⁸בָּרוּךְ אַתָּה, יְיָ אֱלֹהֵינוּ, מֶלֶךְ הָעוֹלָם, אֲשֶׁר בָּחַר בָּנוּ מִכָּל הָעַמִּים, וְנָתַן לָנוּ אֶת תּוֹרָתוֹ. ⁹בָּרוּךְ אַתָּה, יְיָ, נוֹתֵן הַתּוֹרָה.

BRETTLER (BIBLE)

class (Jer. 18:18; Ezek. 7:26); only after the exile does public study arise (Neh. 8). Joshua 1:8, a late biblical text, explicitly demands, "This Torah book should never leave your mouth; you should recite it day and night so that you will heed everything that is written in it; then your path will succeed, and then you will flourish."

⁶*"Study Your Torah for its own sake"* With the exception of Psalm 119, a late composition, study for its own sake is foreign to biblical culture. The purpose of hearing the law is so that it will be observed (e.g., Deut. 5:1).

⁷*"Who teaches Torah"* A jarring phrase from a biblical perspective, since only a small part of the Bible, the Decalogue, was publicly taught to all Israel (Exod. 20:18–21; Deut. 5:22–33). Also, in the Bible, Moses, not God, does the teaching.

⁸*"Who chose us...and gave us His Torah"* The chosenness of Israel—a central biblical idea (e.g., Deut. 7:6–7; Isa. 41:8–9; Ps. 33:12)—confers not blessing but responsibility:

"Only you have I been intimate with from all the nations of the earth; therefore I will requite you all of your sins" (Amos 3:2). "Who chose us" is therefore followed by "and gave us His Torah"—that is, Israel is chosen to receive the Torah, an idea never made explicit in the Bible, but suggested by Genesis 18:19, "For I [God] have been intimate with him [Abraham], so that he will command his children and his house after him to observe the way of the Lord."

◆

DORFF (THEOLOGY)

fourth-century Sages, Abaye and Rav Papa) articulates our dependence on the intricate functioning of our body, warning us not to take bodily operations for granted: rather, we are to see in our very bodies a wondrous sign of God's providence, which extends beyond our prayers; before we ever learned to pray, we were created with the miraculous ability to flourish.

⁵ *"Commanded us to engage in words of Torah"* These three blessings thanking God for giving us the Torah are ascribed to third-century scholars, Rav Judah, Rabbi Johanan, and Rav Hamnuna, the last of whom suggests we say them all (Ber. 11b). The Talmud requires them each time we study, but the liturgy defines the early morning service as one such occasion, so inserts the blessings here, prior to selections from the Torah and from rabbinic literature. Thus at the very beginning of the morning we recognize our joint dependence on the smooth functioning of our bodies and the linking of our lives to Torah.

Each blessing describes our connections to Torah differently. The first puts the burden on us: *we* are commanded not just to study it, but to engage in it, to wrestle with it in all areas of our lives. The second depicts God as a master teacher, who can make Torah sweet in our mouths. The third depicts us passively receiving Torah as God's gift toHis chosen people. All three blessings combined portray the spectrum of divine relationships through Torah: active engagement, student-teacher interaction, and passive acceptance of a divine gift.

Moreover, the source of the three study selections that follow teaches us something important about Torah. One comes from the Torah, one from the Mishnah, and one from the Talmud. Jewish tradition is not fundamentalist, then, contained in the written Torah alone. Torah is a matter of ongoing revelation, where God's instruction (the literal meaning of "Torah") begins with the written Torah but continues through the Oral Tradition: the Mishnah first (c. 200 C.E.), then the Talmud (c. 500 C.E.), and then expanded sources throughout the generations.

◆

awakening from sleep. *SVT* also offers halakhic instructions as to how, ritually, to wash one's hands, along with a detailed explanation as to why the Sages deemed handwashing to be a necessary "preparation for prayer."

[2] *"Blessed are You, Adonai our God"* Here, as elsewhere, regularly, the Reconstructionist *Kol Haneshamah* offers a variety of English metaphors when translating the ineffable Hebrew name of God, Adonai. In an attempt to capture a sense of the infinite reality that marks the divine, the Reconstructionist rite translates the name of God here as "Blessed are You, THE ARCHITECT, our God...." The benediction ends by addressing God as "Blessed are You, the wondrous Healer of all flesh." Diverse representations of God's name are found throughout the prayer book, depending on context, to reflect the Reconstructionist conviction that the divine fullness can never be captured by a single word, but can only be approached by a variety of images.

[2] *"Who formed humans with wisdom"* A significant number of contemporary liberal liturgies now include this talmudic benediction for the body in their prayer books. Among them are *Gates of Prayer, Kol Haneshamah, Siddur Va'ani T'fillati,* and *Siddur Sim Shalom*. All of them deem this blessing an appropriate vehicle for expressing gratitude for the gift of body and health.

Nineteenth-century non-Orthodox prayer books stand in sharp contrast to their twentieth-century successors on this matter. The Victorian sensibilities that informed the authors of these works did not allow them to feel comfortable with a detailed liturgical allusion to bodily functions. Hence, they generally omitted this passage. This was true even of the 1885 *Avodat Yisrael* by Marcus Jastrow, a founder of American Conservative Judaism. Isaac Mayer Wise alone did not want to abandon this benediction, which he resolved by recasting it without any reference to the body at all: "Praised be Thou, O God, our Lord, universal King, who hast made man with wisdom, and created in him a pure soul in Thy image, that he do Thy will, in love, and behold Thy goodness, O God, in the Land of life. Praised be Thou, O God, who workest wonders."

[5] *"Blessed are You...who...commanded us* [v'tsivanu] *to engage in words of Torah"* Unlike earlier Reform prayer books, *Gates of Prayer* includes this blessing. Furthermore, here (in relationship to Torah study), it translates *v'tsivanu* as "commanded us." This stands in sharp contrast to how *GOP* rendered the Hebrew in regard to the ritual acts of *tallit* and *t'fillin* (see above, "commanded us to wrap ourselves"). *Kol Haneshamah* names God here "THE ONE OF SINAI," thereby reflecting once again its commitment to multiple images for envisioning and representing the divine.

[6] *"Adonai our God, make the words of Your Torah sweet to us" Kol Haneshamah* here translates the name of God as "WISE ONE." It is also significant that the 1998 edition of *Siddur Sim Shalom*, here as elsewhere, refuses to render "Adonai" as "Lord," in

deference to feminist objections to translating the name of God with a masculine term. Instead, the most recent American Conservative rite simply transliterates the name of God, "Adonai," with no translation at all. In this way, the 1998 *SSS* testifies to the powerful hold that feminist concerns have on modern-day liberal Judaism generally.

[8] *"Who chose us from all peoples, and gave us His Torah"* While both Conservative liturgies *(Siddur Va'ani T'fillati and Siddur Sim Shalom)* include the traditional Torah blessing here, *Ha'avodah Shebalev* is the only twentieth-century Reform Siddur that does so. The blessing seemed out of order for a rite that did not include significant study passages in its condensed early morning service. However, in the nineteenth century, I. M. Wise included an altered version that addresses "the universal King, who hast chosen us from among all peoples and intrusted us with Thy Law, that we be unto Thee a kingdom of priests, and a holy people." Wise's reformulation voiced the universalistic ethics that marked classical Reform Judaism.

◆

FRANKEL (A WOMAN'S VOICE)

study! But on the other, how healing it can be for us to "make the words of Your Torah sweet to us and to the house of Israel, Your people," despite our physical distress.

For women, whose anatomical system is far more complex than men's, this blessing is especially meaningful. The very word for "duct," *n'kavim,* shares its root with *n'kevah,* the Hebrew word for "female." Specifically, this word means to "perforate" or "make hollow" (as does its synonym in this passage, *challul*). Women are thus characterized by the spaces and hollows within them, the womb that will cradle the next generation, the vagina that admits the seed of life and that fills with and disgorges blood each month when the womb remains empty of new life. Aware of this natural ebb and flow, we can understand the double nature of the concluding blessing of this paragraph: God not only heals us, *rofei kol basar,* when our internal passageways malfunction, but also performs wonders, *mafli la'asot,* precisely when they operate as they are supposed to.

◆

J. HOFFMAN (TRANSLATION)

[1] *"Washing"* The Hebrew comes from the verbal root *n.t.l.,* which means "to lift" or "to take." (It is the same verb usually translated as "to shake" in the blessing for the *lulav.*) It is not clear how it came to mean "to wash." A Greek word *antlion* ("bucket") has letters in common with the Hebrew *natla,* "the bowl for washing one's hands," but that connection seems coincidental.

Alternatively, the "washing" here may mean "taking away of" = "cleansing" metaphorically.

[2] *"Formed"* Following Birnbaum and others. "Created" would be better, but we will need that verb below for a different Hebrew original. On principle, assuming that doubling a word has a different effect than using two similar words, we try not to use the same English word for different Hebrew originals.

[2] *"With wisdom"* The Hebrew is likewise ambiguous as to whether God or humans have the wisdom, but context makes it clear that God, using God's wisdom, created us so well.

[2] *"A system of ducts and conduits"* The Hebrew relies poetically on two words, each appearing twice in a row, once as a noun and once as an adjective: *n'kavim n'kavim,* "pierced holes," and *chalulim chalulim,* "hollow conduits." Because we cannot duplicate this effect in English (although "hollow hollows" is a step in the right direction), we rewrite the phrase in our own idiom.

[3] *"Well-known"* Literally, "evident and known." Hebrew often uses parallel linguistic forms (here, two adjectives) where English uses a modifier (adjective or adverb) and a term that is modified (here, an adjective ["known"] and an adverb ["evident and" = "well…"]).

[3] *"Stand before You"* Continuing the theme of standing before a throne, begun above with *kisei,* literally, "chair," but used liturgically, usually, as "throne [of glory]."

[5] *"Engage in words of Torah"* Others, simply "study." Our translation adheres more closely to the original, on the assumption that the original authors chose this phrase over "to study" (which is used below) for a reason. The Hebrew word for "word" also means "things," and so the Hebrew phrase is actually broader than the English, perhaps even as broad as "engage in Torah."

[6] *"Sweet to us"* Or, "pleasant in our mouth." That translation would work here, but immediately following we would then need "and in the mouth of the house of Israel, Your people," which, we think, misses the mark.

[6] *"Know Your name"* To "know God's name" meant to recognize God's sovereignty.

———◆———

L. HOFFMAN (HISTORY)

prayer book (composed around 860) were these postponed to the public synagogue service. Thereafter, public practice followed the precedent of Jacob ben Asher (c. 1275–1340), as recorded in his influential law code, the *Tur.* (See "Blessings and Study: The Jewish Way to Begin a Day," pp. 6–16.)

In our custom, though not universally, the blessing over handwashing comes first, an echo of the time when all the blessings were said at home. It precedes the blessings over Torah study because sacred study requires clean hands, and human hands (which might rove over the body during sleep) are considered unclean upon awakening.

²,⁴ *"Formed humans…heals all creatures"* The parallelism here gives us acute insight into the rabbinic conceptualization of healing: First, "Blessed are You…who *formed* (= *created*) humans…," and then, "Blessed are You…who *heals* all creatures." So in rabbinic algebra, "Formed (Created) = Healed." That is, healing is a kind of creating. Primo Levi intuits this age-old Jewish insight in his Holocaust memoir: he remembers being forced to watch a man die slowly on the gallows in Auschwitz. As the victim twists in agony, Levi thinks, "To destroy a man is difficult, almost as difficult as to create one." Disease, like the gallows, destroys what God has made. Surely, the reverse too is true: those who heal, create (or re-create) as God once did.

The Halakhah, incidentally, bans administering medicine on Shabbat if a patient is not at least sick enough to be bedridden. Technically, the reason given is that giving the medicine might entail grinding, one of the categories of forbidden Sabbath work laid down by Torah. But that reasoning is after the fact. Already in the first century, the Gospels (Matt. 12:9–13; Mark 3:1–6; Luke 6:6–11) report the Jewish authorities accusing Jesus of healing a man with a withered hand on Shabbat. The underlying issue is that healing is creating. As God rested from creation on Shabbat, so the Rabbis prefer that we rest from healing then—except in cases of absolute necessity, of course.

This identification of doctors' work with God's explains the Talmud's wonderment that human beings may effect cures at all. Surely that is God's work. We may heal, the Talmud concludes, because "God has given us permission" to do God's work—the work of continuing creation.

⁸ *"Gave us His Torah"* One of several Torah blessings inserted here. We know of others that were once current also, for example, "Blessed…who chose this Torah and sanctified it and took pleasure in it for those who fulfill it" (Deut. Rab. 11). Of all the blessings created in antiquity, only blessings for Torah have come down to us in so many different versions—a testimonial to the centrality of Torah to Judaism.

◆

KUSHNER & POLEN (CHASIDISM)

and vice versa. How do we enter into life-sustaining intercourse with the outside world while still maintaining a physiological boundary?

We read (Gen. Rab. 1:3): "Rabbi Tanchuma opened his teaching by citing Psalm 86:10, 'For You are great and do wondrous things….' Rabbi Tanchum ben Rabbi Chiya said that if a goatskin bag has a hole, even one as small as the eye of a needle, all its air escapes; yet though a person is formed with many different orifices, the person's breath does not escape through them. Who achieved this? As the psalm verse concludes, 'Only You God!'"

In his commentary to the *Shulchan Arukh* ("Laws of Washing Hands in the

Morning," Section 6), Moses Isserles speaks of the mystery of life. While in utero, the mouth, for instance, must be closed, but upon birth, it must be opened or we would perish. There seems to be a kind of reversal of fetal openings and closings necessary for the maintenance of human life. In the final analysis, a human being bears humbling similarities to a goatskin sack filled with wind, a bag of breath. God graciously keeps enough breath or spirit within the body to sustain it. Thus the daily continuation of life is even more than just openings and closings, or delicate organic balance; life is a matter of getting the right things into the body and the right things out of the body—all in the proper order. For this reason, says Isserles, the blessing concludes with an image of God as wondrous healer.

[2] *"Ducts and conduits"* According to *Tzava'at Harivash,* the popular Chasidic manual of spiritual discipline, attributed to the Baal Shem Tov (Section 22):

> Let whatever you experience remind you of the Holy One. If love, let it remind you of the love of God; if fear, let it remind you of the fear of God. When you go to sleep, think, my consciousness is now going to God. Even when you use the toilet, you should think, "I am now separating bad from good. Now only the good remains for the service of God." In this way you will be strengthened in your service of God.

And just this is the real meaning of the spiritual-meditative practices known as *yichudim,* that is, "unifications," the joining of deed to God. In earlier kabbalistic traditions, *yichudim* had meant unifying the potencies of different and often arcane divine names. Here, however, we encounter an example of Chasidism's revolutionary dimension. *Yichudim* have now become exercises of meditative awareness that bring every aspect of life—even bodily functions!—into the realm of the sacred. Everything is part of the universal divine organism. Through such *yichudim*—unifying meditations—even the most ordinary and filthy aspects of life become potentially sacred deeds.

[6] *"Make the words of Your Torah sweet"* Ya'akov Yosef of Polnoye, a second-generation Chasidic master (d. 1782), offers a parable (*Toldot Ya'akov Yosef, Sh'elah,* 172) to help us read the words of Torah so as to make them "sweet." He draws on one of the most fundamental principles of Jewish spirituality: doing a sacred deed *lishmah,* "for its own sake," purely and simply in response to a divine request. Indeed, as we see in the following teaching, not only do we sweeten the sacred words of scripture, we literally liberate the letters and return them to their divine source or root.

> It once happened that some travelers lost their way and decided to go to sleep until someone came along who could show them the way. Someone first came along and led them to a place of wild beasts and brigands but then someone else came and showed them the right path. It is the same way with the letters of the Torah, through which the world was created. They came to this world in the form of travelers who have lost their way and fallen asleep. When someone comes along and studies Torah for its own sake, such a one leads them on the right path so that they can cleave to their root.

LANDES (HALAKHAH)

The most notable exception to the opinion that blessings may be said in any language is that of *Arukh Hashulchan,* who argues that the talmudic license to say prayers in any language no longer applies, because we are no longer sensitive to the deeply mystical nature of the Hebrew language. If we translate them, we are likely to lose their deeper meanings, without realizing it (O. Ch. 62:3–4; 185:2–3).

In any case, a person saying a blessing as an emissary for others, such as a cantor, should be able to understand it in Hebrew (*Magen Avraham,* O. Ch. 102).

◆ ◆ ◆

3 | *Study and Blessings*

¹May Adonai bless you and keep you. ²May Adonai shine His face toward you and treat you graciously. ³May Adonai lift His face toward you and grant you peace.

⁴These are things that are priceless: leaving the corners of your fields for the poor, bringing your first fruits to the Temple, bringing offerings at each festival, doing kindness, and studying Torah. ⁵These are things that yield interest during your life, while the principal remains for you in the world-to-come: honoring your father and mother, doing kindness, arriving early to study morning and evening, welcoming strangers, visiting the sick, providing for the bride, burying the dead, paying attention to prayer, bringing peace between one person and another; and the study of Torah is like them all.

⁶My God, the soul You have put within me is a pure one. ⁷You created it; You formed it; You breathed it into me; You keep it within me; and You will take it from me and return it to me in the hereafter. ⁸So long as my soul is within me, I gratefully acknowledge You, Adonai my God and my ancestors' God, Master of all creatures, Lord of all souls. ⁹Blessed are You, Adonai, who restores souls to dead corpses.

¹יְבָרֶכְךָ יְיָ וְיִשְׁמְרֶךָ.

²יָאֵר יְיָ פָּנָיו אֵלֶיךָ וִיחֻנֶּךָּ.

³יִשָּׂא יְיָ פָּנָיו אֵלֶיךָ, וְיָשֵׂם לְךָ שָׁלוֹם.

⁴אֵלּוּ דְבָרִים שֶׁאֵין לָהֶם שֶׁעוּר: הַפֵּאָה, וְהַבִּכּוּרִים, וְהָרֵאָיוֹן, וּגְמִילוּת חֲסָדִים, וְתַלְמוּד תּוֹרָה. ⁵אֵלּוּ דְבָרִים שֶׁאָדָם אוֹכֵל פֵּרוֹתֵיהֶם בָּעוֹלָם הַזֶּה וְהַקֶּרֶן קַיֶּמֶת לוֹ לָעוֹלָם הַבָּא, וְאֵלּוּ הֵן: כִּבּוּד אָב וָאֵם, וּגְמִילוּת חֲסָדִים, וְהַשְׁכָּמַת בֵּית הַמִּדְרָשׁ שַׁחֲרִית וְעַרְבִית, וְהַכְנָסַת אוֹרְחִים, וּבִקּוּר חוֹלִים, וְהַכְנָסַת כַּלָּה, וְהַלְוָיַת הַמֵּת, וְעִיּוּן תְּפִלָּה, וַהֲבָאַת שָׁלוֹם בֵּין אָדָם לַחֲבֵרוֹ; וְתַלְמוּד תּוֹרָה כְּנֶגֶד כֻּלָּם.

⁶אֱלֹהַי, נְשָׁמָה שֶׁנָּתַתָּ בִּי טְהוֹרָה הִיא. ⁷אַתָּה בְרָאתָהּ, אַתָּה יְצַרְתָּהּ, אַתָּה נְפַחְתָּהּ בִּי, וְאַתָּה מְשַׁמְּרָהּ בְּקִרְבִּי, וְאַתָּה עָתִיד לִטְּלָהּ מִמֶּנִּי וּלְהַחֲזִירָהּ בִּי לֶעָתִיד לָבֹא. ⁸כָּל זְמַן שֶׁהַנְּשָׁמָה בְקִרְבִּי מוֹדֶה אֲנִי לְפָנֶיךָ, יְיָ אֱלֹהַי וֵאלֹהֵי אֲבוֹתַי, רִבּוֹן כָּל הַמַּעֲשִׂים, אֲדוֹן

119

¹⁰Blessed are You, Adonai our God, Ruler of the world, who gave the cunning rooster its ability to distinguish between day and night.

¹¹Blessed are You, Adonai our God, Ruler of the world, who did not make me a gentile.

¹²Blessed are You, Adonai our God, Ruler of the world, who did not make me a slave.

[Men say:]

¹³Blessed are You, Adonai our God, Ruler of the world, who did not make me a woman.

[Women say:]

¹⁴Blessed are You, Adonai our God, Ruler of the world, who made me as He desired.

[Everyone continues:]

¹⁵Blessed are You, Adonai our God, Ruler of the world, who opens the eyes of the blind.

¹⁶Blessed are You, Adonai our God, Ruler of the world, who clothes the naked.

¹⁷Blessed are You, Adonai our God, Ruler of the world, who frees the captive.

¹⁸Blessed are You, Adonai our God, Ruler of the world, who raises those who are bent over.

¹⁹Blessed are You, Adonai our God, Ruler of the world, who spreads out the land on the water.

²⁰Blessed are You, Adonai our God, Ruler of the world, who has provided my every need.

²¹Blessed are You, Adonai our God, Ruler of the world, who makes firm man's steps.

²²Blessed are You, Adonai our God, Ruler of the world, who girds Israel with might.

²³Blessed are You, Adonai our God, Ruler of the world, who crowns Israel with glory.

כָּל הַנְּשָׁמוֹת. ⁹בָּרוּךְ אַתָּה, יְיָ, הַמַּחֲזִיר נְשָׁמוֹת לִפְגָרִים מֵתִים.

¹⁰בָּרוּךְ אַתָּה, יְיָ אֱלֹהֵינוּ, מֶלֶךְ הָעוֹלָם, אֲשֶׁר נָתַן לַשֶּׂכְוִי בִינָה לְהַבְחִין בֵּין יוֹם וּבֵין לָיְלָה.

¹¹בָּרוּךְ אַתָּה, יְיָ אֱלֹהֵינוּ, מֶלֶךְ הָעוֹלָם, שֶׁלֹּא עָשַׂנִי גוֹי.

¹²בָּרוּךְ אַתָּה, יְיָ אֱלֹהֵינוּ, מֶלֶךְ הָעוֹלָם, שֶׁלֹּא עָשַׂנִי עָבֶד.

[Men say:]

¹³בָּרוּךְ אַתָּה, יְיָ אֱלֹהֵינוּ, מֶלֶךְ הָעוֹלָם, שֶׁלֹּא עָשַׂנִי אִשָּׁה.

[Women say:]

¹⁴בָּרוּךְ אַתָּה, יְיָ אֱלֹהֵינוּ, מֶלֶךְ הָעוֹלָם, שֶׁעָשַׂנִי כִּרְצוֹנוֹ.

[Everyone continues:]

¹⁵בָּרוּךְ אַתָּה, יְיָ אֱלֹהֵינוּ, מֶלֶךְ הָעוֹלָם, פּוֹקֵחַ עִוְרִים.

¹⁶בָּרוּךְ אַתָּה, יְיָ אֱלֹהֵינוּ, מֶלֶךְ הָעוֹלָם, מַלְבִּישׁ עֲרֻמִּים.

¹⁷בָּרוּךְ אַתָּה, יְיָ אֱלֹהֵינוּ, מֶלֶךְ הָעוֹלָם, מַתִּיר אֲסוּרִים.

¹⁸בָּרוּךְ אַתָּה, יְיָ אֱלֹהֵינוּ, מֶלֶךְ הָעוֹלָם, זוֹקֵף כְּפוּפִים.

¹⁹בָּרוּךְ אַתָּה, יְיָ אֱלֹהֵינוּ, מֶלֶךְ הָעוֹלָם, רוֹקַע הָאָרֶץ עַל הַמָּיִם.

²⁰בָּרוּךְ אַתָּה, יְיָ אֱלֹהֵינוּ, מֶלֶךְ הָעוֹלָם, שֶׁעָשָׂה לִי כָּל צָרְכִּי.

²¹בָּרוּךְ אַתָּה, יְיָ אֱלֹהֵינוּ, מֶלֶךְ הָעוֹלָם,

²⁴Blessed are You, Adonai our God, Ruler of the world, who gives strength to the tired.

²⁵Blessed are You, Adonai our God, Ruler of the world, who removes sleep from my eyes, slumber from my eyelids.

²⁶So may it be Your will, Adonai my God and my ancestors' God, that You make us familiar with Your Torah and make us cling to Your commandments. ²⁷Don't bring us to sin, transgression, iniquity, temptation, or disgrace. ²⁸Let our evil inclination not rule over us.

²⁹Distance us from bad people and bad friends. ³⁰Make us cling to our good inclination and to good deeds. ³¹And bend our will so it subjugates itself to You. ³²Today and every day, may we be found to have grace, favor, and mercy, in Your eyes and in the eyes of all who behold us. ³³Reward us with great kindness. ³⁴Blessed are You, Adonai, who rewards His people Israel with great kindness.

³⁵May it be Your will, Adonai my God and my ancestors' God, that You deliver me today and every day from impudence and insolence, from bad people and from bad friends, from bad neighbors and from bad encounters, and from the destructive Adversary, from oppressive judgments and oppressive opponents at law, whether of the covenant or not.

הַמֵּכִין מִצְעֲדֵי גָבֶר.

²²בָּרוּךְ אַתָּה, יְיָ אֱלֹהֵינוּ, מֶלֶךְ הָעוֹלָם, אוֹזֵר יִשְׂרָאֵל בִּגְבוּרָה.

²³בָּרוּךְ אַתָּה, יְיָ אֱלֹהֵינוּ, מֶלֶךְ הָעוֹלָם, עוֹטֵר יִשְׂרָאֵל בְּתִפְאָרָה.

²⁴בָּרוּךְ אַתָּה, יְיָ אֱלֹהֵינוּ, מֶלֶךְ הָעוֹלָם, הַנּוֹתֵן לַיָּעֵף כֹּחַ.

²⁵בָּרוּךְ אַתָּה, יְיָ אֱלֹהֵינוּ, מֶלֶךְ הָעוֹלָם, הַמַּעֲבִיר שֵׁנָה מֵעֵינָי וּתְנוּמָה מֵעַפְעַפָּי.

²⁶וִיהִי רָצוֹן מִלְפָנֶיךָ, יְיָ אֱלֹהֵינוּ וֵאלֹהֵי אֲבוֹתֵינוּ, שֶׁתַּרְגִּילֵנוּ בְּתוֹרָתֶךָ וְדַבְּקֵנוּ בְּמִצְוֹתֶיךָ; ²⁷וְאַל תְּבִיאֵנוּ לֹא לִידֵי חֵטְא, וְלֹא לִידֵי עֲבֵרָה וְעָוֹן, וְלֹא לִידֵי נִסָּיוֹן, וְלֹא לִידֵי בִזָּיוֹן; ²⁸וְאַל תַּשְׁלֶט־בָּנוּ יֵצֶר הָרָע;

²⁹וְהַרְחִיקֵנוּ מֵאָדָם רָע וּמֵחָבֵר רָע; ³⁰וְדַבְּקֵנוּ בְּיֵצֶר הַטּוֹב וּבְמַעֲשִׂים טוֹבִים; ³¹וְכֹף אֶת יִצְרֵנוּ לְהִשְׁתַּעְבֶּד־לָךְ. ³²וּתְנֵנוּ הַיּוֹם וּבְכָל יוֹם לְחֵן וּלְחֶסֶד וּלְרַחֲמִים בְּעֵינֶיךָ וּבְעֵינֵי כָל רוֹאֵינוּ, ³³וְתִגְמְלֵנוּ חֲסָדִים טוֹבִים. ³⁴בָּרוּךְ אַתָּה, יְיָ, גּוֹמֵל חֲסָדִים טוֹבִים לְעַמּוֹ יִשְׂרָאֵל.

³⁵יְהִי רָצוֹן מִלְפָנֶיךָ, יְיָ אֱלֹהַי וֵאלֹהֵי אֲבוֹתַי, שֶׁתַּצִּילֵנִי הַיּוֹם וּבְכָל יוֹם מֵעַזֵּי פָנִים וּמֵעַזּוּת פָּנִים, מֵאָדָם רָע וּמֵחָבֵר רָע, וּמִשָּׁכֵן רָע וּמִפֶּגַע רָע וּמִשָּׂטָן הַמַּשְׁחִית, מִדִּין קָשֶׁה וּמִבַּעַל דִּין קָשֶׁה, בֵּין שֶׁהוּא בֶן־בְּרִית וּבֵין שֶׁאֵינוֹ בֶן־בְּרִית.

BRETTLER (BIBLE)

[1] *"May Adonai bless you"* The well-known Priestly Blessing of Numbers 6:24–26, structurally compact, with each verse longer than the one before it, as if to suggest the growing outpouring of divine blessings. The context in Numbers does not indicate how, when or where the blessing was used, but we know that it was popular in antiquity. There are several significant Mesopotamian parallels, and a version of the Bible's wording, from the seventh or sixth century B.C.E. and written on silver, was found in a burial trove in Jerusalem; it presumably functioned as an amulet. Biblical texts both before the exile *(p. 127)*

DORFF (THEOLOGY)

[1] *"May Adonai bless you"* The Priestly Blessing (as this is called) consists of three Hebrew sentences—presumably three separate blessings, but related to reach other through the repetition of similar wording: *(p. 129)*

ELLENSON (MODERN LITURGIES)

[1] *"May Adonai bless you and keep you"* The traditional Priestly Blessing (Numb. 6:24–26) is found in both *Siddur Sim Shalom* and *Siddur Va'ani T'fillati* (American and Israeli Conservative), as well as *Ha'avodah Shebalev* (Israeli Reform). *(p. 133)*

FRANKEL (A WOMAN'S VOICE)

[4] *"Doing kindness"* Although the phrase "unsung hero" seems like an oxymoron, Judaism has long recognized that those who perform behind-the-scenes acts of kindness constitute the real champions of an enduring society. However, such acts rarely receive ample recognition in this life; rather, their full harvest comes in the ethical ripening of succeeding generations. Among these unsung heroes are countless women of valor who, in their homes and communities, welcome strangers, visit the *(p. 135)*

[1]May Adonai bless you and keep you.

[2]May Adonai shine His face toward you and treat you graciously.

[3]May Adonai lift His face toward you and grant you peace.

[4]These are things that are priceless: leaving the corners of your fields for the poor, bringing your first fruits to the Temple, bringing offerings at each festival, doing kindness, and studying Torah. [5]These

J. HOFFMAN (TRANSLATION)

[1] *"May Adonai bless you and keep you"* It is difficult to capture the beauty of these famous lines without sacrificing the content. Each line begins with a verb, followed by "Adonai," followed, in turn, by another verb. (Ps. 67:2 repeats part of the content of these lines, but without the lyric beauty.) An English version with the same poetic feel might read: "May you be blessed by Adonai and kept. / May you be emblazened by Adonai's face and treated graciously. / May you *(p. 136)*

L. HOFFMAN (HISTORY)

FOLLOWING BLESSINGS FOR STUDY, WITH WHICH THE PRIOR SECTION ENDED, WE NOW GET STUDY PASSAGES FROM BIBLE, MISHNAH, AND TALMUD. THE LAST OF THESE IS A TALMUDIC LIST OF MORE BLESSINGS TO SAY, HENCE THE TITLE— "STUDY [BUT SIMULTANEOUSLY] MORE BLESSINGS."

[6] *"The soul You have put within me"* Sefardi custom demands that the blessing for the body ("Blessed…who formed humans," above)   *(p. 139)*

LANDES (HALAKHAH)

[4] *"Things that are priceless"* Several items in this list are moral commandments— positive things we do with moral consequences, like (here), "doing kindness" and "honoring your father and mother." It is often asked why we do not say blessings over such things. The fact is, we do say blessings before performing a commandment or before partaking of something that gives us enjoyment. The former category applies specifically to positive commandments *between humans and God*. These are said immediately before a commandment's performance (Maimonides, Laws of Blessings, 11: 2). *Kesef Mishneh* (Rabbi Joseph Caro, sixteenth-century, Land of Israel) clarifies, "Our teacher [Maimonides] deliberately specified 'commandments between human and God.' But interpersonal commandments such as charity and the like do not require a blessing."

Abudraham (thirteenth to fourteenth century, Spain) explains this distinction ("Introduction to Prayer"): "We do not say blessings over commandments that depend on the cooperation of others. Examples of this are *ts'dakah* ["charity"] to the poor, or bestowing happiness upon strangers, widows, or orphans on the festivals…since the beneficiaries may choose not to accept our gifts, or to reject our kindness altogether," thereby voiding the performance of the commandment. In his commentary to Exodus 24: 30, *Torah T'mimah*   *(p. 142)*

[1] יְבָרֶכְךָ יְיָ וְיִשְׁמְרֶךָ.

[2] יָאֵר יְיָ פָּנָיו אֵלֶיךָ וִיחֻנֶּךָ.

[3] יִשָּׂא יְיָ פָּנָיו אֵלֶיךָ, וְיָשֵׂם לְךָ שָׁלוֹם.

[4] אֵלּוּ דְבָרִים שֶׁאֵין לָהֶם שִׁעוּר: הַפֵּאָה, וְהַבִּכּוּרִים, וְהָרֵאָיוֹן, וּגְמִילוּת חֲסָדִים, וְתַלְמוּד תּוֹרָה. [5] אֵלּוּ דְבָרִים שֶׁאָדָם אוֹכֵל פֵּרוֹתֵיהֶם בָּעוֹלָם הַזֶּה וְהַקֶּרֶן קַיֶּמֶת לוֹ לָעוֹלָם הַבָּא, וְאֵלּוּ הֵן: כִּבּוּד אָב וָאֵם, וּגְמִילוּת

KUSHNER & POLEN (CHASIDISM)

[4] *"These are things that are priceless… offerings at each festival"* [Lit., These are the things that have no fixed measure…] Yehudah Aryeh Lieb of Ger (d. 1905) explains *(S'fas Emes, s.v. Pesach)* that the sense of the divine presence during the time of the festival pilgrimage offerings in the Temple was beyond measure. The holiness of the festival bestowed blessing upon what the *S'fas Emes* identifies as the three primary modes of all being: space *(makom)*, time *(z'man)*, and   *(p. 140)*

are things that yield interest during your life, while the principal remains for you in the world-to-come: honoring your father and mother, doing kindness, arriving early to study morning and evening, welcoming strangers, visiting the sick, providing for the bride, burying the dead, paying attention to prayer, bringing peace between one person and another, and the study of Torah is like them all.

[6]My God, the soul You have put within me is a pure one. [7]You created it; You formed it; You breathed it into me; You keep it within me; and You will take it from me and return it to me in the hereafter. [8]So long as my soul is within me, I gratefully acknowledge You, Adonai my God and my ancestors' God, Master of all creatures, Lord of all souls. [9]Blessed are You, Adonai, who restores souls to dead corpses.

[10]Blessed are You, Adonai our God, Ruler of the world, who gave the cunning rooster its ability to distinguish between day and night.

[11]Blessed are You, Adonai our God, Ruler of the world, who did not make me a gentile.

[12]Blessed are You, Adonai our God, Ruler of the world, who did not make me a slave.

[Men say:]

[13]Blessed are You, Adonai our God, Ruler of the world, who did not make me a woman.

חֲסָדִים, וְהַשְׁכָּמַת בֵּית הַמִּדְרָשׁ שַׁחֲרִית וְעַרְבִית, וְהַכְנָסַת אוֹרְחִים, וּבִקּוּר חוֹלִים, וְהַכְנָסַת כַּלָּה, וְהַלְוָיַת הַמֵּת, וְעִיּוּן תְּפִלָּה, וַהֲבָאַת שָׁלוֹם בֵּין אָדָם לַחֲבֵרוֹ; וְתַלְמוּד תּוֹרָה כְּנֶגֶד כֻּלָּם.

[6]אֱלֹהַי, נְשָׁמָה שֶׁנָּתַתָּ בִּי טְהוֹרָה הִיא. [7]אַתָּה בְרָאתָהּ, אַתָּה יְצַרְתָּהּ, אַתָּה נְפַחְתָּהּ בִּי, וְאַתָּה מְשַׁמְּרָהּ בְּקִרְבִּי, וְאַתָּה עָתִיד לִטְּלָהּ מִמֶּנִּי וּלְהַחֲזִירָהּ בִּי לֶעָתִיד לָבֹא. [8]כָּל זְמַן שֶׁהַנְּשָׁמָה בְקִרְבִּי מוֹדֶה אֲנִי לְפָנֶיךָ, יְיָ אֱלֹהַי וֵאלֹהֵי אֲבוֹתַי, רִבּוֹן כָּל הַמַּעֲשִׂים, אֲדוֹן כָּל הַנְּשָׁמוֹת. [9]בָּרוּךְ אַתָּה, יְיָ, הַמַּחֲזִיר נְשָׁמוֹת לִפְגָרִים מֵתִים.

[10]בָּרוּךְ אַתָּה, יְיָ אֱלֹהֵינוּ, מֶלֶךְ הָעוֹלָם, אֲשֶׁר נָתַן לַשֶּׂכְוִי בִינָה לְהַבְחִין בֵּין יוֹם וּבֵין לָיְלָה.

[11]בָּרוּךְ אַתָּה, יְיָ אֱלֹהֵינוּ, מֶלֶךְ הָעוֹלָם, שֶׁלֹּא עָשַׂנִי גּוֹי.

[12]בָּרוּךְ אַתָּה, יְיָ אֱלֹהֵינוּ, מֶלֶךְ הָעוֹלָם, שֶׁלֹּא עָשַׂנִי עָבֶד.

[Men say:]

[13]בָּרוּךְ אַתָּה, יְיָ אֱלֹהֵינוּ, מֶלֶךְ הָעוֹלָם, שֶׁלֹּא עָשַׂנִי אִשָּׁה.

[Women say:]

[14]בָּרוּךְ אַתָּה, יְיָ אֱלֹהֵינוּ, מֶלֶךְ הָעוֹלָם, שֶׁעָשַׂנִי כִּרְצוֹנוֹ.

[Everyone continues:]

[15]בָּרוּךְ אַתָּה, יְיָ אֱלֹהֵינוּ, מֶלֶךְ הָעוֹלָם,

[Women say:]

¹⁴Blessed are You, Adonai our God, Ruler of the world, who made me as He desired.

[Everyone continues:]

¹⁵Blessed are You, Adonai our God, Ruler of the world, who opens the eyes of the blind.

¹⁶Blessed are You, Adonai our God, Ruler of the world, who clothes the naked.

¹⁷Blessed are You, Adonai our God, Ruler of the world, who frees the captive.

¹⁸Blessed are You, Adonai our God, Ruler of the world, who raises those who are bent over.

¹⁹Blessed are You, Adonai our God, Ruler of the world, who spreads out the land on the water.

²⁰Blessed are You, Adonai our God, Ruler of the world, who has provided my every need.

²¹Blessed are You, Adonai our God, Ruler of the world, who makes firm man's steps.

²²Blessed are You, Adonai our God, Ruler of the world, who girds Israel with might.

²³Blessed are You, Adonai our God, Ruler of the world, who crowns Israel with glory.

²⁴Blessed are You, Adonai our God, Ruler of the world, who gives strength to the tired.

פּוֹקֵחַ עִוְרִים.

¹⁶בָּרוּךְ אַתָּה, יְיָ אֱלֹהֵינוּ, מֶלֶךְ הָעוֹלָם, מַלְבִּישׁ עֲרֻמִּים.

¹⁷בָּרוּךְ אַתָּה, יְיָ אֱלֹהֵינוּ, מֶלֶךְ הָעוֹלָם, מַתִּיר אֲסוּרִים.

¹⁸בָּרוּךְ אַתָּה, יְיָ אֱלֹהֵינוּ, מֶלֶךְ הָעוֹלָם, זוֹקֵף כְּפוּפִים.

¹⁹בָּרוּךְ אַתָּה, יְיָ אֱלֹהֵינוּ, מֶלֶךְ הָעוֹלָם, רוֹקַע הָאָרֶץ עַל הַמָּיִם.

²⁰בָּרוּךְ אַתָּה, יְיָ אֱלֹהֵינוּ, מֶלֶךְ הָעוֹלָם, שֶׁעָשָׂה לִי כָּל צָרְכִּי.

²¹בָּרוּךְ אַתָּה, יְיָ אֱלֹהֵינוּ, מֶלֶךְ הָעוֹלָם, הַמֵּכִין מִצְעֲדֵי גָבֶר.

²²בָּרוּךְ אַתָּה, יְיָ אֱלֹהֵינוּ, מֶלֶךְ הָעוֹלָם, אוֹזֵר יִשְׂרָאֵל בִּגְבוּרָה.

²³בָּרוּךְ אַתָּה, יְיָ אֱלֹהֵינוּ, מֶלֶךְ הָעוֹלָם, עוֹטֵר יִשְׂרָאֵל בְּתִפְאָרָה.

²⁴בָּרוּךְ אַתָּה, יְיָ אֱלֹהֵינוּ, מֶלֶךְ הָעוֹלָם, הַנּוֹתֵן לַיָּעֵף כֹּחַ.

²⁵בָּרוּךְ אַתָּה, יְיָ אֱלֹהֵינוּ, מֶלֶךְ הָעוֹלָם, הַמַּעֲבִיר שֵׁנָה מֵעֵינָי וּתְנוּמָה מֵעַפְעַפָּי.

²⁶וִיהִי רָצוֹן מִלְפָנֶיךָ, יְיָ אֱלֹהֵינוּ וֵאלֹהֵי אֲבוֹתֵינוּ, שֶׁתַּרְגִּילֵנוּ בְּתוֹרָתֶךָ וְדַבְּקֵנוּ בְּמִצְוֹתֶיךָ; ²⁷וְאַל תְּבִיאֵנוּ לֹא לִידֵי חֵטְא, וְלֹא לִידֵי עֲבֵרָה וְעָוֹן, וְלֹא לִידֵי נִסָּיוֹן, וְלֹא לִידֵי בִזָּיוֹן; ²⁸וְאַל תַּשְׁלֶט־בָּנוּ יֵצֶר הָרָע;

²⁹וְהַרְחִיקֵנוּ מֵאָדָם רָע וּמֵחָבֵר רָע;

25Blessed are You, Adonai our God, Ruler of the world, who removes sleep from my eyes, slumber from my eyelids.

26So may it be Your will, Adonai my God and my ancestors' God, that You make us familiar with Your Torah and make us cling to Your commandments. 27Don't bring us to sin, transgression, iniquity, temptation, or disgrace. 28Let our evil inclination not rule over us.

29Distance us from bad people and bad friends. 30Make us cling to our good inclination and to good deeds. 31And bend our will so it subjugates itself to You. 32Today and every day, may we be found to have grace, favor, and mercy, in Your eyes and in the eyes of all who behold us. 33Reward us with great kindness. 34Blessed are You, Adonai, who rewards His people Israel with great kindness.

35May it be Your will, Adonai my God and my ancestors' God, that You deliver me today and every day from impudence and insolence, from bad people and from bad friends, from bad neighbors and from bad encounters, and from the destructive Adversary, from oppressive judgments and oppressive opponents at law, whether of the covenant or not.

30וְדַבְּקֵנוּ בְּיֵצֶר הַטּוֹב וּבְמַעֲשִׂים טוֹבִים; 31וְכֹף אֶת יִצְרֵנוּ לְהִשְׁתַּעְבֶּד־לָךְ. 32וּתְנֵנוּ הַיּוֹם וּבְכָל יוֹם לְחֵן וּלְחֶסֶד וּלְרַחֲמִים בְּעֵינֶיךָ וּבְעֵינֵי כָל רוֹאֵינוּ, 33וְתִגְמְלֵנוּ חֲסָדִים טוֹבִים. 34בָּרוּךְ אַתָּה, יְיָ, גּוֹמֵל חֲסָדִים טוֹבִים לְעַמּוֹ יִשְׂרָאֵל.

35יְהִי רָצוֹן מִלְּפָנֶיךָ, יְיָ אֱלֹהַי וֵאלֹהֵי אֲבוֹתַי, שֶׁתַּצִּילֵנִי הַיּוֹם וּבְכָל יוֹם מֵעַזֵּי פָנִים וּמֵעַזּוּת פָּנִים, מֵאָדָם רָע וּמֵחָבֵר רָע, וּמִשָּׁכֵן רָע וּמִפֶּגַע רָע וּמִשָּׂטָן הַמַּשְׁחִית, מִדִּין קָשֶׁה וּמִבַּעַל דִּין קָשֶׁה, בֵּין שֶׁהוּא בֶן־בְּרִית וּבֵין שֶׁאֵינוֹ בֶן־בְּרִית.

126

(Pss. 4 and 67) and after the exile (Ps. 119:130–135 and Mal. 1:6–2:9) know of it.

The blessing is strikingly anthropomorphic: Adonai shines and lifts His face on the recipient of the blessing. But biblical texts are quite comfortable with anthropomorphisms, and even rabbinic culture, which is often thought to reject them, very frequently views God in distinctly anthropomorphic form.

[4] *"Corners of your fields* [pe'ah]*"* Leviticus 19:9 and 23:22 mandate that the corner of the field be left for the poor and the resident alien.

[4] *"First fruits* [bikurim]"* Deuteronomy 26:1–11 describes a ritual of bringing the first fruits to the priest.

[4] *"Offering at each festival* [ra'ayon]*"* Deuteronomy 16:16–17 generalizes Exodus 23:15, suggesting that on all three pilgrimage festivals a gift must be brought to God— "my face shall not be seen empty-handed."

[4] *"Studying Torah* [Talmud Torah]"* See "Engage in words of Torah," pp. 108, 110.

[5] *"Honoring your father and mother"* The family was stressed in biblical culture, and legislation gave parents total rights to discipline their children (Deut. 21:18–21). Obligation toward parents is mentioned in the Decalogue (Exod. 20:12; Deut. 5:16), elsewhere in the Torah (e.g., Lev. 19:3), and especially in wisdom literature (e.g., Prov. 23:22).

[6] *"The soul* [n'shamah]*"* The fundamental premise here—that a person consists of a body and a separate soul—is foreign to the Bible, where *n'shamah* means "breath" and, by extension, "breathing [living] person," but not "soul." God controls who breathes, and breathed life into the first person (Gen. 2:7). This prayer assimilates the Hebrew *n'shamah* to the late idea of resurrection, found biblically only in Daniel 12:2, giving us the novel notion that the soul will be re-breathed back into the body.

[10] *"Who gave the cunning rooster its ability to distinguish"* From Job 38:36, where God points out Job's limited understanding of the universe. "Who put wisdom in the hidden parts? Who gave the cunning rooster its ability to distinguish?"

[11] *"A gentile* [goy]*"* In biblical Hebrew, *goy* denotes a nation attached to a territory, including Israel (e.g., Gen. 12:2; 2 Sam. 7:23). In exilic texts, it begins to mean "*other* nations" (e.g., Ezek. 5:6–8; Lam. 1:3), but it never means that exclusively and is not used derogatorily.

[12] *"A slave* [aved]*"* Either "slave" or "servant." Though a variety of attitudes toward slavery/servantry exist in the Bible, Exodus 21:21 represents the usual view: a servant/slave is another person's property. In addition, slavery/servitude symbolizes a return to Egypt and a denial of God as liberator. Once enslaved to Egypt, Israel is freed to become the servants of God (Lev. 25:42).

[13] *"Did not make me a woman"* In many cases, biblical women have full legal personhood. For example, the law of a goring ox applies equally to men and women (Exod. 21:28). However, a woman's sexuality is owned by her father or husband (Exod. 22:15–16), who may also annul vows (Num. 30). Women typically could not own property, as we see from the Book of Ruth, where Naomi cannot reclaim the field of her deceased husband without the intervention of a male redeemer. The fundamental status of the married woman is reflected in the title of her husband, *ba'al,* "master." It is easy to understand why males would not want to be women in biblical society; in fact calling a man "a woman" is used derogatorily in prophetic literature (Isa. 19:16; Jer. 51:30).

[15] *"Opens the eyes of the blind"* From Psalm 146:8.

[17] *"Frees the captive"* From Psalm 146:7.

[18] *"Raises those who are bent over"* From Psalm 146:8.

[19] *"Spreads out the land on the water"* From Psalm 136:6, using imagery of Genesis 1:6–8.

[21] *"Makes firm man's steps"* From Psalm 37:23 and Proverbs 20:24, reflecting the biblical notion that God controls all of human action.

[22] *"Girds Israel"* From Psalm 65:7, where God is described as "girded with might" to help Israel in battle.

[23] *"Crowns Israel with glory"* A particularistic adaptation of Psalm 8:6, where God crowns all peoples with glory.

[26] *"Make us familiar with Your Torah"* In contrast to the earlier section (see above, "Study Your Torah for its own sake") where Torah is to be studied for its own sake, here such study merely fosters obedience, as in Joshua 1:8: "Let not this Book of Teaching cease from your lips…that you may faithfully observe all that is written there." The inclusion of an evil inclination as the cause of sin is rabbinic, but the power of peer pressure ("Distance us from bad people and bad friends") follows biblical norms, especially in Proverbs.

[32] *"Grace, favor, and mercy* [chen, chesed, rachamim] *"* This triplet never appears in the Bible, but "grace and favor" appear together (e.g., Esther 2:17), as do "favor and mercy" (e.g., Hos. 2:21). The combined phrase here orders the three words from short to long, a well-known cross-linguistic feature called "the law of increasing members."

[35] *"May it be Your will"* Largely post-biblical, but "bad men" *(adam ra)* occurs in Psalm 140:2. Deuteronomy 28:50 imputes "impudence" *(az panim)* to nations that withhold honor from the elderly and compassion from the very young.

DORFF (THEOLOGY)

1. May Adonai bless you and keep [or protect, or guard] you.
2. May Adonai shine His face toward [or cause His presence to shine upon, or lift up His countenance upon, or deal kindly with, or look kindly upon] you [or show you favor] and treat you graciously [or show you favor, or favor you with enlightenment and grace].
3. May Adonai lift His face toward [or turn His countenance (or face) upon, or turn with favor unto] you [or show you kindness] and grant you *shalom,* "peace" [or establish peace for you].

Each line addresses a different context in our relationship to God.

The first blessing speaks generally: "May Adonai bless" us with all good things, whether material, intellectual, emotional, communal, or spiritual—"and keep [or guard]" us from the bad.

In the second blessing, we address a situation when relations with God are especially good. Then God causes "His face" to "shine" on us, that is, God "smiles" on us. God is then "gracious" to us, in that God seems to give us even more than we deserve. The first clause may also imply that God "smiles" on us in the sense that He is not embarrassed to demonstrate His good feelings for us, since the relationship between us is good. The second blessing, then, asks God to be unjustifiably generous to us, materially and emotionally, when we and God are on good terms.

The third blessing, however, obtains when we have offended God. It prays that God not turn His back or hide His face from us, cutting us off as parents might when they send naughty children to their room. Instead, "May Adonai lift His face toward" us, or, as we say, may God "face" us, taking us back in forgiveness and favor; may He make "peace" with us despite our transgressions.

The Bible describes God's anger as "hiding His face" from us, cutting off communication as an act of punishment. Jeremiah (23:39), for instance, quotes God as saying, "I will cast you away from My face." Conversely, "to lift up one's face" means to face someone in compassion and to grant a favor or show partiality beyond what justice demands or even allows. The third blessing, then, assures us that even if we offend, God will nevertheless not cut us off but rather turn toward us in the hope of making peace.

The original intent of this biblical prayer is therefore this:

1. May Adonai give you all life's good and keep you from the bad.
2. [When your relationship with God is good,] may Adonai smile on you and give you more than you deserve.
3. [And when you have offended God,] may Adonai face you and make peace with you.

The Priestly Blessing thus articulates the Jewish conception of our relationship with God.

First, God has an abiding and caring relationship with us. God is not only a creative force in nature ("deism"); God is personally engaged with us ("theism").

Second, God has a sense of justice, so can be angered by our transgressions and both willing and able to punish us for them. At the same time, God's justice is not blind; it is tempered with compassion, born out of love for us. God is like a parent—a metaphor for God in the Bible and the liturgy. Conversely, God's balancing of justice with compassion is a model for human parents: to know when to punish and when to forgive is a godly trait.

Third, God's relationships with us range from unusually close to angry and judgmental. Most of the time, we are on an even keel; God grants us the good and keeps us from the bad. Sometimes, things become particularly wonderful between us, and we get more than we deserve. But sometimes, too, we hurt each other and must remember that the relationship is too important to founder. Then both God and we must take the initiative to face each other and forgive.

The divine-human relationship models human relationships also. The mark of a good relationship is not that everything is always fine. It is, rather, the ability to live through both highs and lows. We must know how to support each other in the everyday (the first blessing), be undeservedly generous to each other during the special moments of good feeling (the second blessing), and seek reconciliation when the relationship falters (the third blessing).

[4] *"These are things that are priceless"* The Rabbis regularly stipulate the limits of what God requires. For example, even though, theoretically, Jews should have as many children as possible (Yeb. 62b), they define the commandment to "be fruitful and multiply" (Gen. 1:28) as requiring a son and a daughter (M. Yeb. 6:6).

The commandments listed here, however, have no prescribed limit, minimum or maximum, so fulfilling them depends on a person's character: kinder and better people will give more of the edge of their fields to the poor (Lev. 19:9), for instance. They will engage in many acts of kindness and will study much Torah; others will do less. Despite Judaism's penchant toward translating morality into legal requirements, the Mishnah (Pe'ah 1:1) recognizes that in some matters, full specificity is impossible. Ultimately, we have to shape people's character so that they want to do more, not less.

[5] *"These are the things that yield interest during your life, while the principal remains for you in the world-to-come"* From Talmud (Shab. 127a). The Rabbis use the economic metaphor of a monetary fund, with interest that can be drawn upon without diminishing the principal. Some believe the passage refers to life after death: God rewards us now without diminishing the ultimate reward available when we die. The passage may also be this-worldly: the benefits of fulfilling the commandments on this list accrue to the agent (and, in the relevant examples, to the recipients) not only immediately, but in the future too, since the "principal" never runs out.

[5] *"Study of Torah is like them all"* Some believe this means that study is better than all of the other actions on the list, but that can hardly be the case, since as much as Judaism values study, it is only because study leads to action (Kid. 40b). This faulty understanding has unfortunately been used by some institutions of Jewish learning to

justify immoral or illegal activity, like failing to pay taxes.

More plausible interpretations might be that study of Torah "undergirds them all" or "frames the background of them all." This is another form of Hillel's lesson, "An ignoramus cannot be pious" (M. Avot 2:6). Torah is indispensable, in that without it, even the most well-intentioned people would not know how to act properly.

⁶ *"My God, the soul"* First Temple literature (written before 586 B.C.E.)—with the exception of Isaiah 26:19, which most scholars date later—does not express a belief in a life after death. Those who die go down to the grave, *sh'ol*, where nobody remembers or praises God (Ps. 6:6; cf. 115:17; 118:17; etc.). Eternity comes through our descendants and the memory of what we did. Second Temple books like Job (c. 400 B.C.E.) and Ecclesiastes (c. 250 B.C.E.) know about the belief in a life after death, but deny it (Job 7:6–10; 14:12, 14; 16:22; etc.; Eccles 3:19–22; 9:4–6, 10; 11:8; 12:7). That is why Job finds it so troubling that good people like him suffer and why Ecclesiastes thinks life is meaningless. Only in what is chronologically the last book of the Bible, Daniel (c. 165 B.C.E.), do we get a clear belief in resurrection of the dead (Dan. 12:1–3).

In the last two centuries B.C.E. and the first century C.E., the Sadducees, who believed only in the written Torah, accordingly denied a resurrection of the dead, while the Pharisees (and their descendants, the Rabbis) affirmed it (M. San. 10:1). Some Rabbis believed that at death people die completely, body and soul, and at the time of resurrection they are brought back to life as whole persons. Others held that only the body dies; the soul remains alive until it is reunited with the body at the time of resurrection. This talmudic prayer (Ber. 60b) clearly assumes the latter. On the analogy of sleep, our soul (like our waking consciousness) departs, but then, upon awakening, God "restores souls to dead corpses."

¹⁰ *"Who gave the cunning rooster its ability to distinguish"* The Talmud (R.H. 26a) understands the word *sekhvi* (from Job 38:36) to mean rooster, and on that interpretation, we thank God for the alarm clocks in nature with which we pace our lives. In the context of Job, however, the word may denote the human mind, in which case we thank God for enabling *us* to distinguish day from night. As anyone who has ever taken a "redeye" flight will know, we suffer when we violate the rhythms that God has created in nature, and so we thank God for making us aware of them (with the help of roosters or not) so that normally, at least, we can live by them.

¹¹⁻¹³ *"Who did not make me a gentile...a slave...a woman"* Although the blessings sound both chauvinistic and sexist, and although there are both chauvinistic and sexist parts of the Jewish tradition, the blessings here are neither, in that they are intended as ways to thank God for the duty of obeying the commandments. The order of the blessings becomes important here. Jews first thank God for not making them gentiles—because Jews are subject to all 613 of the Torah's commandments, while non-Jews are bound (San. 56a) by only the seven universal commandments given to all children of Noah ("the Noahide Covenant"). We then thank God for not making us slaves—

because servitude restricts slaves to just the 365 negative commandments of the Torah. Finally, Jewish men praise God for not making them women—because women are exempted from about a dozen commandments, while men are bound by them all (cf. PT Ber. 9:2).

Beginning in 1945, the Conservative Movement tried to provide an inoffensive version of these blessings that captures the Rabbis' intention of expressing gratitude for the commandments. It expressed them positively, thanking God for making me "in his image," "an Israelite," and "free." In so doing, it altered the original order, which would have required thanking God for making me "an Israelite," then "free," and, finally, "in his image." The shift in order was motivated by the desire to maintain the theory behind the original order—going from the most general to the most particular, for all human beings are made in God's image, some are Jews, and only some (thankfully, in our day, most) are free to practice their religion.

[15] *"Opens the eyes of the blind"* Blind people say this blessing too, just as they say the blessing for light before the *Sh'ma* (see Volume 1, *The Sh'ma and Its Blessings*, pp. 41–43), for even though they cannot see, they derive benefit from those who do (Meg. 24b).

[17–18] *"Frees…raises"* Two blessings for sitting up in bed, then standing up. Anyone who has ever been bedridden, or who has seen others who are, will recognize the miraculous neurological, muscular, and skeletal structure that enables most of us just to sit and stand—abilities that we all too often take for granted.

[20] *"Has provided me my every need"* For tying our shoes—a blessing composed when shoes were a luxury. Few readers of this commentary would think of shoes that way, but the Rabbis knew people who had to walk barefoot, just as many in impoverished countries must today.

[21] *"Makes firm man's steps"* Anyone who has broken a leg or ankle (as I did) will have renewed appreciation for a blessing of appreciation for the ability to walk.

[22–23] *"Girds Israel with might…crowns Israel with glory"* For putting on a belt and head covering, two acts that the blessings transform from the concrete to the symbolic and from the personal to the national. We are motivated to think of God and Israel even in the personal act of dressing ourselves.

[26] *"May it be Your will"* After washing and dressing, the Rabbis have us express our hopes for the day—to avoid evil, be spared trials and shame, and benefit from God's goodness. We may not begin our day without identifying what is really important in life.

We actually have two paragraphs beginning "May it be Your will." The Talmud framed the first in the plural (Ber. 60b) and the second in the singular (Shab. 39b). By saying both, we identify first as part of the entire Jewish people and only then as an individual. The liturgy thus moves us beyond our egocentric selves before giving us the language to pray for ourselves alone. This is one of many examples in which the Jewish emphasis on communal identity stands in sharp contrast to the Enlightenment view embedded in contemporary Western society, where we are primarily individuals and only secondarily members of a community.

—◆—

ELLENSON (MODERN LITURGIES)

SSS supplements this passage with verses from Leviticus 19 that command the Jewish people to be holy and to manifest that holiness through ethical behavior.

Interestingly, the Reconstructionist *Kol Haneshamah,* despite its traditionalist penchant, does not provide this or any other scriptural or rabbinic reading here. A note by Rabbi David Teutsch, President of the Reconstructionist Rabbinical College, explains, "Traditionally, brief sections of classical texts are studied as part of *Birkhot Hashahar.* Together these comprised the daily minimum of Jewish study. While there has been disagreement within Jewish tradition about which sources must be included, passages of Torah, Mishnah, and Talmud have come to dominate. More contemporary sources can be used in our time as well. What matters is making Jewish study a daily activity."

Obviously, the decision of *Kol Haneshamah* not to include specific study texts in *Birkhot Hashachar* is not an indication that such study should not occur. Rather, the choice of text is left up to the individual prayer community. The flexible notion of canon that marks this liberal Jewish denomination allows Rabbi Teutsch to assert that "more contemporary" sources can be as appropriate as traditional ones.

[4] *"These are things that are priceless"* This reading from Mishnah Pe'ah, as well as the talmudic passage from Shabbat that accompanies it, are found in many liberal prayer books *(Siddur Sim Shalom, Siddur Va'ani T'fillati, Ha'avodah Shebalev,* and *Gates of Prayer).* Its ethical sentiments are congenial to the temperament that informs liberal Jews generally.

[4] *"Leaving the corners of your fields..., bringing your first fruits..., bringing offerings..., doing kindness, and studying Torah"* Gates of Prayer omits the imperatives that relate to agriculture and moves directly to ethical responsibilities that speak directly to contemporary Jews.

[5] *"Bringing peace between one person and another"* The Israeli Reform *Ha'avodah Shebalev* adds "between a man and his wife."

[5] *"The study of Torah is like them all"* Siddur Sim Shalom (American Conservative) translates, "The study of Torah is the most basic of them all." Neither *SSS* nor the Orthodox Birnbaum Siddur, which translates, "The study of Torah excels them all," shrinks from affirming Torah study as a value in and of itself. By saying, "The study of

Torah is equal to them all," *Gates of Prayer* reflects a Reform view of Torah that assigns instrumental value to its study and regards ethical acts as above and beyond ritual deeds—even Torah learning.

[6] *"The soul You have put within me"* Many modern Jews have had little difficulty confirming the immortality of the soul. But they have generally rejected the promise of bodily resurrection. As a result, the *Hamburg Temple Prayer Books* and David Einhorn offered vernacular renditions of this meditation that affirmed spiritual immortality while excluding all reference to bodily resurrection. Abraham Geiger retained the Hebrew text in its entirety in his 1854 and 1870 Siddurim, but offered a translation that de-emphasized resurrection. Wise omitted the entire passage from *Minhag America,* believing, perhaps, that his reworking of "Who hast formed man in wisdom…" (see above, "Who formed humans with wisdom"), sufficiently addressed the issue of the soul's immortality.

In the 1900s, the *Union Prayer Book, Gates of Prayer, Ha'avodah Shebalev,* and *Kol Haneshamah* (Reform and Reconstructionist) all followed the direction of nineteenth-century Reform, refusing also to affirm a belief in bodily resurrection. *UPB* (American Reform) omitted the line "You will take it from me and return it to me in the hereafter" even from its Hebrew, for instance, and *Ha'avodah Shebalev* (Israeli Reform) substitutes *l'chayei olam* ("eternal life") for *le'atid lavo* ("the hereafter"). *Kol Haneshamah* (Reconstructionist) makes the same Hebrew change, but translates, "everlasting life." *Siddur Sim Shalom* (American Conservative), retains the traditional Hebrew, but offers "life eternal" in English. Immortality of the soul is thus everywhere affirmed, even as bodily resurrection is universally rejected.

[9] *"Who restores souls to dead corpses"* According to the late Jacob Petuchowski, the closing promise does not even refer to bodily resurrection. It is rather a prayer of gratitude for the return of the soul after sleep, which the Rabbis understood as "partial death." Nevertheless, most editors have interpreted it otherwise. Abraham Geiger left it untranslated. Einhorn transformed resurrection into the soul's immortality by substituting "who hast given us an immortal soul." Marcus Jastrow (1885, early Conservative) adapted the penultimate words of this prayer as its conclusion, saying, "Author of all works, Source of all souls." The *Union Prayer Book* (classical Reform), quoting Job 12:10, states, "in whose hands are the souls of all the living and the spirits of all flesh." *Gates of Prayer* (current American Reform) offers the same concluding phrase, but in Hebrew as well. *Ha'avodah Shebalev* (Israeli Reform) and *Kol Haneshamah* (Reconstructionist) follow the Hebrew of *GOP,* though the latter translates, "Blessed are You, THE HOLY SPIRIT, in whose possession are the soul of every living thing, the animation of all flesh." The commentary by Rabbi Arthur Green states, "The traditional formula of this blessing, referring to the future resurrection of the dead, has been emended."

[11–13] *"Who did not make me"* For the last two centuries, non-Orthodox prayer books have not countenanced such wording in their liturgies. Universally, they have condemned these prayers as xenophobic and sexist. In his 1854 Siddur, Abraham Geiger substituted a single blessing, *she'asani l'ovdo,* "who has made me to serve Him [God]," for all three. Wise's *Minhag America* and Jastrow's *Avodat Yisrael* (early American Reform and Conservative) placed the talmudic benediction *she'asani yisra'el,* "who has made me a Jew," in their stead. The twentieth-century *Siddur Va'ani T'fillati* (Israeli Conservative) followed Wise and Jastrow.

Other liberal liturgies *(Kol Haneshamah, Siddur Sim Shalom, Ha'avodah Shebalev,* and *Gates of Prayer)* have all transformed these blessings into positive statements: "who has made me a Jew," "who has made me in His image," and "who has made me free." *SVT* offers these formulations as an option, but prefers the alternative outlined above. *GOP* includes the first and third of these benedictions, omitting the second altogether.

[25] *"Who removes sleep from my eyes, slumber from my eyelids"* Geiger (1854) and Mordecai Kaplan both place this blessing first in the litany of blessings here—since, presumably, consciousness of being awake is our first act each morning.

[34] *"Who rewards His people Israel with great kindness"* Disturbed by the particularity of these words, Geiger's more radical 1870 Siddur, as well as Wise's 1857 *Minhag America,* universalized the language. Geiger substituted "His creatures" for "His people Israel," while Wise wrote, "Thy creatures." Interestingly, the Conservative Marcus Jastrow maintained the Hebrew, but instead of a literal translation, wrote, "who bestowest bountifully goodness and beneficence." Twentieth-century liberal Siddurim include the original Hebrew and a faithful English equivalent—a sign of renewed Jewish particularity that typifies the period following the 1967 Six-Day War in Israel, especially.

[35] *"Deliver me today"* Though it is not clear exactly why, most non-Orthodox liturgies omit this paragraph, Geiger (1854), *Siddur Sim Shalom* (Conservative), and *Ha'avodah Shebalev* (Israeli Reform) being the exceptions. Typically, Geiger supplied the Hebrew, without translation.

◆————

FRANKEL (A WOMAN'S VOICE)

sick, comfort mourners, mend fences, bind wounds, and inspire us all with their abiding faith. Even though many of them do not attend the study house, their love of Torah sustains the world.

[6] *"The soul You have put within me"* Much has been written recently about our "inner child," the primal root of our psyche from which our later selves emerge, our intrinsic nature, our uncorrupted essence. In Judaism, this inner child is called our *n'shamah,* usually translated as "soul," but literally meaning "breath." This *n'shamah* is the image of God within us, incorruptible, deriving its life force from the divine breath. Here in

this prayer, we acknowledge our status as debtors. One day God will reclaim our borrowed soul and then return it to us in some other form. The only way we can repay our debt in this life is to offer thanks.

[13] *"Who did not make me a woman"* Few lines in the liturgy have provoked as much passion in modern times as this one, a prayer in which Jewish men express their gratitude to God for not having been made female. In contemporary times, as feminism has gained a firmer foothold even in the more traditional Jewish communities, various strategies have been offered to rationalize, neutralize, or eradicate the exclusionary message implicit in this blessing.

In more traditional prayer books, women long ago were given alternate words to substitute for this exclusively male blessing. Of the many medieval options (see "On Gentiles, Slaves, and Women: The Blessings 'Who Did Not Make Me'—Historical Survey," pp. 17–27), the one that stuck is "Blessed...who has made me according to Your will." In response to the contemporary argument that men too have been made according to God's will and so could recite the same words assigned here to women, traditionalists reply that the men's blessing thanks God not for their superior status but for the privilege of being obligated to perform time-bound commandments, a burden from which women have been released in order to perform their equally sacred duties to home, husband, and children.

Liberal Judaism, rejecting such arguments as patronizing or specious, has created an altogether new blessing to be recited by both genders: *she'asani b'tsalmo* or *b'tsalmah*—"Who has made me in [God's = His] image" or "[God's = Her] image." Although this new blessing could replace the male/female double blessing of the traditional prayer book and still be interpreted to validate different ritual roles for men and women, no such innovation has even been considered in traditional circles. Liturgical conservatism, even in the face of a growing Orthodox feminism, is hard to overcome, especially since this particular blessing dates back to the Talmud (and its alternative for women, to the fourteenth century).

◆

J. HOFFMAN (TRANSLATION)

be witness to Adonai's face, and may He grant you peace." But the passive is unacceptable here for other reasons. Also in terms of content, the most serious question is whether "[May Adonai] shine His face" and "[May Adonai] lift His face" are idioms whose meanings we no longer know or poetic similes best translated word for word. Here we (following Fox, *NSRV*, Artscroll, and others) assume the latter. *JPS* suggests, "deal kindly" and "bestow favor," respectively. Birnbaum gives us "countenance" (a nice word play on "face") and "favor." *SSS* uses "favor" for "shine His face," and "show kindness" for "lift His face." There is also a question whether the blessing is predictive ("Adonai will") or jussive ("May Adonai").

[4] *"These are things"* "These…" is the first of two lists, that is, of those "[things] that are 'priceless'"; the second list here is of those things whose rewards are enjoyed in the world-to-come. Reform tradition *(GOP)*, curiously, has combined the headings of both lists as a title for the second list, but omitting the items in the first list completely. Later Reform versions (1994 *GOP*) and some songs (e.g., Klepper) apparently based on it then omit the second half of the double heading, with the result that the first heading appears before the second list.

[4] *"Priceless"* The legal point of the Hebrew is that one can never do too much of these things. The Hebrew phrase "without value" is like the English "priceless," not "valueless" but "invaluable." A similar concept is expressed by Artscroll's "…things that have no prescribed measure."

[4] *"Leaving the corners of your fields for the poor"* Hebrew, *pe'ah,* a technical term lacking in English, and so we spell out what it refers to. Four technical terms follow, and of them the first two have no equivalent in English, and so they too are spelled out.

[4] *"Festival"* Passover, Shavuot, and Sukkot, the three "pilgrimage" holidays, during which one was supposed to make a pilgrimage journey to Jerusalem. These might be considered, then, "pilgrimage" offerings.

[5] *"Like them all"* Hebrew, *k'neged,* the same word translated above as "next to" (p. 78.) Again, the point is that they are parallel is some sense. "Like" maintains the ambiguity of the Hebrew, which leaves open the way in which Torah is like "them all." It is not clear from the text if the Torah is like each of "them" or only like the group together, that is, for example, if Torah is like visiting the sick, or only like visiting the sick when taken with all the others.

[6] *"Soul"* Curiously, the Hebrew simply reads "a soul." It is not clear what to make of this seemingly incorrect Hebrew; the word "the" may have been omitted for purposes of meter. But see L. Hoffman, "The soul You have put within me," p. 123, 139.

[9] *"Dead corpses"* So reads the Hebrew. It's not clear if this was supposed to indicate anything more than just "the dead." In Hebrew, as in English, there are no live corpses.

[10] *"Cunning rooster"* Others, "cock." We prefer "rooster" to "cock" because of the other connotations of "cock." The Hebrew is *sekhvi,* a word of unclear origin, occurring only once in the Bible (Job 38:36, from which this blessing is adapted). To judge from its use in rabbinic times, it meant either "rooster" or "mind," and so we guess that it might refer to the clever aspect of the rooster.

[10] *"Ability"* Literally, "wisdom."

[11] *"Who did not make"* More idiomatic might be "for not making me," but this, like most blessings, starts off in second person and continues in third person. We want to preserve that (odd) effect in our translation.

15 *"Opens the eyes"* The Hebrew *poke'ach* means "to open the eyes," and so the Hebrew here consists of a nice pithy pair of words ("open-the-eyes-of" and "the-blind") as it does in the next three blessings ("clothes" and "the-naked"; "frees" and "the captive"; and "raises" and "those-who-are-bent-over"). Unfortunately, we see no way to translate this aspect of the Hebrew.

18 *"Those who are bent over"* Perhaps "downtrodden" might be the point here.

19 *"On the water"* Or "above the water." The notion of spreading out the land on the water refers to an ancient conception of the world in which there are seas beneath the continents upon which the continents lie.

22 *"Girds"* Following standard translations. (The Hebrew root *alef-zian-resh* should not be confused with the similar sounding root *ayin-zian-resh*, which means "to help.") The idea is that God makes Israel strong.

24 *"Tired"* From the Hebrew root *yud-ayin-peh*. This is one of a small group of roots that undergo metathesis, that is, reversal of letters. The reversed form, *ayin-yud-peh*, is more commonly known.

25 *"Slumber"* Following standard translations. The Hebrew has two words for sleep, one used immediately above, and a fancier one here.

29 *"Friends"* Hebrew, *chaver*, which ranges in meaning from "friend" to "member." The notion here is probably a combination of both, something like "our crowd," the point being that even our crowd may contain bad people. Below we will talk about oppressive opponents "whether of the covenant or not" (that is, whether Jewish or not). Perhaps this expresses the same idea.

32 *"Behold"* Literally, "see."

35 *"Impudence and insolence"* The Hebrew for both words is a phrase ending in *panim*. We hope that "impudence" and "insolence" sound sufficiently alike to convey the similarity.

35 *"Bad friends"* See above, "Friends."

35 *"Adversary"* Hebrew, *satan*, which has progressed in meaning from Adversary to Devil.

138

immediately precede this one, giving us a perfect parallelism: thanks to God for body and for soul. The Hebrew does not say "the soul," but just "soul," without the definite object. Early rites (geonic) often have "the soul," however, so the definite article may just have dropped out accidentally. Alternatively, its absence here is purposeful, alluding to a similar usage in the Talmud (Nid. 30b) where we are reminded of a vow we are said to have made to God to keep our soul pure. The theme of the soul's necessary purity is carried over eventually into Western culture through the tale of Faust, an actual historical character in the sixteenth century and, later, the chief character in literature, drama, and opera, who sullies his soul by selling it to the devil.

[9] *"Who restores souls to dead corpses"* The morning service is conceived halakhically as a celebration of being resurrected from our sleep, which is likened to death (see "The Halakhah of Waking Up," pp. 35–42)—an idea the Rabbis inherited from the Greeks (Homer [*Iliad*, 14:277] calls sleep the "twin brother of death"). Part of classical Judaism's promise for the future is personal resurrection. In fact, an alternative talmudic tradition (PT R.H. 1) prescribes that when we wake up, we say, "Blessed are You, who resurrects the dead." (See, "Remember us with fondness, and visit us with salvation," pp. 147, 155.) The language here is also talmudic, however (San. 108a).

[11–13] *"Who did not make me"* These three blessings are talmudic (cf. T. Ber. 6:18, Men. 43a) but are not part of the standard list of talmudic blessings whence most of the others here derive (Ber. 60a). (See "On Gentiles, Slaves, and Women: The Blessings 'Who Did Not Make Me,'" pp. 17–34.) Though intertwined in our rite, the Spanish-Portuguese custom is to say them separately, only after the other blessings are completed.

[24] *"Who gives strength to the tired"* In human affairs, says the midrash, we loan something to someone and get it back more worn and frayed. By contrast, we loan our tired soul to God for the night, and it gets returned renewed the next morning. Hence God gives strength to the tired.

The other blessings in the list are talmudic (mostly from Ber. 60a). This one was added later by Ashkenazi congregations, but was not adopted by the Spanish-Portuguese Sefardim. It is cited by the *Tur* (thirteenth century), but heated debate continued for some time as to whether it should be included, given its absence from the original talmudic list. As late as the seventeenth century, authorities like Polish talmudist Joel Sirkes (1561–1640) justified its inclusion on the grounds that the Rabbis who had first introduced it would never have done so if they had not seen it in at least some manuscripts of the Talmud, albeit not in the editions known to Sirkes.

[26] *"Make us familiar with Your Torah"* Early authorities believed this paragraph was a continuation of the blessing prior ("Blessed…who removes sleep from my eyes…"). As we have it, the prior blessing is in the first person singular ("my eyes"), however, and this is the first person plural ("make us familiar"); but many early versions use the first

person singular throughout, and the Spanish-Portuguese custom is to say both prayers in the plural ("our eyes"). The combined thought of the two prayers together would then be that removal of sleep opens our eyes to the greater possibilities of Torah and ethical behavior. Just waking up is insufficient. Much as we thank God for removal of sleep, we are far more grateful for awakening to the highest possibilities of human potential.

35 *"Deliver me"* Originally a private prayer attributed to Judah Hanasi (end second century C.E.). The Talmud (Ber. 7a) gives several such private prayers said by one Rabbi or another after reciting the *Amidah*. As the liturgy developed, some of them were taken out of context and added elsewhere. This one found its way here as a fitting early morning aspiration.

◆

KUSHNER & POLEN (CHASIDISM)

consciousness *(nefesh)*. (Indeed, this tripartite scheme goes all the way back to *Sefer Y'tsirah,* one of the earliest Jewish mystical texts, dating from the first or second century.) Chagigah 2a discusses pilgrims who come to fulfill the *mitzvah* of "being seen" at the Temple with the words of the following maxim: "Just as the One [God] comes to see, so one [the pilgrim] is seen." This may also be read reflexively: You may come to give, but you wind up receiving. Thus in the Temple, the spiritual center of the universe, holiness radiates outward in all directions, especially during the time of festival offerings. In this way, with the right preparation and prayer, one can access this source of infinite sanctity. It has no fixed measure.

25 *"Who removes sleep from my eyes"* "One should awaken oneself early in the morning like a lion, rousing the dawn, to serve his Creator." With these words, Joseph Caro (1488–1575) commences his *Shulchan Arukh,* the definitive code of Jewish law. Written originally for Sefardi Jews, the *Shulchan Arukh,* or "Set Table," did not specifically address Ashkenazi customs. Then, between 1569 and 1571, Moses Isserles (1530–1572) published his commentary on the *Shulchan Arukh,* the *Mapa,* the "Tablecloth," for German Jews. The *Mapa* opens with Psalm 16:8, "Continually, I set Adonai before me...." Taken together, Nosson Sternhartz of Nemirov, in his *Likkutei Halakhot,* suggests that the opening lines of each text, "Arise like a lion..." and "Set Adonai before me" describe the paradigm of awakening: Like a lion in service of God, who is ever before me.

He cites his master, Nachman of Bratslav (1772–1810), who warns that too much self-examination and introspection will inevitably create anxiety over your distance from God. Such preoccupation with your defects only leads to depression; but since depression effectively incapacitates you, making you unable to serve your Creator, sadness of any kind is an enemy of right acting. You must therefore continually strive, counsels Nachman, to find something good in yourself. Always be on guard against the arguments of the insidious inner voice trying to persuade you that you're no damn good, that you've never done anything of value, that even the good you've attempted is defective. This is the voice of the enemy.

Your most effective defense is the simple fact that it's inconceivable you don't have some good points. Find one, advises Nachman; then find another. Keep looking. Begin by giving yourself the benefit of the doubt. Of course you've made mistakes. Nevertheless, by adding one good point to another, you gradually move from self-deprecation to self-respect. And only through such self-affirmation will you merit to make *t'shuvah,* "return" to God. (Indeed, one old tradition counsels that if your atonement leaves you feeling bad, then it was not real atonement.)

It is with this in mind that we now understand Psalm 37:10, "Yet *[od]* a little bit more and the wickedness [the wicked dimension of your psyche] will be gone" *(V'od m'at v'ein rasha).* In other words, if you acknowledge within yourself even the littlest bit of good—that *od,* that "yetness"—you will no longer think yourself wicked. And once that happens you will be able to raise yourself in joy—now finally able to pray. And this, in turn, is confirmed in Psalm 146:2, *azamrah leiloha'i b'odi,* literally, "I will sing to God with my 'yetness.'" By means of just that littlest bit of "yet," you will be able to sing praises to God. (Nosson Sternhartz pushes the implication to teach that only someone who learned how to find good points—even in someone else who may be a sinner—is qualified to lead the congregation in prayer.)

And this, then, is how you should rouse yourself from sleep and begin each new day. Sleep, according to Sternhartz is not unconsciousness but a metaphor for the stupor of thinking you're no damn good—and neither is anyone else. You must roar like a lion for the goodness you will find in yourself and others (based on Nachman of Bratslav's *Likkutei Moharan,* 282). And now you are ready to serve God and start your day.

[33] *"Reward us with great kindness* [chasadim tovim]*"* Meshullam Zusya of Anipol (d. 1800) is puzzled by the apparent redundancy of *chasadim* (from the word *chesed*) and *tovim* (from the word *tov*). *Chesed* means "love," and *tov* means good. Surely, if we receive love, then it is also obviously good. One explanation, suggests Zusya, comes from the case of a precious stone densely wrapped in thorns and thistles. Any attempt even to touch the jewel would scratch one's hand. The gem might be beautiful, but its covering renders it effectively useless, worthless. It is often the same way with love. For this reason, we pray not only to receive love but that the love should be clothed in goodness, in a way that it is accessible (*Bet Aharon; Y'sod Ha'avodah,* 6).

—◆—

LANDES (HALAKHAH)

(R. Barukh Epstein, Russia/U.S., 1860–1931), he further elaborates:

> Many have asked why we do not say blessings over the performance of commandments such as *ts'dakah,* kindness, returning lost objects, or visiting the sick…. The answer, in my opinion, is simple. The formula of the blessing, "Who has sanctified us through His commandments and commanded us," implies that through the performance of the particular commandment, we become holier than, and therefore distinguished from, other peoples, who do not perform it. This can only apply to commandments "between man and God," such as: *t'fillin, tsitsit, sukkah, lulav,* and so forth, which other nations do not observe. However, this can not be the case regarding commandments "between man and man," since these are performed by other nations as well. We cannot say, "Who has sanctified us"—that is, set us apart—"through His commandments," since we are no different in this respect from any other civilized nation.

Professor Saul Lieberman (*Tosefta Kifshutah,* Ber. p. 112) cites a dissenting view: "The commentary by the author of the *Sefer Hacharedim* (R. Eliezer Azkari—or Azikri, sixteenth-century kabbalist and philosopher, Safed) to the Yerushalmi, Berakhot 6:1, states:

> All commandments require blessings. I have discovered that R. Elijah [of London] would say a blessing when giving charity or loaning funds to the poor, or performing any of the commandments, although this practice never became widely accepted. In the halakhic rulings of R. Elijah, we read: "It seems that all positive commandments require a blessing. I often say 'Who has hallowed us with His commandments and commanded us to respect the elderly,' 'to honor the aged,' and so forth.

[10] *"Who gave the cunning rooster* [sekhvi] *its ability to distinguish" Sekhvi,* "rooster," also means "heart," which is the source of all understanding.

[11] *"Who did not make me a gentile"* According to R. Meir Halevi Abulafia of Toledo (1175–1244), a convert cannot say this blessing, since it refers to origins, and such a person began as a gentile. Various authorities (e.g., *Magen Abraham,* Taz, and Gra) require that he say *she'asani ger,* ("Who made me a convert"). Others suggest *shehikhnisani tachat kanfei hashekhinah* ("Who has brought me under the wings of the divine presence"). But the *Yad Aharon* decides that a convert can say the blessing in question (*B'er Haiteiv* 46:5). The final opinion should be whatever practice is customary. See also "On Gentiles, Slaves, and Women: The Blessings 'Who Did Not Make Me,'" pp. 17–34.

[17–18] *"Who frees the captive…raises those who are bent over"* If, by mistake, one recites "raises those" before "frees the captive," one no longer should recite the latter, for it is contained within the former (*Shulchan Arukh,* O. Ch. 46:5; *Mishnah B'rurah* 20).

◆ ◆ ◆

4 *The* Akedah

[1] Our God and our ancestors' God, remember us with fondness, and visit us with salvation and mercy from the highest heavens of old. [2] And in our favor, Adonai our God, remember the love of our ancestors, Abraham, Isaac, and Israel, Your servants; remember the covenant, and the kindness, and the oath You swore to our ancestor Abraham on Mount Moriah, and the binding of Isaac his son on the altar, as written in Your Torah:

[3] And after these things God tested Abraham. [4] He said to him, "Abraham," and Abraham answered, "Yes?" [5] And God said, "Take your son, your only one, whom you love, Isaac, and go to the land of Moriah, and offer him there as a sacrifice on one of the mountains that I mention." [6] So Abraham got up early in the morning, and saddled his donkey, and took his two boys with him and also Isaac, his son. [7] He split wood for the sacrifice and got up and went to the place that God had told him. [8] On the third day, Abraham lifted his eyes and saw the place from afar. [9] Abraham said to his boys, "You stay here with the donkey, while the boy and I go up there, and after we worship we will return to you." [10]Abraham took the wood for the sacrifice and put it on Isaac, his son,

¹אֱלֹהֵינוּ וֵאלֹהֵי אֲבוֹתֵינוּ, זָכְרֵנוּ בְּזִכָּרוֹן טוֹב לְפָנֶיךָ, וּפָקְדֵנוּ בִּפְקֻדַּת יְשׁוּעָה וְרַחֲמִים מִשְּׁמֵי שְׁמֵי קֶדֶם; ²וּזְכָר-לָנוּ, יְיָ אֱלֹהֵינוּ, אַהֲבַת הַקַּדְמוֹנִים, אַבְרָהָם יִצְחָק וְיִשְׂרָאֵל עֲבָדֶיךָ, אֶת הַבְּרִית וְאֶת הַחֶסֶד, וְאֶת הַשְּׁבוּעָה שֶׁנִּשְׁבַּעְתָּ לְאַבְרָהָם אָבִינוּ בְּהַר הַמּוֹרִיָּה, וְאֶת הָעֲקֵדָה שֶׁעָקַד אֶת יִצְחָק בְּנוֹ עַל גַּבֵּי הַמִּזְבֵּחַ, כַּכָּתוּב בְּתוֹרָתֶךָ:

³וַיְהִי אַחַר הַדְּבָרִים הָאֵלֶּה, וְהָאֱלֹהִים נִסָּה אֶת אַבְרָהָם, ⁴וַיֹּאמֶר אֵלָיו: אַבְרָהָם, וַיֹּאמֶר הִנֵּנִי. ⁵וַיֹּאמֶר: קַח נָא אֶת בִּנְךָ, אֶת יְחִידְךָ, אֲשֶׁר אָהַבְתָּ, אֶת יִצְחָק, וְלֶךְ לְךָ אֶל אֶרֶץ הַמֹּרִיָּה, וְהַעֲלֵהוּ שָׁם לְעֹלָה עַל אַחַד הֶהָרִים אֲשֶׁר אֹמַר אֵלֶיךָ. ⁶וַיַּשְׁכֵּם אַבְרָהָם בַּבֹּקֶר, וַיַּחֲבֹשׁ אֶת חֲמֹרוֹ, וַיִּקַּח אֶת שְׁנֵי נְעָרָיו אִתּוֹ וְאֵת יִצְחָק בְּנוֹ; ⁷וַיְבַקַּע עֲצֵי עֹלָה, וַיָּקָם וַיֵּלֶךְ אֶל הַמָּקוֹם אֲשֶׁר אָמַר לוֹ הָאֱלֹהִים. ⁸בַּיּוֹם הַשְּׁלִישִׁי, וַיִּשָּׂא אַבְרָהָם

143

and he took the fire and the knife in his own hand. 11And the two of them went off together. 12Isaac said to Abraham, his father, "Dad," and Abraham answered, "Yes, my son?" And Isaac said, "Here is the fire and the wood, but where is the lamb to sacrifice?" 13Abraham said, "God will see to the lamb to sacrifice, my son." 14And the two of them went off together. 15And they came to the place that God had told him, and Abraham built the altar there, arranged the wood, and bound Isaac, his son, and put him on the altar on the wood. 16And Abraham extended his hand to take the knife and slaughter his son. 17But Adonai's angel called to him from heaven, "Abraham! Abraham!" 18Abraham answered, "Yes?" 19And the angel said, "Do not put your hand forward toward the boy and do not do anything to him, for now I know that you revere God, for you did not withhold your son, your only one, from Me." 20As Abraham lifted his eyes he saw a ram, behind, caught in the thicket by its horns; so Abraham went and got the ram and offered it up as a sacrifice instead of his son. 21Abraham called that place "God will see," which nowadays would be "On the mountain of God will be seen." 22One of Adonai's angels called to Abraham a second time from heaven: 23"'By Myself have I sworn,' said Adonai, 'that because you did this thing, and you did not withhold your son, your only one, I will bless you greatly, and make your descendants as numerous as the stars in the sky and as the sand upon the seashore. 24Your descendants shall possess their enemies' cities. 25And through your descendants all the peoples of the earth shall be blessed, because you listened to My voice.'" 26Abraham returned to his boys. 27They got up and went off together to Be'er Sheva, and Abraham lived in Be'er Sheva.

אֶת עֵינָיו וַיַּרְא אֶת הַמָּקוֹם מֵרָחֹק. 9וַיֹּאמֶר אַבְרָהָם אֶל נְעָרָיו: שְׁבוּ לָכֶם פֹּה עִם הַחֲמוֹר, וַאֲנִי וְהַנַּעַר נֵלְכָה עַד כֹּה, וְנִשְׁתַּחֲוֶה וְנָשׁוּבָה אֲלֵיכֶם. 10וַיִּקַּח אַבְרָהָם אֶת עֲצֵי הָעֹלָה וַיָּשֶׂם עַל יִצְחָק בְּנוֹ, וַיִּקַּח בְּיָדוֹ אֶת הָאֵשׁ וְאֶת הַמַּאֲכֶלֶת, 11וַיֵּלְכוּ שְׁנֵיהֶם יַחְדָּו. 12וַיֹּאמֶר יִצְחָק אֶל אַבְרָהָם אָבִיו, וַיֹּאמֶר: אָבִי, וַיֹּאמֶר הִנֶּנִּי בְנִי; וַיֹּאמֶר: הִנֵּה הָאֵשׁ וְהָעֵצִים, וְאַיֵּה הַשֶּׂה לְעֹלָה. 13וַיֹּאמֶר אַבְרָהָם: אֱלֹהִים יִרְאֶה לּוֹ הַשֶּׂה לְעֹלָה, בְּנִי; 14וַיֵּלְכוּ שְׁנֵיהֶם יַחְדָּו. 15וַיָּבֹאוּ אֶל הַמָּקוֹם אֲשֶׁר אָמַר לוֹ הָאֱלֹהִים, וַיִּבֶן שָׁם אַבְרָהָם אֶת הַמִּזְבֵּחַ, וַיַּעֲרֹךְ אֶת הָעֵצִים, וַיַּעֲקֹד אֶת יִצְחָק בְּנוֹ, וַיָּשֶׂם אֹתוֹ עַל הַמִּזְבֵּחַ מִמַּעַל לָעֵצִים. 16וַיִּשְׁלַח אַבְרָהָם אֶת יָדוֹ וַיִּקַּח אֶת הַמַּאֲכֶלֶת לִשְׁחֹט אֶת בְּנוֹ. 17וַיִּקְרָא אֵלָיו מַלְאַךְ יְיָ מִן הַשָּׁמַיִם, וַיֹּאמֶר: אַבְרָהָם, אַבְרָהָם, 18וַיֹּאמֶר הִנֵּנִי. 19וַיֹּאמֶר: אַל תִּשְׁלַח יָדְךָ אֶל הַנַּעַר וְאַל תַּעַשׂ לוֹ מְאוּמָה, כִּי עַתָּה יָדַעְתִּי כִּי יְרֵא אֱלֹהִים אַתָּה, וְלֹא חָשַׂכְתָּ אֶת בִּנְךָ אֶת יְחִידְךָ מִמֶּנִּי. 20וַיִּשָּׂא אַבְרָהָם אֶת עֵינָיו וַיַּרְא וְהִנֵּה אַיִל, אַחַר, נֶאֱחַז בַּסְּבַךְ בְּקַרְנָיו; וַיֵּלֶךְ אַבְרָהָם וַיִּקַּח אֶת הָאַיִל, וַיַּעֲלֵהוּ לְעֹלָה תַּחַת בְּנוֹ. 21וַיִּקְרָא אַבְרָהָם שֵׁם הַמָּקוֹם הַהוּא: יְיָ

28Master of the world, may it be Your will, Adonai, our God and our ancestors' God, that You remember in our favor the covenant with our ancestors. 29Just as our ancestor Abraham overpowered his mercy toward his only son, willing to slay him in order to do Your will, so may Your mercy overpower Your anger toward us, and may Your mercy prevail over Your retribution. 30Adonai our God, be lenient with us and deal with us kindly and mercifully. 31In Your great goodness, may Your anger turn away from Your people, Your city, Your land, and Your heritage. 32Adonai our God, fulfill what You promised us through Moses, Your servant: 33 "I will remember My covenant with Jacob, and My covenant with Isaac, and My covenant with Abraham; and I will remember the land."

יֵרָאֶה, אֲשֶׁר יֵאָמֵר הַיּוֹם: בְּהַר יְיָ יֵרָאֶה.

22וַיִּקְרָא מַלְאַךְ יְיָ אֶל אַבְרָהָם שֵׁנִית מִן הַשָּׁמָיִם. וַיֹּאמֶר: 23בִּי נִשְׁבַּעְתִּי, נְאֻם יְיָ, כִּי יַעַן אֲשֶׁר עָשִׂיתָ אֶת הַדָּבָר הַזֶּה, וְלֹא חָשַׂכְתָּ אֶת בִּנְךָ, אֶת יְחִידֶךָ. כִּי בָרֵךְ אֲבָרֶכְךָ, וְהַרְבָּה אַרְבֶּה אֶת זַרְעֲךָ כְּכוֹכְבֵי הַשָּׁמַיִם, וְכַחוֹל אֲשֶׁר עַל שְׂפַת הַיָּם, 24וְיִרַשׁ זַרְעֲךָ אֵת שַׁעַר אֹיְבָיו. 25וְהִתְבָּרְכוּ בְזַרְעֲךָ כֹּל גּוֹיֵי הָאָרֶץ, עֵקֶב אֲשֶׁר שָׁמַעְתָּ בְּקֹלִי. 26וַיָּשָׁב אַבְרָהָם אֶל נְעָרָיו, 27וַיָּקֻמוּ וַיֵּלְכוּ יַחְדָּו אֶל בְּאֵר שָׁבַע; וַיֵּשֶׁב אַבְרָהָם בִּבְאֵר שָׁבַע.

28רִבּוֹנוֹ שֶׁל עוֹלָם, יְהִי רָצוֹן מִלְּפָנֶיךָ, יְיָ אֱלֹהֵינוּ וֵאלֹהֵי אֲבוֹתֵינוּ, שֶׁתִּזְכָּר־לָנוּ בְּרִית אֲבוֹתֵינוּ. 29כְּמוֹ שֶׁכָּבַשׁ אַבְרָהָם אָבִינוּ אֶת רַחֲמָיו מִבֶּן־יְחִידוֹ, וְרָצָה לִשְׁחֹט אוֹתוֹ כְּדֵי לַעֲשׂוֹת רְצוֹנֶךָ, כֵּן יִכְבְּשׁוּ רַחֲמֶיךָ אֶת כַּעַסְךָ מֵעָלֵינוּ, וְיָגֹלּוּ רַחֲמֶיךָ עַל מִדּוֹתֶיךָ, 30וְתִתְכַּנֵּס אִתָּנוּ לִפְנִים מִשּׁוּרַת דִּינֶךָ, וְתִתְנַהֵג עִמָּנוּ, יְיָ אֱלֹהֵינוּ, בְּמִדַּת הַחֶסֶד וּבְמִדַּת הָרַחֲמִים. 31וּבְטוּבְךָ הַגָּדוֹל, יָשׁוּב חֲרוֹן אַפְּךָ מֵעַמְּךָ וּמֵעִירְךָ וּמֵאַרְצְךָ וּמִנַּחֲלָתֶךָ. 32וְקַיֶּם־לָנוּ, יְיָ אֱלֹהֵינוּ, אֶת הַדָּבָר שֶׁהִבְטַחְתָּנוּ עַל יְדֵי מֹשֶׁה עַבְדֶּךָ, כָּאָמוּר: 33וְזָכַרְתִּי אֶת בְּרִיתִי יַעֲקוֹב, וְאַף אֶת בְּרִיתִי יִצְחָק, וְאַף אֶת בְּרִיתִי אַבְרָהָם אֶזְכֹּר, וְהָאָרֶץ אֶזְכֹּר.

BRETTLER (BIBLE)

[2] *"Love of our ancestors"* The Bible does not depict the patriarchs as "loving God." Rather, God loves them (Deut. 7:8; 10:15). Only in Isaiah 41:8 is Abraham called *ohavi*, but *ohavi* may not mean "who loves Me." It probably should be translated as "the one who obeyed Me" (see Volume 1, *The Sh'ma and Its Blessings*, p. 101).

The prayer epitomizes the rabbinic doctrine of *z'khut avot* ("merits of the ancestors"), according to which later generations benefit from the meritorious deeds of their predecessors, especially the *Akedah,* "the binding of Isaac." The Bible does not explicitly recognize this idea, though the Decalogue states that the *(p. 150)*

DORFF (THEOLOGY)

[2] *"Remember the love of our ancestors"* An invocation of the doctrine of *z'khut avot,* "the merit of the ancestors," by which we may attain reward not for own deeds but as a consequence of the extra merit laid up by our pious ancestors. The question is whether we also suffer for our *(p. 152)*

ELLENSON (MODERN LITURGIES)

[1] *"Our God and our ancestors' God"* An introduction to Genesis 22:1–19, the binding of Isaac (the *Akedah*), a story that most liberal Jews have found troubling. They have not viewed the Abraham of this passage positively as "a knight of faith" (in the words *(p. 152)*

FRANKEL (A WOMAN'S VOICE)

[1] *"Remember us with fondness"* In eastern Europe over a period of a thousand years, Jewish women would visit the cemetery during the High Holy Day season, as well as during times of distress, in order to measure out candle wicking equal in length to the circumference of certain graves. These strands were then cut into individual wicks and burned in candles on Yom Kippur, both at home and at synagogue, as the women recited *t'khines,* Yiddish prayers for *(p. 153)*

[1] Our God and our ancestors' God, remember us with fondness, and visit us with salvation and mercy from the highest heavens of old. [2] And in our favor, Adonai our God, remember the love of our ancestors, Abraham, Isaac, and Israel, Your servants; remember the covenant, and the kindness, and the oath You swore to our ancestor Abraham on Mount Moriah, and the binding of Isaac his son on the altar, as written in Your Torah:

J. HOFFMAN (TRANSLATION)

[1] *"Remember"* From the Hebrew root *z-kh-r.* We have probably misunderstood this root, at least partially. "Remember us fondly" makes sense here, but this same root is used, for example, in "remember us to life" during the High Holy Days, and "remember us to life" is devoid of meaning.

[1] *"With fondness"* If it were English, "remember us with a fond remembrance" would better capture the Hebrew, especially in light of *(p. 153)*

L. HOFFMAN (HISTORY)

THE STORY OF ABRAHAM'S NEAR SACRIFICE OF ISAAC (GEN. 22:1–19), PRECEDED AND FOLLOWED BY PETITIONS FOR GOD TO "REMEMBER" US ON ACCOUNT OF GOD'S COVENANTAL RELATIONSHIP WITH OUR BIBLICAL ANCESTORS.

[1] *"Remember us with fondness* [b'zikaron tov], *and visit us with salvation"* The promise that God remembers us is ubiquitous in Jewish liturgy. It appears most prominently on Rosh Hashanah, where one-third of the portion of the

¹אֱלֹהֵינוּ וֵאלֹהֵי אֲבוֹתֵינוּ, זָכְרֵנוּ בְּזִכָּרוֹן טוֹב לְפָנֶיךָ,
וּפָקְדֵנוּ בִּפְקֻדַּת יְשׁוּעָה וְרַחֲמִים מִשְּׁמֵי שְׁמֵי קֶדֶם;
²וּזְכָר־לָנוּ, יְיָ אֱלֹהֵינוּ, אַהֲבַת הַקַּדְמוֹנִים, אַבְרָהָם
יִצְחָק וְיִשְׂרָאֵל עֲבָדֶיךָ, אֶת הַבְּרִית וְאֶת הַחֶסֶד, וְאֶת
הַשְּׁבוּעָה שֶׁנִּשְׁבַּעְתָּ לְאַבְרָהָם אָבִינוּ בְּהַר הַמּוֹרִיָּה,
וְאֶת הָעֲקֵדָה שֶׁעָקַד אֶת יִצְחָק בְּנוֹ עַל גַּבֵּי הַמִּזְבֵּחַ,
כַּכָּתוּב בְּתוֹרָתֶךָ:

service where the shofar is blown celebrates God's memory. On festivals, too, we pray that memory of us will ascend to God "for good" *[l'tovah]*—a reflection of what is prayed for here. But what does it mean to say that God remembers? How can a God who is supposed to know everything "forget"? And if God cannot forget, how can God "remember"?

It is not that God forgets and then has to be reminded. Only humans have the sense that things happen in time, which passes before our consciousness like a videotape, so that we may not remember the part that is now long past. God, by contrast, knows everything all at once. Memory, for God, has the sense of mindfulness with the intent of visiting something upon us—hence the verb in apposition to "remember [us]": "visit us." These are two sides of the same coin. God remembers us in that God's attention is drawn to us, and as a result, we are visited for good (i.e. "with fondness") or for evil. In English, we have the negative sense of a such a visit when we speak of a visitation. In Hebrew, it usually means just the opposite: a positive visit of divine mercy, as when (Gen. 21) "God visited Sarah," meaning that God's attention was drawn to Sarah such that God granted her request to bear Isaac.

"With fondness" implies that the memory God has of us will result in our "good." But the word "good," is used technically to mean "ultimate good," namely, salvation. The prayer is composed poetically: "Remember us with fondness" and "Visit us with salvation" are parallel petitions that amount to the same thing—God's being sufficiently mindful of us to save us.

Salvation has many different meanings in Jewish thought. Unlike Christianity, where it connotes being individually saved from our sins, in Judaism, it generally has a corporate meaning: having a messiah come to save us all, or seeing the dawn of "the world-to-come." The Talmud *(p. 155)*

3 And after these things God tested Abraham. 4 He said to him, "Abraham," and Abraham answered, "Yes?" 5 And God said, "Take your son, your only one, whom you love, Isaac, and go to the land of Moriah, and offer him there as a sacrifice on one of the mountains that I mention." 6 So Abraham got up early in the morning, and saddled his donkey, and took his two boys with him and also Isaac, his son. 7 He split wood for the sacrifice and got up and went to the place that God had told him. 8 On the third day, Abraham lifted his eyes and saw the place from afar. 9 Abraham said to his boys, "You stay here with the donkey, while the boy and I go up there, and after we worship we will return to you." 10 Abraham took the wood for the sacrifice and put it on Isaac, his son, and he took the fire and the knife in his own hand. 11 And the two of them went off together. 12 Isaac said to Abraham, his father, "Dad," and Abraham answered, "Yes, my son?" And Isaac said, "Here is the fire and the wood, but where is the lamb to sacrifice?" 13 Abraham said, "God will see to the lamb to sacrifice, my son." 14 And the two of them went off together. 15 And they came to the place that God had told him, and Abraham built the altar there, arranged the wood, and bound Isaac, his son, and put him on the altar on the wood. 16 And Abraham extended his hand to take the knife

³וַיְהִי אַחַר הַדְּבָרִים הָאֵלֶּה, וְהָאֱלֹהִים נִסָּה אֶת אַבְרָהָם, ⁴וַיֹּאמֶר אֵלָיו: אַבְרָהָם, וַיֹּאמֶר הִנֵּנִי. ⁵וַיֹּאמֶר: קַח נָא אֶת בִּנְךָ, אֶת יְחִידְךָ, אֲשֶׁר אָהַבְתָּ, אֶת יִצְחָק, וְלֶךְ לְךָ אֶל אֶרֶץ הַמֹּרִיָּה, וְהַעֲלֵהוּ שָׁם לְעֹלָה עַל אַחַד הֶהָרִים אֲשֶׁר אֹמַר אֵלֶיךָ. ⁶וַיַּשְׁכֵּם אַבְרָהָם בַּבֹּקֶר, וַיַּחֲבֹשׁ אֶת חֲמֹרוֹ, וַיִּקַּח אֶת שְׁנֵי נְעָרָיו אִתּוֹ וְאֵת יִצְחָק בְּנוֹ; ⁷וַיְבַקַּע עֲצֵי עֹלָה, וַיָּקָם וַיֵּלֶךְ אֶל הַמָּקוֹם אֲשֶׁר אָמַר לוֹ הָאֱלֹהִים. ⁸בַּיּוֹם הַשְּׁלִישִׁי, וַיִּשָּׂא אַבְרָהָם אֶת עֵינָיו וַיַּרְא אֶת הַמָּקוֹם מֵרָחֹק. ⁹וַיֹּאמֶר אַבְרָהָם אֶל נְעָרָיו: שְׁבוּ לָכֶם פֹּה עִם הַחֲמוֹר, וַאֲנִי וְהַנַּעַר נֵלְכָה עַד כֹּה, וְנִשְׁתַּחֲוֶה וְנָשׁוּבָה אֲלֵיכֶם. ¹⁰וַיִּקַּח אַבְרָהָם אֶת עֲצֵי הָעֹלָה וַיָּשֶׂם עַל יִצְחָק בְּנוֹ, וַיִּקַּח בְּיָדוֹ אֶת הָאֵשׁ וְאֶת הַמַּאֲכֶלֶת, ¹¹וַיֵּלְכוּ שְׁנֵיהֶם יַחְדָּו. ¹²וַיֹּאמֶר יִצְחָק אֶל אַבְרָהָם אָבִיו, וַיֹּאמֶר: אָבִי, וַיֹּאמֶר הִנֶּנִּי בְנִי; וַיֹּאמֶר: הִנֵּה הָאֵשׁ וְהָעֵצִים, וְאַיֵּה הַשֶּׂה לְעֹלָה. ¹³וַיֹּאמֶר אַבְרָהָם: אֱלֹהִים יִרְאֶה לּוֹ הַשֶּׂה לְעֹלָה, בְּנִי; ¹⁴וַיֵּלְכוּ שְׁנֵיהֶם יַחְדָּו. ¹⁵וַיָּבֹאוּ אֶל הַמָּקוֹם אֲשֶׁר אָמַר לוֹ הָאֱלֹהִים, וַיִּבֶן שָׁם אַבְרָהָם אֶת הַמִּזְבֵּחַ, וַיַּעֲרֹךְ אֶת הָעֵצִים, וַיַּעֲקֹד אֶת יִצְחָק בְּנוֹ, וַיָּשֶׂם אֹתוֹ עַל הַמִּזְבֵּחַ מִמַּעַל לָעֵצִים. ¹⁶וַיִּשְׁלַח אַבְרָהָם אֶת יָדוֹ וַיִּקַּח אֶת

and slaughter his son. [17]But Adonai's angel called to him from heaven, "Abraham! Abraham!" [18]Abraham answered, "Yes?" [19]And the angel said, "Do not put your hand forward toward the boy and do not do anything to him, for now I know that you revere God, for you did not withhold your son, your only one, from Me." [20]As Abraham lifted his eyes he saw a ram, behind, caught in the thicket by its horns; so Abraham went and got the ram and offered it up as a sacrifice instead of his son. [21]Abraham called that place "God will see," which nowadays would be "On the mountain of God will be seen." [22]One of Adonai's angels called to Abraham a second time from heaven: [23]"'By Myself have I sworn,' said Adonai, 'that because you did this thing, and you did not withhold your son, your only one, I will bless you greatly, and make your descendants as numerous as the stars in the sky and as the sand upon the seashore. [24]Your descendants shall possess their enemies' cities. [25]And through your descendants all the peoples of the earth shall be blessed, because you listened to My voice.'" [26]Abraham returned to his boys. [27]They got up and went off together to Be'er Sheva, and Abraham lived in Be'er Sheva.

[28]Master of the world, may it be Your will, Adonai, our God and our ancestors' God, that You remember in

הַמַּאֲכֶלֶת לִשְׁחֹט אֶת בְּנוֹ. [17]וַיִּקְרָא אֵלָיו מַלְאַךְ יְיָ מִן הַשָּׁמַיִם, וַיֹּאמֶר: אַבְרָהָם, אַבְרָהָם, [18]וַיֹּאמֶר הִנֵּנִי. [19]וַיֹּאמֶר: אַל תִּשְׁלַח יָדְךָ אֶל הַנַּעַר וְאַל תַּעַשׂ לוֹ מְאוּמָה, כִּי עַתָּה יָדַעְתִּי כִּי יְרֵא אֱלֹהִים אַתָּה, וְלֹא חָשַׂכְתָּ אֶת בִּנְךָ אֶת יְחִידְךָ מִמֶּנִּי. [20]וַיִּשָּׂא אַבְרָהָם אֶת עֵינָיו וַיַּרְא וְהִנֵּה אַיִל, אַחַר, נֶאֱחַז בַּסְּבַךְ בְּקַרְנָיו; וַיֵּלֶךְ אַבְרָהָם וַיִּקַּח אֶת הָאַיִל, וַיַּעֲלֵהוּ לְעֹלָה תַּחַת בְּנוֹ. [21]וַיִּקְרָא אַבְרָהָם שֵׁם הַמָּקוֹם הַהוּא: יְיָ יִרְאֶה, אֲשֶׁר יֵאָמֵר הַיּוֹם: בְּהַר יְיָ יֵרָאֶה. [22]וַיִּקְרָא מַלְאַךְ יְיָ אֶל אַבְרָהָם שֵׁנִית מִן הַשָּׁמַיִם. וַיֹּאמֶר: [23]בִּי נִשְׁבַּעְתִּי, נְאֻם יְיָ, כִּי יַעַן אֲשֶׁר עָשִׂיתָ אֶת הַדָּבָר הַזֶּה, וְלֹא חָשַׂכְתָּ אֶת בִּנְךָ, אֶת יְחִידֶךָ. כִּי בָרֵךְ אֲבָרֶכְךָ, וְהַרְבָּה אַרְבֶּה אֶת זַרְעֲךָ כְּכוֹכְבֵי הַשָּׁמַיִם, וְכַחוֹל אֲשֶׁר עַל שְׂפַת הַיָּם, [24]וְיִרַשׁ זַרְעֲךָ אֵת שַׁעַר אֹיְבָיו. [25]וְהִתְבָּרְכוּ בְזַרְעֲךָ כֹּל גּוֹיֵי הָאָרֶץ, עֵקֶב אֲשֶׁר שָׁמַעְתָּ בְּקֹלִי. [26]וַיָּשָׁב אַבְרָהָם אֶל נְעָרָיו, [27]וַיָּקֻמוּ וַיֵּלְכוּ יַחְדָּו אֶל בְּאֵר שָׁבַע; וַיֵּשֶׁב אַבְרָהָם בִּבְאֵר שָׁבַע. [28]רִבּוֹנוֹ שֶׁל עוֹלָם, יְהִי רָצוֹן מִלְּפָנֶיךָ, יְיָ אֱלֹהֵינוּ וֵאלֹהֵי אֲבוֹתֵינוּ, שֶׁתִּזְכָּר־לָנוּ בְּרִית אֲבוֹתֵינוּ. [29]כְּמוֹ שֶׁכָּבַשׁ אַבְרָהָם אָבִינוּ אֶת רַחֲמָיו מִבֶּן־יְחִידוֹ, וְרָצָה לִשְׁחֹט אוֹתוֹ כְּדֵי לַעֲשׂוֹת רְצוֹנֶךָ, כֵּן

our favor the covenant with our ancestors. [29]Just as our ancestor Abraham overpowered his mercy toward his only son, willing to slay him in order to do Your will, so may Your mercy overpower Your anger toward us, and may Your mercy prevail over Your retribution. [30]Adonai our God, be lenient with us and deal with us kindly and mercifully. [31]In Your great goodness, may Your anger turn away from Your people, Your city, Your land, and Your heritage. [32]Adonai our God, fulfill what You promised us through Moses, Your servant: [33] "I will remember My covenant with Jacob, and My covenant with Isaac, and My covenant with Abraham; and I will remember the land."

יִכְבְּשׁוּ רַחֲמֶיךָ אֶת כַּעַסְךָ מֵעָלֵינוּ, וְיִגֹּלּוּ רַחֲמֶיךָ עַל מִדּוֹתֶיךָ, וְתִכָּנֵס אִתָּנוּ לִפְנִים מִשּׁוּרַת דִּינֶךָ, [30]וְתִתְנַהֵג עִמָּנוּ, יְיָ אֱלֹהֵינוּ, בְּמִדַּת הַחֶסֶד וּבְמִדַּת הָרַחֲמִים. [31]וּבְטוּבְךָ הַגָּדוֹל, יָשׁוּב חֲרוֹן אַפְּךָ מֵעַמְּךָ וּמֵעִירְךָ וּמֵאַרְצְךָ וּמִנַּחֲלָתֶךָ. [32]וְקַיֶּם־לָנוּ, יְיָ אֱלֹהֵינוּ, אֶת הַדָּבָר שֶׁהִבְטַחְתָּנוּ עַל יְדֵי מֹשֶׁה עַבְדֶּךָ, כָּאָמוּר: [33]וְזָכַרְתִּי אֶת בְּרִיתִי יַעֲקוֹב, וְאַף אֶת בְּרִיתִי יִצְחָק, וְאַף אֶת בְּרִיתִי אַבְרָהָם אֶזְכֹּר, וְהָאָרֶץ אֶזְכֹּר.

BRETTLER (BIBLE)

benefit of good deeds in general may last for "one thousand" generations (see Exod. 20:6; Deut. 5:10; Exod. 34:7; and Jer. 32:18) and the conclusion of the *Akedah* suggests future blessing as a result of Abraham's actions (Gen. 22:16–18).

[2]*"Remember the covenant"* According to Deuteronomy 7:12, if Israel heeds the covenant, God will maintain "the covenant benefits" as promised. Deuteronomy reverses Genesis 22:16–18, where God's original promise is unconditional, independent of Israel's behavior.

The *Akedah* ("The binding of Isaac").

This noun *Akedah,* from the verb *vaya'akod,* "he [Abraham] bound," is never found in the Bible, which in general downplays the binding of Isaac; no biblical text ever asks God to recall the *Akedah.*

The biblical account (Gen. 22) is pre-exilic. It is popularly, but incorrectly, understood as a polemic against child sacrifice. It nowhere suggests that such sacrifice should be generally banned. In fact, later biblical texts view child sacrifice as an extreme but effective measure to call upon God to perform a desired action (2 Kings 3:27). Genesis simply states that because Abraham showed his willingness to carry out this most difficult request, he will be blessed by many descendants who will control the Land of Israel, and others shall bless themselves by him (Gen. 22:16–18). Thus, the *Akedah* functions to explain why Israel is worthy of blessing.

[3] *"After these things"* Rabbinic commentary speculates what "these things" are, but biblical idiom probably used the phrase as a paragraph marker to indicate the opening of a new unit.

[4] *"Yes?"* Biblical Hebrew has no word for "yes." *Hineni* approaches this meaning, with the sense of "I'm listening."

[5] *"Your son, your only one, whom you love, Isaac"* Piling on epithets for Isaac increases the pain of the narration. Isaac is Abraham's "only" son after the banishment of Ishmael in the previous chapter.

[5] *"Go [lekh l'kha]"* A reminder of Genesis 12:1, where Abraham's story begins with the command *lekh l'kha*, "Go," and thus a clever stylistic bracket for the main section of the Abraham narratives. These units share other elements too, including the fact that the place to which Abraham is sent is not noted in advance.

[5] *"Moriah"* Mentioned only here and in 2 Chronicles 3:1, where it is identified with the Temple site.

[6] *"Abraham got up early"* The command to "go" may have been a dream revelation.

[6] *"Also Isaac his son"* The literary device of positioning Isaac only after everything else that Abraham took reflects Abraham's ambivalence. He takes Isaac last.

[7] *"He split wood"* Literally, "to cleave," a violent word reflecting the chapter's violence overall.

[8] *"On the third day"* The day that the climax is expected, as in Exodus 19:16, where revelation transpires "on the third day" also.

[10] *"The knife [ma'achelet]"* A word denoting a knife large enough to dismember a body (Judg. 19:29)—again expressing the chapter's overall violence.

[12] *"Dad…my son"* Used redundantly here to heighten the anguish.

[14] *"The two of them went off together"* Recited twice. By the second time (here), Isaac should know that he is the likely sacrifice. Reusing the phrase reflects his willing participation.

[15] *"They came"* The succession of verbs and their objects in this and the next verse conveys a picture of Abraham almost sleepwalking through his actions.

[16] *"Slaughter"* A very strong word, typical of cattle, depicting Isaac as a sacrificial victim.

¹⁷ *"Abraham! Abraham!"* The name is doubled to command attention (as in Exod. 3:4 and 1 Sam. 3:10) from Abraham who is intent on completing what he has begun.

²⁰ *"A ram [ayil acher]"* This is grammatically impossible in Hebrew. Following the Septuagint (the ancient Greek Bible translation), the Samaritan Pentateuch, some Targumim (ancient Jewish Aramaic translations), and other evidence, the word *acher* should be emended to *echad,* meaning "one." The final letters of the two words *dalet* and *resh* are easily confused.

²⁶ *"Abraham returned"* The text suggests that Isaac does not return with his father; throughout the rest of Genesis, they never interact again.

³¹ *"In Your great goodness"* From Nehemiah 9:25.

³³ *"I will remember My covenant"* Leviticus 26 features "the great rebuke"—a lengthy description of the destruction and exile awaiting Israel if they reject God's commandments. But it ends (Lev. 26:42) as here, with the assurance that even then, God will regather Israel because God will remember the covenant.

◆

DORFF (THEOLOGY)

ancestors' sins. According to the Decalogue, we do, although later biblical sources (Jeremiah and Ezekiel) object to the idea and promise instead that we will suffer for our own sins alone (see Brettler, "Love of our ancestors," pp. 146, 150). Indeed, God commands that standard for our own human systems of justice (Deut. 24:16), far ahead of many other legal systems. In England, for example, "attaint" (by which descendants could be punished for their ancestors' treason) was abolished only about 1830. The U.S. Constitution (Article 3, Section 3) specifically had to ban such attaints. Unfortunately, in real life, children do prosper or suffer for what their parents have done. Thus the biblical doctrine, while morally problematic, is an accurate description of life as we know it.

◆

ELLENSON (MODERN LITURGIES)

of Protestant theologian Søren Kierkegaard). Instead, they have questioned the propriety of Abraham's willing suspension of the ethical imperative not to murder for the sake of showing faith in God. Liberal prayer books have therefore omitted this introductory paragraph, as well as the *Akedah* passage itself and the "Eternal Lord" prayer *(Adon Olam)* following it.

◆

FRANKEL (A WOMAN'S VOICE)

the benefit of the living and the dead. One such prayer, written by the eighteenth century Yiddish liturgist Sarah bas Tovim and translated by Chava Weissler, a prominent scholar of this special genre of personal petition, refers to Sarah's role in the *Akedah*, the binding of Isaac. Significantly, Abraham's wife, Sarah, does not appear in the passage from Genesis cited here in the liturgy. Our poet adds it in her prayer: "By the merit of my laying the thread for our Mother Sarah, may God, blessed be He, remember for us the merit of her pain when her dear son Isaac was led away to be bound on the altar. May she be a [good] advocate for us before God; may we be blessed, that this year we not, God forbid, become widows, and that our little children may not, God forbid, be taken away from the world during our lives" (From Chava Weissler, *Voices of the Matriarchs* [Boston: Beacon Press, 1998], p. 140).

Indeed, as we now ask God to "remember us favorably," how appropriate to invoke the merits of Mother Sarah in our appeal, thus honoring her trial, along with that of her husband and son.

[28] *"The covenant with our ancestors"* Here, as in so many other places in the liturgy, we remind God of the biblical covenant with the patriarchs, God's eternal promise that we, their descendants, will inherit God's protective favor and ultimate redemption. Reprising the leitmotif of the previous several paragraphs—Abraham's demonstration of faith during the *Akedah*—we bring this section to a close by invoking the patriarchs' names one last time.

To these names we can add Mother Rachel, as in the following *t'khinah* written almost one hundred years ago by Rochel-Esther Bas Avi-chayil of Jerusalem and translated by Norman Tarnor: "Remember Your holy promise made to our faithful Mother Rachel. When the Jews were being led out of Jerusalem into exile…her weeping rent the heavens. The voice, as recorded in the Midrash, was that of a sheep among seventy wolves. And God replied [to her]: 'Moderate your weeping. There will come a time of Redemption when they will return joyfully from foreign lands to their own borders in the Land of Israel and will serve God in sanctity and purity…, Accept, therefore, the weeping of holy Rachel, together with our tears, so that we may merit to behold the [return of the children to their border] quickly and in our own day" (Norman Tarnor, *A Book of Jewish Women's Prayers* [Northvale, N.J.: Jason Aronson, 1995], pp. 116–117).

———◆———

J. HOFFMAN (TRANSLATION)

the next line, which also repeats the verb's root in the object. Our translation misses the parallelism.

[2] *"Ancestors"* This is not the usual Hebrew word for ancestors (*avot*). Rather, *kadmonim* is used here, with a connotation of "early" or "original" people.

2 *"Israel"* That is, Jacob.

3 *"After these things"* This phrase, coming as it does at the beginning of the story, is confusing and has yielded a lot of midrashic interpretation.

4 *"Abraham answered"* Literally, just "he answered." The Hebrew does not repeat the names. But this is a story-type text, and in our narrative style, names are repeated before quotations.

4 *"Yes?"* Others, "Here I am" or "I am here." Those translations seem too literal to us.

5 *"Take"* We leave untranslated the Hebrew word *na,* often translated "please," which serves to add a certain poetic, formal, or urgent tone to the text, similar to Shakespeare's "pray...."

5 *"Moriah"* The name "Moriah" looks like it might have come from the root for "to show," which is a theme running throughout this story.

5 *"Sacrifice"* Birnbaum, "burnt offering." There are two kinds of sacrifices in the Torah, one that is totally consumed (a "burnt offering") and one that is not. This is the former. But because "burnt offering" is not a common phrase in English, we prefer "sacrifice."

6 *"Boys"* Others, "servants." They probably were servants, but the text plays with the term "boy" or "youth," using it below for the servants and for Isaac also.

6 *"Also"* The connotations from "also" come from the word order in Hebrew.

9 *"After we worship"* Or, "so that we can worship and return to you."

12 *"Yes, my son?"* Abraham uses the same word when his son calls his name that he did when God called his name.

15 *"On the wood"* Or, "over the wood"

17 *"Heaven"* Others, "the heavens," which is not English. Either "heaven" or "the sky."

20 *"Behind"* Behind what is not clear. Almost certainly this is a "typo" in the Torah, which should read "one *[echad]* ram," as opposed to our reading, *acher.* The word, being unpointed, would be the same except for the final consonant, a *resh* rather than a *dalet.* Midrash suggests that it can be read "another ram."

21 *"Would be"* The text illustrates two periods in the development of Hebrew. In the first, *yireh* ("will see") was properly grammatical; in the second, *yeira'eh* ("will be seen") had become properly grammatical. A similar example in English would be, "methinks," which nowadays would be "I think."

Attempting to reconcile both Hebrew dialects, *JPS* offers: "Abraham named that site Adonai-yireh, whence the present saying, 'On the mount of the Lord there is vision.'" But that is not so much a reconciliation as it is a renaming of the two options without differentiating the reason why they both exist.

[24] *"Cities"* Literally, "gates," but used metonymically (i.e., mentioning the part as symbolic of the whole).

[26] *"Boys"* The text does not indicate if Isaac is among "his boys." Tradition holds that Isaac is not.

[27] *"And Abraham lived"* Or, perhaps, "Because Abraham lived...."

[29] *"So may Your"* An ironic use of "so."

[29] *"Prevail"* Literally, "roll over."

[30] *"Be lenient with us"* A technical term in Hebrew. Literally, "from the absolute law," in which "from" means "less than," in the way that something taken from a whole is less than the whole.

[30] *"Kindly and mercifully"* Literally, "according to the *midah* of kindness and the *midah* of mercy," where a *midah* is one of the ways God can treat us. Another way is the *midah* of the law. If God were to treat us that way, the idea is, we would be doomed.

[31] *"May Your anger"* The Hebrew, a fairly common idiom, literally means "the burning wrath of Your nose." Birnbaum's "fierce wrath" is poetic but too strong.

[33] *"My covenant with Jacob"* Curiously, this line (from Lev. 26:42), lacks the word "with" in all three cases, so literally reads "my covenant Jacob," "my covenant Isaac," etc.

◆——————

L. HOFFMAN (HISTORY)

debates the nature of "the world-to-come," one third-century Sage (Samuel) saying it will be just like the world of today but without oppression, and the other (Samuel's classic opponent, Rav) characterizing it as a purely spiritual existence without the need to eat, drink, or otherwise care for our bodies. Judaism never codified either view, both of which remain valid options.

There is, of course, a personal side to this communal promise: the reward to the righteous that permits them to inherit their share in such a post-historical world of the future. That is where the immortality of the soul and the resurrection of the body come in. As we saw above (see "Who restores souls to dead corpses," p. 139), the Rabbis assumed that when we die, our bodies decay ("dust to dust") but will be resurrected and reunited with their animating souls. Here is where Judaism and Christianity overlap in belief. Also, as in Christianity, inheriting resurrection and a share in the ultimate world of the future depends on our merit.

But classical Christianity denied the possibility that human beings can ever be good enough to merit salvation. People are saved from their sins, therefore, not by their own good deeds but by faith in Christ, who, says the Christian, "died for our sins." Judaism never gave such weight to faith; rather, human action in the world through the *mitzvot* is primary.

But Judaism too questioned whether any of us can really be good enough on our own to warrant being saved. It therefore adopted the notion that we can draw upon the merit of our ancestors, whose good deeds are saved up in what amounts to a merit bank account, the "interest" of which is available for our use. Abraham and Isaac, especially, are cited as having been so righteous that we can draw upon their extra merit, because the two of them, jointly (as the Rabbis saw it), were prepared to perform the ultimate sacrifice: Isaac was ready to die, and Abraham, his father, prepared to slaughter him.

This request that God visit us with salvation therefore introduces the classic account of the binding of Isaac (the *Akedah*). That account will conclude with a reiteration of the plea that God remember us.

◆ ◆ ◆

5 | *The Sh'ma*

¹You should always fear God inwardly and outwardly, and gratefully acknowledge the truth, and speak truth in your hearts, and rise up early to say:

²Master of all worlds, we do not offer our supplications before You based on our righteousness, but rather based on Your great mercy. ³What are we? ⁴What are our lives? ⁵What is our love? ⁶What is our righteousness? ⁷What is our salvation? ⁸What is our strength? ⁹What is our might? ¹⁰What can we say before You, Adonai our God and our ancestors' God? ¹¹Are not all mighty ones as though they were nothing before You, men of fame as though they never existed, the educated as though without knowledge, and the wise as though without insight, for most of their acts are without value and the days of their life worthless before You! ¹²Man barely rises above beast, for everything is worthless.

¹³But we are Your people, the children of Your covenant, the children of Abraham, Your love, to whom You took an oath on Mount Moriah; the descendants of Isaac, his only son, who was bound on the altar; the community of Jacob, Your first-born, whom You called Israel and Jeshurun on account of Your love for him and joy with him. ¹⁴Therefore we must gratefully acknowledge, praise, and glorify You, and bless,

¹לְעוֹלָם יְהֵא אָדָם יְרֵא שָׁמַיִם בַּסֵּתֶר וּבַגָּלוּי, וּמוֹדֶה עַל הָאֱמֶת, וְדוֹבֵר אֱמֶת בִּלְבָבוֹ, וְיַשְׁכֵּם וְיֹאמַר:

²רִבּוֹן כָּל הָעוֹלָמִים, לֹא עַל צִדְקוֹתֵינוּ אֲנַחְנוּ מַפִּילִים תַּחֲנוּנֵינוּ לְפָנֶיךָ, כִּי עַל רַחֲמֶיךָ הָרַבִּים. ³מָה אֲנַחְנוּ, ⁴מֶה חַיֵּינוּ, ⁵מֶה חַסְדֵּנוּ, ⁶מַה צִּדְקֵנוּ, ⁷מַה יְשׁוּעָתֵנוּ, ⁸מַה כֹּחֵנוּ, ⁹מַה גְּבוּרָתֵנוּ. ¹⁰מַה נֹּאמַר לְפָנֶיךָ, יְיָ אֱלֹהֵינוּ וֵאלֹהֵי אֲבוֹתֵינוּ, ¹¹הֲלֹא כָּל הַגִּבּוֹרִים כְּאַיִן לְפָנֶיךָ, וְאַנְשֵׁי הַשֵּׁם כְּלֹא הָיוּ, וַחֲכָמִים כִּבְלִי מַדָּע, וּנְבוֹנִים כִּבְלִי הַשְׂכֵּל, כִּי רֹב מַעֲשֵׂיהֶם תֹּהוּ, וִימֵי חַיֵּיהֶם הֶבֶל לְפָנֶיךָ; ¹²וּמוֹתַר הָאָדָם מִן הַבְּהֵמָה אָיִן, כִּי הַכֹּל הָבֶל.

¹³אֲבָל אֲנַחְנוּ עַמְּךָ בְּנֵי בְרִיתֶךָ, בְּנֵי אַבְרָהָם אֹהַבְךָ שֶׁנִּשְׁבַּעְתָּ לּוֹ בְּהַר הַמּוֹרִיָּה, זֶרַע יִצְחָק יְחִידוֹ שֶׁנֶּעֱקַד עַל גַּב הַמִּזְבֵּחַ, עֲדַת יַעֲקֹב בִּנְךָ בְּכוֹרֶךָ, שֶׁמֵאַהֲבָתְךָ שֶׁאָהַבְתָּ אוֹתוֹ, וּמִשִּׂמְחָתְךָ שֶׁשָּׂמַחְתָּ בּוֹ, קָרָאתָ אֶת שְׁמוֹ יִשְׂרָאֵל וִישֻׁרוּן.

sanctify, and render honor and grateful acknowledgment to Your name. [15]We are happy! [16]How wonderful is our lot, how great our destiny, and how beautiful our heritage. [17]We are happy, we who, early and late, by night and morning, twice a day, say:

[18]Hear O Israel: Adonai is our God; Adonai is One.

[19]Blessed is the One the glory of whose kingdom is renowned forever.

[20]You are You, before the world was created, after the world was created, in this world, and in the world-to-come. [21]Sanctify Your name through those who sanctify Your name. [22]Sanctify Your name throughout Your world. [23]Through Your deliverance may we become mighty and proud. [24]Blessed are You, Adonai, who sanctifies Your name among the multitudes.

[25]Adonai our God, You are in heaven and on earth and in the highest heavens above. [26]Truly, You are first and You are last, and other than You there are no gods. [27]Gather those who yearn for You from the four corners of the earth. [28]All who walk the earth will recognize and know that only You are God over all the kingdoms of the earth. [29]You made heaven and earth, the sea, and everything in them. [30]Who among all the works of Your hands, among the heavenly or earthly creatures, can tell You what to do!

[14]לְפִיכָךְ אֲנַחְנוּ חַיָּבִים לְהוֹדוֹת לְךָ וּלְשַׁבֵּחֲךָ וּלְפָאֶרְךָ, וּלְבָרֵךְ וּלְקַדֵּשׁ וְלָתֵת שֶׁבַח וְהוֹדָיָה לִשְׁמֶךָ. [15]אַשְׁרֵינוּ, [16]מַה טּוֹב חֶלְקֵנוּ וּמַה נָּעִים גּוֹרָלֵנוּ וּמַה יָּפָה יְרֻשָּׁתֵנוּ. [17]אַשְׁרֵינוּ, שֶׁאֲנַחְנוּ מַשְׁכִּימִים וּמַעֲרִיבִים, עֶרֶב וָבֹקֶר, וְאוֹמְרִים פַּעֲמַיִם בְּכָל יוֹם:

[18]שְׁמַע יִשְׂרָאֵל, יְיָ אֱלֹהֵינוּ, יְיָ אֶחָד. [19]בָּרוּךְ שֵׁם כְּבוֹד מַלְכוּתוֹ לְעוֹלָם וָעֶד.

[20]אַתָּה הוּא עַד שֶׁלֹּא נִבְרָא הָעוֹלָם, אַתָּה הוּא מִשֶּׁנִּבְרָא הָעוֹלָם, אַתָּה הוּא בָּעוֹלָם הַזֶּה וְאַתָּה הוּא לָעוֹלָם הַבָּא. [21]קַדֵּשׁ אֶת שִׁמְךָ עַל מַקְדִּישֵׁי שְׁמֶךָ, [22]וְקַדֵּשׁ אֶת שִׁמְךָ בְּעוֹלָמֶךָ, [23]וּבִישׁוּעָתְךָ תָּרוּם וְתִגְבַּהּ קַרְנֵנוּ. [24]בָּרוּךְ אַתָּה, יְיָ, מְקַדֵּשׁ אֶת שִׁמְךָ בָּרַבִּים.

[25]אַתָּה הוּא, יְיָ אֱלֹהֵינוּ, בַּשָּׁמַיִם וּבָאָרֶץ וּבִשְׁמֵי הַשָּׁמַיִם הָעֶלְיוֹנִים. [26]אֱמֶת, אַתָּה הוּא רִאשׁוֹן וְאַתָּה הוּא אַחֲרוֹן, וּמִבַּלְעָדֶיךָ אֵין אֱלֹהִים. [27]קַבֵּץ קֹוֶיךָ מֵאַרְבַּע כַּנְפוֹת הָאָרֶץ; [28]יַכִּירוּ וְיֵדְעוּ כָּל בָּאֵי עוֹלָם כִּי אַתָּה הוּא הָאֱלֹהִים לְבַדְּךָ לְכָל מַמְלְכוֹת הָאָרֶץ. [29]אַתָּה עָשִׂיתָ אֶת הַשָּׁמַיִם וְאֶת הָאָרֶץ, אֶת הַיָּם, וְאֶת כָּל אֲשֶׁר בָּם, [30]וּמִי בְּכָל מַעֲשֵׂה יָדֶיךָ, בָּעֶלְיוֹנִים אוֹ בַתַּחְתּוֹנִים, שֶׁיֹּאמַר לְךָ מַה תַּעֲשֶׂה. [31]אָבִינוּ

³¹Our father in heaven, deal kindly with us for the sake of Your great name by which we are called, and, Adonai our God, bring about that which is written: ³²At that time I will bring you in; at the time that I gather you I will make you famous and glorious among all the nations of the earth, when I return your returnees before your very eyes. ³³So says Adonai.

שֶׁבַּשָּׁמַיִם, עֲשֵׂה עִמָּנוּ חֶסֶד בַּעֲבוּר שִׁמְךָ הַגָּדוֹל שֶׁנִּקְרָא עָלֵינוּ, וְקַיֶּם־לָנוּ, יְיָ אֱלֹהֵינוּ, מַה שֶּׁכָּתוּב: ³²בָּעֵת הַהִיא אָבִיא אֶתְכֶם, וּבָעֵת קַבְּצִי אֶתְכֶם, כִּי אֶתֵּן אֶתְכֶם לְשֵׁם וְלִתְהִלָּה בְּכל עַמֵּי הָאָרֶץ, בְּשׁוּבִי אֶת שְׁבוּתֵיכֶם לְעֵינֵיכֶם, ³³אָמַר יְיָ.

159

BRETTLER (BIBLE)

[1] *"Inwardly"* The *Akedah* assumes that God does not know our innermost thoughts—otherwise, why test Abraham? Jeremiah 20:12, however, states that God "examines the heart and mind," as here.

[1] *"Acknowledge the truth"* In the four times this idiom is used in the Bible, it means to acknowledge God's reliability (Pss. 30:10; 71:22; 138:2; Isa. 38:19).

[1] *"And speak truth in your hearts"* From Psalm 15:2, a description of those who reside in the Temple.

[2] *"Based on our righteousness…based on Your great mercy"* From Daniel 9:18. Psalms too contain confessions of guilt and *(p. 164)*

DORFF (THEOLOGY)

[3-4] *"What are we? What are our lives?"* The stark reality of this prayer reminds us of *Un'taneh Tokef,* a prayer from the High Holy Days, in which we face the fact that who shall live and who shall die is in God's hands; and also of Ecclesiastes, for whom life is without purpose or value, for *(p. 165)*

ELLENSON (MODERN LITURGIES)

[1] *"You should always fear God"* Abraham Geiger included this in his 1854 prayer book, but not in the more radical 1870 edition. More modern editors have restored it, though all Reconstructionist services still omit it. The words themselves were not considered *(p. 165)*

FRANKEL (A WOMAN'S VOICE)

[1] *"Speak truth in your hearts"* Because the world seems to conspire against unconditional caring, most children (at some point) doubt that their parents truly love them, no matter what. To reclaim that potentially absent love, they may resort to desperate tactics: blackmail, threats, displays of helplessness, aloofness, and self-injury. Even when we come to recognize as adults that we can take care of ourselves, we still long for that unconditional love that inevitably eluded us at *(p. 166)*

[1] You should always fear God inwardly and outwardly, and gratefully acknowledge the truth, and speak truth in your hearts, and rise up early to say:

[2] Master of all worlds, we do not offer our supplications before You based on our righteousness, but rather based on Your great mercy. [3] What are we? [4] What are our lives? [5] What is our love? [6] What is our righteousness? [7] What is our salvation? [8] What is our strength? [9] What is our might? [10] What can we say

J. HOFFMAN (TRANSLATION)

[1] *"You"* Literally, "man."

[1] *"Fear God"* Literally, "fear heaven."

[1] *"Inwardly and outwardly"* Others, "in private and in public," probably based on the erroneous assumption that this passage refers to persecution and the inability of Jews during certain time periods to pray publicly.

[2] *"Supplications"* Hebrew, *tachanunim,* a technical term for a genre of *(p. 167)*

L. Hoffman (History)

The Sh'ma *that occurs in the Morning Blessings, as opposed to the official one that follows the Call to Prayer (the* Bar'khu*), known as the* Sh'ma *and Its Blessings.*

[1] *"Fear God inwardly and outwardly"* In a way, this paragraph is part of our prayers by mistake! It introduces the *Sh'ma* that is included in the Morning Blessings. The official recitation of the *Sh'ma* comes later, after the Call to Prayer (the *Bar'khu*). Why, then, does it

¹לְעוֹלָם יְהֵא אָדָם יְרֵא שָׁמַיִם בַּסֵּתֶר וּבַגָּלוּי, וּמוֹדֶה עַל הָאֱמֶת, וְדוֹבֵר אֱמֶת בִּלְבָבוֹ, וְיַשְׁכֵּם וְיֹאמַר:

²רִבּוֹן כָּל הָעוֹלָמִים, לֹא עַל צִדְקוֹתֵינוּ אֲנַחְנוּ מַפִּילִים תַּחֲנוּנֵינוּ לְפָנֶיךָ, כִּי עַל רַחֲמֶיךָ הָרַבִּים. ³מָה אֲנַחְנוּ, ⁴מֶה חַיֵּינוּ, ⁵מֶה חַסְדֵּנוּ, ⁶מַה צִּדְקֵנוּ, ⁷מַה יְשׁוּעָתֵנוּ, ⁸מַה כֹּחֵנוּ, ⁹מַה גְּבוּרָתֵנוּ. ¹⁰מַה נֹּאמַר לְפָנֶיךָ, יְיָ אֱלֹהֵינוּ וֵאלֹהֵי אֲבוֹתֵינוּ, ¹¹הֲלֹא כָּל הַגִּבּוֹרִים כְּאַיִן

appear here as well? The two lines of this paragraph were apparently provided as an answer to that question, namely, "Fear God inwardly"—that is, during this private rubric, the Morning Blessings that were originally said privately at home as part of a spiritual regimen of greeting the new day.

The words "and outwardly" were added later, because without them, one might falsely conclude that one should fear God *only* in private.

In any event, the paragraph is akin to modern-day prayerbook instructions on how to pray, not prayer. Early printers with only a single font printed the line so it looked like the prayer following, and it became common to pray the instructions—not altogether unlike contemporary Jews praying the words, "Congregation is seated."

[1] *"Speak truth in your hearts"* Tradition draws moral implications from this. What we say as truth in our heart should correspond to what we represent as truth to others. The example given is a talmudic tale of Rav Safra, who is offered money for one of his possessions. He agrees within his heart, but says nothing out loud at the time because he does not want to interrupt the prayer in which he happens to be engaged. Hearing no response, the would-be purchaser mistakenly concludes that his offer is too low, and he ups the offer. After ending his prayer, Rav Safra sells the item to the purchaser for the original offer, since in his heart, he had decided the first price was fair.

Judaism has a unique ethical category of *g'neivat da'at,* loosely translated as "deceit," but literally meaning "stealing the mind." This is an instance of *g'neivat da'at,* since allowing people to think that an item requires a higher bid when in fact it doesn't would be to deceive would-be buyers by, as it were, stealing their mind and implanting false information about the pending purchase.

before You, Adonai our God and our ancestors' God? ¹¹Are not all mighty ones as though they were nothing before You, men of fame as though they never existed, the educated as though without knowledge, and the wise as though without insight, for most of their acts are without value and the days of their life worthless before You! ¹²Man barely rises above beast, for everything is worthless.

¹³But we are Your people, the children of Your covenant, the children of Abraham, Your love, to whom You took an oath on Mount Moriah; the descendants of Isaac, his only son, who was bound on the altar; the community of Jacob, Your first-born, whom You called Israel and Jeshurun on account of Your love for him and joy with him. ¹⁴Therefore we must gratefully acknowledge, praise, and glorify You, and bless, sanctify, and render honor and grateful acknowledgment to Your name. ¹⁵We are happy! ¹⁶How wonderful is our lot, how great our destiny, and how beautiful our heritage. ¹⁷We are happy, we who, early and late, by night and morning, twice a day, say:

¹⁸Hear O Israel: Adonai is our God; Adonai is One.

¹⁹Blessed is the One the glory of whose kingdom is renowned forever.

²⁰You are You, before the world was created, after the world was created,

לְפָנֶיךָ, וְאַנְשֵׁי הַשֵּׁם כְּלֹא הָיוּ, וַחֲכָמִים כִּבְלִי מַדָּע, וּנְבוֹנִים כִּבְלִי הַשְׂכֵּל, כִּי רֹב מַעֲשֵׂיהֶם תְּהוּ, וִימֵי חַיֵּיהֶם הֶבֶל לְפָנֶיךָ; ¹²וּמוֹתַר הָאָדָם מִן הַבְּהֵמָה אָיִן, כִּי הַכֹּל הָבֶל.

¹³אֲבָל אֲנַחְנוּ עַמְּךָ בְּנֵי בְרִיתֶךָ, בְּנֵי אַבְרָהָם אֹהַבְךָ שֶׁנִּשְׁבַּעְתָּ לּוֹ בְּהַר הַמֹּרִיָּה, זֶרַע יִצְחָק יְחִידוֹ שֶׁנֶּעֱקַד עַל גַּב הַמִּזְבֵּחַ, עֲדַת יַעֲקֹב בִּנְךָ בְּכוֹרֶךָ, שֶׁמֵּאַהֲבָתְךָ שֶׁאָהַבְתָּ אוֹתוֹ, וּמִשִּׂמְחָתְךָ שֶׁשָּׂמַחְתָּ בּוֹ, קָרָאתָ אֶת שְׁמוֹ יִשְׂרָאֵל וִישֻׁרוּן.

¹⁴לְפִיכָךְ אֲנַחְנוּ חַיָּבִים לְהוֹדוֹת לְךָ וּלְשַׁבֵּחֲךָ וּלְפָאֶרְךָ, וּלְבָרֵךְ וּלְקַדֵּשׁ וְלָתֵת שֶׁבַח וְהוֹדָיָה לִשְׁמֶךָ. ¹⁵אַשְׁרֵינוּ, ¹⁶מַה טּוֹב חֶלְקֵנוּ וּמַה נָּעִים גּוֹרָלֵנוּ וּמַה יָּפָה יְרֻשָּׁתֵנוּ. ¹⁷אַשְׁרֵינוּ, שֶׁאֲנַחְנוּ מַשְׁכִּימִים וּמַעֲרִיבִים, עֶרֶב וָבֹקֶר, וְאוֹמְרִים פַּעֲמַיִם בְּכָל יוֹם:

¹⁸שְׁמַע יִשְׂרָאֵל, יְיָ אֱלֹהֵינוּ, יְיָ אֶחָד. ¹⁹בָּרוּךְ שֵׁם כְּבוֹד מַלְכוּתוֹ לְעוֹלָם וָעֶד.

²⁰אַתָּה הוּא עַד שֶׁלֹּא נִבְרָא הָעוֹלָם, אַתָּה הוּא מִשֶּׁנִּבְרָא הָעוֹלָם, אַתָּה הוּא בָּעוֹלָם הַזֶּה וְאַתָּה הוּא לָעוֹלָם הַבָּא. ²¹קַדֵּשׁ אֶת שִׁמְךָ עַל מַקְדִּישֵׁי שְׁמֶךָ, ²²וְקַדֵּשׁ אֶת שִׁמְךָ בְּעוֹלָמֶךָ, ²³וּבִישׁוּעָתְךָ תָּרוּם וְתַגְבִּהַּ קַרְנֵנוּ. ²⁴בָּרוּךְ אַתָּה, יְיָ, מְקַדֵּשׁ אֶת שִׁמְךָ בָּרַבִּים.

in this world, and in the world-to-come. [21]Sanctify Your name through those who sanctify Your name. [22]Sanctify Your name throughout Your world. [23]Through Your deliverance may we become mighty and proud. [24]Blessed are You, Adonai, who sanctifies Your name among the multitudes.

[25]Adonai our God, You are in heaven and on earth and in the highest heavens above. [26]Truly, You are first and You are last, and other than You there are no gods. [27]Gather those who yearn for You from the four corners of the earth. [28]All who walk the earth will recognize and know that only You are God over all the kingdoms of the earth. [29]You made heaven and earth, the sea, and everything in them. [30]Who among all the works of Your hands, among the heavenly or earthly creatures, can tell You what to do! [31]Our father in heaven, deal kindly with us for the sake of Your great name by which we are called, and, Adonai our God, bring about that which is written: [32]At that time I will bring you in; at the time that I gather you I will make you famous and glorious among all the nations of the earth, when I return your returnees before your very eyes. [33]So says Adonai.

אַתָּה הוּא, יְיָ אֱלֹהֵינוּ, בַּשָּׁמַיִם וּבָאָרֶץ [25]
וּבִשְׁמֵי הַשָּׁמַיִם הָעֶלְיוֹנִים. [26]אֱמֶת, אַתָּה
הוּא רִאשׁוֹן וְאַתָּה הוּא אַחֲרוֹן,
וּמִבַּלְעָדֶיךָ אֵין אֱלֹהִים. [27]קַבֵּץ קֹוֶיךָ
מֵאַרְבַּע כַּנְפוֹת הָאָרֶץ; [28]יַכִּירוּ וְיֵדְעוּ
כָּל בָּאֵי עוֹלָם כִּי אַתָּה הוּא
הָאֱלֹהִים לְבַדְּךָ לְכֹל מַמְלְכוֹת הָאָרֶץ.
[29]אַתָּה עָשִׂיתָ אֶת הַשָּׁמַיִם וְאֶת הָאָרֶץ,
אֶת הַיָּם, וְאֶת כָּל אֲשֶׁר בָּם, [30]וּמִי בְּכָל
מַעֲשֵׂה יָדֶיךָ, בָּעֶלְיוֹנִים אוֹ בַתַּחְתּוֹנִים,
שֶׁיֹּאמַר לְךָ מַה תַּעֲשֶׂה. [31]אָבִינוּ
שֶׁבַּשָּׁמַיִם, עֲשֵׂה עִמָּנוּ חֶסֶד בַּעֲבוּר
שִׁמְךָ הַגָּדוֹל שֶׁנִּקְרָא עָלֵינוּ, וְקַיֶּם־לָנוּ,
יְיָ אֱלֹהֵינוּ, מַה שֶּׁכָּתוּב: [32]בָּעֵת הַהִיא
אָבִיא אֶתְכֶם, וּבָעֵת קַבְּצִי אֶתְכֶם, כִּי
אֶתֵּן אֶתְכֶם לְשֵׁם וְלִתְהִלָּה בְּכֹל עַמֵּי
הָאָרֶץ, בְּשׁוּבִי אֶת שְׁבוּתֵיכֶם לְעֵינֵיכֶם,
[33]אָמַר יְיָ.

requests for compassion, but they also argue the reverse on occasion: the absence of serious sin and inequitable treatment by God. This "protest" tradition is de-emphasized in post-biblical times.

10 "*What can we say before You?*" A statement of our fundamental creatureliness, a view shared, for example, by Job 25, and very popular among the prayers discovered among the Dead Sea Scrolls. An alternative view is found in Psalm 8:6, where humanity is "a little less than divine."

12 "*Man barely rises above beast, for everything is worthless*" From the pessimistic Ecclesiastes 3:19.

13 "*But we are Your people*" In contrast to the previous paragraph, a recap of the previous theme of the *Akedah,* highlighting Israel's worthiness.

13 "*Whom You called Israel and Jeshurun*" Jacob is renamed "Israel" in Gen. 32:29, after his nocturnal struggle with the angel. Jeshurun is a rare, poetic name for Israel (Deut. 32:15; 33:5, 26; Isa. 44:2), but nowhere do we find God naming him that. Neither name is associated in the Bible with God's "love" or "delight" as suggested here.

14 "*We must gratefully acknowledge*" Though this list of praise verbs is not attested in the Bible, several psalms (e.g., 68:5; 105:2–5) use similar lists to suggest that God must be acknowledged. Piling up synonyms stresses the chasm between God and ourselves.

21 "*Sanctify Your name*" God's name is of particular interest to the Bible's priestly writers and is seen especially in Leviticus and Ezekiel. The pun here, with the threefold repetition of "holy," mirrors Leviticus 22:32: "Do not profane My holy name, that I may be sanctified among the Israelites, I, Adonai, who sanctifies you." God's holy name is His reputation. Ezekiel 39:25, for example, promises that God will gather the exiles and restore his reputation. God is also to "sanctify His name" throughout the world, a universalist theme found biblically, for example, in Ezekiel 36:23: "the nations shall know that I am Adonai."

In later Jewish thought, it is not God but humans who sanctify God's name—through acts of martyrdom.

25 "*Heaven,… earth…highest heavens*" From Deuteronomy 10:14.

26 "*You are first and You are last*" This entire prayer cites biblical verses, though with slight changes, like a change in person ("You" instead of "I"), since God is addressed here, whereas in the Bible, God is speaking.

27 "*Gather…from the four corners of the earth*" Paraphrasing Isaiah 11:12.

28 "*All who walk the earth will recognize and know*" Paraphrasing 2 Kings 19:19, Isaiah 37:20, and Isaiah 37:16.

[29] *"You made heaven and earth, the sea, and everything in them"* From Isaiah 37:16 and a paraphrase of Psalm 146:6 (cf. Neh. 9:6).

[30] *"Who…can tell You what to do!"* Paraphrasing Job 9:12.

[31] *"For the sake of Your great name by which we are called"* Psalm 109:21 expresses a similar idea.

[32–33] *"At that time…says Adonai"* From Zephaniah 3:20. The prayer, up to now comprised of paraphrases, concludes with an exact quotation, introduced by the citation formula "That which is written" *(mah shekatuv).*

◆———

DORFF (THEOLOGY)

everything today is exactly as it was yesterday and will be tomorrow. In all three cases we are forced to confront our limitations. But the responses are radically different. For Kohelet, we might as well just enjoy the pleasures of life while we have them. For *Un'taneh Tokef,* "prayer, repentance, and righteous acts avert the severity of the [divine] decree." In many ways, though, it is this prayer that gives the most comprehensive answer, for it asserts that what saves us from meaninglessness is the covenant. That includes rootedness in the covenant of our ancestors and a strong contemporary connection with our partner in covenant, God. Such a partnership provides happiness in the present and hope for the future. Even when temporarily unable to change reality for the better, we can gain both power and purpose through our linkage to God.

◆———

ELLENSON (MODERN LITURGIES)

offensive, but they introduce a unit of prayer that climaxes in an early recitation of the *Sh'ma,* which liberal liturgies omitted as redundant, since the full *Sh'ma* and Its Blessings will follow shortly as one of the two key building blocks of the morning service (see Volume 1, *The Sh'ma and Its Blessings*). (See below, "We must gratefully acknowledge.")

[2] *"We do not offer our supplications…based on our righteousness"* This prayer has found a prominent place in most non-Orthodox liturgies, all of which applaud the appropriate humility by which human beings approach God. They generally provide at least vernacular versions (*Hamburg Temple Prayer Books, Olath Tamid, Union Prayer Book*), or the Hebrew too (Geiger [1854], *Minhag America, Gates of Prayer,* and *Siddur Sim Shalom*). But as the tone of humility has not captured the fancy of Reconstructionist prayerbook authors, no Reconstructionist rite contains this text.

[5–9] *"What is our love…righteousness…salvation…strength…might?"* Wise omitted these particular words from the *Minhag America,* as their abject tone seemed to go too far, unduly demeaning human beings, who, after all, are partners with God in covenant.

¹² *"Man barely rises above beast, for everything is worthless"* Wise mutes the force of this particular statement by adding, in both Hebrew and English, "[all is vain] except the pure soul which, by Thy light, shall be enlightened for evermore."

¹⁴ *"We must gratefully acknowledge"* Most liberal liturgies do not recite the *Sh'ma* here (see above, "You should always fear God"). They therefore remove this introduction to it (e.g., Geiger [1870], *Olath Tamid,* and *Union Prayer Book*). Hamburg provided a vernacular rendition of this paragraph, because the idea was sound enough, but not the *Sh'ma* itself, while *Gates of Prayer* offers an abbreviated version of at least the first line. In his earlier work (1854), Geiger included the whole paragraph and the following *Sh'ma* because he wanted to appeal to traditionalists at that early stage of his career. Wise, too, wishing to avoid any sign of radicalism, provided a truncated version of this paragraph and proudly proclaimed the *Sh'ma* here as a sign that God "crownest Israel with the majesty of truth."

²⁴ *"Blessed are You, Adonai, who sanctifies Your name among the multitudes"* In his *Minhag America,* Wise offered a remarkable and noteworthy translation: "Praised be Thou, O God, who sanctifiest Thy name, by those of superior mind." The added words offer powerful testimony as to the Enlightenment faith in the absolute power of reason that informed the nineteenth century.

FRANKEL (A WOMAN'S VOICE)

moments in our childhood when we found ourselves alone or vulnerable. This prayer admits to that earlier longing and acknowledges the heartfelt truth that only God can offer us this kind of constancy.

Admitting such truth is not simple. It requires that we abandon our grandiose childish sense of entitlement to God's favor. We must admit "inwardly and outwardly" that not only we, but even our larger-than-life heroes—our Goliaths and Olympians—are puny in God's sight. Ultimately, we can only throw ourselves on God's mercy.

But is this abject humility an honest expression of how we feel? Must we really live our lives as though we were so worthless, as though *hakol havel,* "everything is worthless," as Ecclesiastes lamented? No, for we have other heroes to plead our cause, champions handpicked by You, God. We have those with whom You made Your covenant. Though unworthy ourselves, we are descended from Your beloved, Abraham, and Jacob, whom You loved. And we might add—though the traditional liturgy does not—we also have Your champions, Sarah and Rebekah, whose courage and wisdom ensured that their sons survived to establish Your covenant.

[18] *"Hear O Israel"* Normally, this central declaration of faith is preceded by a prayer acknowledging God's love for Israel (see Volume 1, *The Sh'ma and Its Blessings*). Our own faith in God that we here declare in the *Sh'ma* is therefore predicated on God's faithfulness to us. By reciting the *Sh'ma,* we embrace this relationship and declare our own love for God in the normal succeeding paragraph, *V'ahavta,* "You shall love [Adonai your God]."

Here, however, *V'ahavta* is missing, as is the paragraph that usually precedes the *Sh'ma* affirming God's love for Israel. Instead we precede our declaration of faith by first affirming our happiness to be Jews: "How wonderful is our lot, how great our destiny, and how beautiful our heritage." Presumably the same reciprocity operates here as well. Here our hope is that just as we proclaim our joy in being Israel, God likewise rejoices that we are God's people.

[21] *"Who sanctify Your name"* In two succeeding paragraphs, both beginning "You are," we encounter the word *shem,* "name," five times. The people of Israel are characterized as *makdishei sh'mekha,* "those who sanctify [God's] name." For centuries of Jewish history, *kiddush hashem,* "the sanctification of the name," has signified martyrdom—giving up one's life to save God's name from desecration. While that connotation remains implicit here (indeed some traditional prayer books spell it out explicitly in a footnote), the central themes of this prayer focus more on God's universal qualities: God is the One who is unchanging, eternal, whose holiness is manifest throughout the world.

Then this universalist vision narrows its focus to remind us of God's particular promise to Israel: God will one day redeem us from captivity. Then we shall regain our name among the nations, *eten etkhem l'shem,* so that sanctifying God's name will entail not our self-effacement but our self-fulfillment. When that happens, the act of *kiddush hashem,* "making God's name holy" in the world, will be not only *our* birthright and obligation, but will be incumbent upon all creatures on earth.

◆

J. HOFFMAN (TRANSLATION)

prayer that is marked by supplicatory language and theology.

[5] *"What is our love?"* A better translation might be "How are we loving?" but that would destroy the effect of the repeated "what."

[11] *"Without value"* Hebrew, *tohu,* the same word used in Genesis to describe the raw reality ("void [and without form]") immediately before God created it into a world. We'd like to use "worthless" here (following Birnbaum), but we want to save that for *hevel,* immediately below.

[11] *"Worthless"* Hebrew, *hevel.* Often translated as "vanity," this word characterizes the theme of of Ecclesiastes, from which it is taken (3:19).

[13] *"Your love"* Two other possibilities are "who loves you" and "whom you love."

[17] *"Night and morning"* The usual English expression would be "morning and night," but in Hebrew "night" always comes first, since the "day" starts at night and continues into the next morning.

[18] *"Hear"* See Volume 1, *The Sh'ma and Its Blessings,* p. 87.

[20] *"Are You"* An extremely difficult text to convey accurately in English. The Hebrew we translate as "are You" is both tenseless and contentless. Furthermore, this tenseless and contentless phrase is repeated before each time period. If it were possible in English, we would prefer something like "You be before the world was created, you be after the world was created," etc. Birnbaum translates, "[You were] the same," "[You are] the same," etc. Artscroll gives us, "It was You, it is You," etc.

[22] *"Throughout"* Literally, "in."

[23] *"May we become"* Or, "make us…."

[24] *"Among the multitudes"* As in Artscroll, Birnbaum supplies, "in the presence of all men." Another possible reading is "in many ways."

[25] *"You are* [atah hu]*"* Repeated from above, where we translated it, "You are You."

[26] *"Are no gods"* Or, "is no God."

[27] *"Those who yearn for You"* More literally, "your yearners."

[28] *"All who walk the earth"* As in Artscroll. The Hebrew—literally "all who come on the earth"—is surely an idiom, so we translate it idiomatically.

[29] *"Everything in them"* It's not clear what "them" refers to. If it were "heaven, earth, and sea," we would expect "and" between "heaven and earth" and "the sea." As this verse stands, we have "heaven and earth" and then "the sea, and everything in them." Earlier, geonic versions of this prayer lack that ending.

[30] *"Who…can tell You what to do"* This is the most likely reading of the verse. Alternatively, "Who can question what You do?"—as in Birnbaum's, "Who can say to You: what do You do?"

[32] *"At the time that I gather you"* Others, "at that time I will gather you." That translation indicates that at the time we are talking about ("at that time"), God will gather us. Our translation suggests that the Hebrew is defining a time ("at the time") when we will be gathered, and so, might be paraphrased, "When I gather you."

[32] *"Make you famous"* Literally, "Make you of renown."

[32] *"Return your returnees"* The Hebrew for "return" *(b'shuvi)* and "exiled" *(sh'vuteikhem)* are similar, forming a verbal pun that we try to represent in the English.

[33] *"So says Adonai"* "Right from the horse's mouth," as it were.

◆

L. HOFFMAN (HISTORY)

[21] *"Those who sanctify Your name"* By the eleventh century, following the Crusaders' massacre of the Jews in the Rhineland, "to sanctify God's name" took on the technical meaning of suffering martyrdom. But that is not its meaning in this prayer, which is contained already in the ninth-century prayer book of Rav Amram, as well as parallel prayer books from the geonic era, like the old Persian rite. Here, it follows the biblical meaning of demonstrating God's reputation by redeeming the world. (See Brettler.)

◆ ◆ ◆

6 | Korbanot
("Sacrifices")

[Korbanot start here. We do not include them (see commentaries for rationale). We do, however, continue with their conclusion, the Thirteen Principles of Torah Interpretation according to Rabbi Ishmael. Some of these principles are commonly referred to by Hebrew terms, which appear in brackets after the translation, for ease of reference.]

A. THIRTEEN PRINCIPLES OF RABBI ISHMAEL

[1] Rabbi Ishmael says that the Torah can be interpreted through thirteen principles.

[2] 1. By *a fortiori* reasoning *["kal vachomer"]*.

[3] 2. By assuming that similar language expresses similar thoughts *["g'zerah shavah"]*.

[4] 3. By finding general principles from one or two biblical laws *["binyan av"]*.

[5] 4. By reasoning that a generalization preceding a specification sets the stage for that specification *["klal ufrat"]*.

[6] 5. By reasoning that a specification preceding a generalization sets the stage for that generalization *["prat ukhlal"]*.

[7] 6. By reasoning that a generalization preceding a specification that precedes another generalization must be judged based on the specification *["klal ufrat ukhlal"]*.

[8] 7. But rules 4 and 5 do not apply if a generalization requires a specification or if a specification requires a generalization.

[1]רַבִּי יִשְׁמָעֵאל אוֹמֵר: בִּשְׁלֹשׁ עֶשְׂרֵה מִדּוֹת הַתּוֹרָה נִדְרֶשֶׁת:

[2]א) מִקַּל וָחֹמֶר;

[3]ב) וּמִגְּזֵרָה שָׁוָה;

[4]ג) מִבִּנְיַן אָב מִכָּתוּב אֶחָד, וּמִבִּנְיַן אָב מִשְּׁנֵי כְתוּבִים;

[5]ד) מִכְּלָל וּפְרָט;

[6]ה) וּמִפְּרָט וּכְלָל;

[7]ו) כְּלָל וּפְרָט וּכְלָל אִי אַתָּה דָן אֶלָּא כְּעֵין הַפְּרָט;

[8]ז) מִכְּלָל שֶׁהוּא צָרִיךְ לִפְרָט, וּמִפְּרָט שֶׁהוּא צָרִיךְ לִכְלָל;

[9]ח) כָּל דָּבָר שֶׁהָיָה בִּכְלָל וְיָצָא מִן הַכְּלָל לְלַמֵּד, לֹא לְלַמֵּד עַל עַצְמוֹ יָצָא, אֶלָּא לְלַמֵּד עַל הַכְּלָל כֻּלּוֹ יָצָא;

⁹8. Whatever follows from a generalization is intended to be considered as teaching not about itself, but about the generalization.

¹⁰9. When something is first implied in a general law and is followed by a provision similar to the general law, the provision is intended to alleviate, not increase, the severity of that similar provision.

¹¹10. When something is first implied in a general law and is followed by a provision dissimilar to the general law, the provision is intended either to alleviate or to increase the severity of that dissimilar provision.

¹²11. When something is first implied in a general law and followed by a new provision, you cannot connect the new provision to the general law unless Scripture explicitly connects them;

¹³12. By deducing a word's meaning from context or from subsequent usage;

¹⁴13. And similarly, by not reconciling two contradictory verses until a third verse reconciles the two.

¹⁵May it be Your will, Adonai our God and our ancestors' God, that the Temple be quickly rebuilt in our days and that You let us share in Your Torah. ¹⁶There we will serve You with reverence, as in days of old and the early years.

¹⁰ט) כָּל דָּבָר שֶׁהָיָה בִּכְלָל וְיָצָא לִטְעוֹן טְעַן אַחֵר שֶׁהוּא כְעִנְיָנוֹ, יָצָא לְהָקֵל וְלֹא לְהַחֲמִיר;

¹¹י) כָּל דָּבָר שֶׁהָיָה בִּכְלָל וְיָצָא לִטְעוֹן טְעַן אַחֵר שֶׁלֹּא כְעִנְיָנוֹ, יָצָא לְהָקֵל וּלְהַחֲמִיר;

¹²יא) כָּל דָּבָר שֶׁהָיָה בִּכְלָל וְיָצָא לִדּוֹן בַּדָּבָר הֶחָדָשׁ, אִי אַתָּה יָכוֹל לְהַחֲזִירוֹ לִכְלָלוֹ עַד שֶׁיַּחֲזִירֶנּוּ הַכָּתוּב לִכְלָלוֹ בְּפֵרוּשׁ;

¹³יב) דָּבָר הַלָּמֵד מֵעִנְיָנוֹ, וְדָבָר הַלָּמֵד מִסּוֹפוֹ;

¹⁴יג) וְכֵן שְׁנֵי כְתוּבִים הַמַּכְחִישִׁים זֶה אֶת זֶה, עַד שֶׁיָּבוֹא הַכָּתוּב הַשְּׁלִישִׁי וְיַכְרִיעַ בֵּינֵיהֶם.

¹⁵יְהִי רָצוֹן מִלְּפָנֶיךָ, יְיָ אֱלֹהֵינוּ וֵאלֹהֵי אֲבוֹתֵינוּ, שֶׁיִּבָּנֶה בֵּית הַמִּקְדָּשׁ בִּמְהֵרָה בְיָמֵינוּ, וְתֵן חֶלְקֵנוּ בְּתוֹרָתֶךָ. ¹⁶וְשָׁם נַעֲבָדְךָ בְּיִרְאָה, כִּימֵי עוֹלָם וּכְשָׁנִים קַדְמוֹנִיּוֹת.

BRETTLER (BIBLE)

The inclusion of sacrificial readings as prayers reflects the fact that sacrifices were the primary means of worship during Temple times and the rabbinic notion that with the Temple gone, prayer serves as their surrogate.

It is unclear what role prayer played in the First Temple. Leviticus 16:21 has Aaron confess the sins of Israel over the scapegoat on Yom Kippur, but this reference to a prayer as part of the cult stands out precisely because it is so rare. It is unclear if sacrifices were typically accompanied by any prayer, and it is unknown how and when most of the Psalms were recited.

It is possible, however, that the rabbinic idea of   *(p. 177)*

DORFF (THEOLOGY)

[1] *"Rabbi Ishmael says"* In preference to all other conceivable options, the liturgy selects these hermeneutic rules (rules of interpretation) to end our daily morning study, for they are the key to opening the meanings inherent in the Torah. They surely demonstrate   *(p. 179)*

ELLENSON (MODERN LITURGIES)

[1] *"Rabbi Ishmael says"* The 1985 edition of *Siddur Sim Shalom* eliminated this from the North American Conservative rite. In its stead, it introduced a series of rabbinic texts and stories dealing with ethics. This substitution was consistent with past Rabbinical   *(p. 179)*

FRANKEL (A WOMAN'S VOICE)

[11] *"10. When something is first implied in a general law"* As in other logical systems, these rules of Rabbi Ishmael are rather arbitrary, more like articles of faith than natural laws. However, we've become so accustomed to relying on them that we forget that they're merely human inventions, based on our imperfect understanding of God's own logic. And because we forget that they are the product of human minds from a long ago time, we imagine that they are timeless and divinely   *(p. 180)*

A. THIRTEEN PRINCIPLES OF RABBI ISHMAEL

[1] Rabbi Ishmael says that the Torah can be interpreted through thirteen principles.

[2] 1. By *a fortiori* reasoning *["kal vachomer"].*

[3] 2. By assuming that similar language expresses similar thoughts *["g'zerah shavah"].*

[4] 3. By finding general principles from one or two biblical laws *["binyan av"].*

J. HOFFMAN (TRANSLATION)

[2] *"A fortiori"* That is, "even more conclusively," as when a lesser issue is subsumed under a weightier one. This and the following twelve principles contain technical legal terms in Hebrew. Here a common technical term exists in English, and so we use it; elsewhere, we resort to brief interpretive phrases.

[15] *"In our days"* See Volume 4, *Seder K'riat Hatorah (The Torah Service),* p. 168.

L. HOFFMAN (HISTORY)

Passages from the Bible and rabbinic literature that prescribe Temple sacrifices. These are followed by Rabbi Ishmael's classic thirteen principles by which Torah is interpreted, and the Kaddish D'rabbanan, a form of the Kaddish that is used nowadays as a memorial prayer but was once just praise of God following Torah study. We omit the actual sacrificial passages but include Rabbi Ishmael's principles and the Kaddish. (p. 181)

LANDES (HALAKHAH)

[1] *"Rabbi Ishmael says"* Though not exhaustive, these rules cover many interpretive principles and develop a sensitivity to others. They begin by affirming human logic and end with faith in Torah itself to resolve contradictions. Taken all together, they illustrate the need for empathic application of the Oral Law.

[2] *"1. By a fortiori reasoning ['kal vachomer']"* That is, a logical inference drawn from a lenient law to a more severe one. Whatever is severe in the lenient law is assumed to hold true in the severe law; conversely, in an inference from a severe law to a lenient one, whatever is lenient in the severe law is assumed to hold true in the lenient law. When, for example, Miriam is punished by leprosy for speaking ill of Moses, and by extension, of God as well, "Adonai said to Moses, 'If her father had but spit in her face, should she not be ashamed for seven days? Let her be shut out from the camp seven days'" (Num. 12:14). Here the *kal* (the lenient term) is the father and the *chomer* (the severe term) is God. It is assumed that had Miriam wronged her father to the point where he spat in her face—a sign of humiliation in ancient Near Eastern culture—the further punishment would be a seven-day quarantine outside the camp. If Miriam's punishment for wronging her father would have been seven days, surely the same punishment is warranted for questioning God. (p. 182)

[1] רַבִּי יִשְׁמָעֵאל אוֹמֵר: בִּשְׁלֹשׁ עֶשְׂרֵה מִדּוֹת הַתּוֹרָה נִדְרָשֶׁת:

[2] א) מִקַּל וָחֹמֶר;

[3] ב) וּמִגְּזֵרָה שָׁוָה;

[4] ג) מִבִּנְיַן אָב מִכָּתוּב אֶחָד, וּמִבִּנְיַן אָב מִשְּׁנֵי כְתוּבִים;

KUSHNER & POLEN (CHASIDISM)

Yehudah Aryeh Lieb of Ger (d. 1905) offers this teaching about sacrifices (*S'fas Emes*, s. v. *Tzav*). He cites Leviticus 6:1–2, which deals almost exclusively with the laws of burnt offerings: "This the ritual of the burnt offering:…[The priest] shall remove the ashes." How strange, notes the Gerer, that the law of the burnt offering should begin with the removal of the ashes of the preceding day's sacrifices. This implies that every sacrifice depends on the removal of ashes. (p. 181)

5 4. By reasoning that a generalization preceding a specification sets the stage for that specification ["klal ufrat"].

6 5. By reasoning that a specification preceding a generalization sets the stage for that generalization ["prat ukhlal"].

7 6. By reasoning that a generalization preceding a specification that precedes another generalization must be judged based on the specification ["klal ufrat ukhlal"].

8 7. But rules 4 and 5 do not apply if a generalization requires a specification or if a specification requires a generalization.

9 8. Whatever follows from a generalization is intended to be considered as teaching not about itself, but about the generalization.

10 9. When something is first implied in a general law and is followed by a provision similar to the general law, the provision is intended to alleviate, not increase, the severity of that similar provision.

11 10. When something is first implied in a general law and is followed by a provision dissimilar to the general law, the provision is intended either to alleviate or to

ד)5 מִכְּלָל וּפְרָט;

ה)6 וּמִפְּרָט וּכְלָל;

ו)7 כְּלָל וּפְרָט וּכְלָל אִי אַתָּה דָן אֶלָּא כְּעֵין הַפְּרָט;

ז)8 מִכְּלָל שֶׁהוּא צָרִיךְ לִפְרָט, וּמִפְּרָט שֶׁהוּא צָרִיךְ לִכְלָל;

ח)9 כָּל דָּבָר שֶׁהָיָה בִּכְלָל וְיָצָא מִן הַכְּלָל לְלַמֵּד, לֹא לְלַמֵּד עַל עַצְמוֹ יָצָא, אֶלָּא לְלַמֵּד עַל הַכְּלָל כֻּלּוֹ יָצָא;

ט)10 כָּל דָּבָר שֶׁהָיָה בִּכְלָל וְיָצָא לִטְעוֹן טַעַן אַחֵר שֶׁהוּא כְעִנְיָנוֹ, יָצָא לְהָקֵל וְלֹא לְהַחֲמִיר;

י)11 כָּל דָּבָר שֶׁהָיָה בִּכְלָל וְיָצָא לִטְעוֹן טַעַן אַחֵר שֶׁלֹּא כְעִנְיָנוֹ, יָצָא לְהָקֵל וּלְהַחֲמִיר;

יא)12 כָּל דָּבָר שֶׁהָיָה בִּכְלָל וְיָצָא לִדּוֹן בַּדָּבָר הֶחָדָשׁ, אִי אַתָּה יָכוֹל לְהַחֲזִירוֹ לִכְלָלוֹ עַד שֶׁיַּחֲזִירֶנּוּ הַכָּתוּב לִכְלָלוֹ בְּפֵרוּשׁ;

יב)13 דָּבָר הַלָּמֵד מֵעִנְיָנוֹ, וְדָבָר הַלָּמֵד מִסּוֹפוֹ;

יג)14 וְכֵן שְׁנֵי כְתוּבִים הַמַּכְחִישִׁים זֶה אֶת זֶה, עַד שֶׁיָּבוֹא הַכָּתוּב הַשְּׁלִישִׁי וְיַכְרִיעַ בֵּינֵיהֶם.

יד)15 יְהִי רָצוֹן מִלְּפָנֶיךָ, יְיָ אֱלֹהֵינוּ וֵאלֹהֵי

increase the severity of that dissimilar provision.

¹²11. When something is first implied in a general law and followed by a new provision, you cannot connect the new provision to the general law unless Scripture explicitly connects them;

¹³12. By deducing a word's meaning from context or from subsequent usage;

¹⁴13. And similarly, by not reconciling two contradictory verses until a third verse reconciles the two.

¹⁵May it be Your will, Adonai our God and our ancestors' God, that the Temple be quickly rebuilt in our days and that You let us share in Your Torah. ¹⁶There we will serve You with reverence, as in days of old and the early years.

אֲבוֹתֵינוּ, שֶׁיִּבָּנֶה בֵּית הַמִּקְדָּשׁ בִּמְהֵרָה בְיָמֵינוּ, וְתֵן חֶלְקֵנוּ בְּתוֹרָתֶךָ. ¹⁶וְשָׁם נַעֲבָדְךָ בְּיִרְאָה, כִּימֵי עוֹלָם וּכְשָׁנִים קַדְמוֹנִיּוֹת.

BRETTLER (BIBLE)

prayer replacing sacrifices has biblical roots. Psalm 40:7 claims, "You take no delight in sacrifice and meal offering.... You did not ask for burnt offerings and purification offerings." Three verses earlier (v. 4), the psalmist says, "He put a new song, praising our God, in my mouth; many will see and will revere and trust in Adonai." The juxtaposition suggests that this "new song" does indeed replace sacrificial worship. Even clearer is Psalm 51:17–19: "Adonai, open my lips, so my mouth may speak Your praise. For You do not delight in my bringing sacrifices; You do not desire burnt offerings. Offerings to God are a contrite spirit; a contrite and broken heart, O God, You will not spurn." It is difficult to date these texts or to determine which social group they reflect, but it is clear that some people in ancient Israel already believed that prayer to God was the functional equivalent of sacrifice.

[1] *"Rabbi Ishmael says"* No systematic set of rules for the interpretation of the Torah has been preserved from the biblical period; nor is there any hint that there even were any. But much evidence suggests that both narrative and legal texts were being interpreted back then. This happened for at least two reasons: First, the legal texts are very incomplete, and once the Torah canon was closed, these limited texts needed to be interpreted to cover circumstances that are not addressed directly. Second, the legal and narrative traditions incorporated into the Torah reflect different time periods and geographical locations. Once they were bound together as a single text, natural differences arising from the combinations of different traditions, penned by different authors, needed reconciliation.

Interpretation is therefore inherent to any culture with sacred texts. We know of Mesopotamian interpretations that parallel rabbinic lore—and may even have influenced it—but there, too, we find no systematic listing of interpretive principles.

I offer three types of illustrations of early interpretation:

1. Legal material from Exodus that is interpreted in Deuteronomy: While discussing the Festival of Matzot (later called Passover), Exodus 23:15 states, "None shall be seen by me empty-handed"; that is, pilgrims to the Temple must bring a gift or sacrifice. The law refers specifically to Matzot, since the festival falls before the first new grain, when barley (out of which matzah can be made) is normally harvested. A worshiper might think, therefore, that if a pilgrimage is undertaken on an occasion when new produce is lacking, God may be visited empty-handed. Deuteronomy 16:16 generalizes, yielding the conclusion: "Three times a year every male shall be seen before God…and none shall be seen by Me empty-handed." The legislation of Exodus is recontextualized to refer to all three pilgrimage festivals, not just Matzot. Exodus 23:15 has been generalized through interpretation.

2. Handling a contradiction between Exodus and Deuteronomy: Exodus 12:8–9 discusses the Passover offering: "They should eat the flesh on that night roasted by fire; they should eat it with matzot and bitter herbs. Do not eat it raw, or boiled at all in water…." Deuteronomy 16:7, on the other hand, mandates: "You shall boil it and eat it…." What does a believer in the divine origin of the entire Torah do with these equally authoritative instructions that contradict one another?

    Chronicles was composed after the Torah was canonized. 2 Chronicles 35:13 resolves the difference by narrating that during the reign of King Josiah, "They boiled the Passover offering with fire, as they were supposed to." The two texts are "reconciled" by incorporating elements of each: the offering is boiled, following Deuteronomy, but by fire—which is to say, "roasted," as in Exodus.

3. The interpretation of two conflicting creation stories from Genesis, in the Book of Jubilees: Jubilees is a non-biblical work from the second century B.C.E., the end of the biblical period. It recasts much of Genesis and early Exodus, but interpretively. For example, Jubilees 2:7 says that the Garden of Eden was creat-

ed on day three. This is nowhere stated in the biblical text, which actually has two separate and sometimes conflicting versions of creation. Only the second (Gen. 2:4b–3:24) has a Garden of Eden narrative. Only the first (Gen. 1–2:4a) lists each day of creation and what happened on it. The author of Jubilees thus combined the two stories.

In sum, several of the principles enumerated by Rabbi Ishmael have earlier antecedents in biblical and pre-rabbinic non-biblical texts, the Dead Sea Scrolls, and the New Testament. Rabbinic texts usually cite the biblical text alongside its interpretation. In these earlier works, the original texts are often just reshaped into new ones, so it is harder to appreciate the extent to which interpretation was already being used.

Only in the rabbinic period, which was interested in systematizing interpretations, do Sages articulate interpretive rules. The thirteen principles of Rabbi Ishmael are the results of one such effort.

[15] *"May it be Your will…that the Temple be quickly rebuilt"* After the destruction of the First Temple, similar wishes were articulated (Lam. 5:18–21). The juxtaposition of this wish with "Let us share in Your Torah," however, is striking, since it demonstrates that Torah study, not just prayer, became a surrogate for Temple worship.

———◆———

DORFF (THEOLOGY)

our ancestors' sophistication in discerning the various ways to interpret texts, but more than that, they epitomize the Rabbis' approach to revelation. In contrast to fundamentalists, Jews were to evaluate the multiple ways in which texts like the Torah may be plausibly interpreted. According to the Rabbis, there are "seventy faces to the Torah" (Num. Rab. 13:15–16).

———◆———

ELLENSON (MODERN LITURGIES)

Assembly prayer books, as earlier Conservative Siddurim had already removed all the traditional biblical and rabbinic texts dealing with sacrifices. But *SSS* was the first Conservative rite to remove the thirteen exegetical principles as well.

This innovation was criticized on two fronts. The Union for Traditional Conservative Judaism attacked it on the grounds that it reflected an "anti-ritual platform." Simultaneously, the late Jakob Petuchowski of the Hebrew Union College chided the Conservative rabbinate for removing rules that possess Jewish theological meaning, in that they signify that the rabbinic tradition, as expounded through these rules, legitimately represents Jewish tradition as handed down by God to Moses at Mount Sinai. By removing the passage, the Conservative Movement was undermining its own claim that authority in Judaism is vested in a proper interpretation of Jewish law.

It appears that the framers of the 1998 edition of SSS took these critiques seriously, for the passage has been restored in the revised edition of SSS.

[15] *"May it be Your will...that the Temple be quickly rebuilt"* Given Conservative Movement opposition to the idea that the sacrificial cult be restored, it is hardly surprising that this passage is absent from its Israeli *Siddur Va'ani T'fillati*. Nor is it therefore startling that the 1985 *Siddur Sim Shalom* replaced this passage with a prayer asking that "we be disciples of Aaron...loving peace and pursuing peace, loving our fellow creatures and drawing them near to Torah." Interestingly, the 1998 edition of SSS offers both the traditional meditation as well as the newer one as an alternative.

◆———

FRANKEL (A WOMAN'S VOICE)

ordained. So, for instance, Rabbi Ishmael's tenth principle states that "when something is first implied in a general law and is followed by a provision dissimilar to the general law, the provision is intended either to alleviate or to increase the severity of that dissimilar provision." In other words, when we specify an exception to a general law, our purpose is to make that exception both more liberal and more stringent than the general law.

One of the classic rabbinic instances of this principle is Exodus 21:1–11, a description of the different treatment meted out to male and female Jewish indentured servants. First we hear that a male servant is to go free after six years of service, without pay. If married and childless, he leaves with his wife; if they have children, however, both wife and children remain behind as slaves. The Torah then goes on to state that a female servant, in contrast, can be redeemed from her indenture before her six years are up if her master becomes displeased with her. In this case, he is expressly forbidden to sell her to another. If he bought her for his son, she is to be married to him with all the rights of a free woman, including food, clothing, and sexual fulfillment. And if he falls short on providing her these rights, she is to go free, without pay.

Applying Rabbi Ishmael's tenth rule to this biblical passage, the Rabbis point out that the lot of a female slave is thus more lenient and more stringent than that of her male counterpart: on the one hand, she may be freed in less than six years—not only if her master is displeased with her but also upon reaching puberty (if she is sold as a minor) or upon the death of her master. On the other hand, she can be married against her will to her master or her master's son. Of course, more is at stake here than a mere system of logical principles, for in this case, the boon of a female slave's early release does not restore her virginity, that is, her marriageability, nor does it give her any means of support once she is released from service. What the Rabbis here call "more lenient" is, at best, hypothetical and, at worst, disingenuous.

———◆———

L. HOFFMAN (HISTORY)

At this point, the main study passages occur. They come from Torah, Mishnah, and Talmud, and they detail the laws of sacrifice. (For their rationale, see "Blessings and Study: The Jewish Way to Begin a Day," pp. 6–16.) Because of constraints of space, and because their content makes them relatively inaccessible to modern-day readers, we have omitted them here. They conclude, however, with Rabbi Ishmael's principles of interpretation followed by a special version of the *Kaddish* called the *Kaddish D'rabbanan*, on which, see below.

———◆———

KUSHNER & POLEN (CHASIDISM)

He then cites a teaching (Lev. Rab. 7:3) that sacrifices make atonement for the evil meditations of our hearts. Sacrifice represents the obliteration of sin. All that remains are ashes, but these remnants of evil—purified through conflagration—are now themselves good. In the kabbalistic maxim, every descent [into sin] involves a complementary ascent [into holiness]. Everything—even what first seems evil—must, therefore, also be part of God's creation. As Isaiah says, God creates light *and* darkness. In this way, through the act of burning, evil is transformed into good. Thus the goal of the sacrificial act has been attained. These ashes, these remnants of our evil machinations, have now themselves become holy. For this reason, they precede each day's offering. Indeed, the residue of sins now atoned is the first and highest order of spiritual business.

[1] *"Rabbi Ishmael says"* Elimelekh of Lizhensk (*No'am Elimelekh*, Likkutey Shoshana, 5755) is struck by the fact that thirteen is the number of principles through which the Torah may be interpreted and the number of divine attributes as enumerated in Exodus 34:6–7: "Adonai passed before him [Moses], and proclaimed, (1) Adonai, (2) Adonai (3) God, (4) merciful and (5) gracious, (6) long suffering, and (7) abundant in goodness and (8) truth, (9) keeping mercy for thousands, (10) forgiving iniquity and (11) transgression and (12) sin, and will...(13) clear...." It should be noted that the preceding are attributes of love, compassion, and mercy; there is no mention of judgment, punishment, or anger.

Rabbi Elimelekh of Lizhensk suggests that only a person who lives by these thirteen divine attributes is able to properly interpret Torah according to Rabbi Ishmael's thirteen principles. Indeed, such an interpretation of Torah based only on love and mercy would be a mark of great spiritual maturity. It would fuse hermeneutic logic with our yearning to emulate the divine. For Elimelekh, the goal of Torah interpretation is therefore understood to be the increase of compassion. Or, to put it another way, only one who has internalized the thirteen attributes of God's compassion is fit to nuance Rabbi Ishmael's principles of Torah interpretation (Y'sod Ha'avodah, 10).

◆

LANDES (HALAKHAH)

As an objective method of logic, *kal vachomer* is a principle from which new law can be derived. An exception to that rule is the death penalty.

[3] *"2. By assuming that similar language expresses similar thoughts* [g'zerah shavah]*"* A clarification derived from comparing identical terms used in different biblical texts. Thus, regarding a Hebrew slave who refuses an offer of freedom, we read, "The master shall bore his ear" (Exod. 21:6). Later, regarding the blood purification of the leper, we are told, "The priest shall put it upon the tip of the right ear" (Lev. 14:14). Just as the right ear is specified in Leviticus, so too the right ear must be intended in Exodus. For a *g'zerah shavah* to hold, it must be based on a tradition, imply a potential mutuality of learning from each to the other, and (ideally) be derived from terms that are not necessary for general comprehension, so may be assumed to be left specifically to imply a *g'zerah shavah* lesson.

[4] *"3. By finding general principles from one or two biblical laws* ['binyan av']*"* Such a principle is applicable to all related laws. Deuteronomy 19:15, for instance, rules, "A single witness may not validate guilt or blame. The case can be validated only on the testimony of two or more witnesses." The next verse states, "If a false witness arise...." In the second verse, "witness" can hardly refer to a single witness, who would have no standing in any event. It must accordingly refer to a pair of witnesses in collusion. The *binyan av* is perhaps the most common of all the rules, but lacking the theological precision of *kal vachomer* or the exact specificity of *g'zerah shavah,* its use is subject to some debate.

[5] *"4. By reasoning that a generalization preceding a specification sets the stage for that specification* ['klal ufrat']*"* When a general rule *(klal)* is followed by a specific detail *(prat),* we follow only the specific detail. Leviticus 1:2 reads, "When any of you present an offering of cattle...the offering shall be chosen from the herd or from the flock." "Cattle" is the *klal,* the general term; "herd" and "flock" are each a *prat,* a detail. We derive the lesson that the offering must come from the herd or the flock. If so, why is there a need for the *klal* altogether? The classic answer is if the details alone were provided, we might be tempted inappropriately to apply other principles such as *binyan av* or *kal vachomer* to the passage.

⁶ *"5. By reasoning that a specification preceding a generalization sets the stage for that generalization* ['prat ukhlal']*"* In such a case, we follow the general rule, not the detailed specification. Exodus 22:9, for instance, discusses a law of bailments involving livestock. "If a man deliver to his neighbor an ass or an ox or a sheep or any beast…" "Ass," "ox," and "sheep" are specifics; "any beast" is the generalization that defines the class of things under discussion here. The specifics are there only for the purposes of narrative clarity.

⁷ *"6. By reasoning that a generalization preceding a specification that precedes another generalization must be judged on the specification* ['klal ufrat ukhlal']*"* Here we have a generalization *(klal),* followed by a specification *(prat),* which is then followed by another generalization *(klal).* In such a case, we draw inference only to other things that are akin to the specification. The laws of theft, for instance, discuss "all manner of misappropriation, pertaining to an ox, an ass, a sheep, a garment, or any other loss…." (Exod. 22:8). "All manner of appropriation" and "any other loss" are bracketing cases of a *klal*; "an ox, an ass, a sheep, a garment" are instances of *prat.* The Rabbis conclude that any other examples that are subsumed here must follow the dual nature of the *prat:* movable property, not landed property; and of real as opposed to symbolic value (such as monetary payment).

⁸ *"7. Rules 4 and 5 do not apply if a generalization requires a specification or if a specification requires a generalization* [miklal shehu tsarikh lifrat umiprat shehu tsarikh likhlal]*"* In such cases, where the issue is clarity alone, we assume that nothing further can be learned from the terms in question, and we ignore the above rules. Following the slaughter of an animal or bird, for example, Leviticus 17:13 instructs us to "pour out its blood and cover it with earth." "Cover" is a *klal,* since it does not specify how the covering should occur. "With earth" is the *prat.* Following the rule of *klal ufrat,* we would assume that only earth may be used to cover the blood. But the Torah stipulates "with earth" here only for clarity's sake. "Cover" might just mean "hide from sight," which could imply hiding the blood in a closed container. "With earth" here specifies that the intent is "cover" in its plain and accepted meaning. The rule of *klal ufrat* is therefore inapplicable, and we take the verse to mean that earth is only an example of all those things that can cover the blood.

⁹ *"8. Whatever follows from a generalization is intended to be considered as teaching not about itself but about the generalization* [kol davar shehayah bikhlal v'yatsa min haklal]*"* A specification (a *prat*) that emerges from a generalization (a *klal*), but teaches us something independently as well, applies not to itself alone but to the *klal* as a whole—that is, it teaches us something new about the rule of which it is a part. According to Leviticus 7:19, a person who is ritually impure is not allowed to eat sacrificial meat. "It shall not be eaten" is the generalization (the *klal*). Verse 20 then stipulates a detail that belongs conceptually to it: "But the person who, in a state of impurity, eats the sacrifice of peace offering—that person shall be cut off from his kin." We might have thought that verse 20 means that only in the case of peace offerings will the culprit be "cut off from his kin," whereas according to the rule under discussion, the consequences of verse 20 apply to the entire *klal.*

[10] *"9. When something is first implied in a general law and is followed by a provision similar to the general law, the provision is intended to alleviate, not increase, the severity of that similar provision* [kol davar shehayah bikhlal v'yatsa lit'on to'an acher shehu kh'inyano]*"*An aspect of a general rule (a *klal*) that emerges independently in a case that is *similar* to the *klal* must be interpreted as adding leniency, not severity, to the *klal*. The Torah pronounces, "Anyone who kills a human being shall be put to death" (Lev. 24:17). But Deuteronomy 19:5 maintains, "If a man accompanies his neighbor into a forest to cut wood, and as his hand swings the ax to cut down a tree, the ax-head flies off the handle and strikes the other so that he dies, that man shall flee to a city [of refuge] and live." (The Bible sets aside such cities where avengers of the victim are not allowed to follow.) We thus may distinguish intentional from unintentional homicide. The specific instance of the woodcutter can be applied back to the *klal* of homicide in general to give us the entire category of unintentional homicide that is to be treated with greater leniency.

[11] *"10. When something is first implied in a general law and is followed by a provision dissimilar to the general law, the provision is intended either to alleviate or to increase the severity of that dissimilar provision* [kol davar shehayah bikhlal v'yatsa lit'on to'an acher shelo kh'inyano]*"*An aspect of a general rule (a *klal*) that emerges independently in a case that is *dissimilar* to the *klal* may be applied leniently or severely. A Hebrew maidservant is part of the *klal* of Hebrew servants in general, as we see from Deuteronomy 15:12, which classifies together "a fellow Hebrew, man or woman, who is sold to you." But Exodus 21:2 adds, about men only, "If you buy a Hebrew manservant, he shall serve six years; in the seventh year, he shall go free." We might assume that the maidservant is included fully by the *klal* of the Hebrew manservant. But Exodus 21:7 says, "If a man sells his daughter to be a servant, she shall not be freed as male servants are." A lenient implication that follows is that the minute she shows signs of puberty, she may not be retained in servitude. Alternatively—the severe implication—her master has the option of marrying her to himself or to his son against her will.

[12] *"11. When something is first implied in a general law and followed by a new provision, you cannot connect the new provision to the general law unless Scripture explicitly connects them* [kol davar shehayah bikhlal v'yatsa lidon badavar hechadash]*"*If an aspect of a generalization (a *klal*) is used to settle an altogether different matter, that matter may no longer be subsumed under the original *klal* unless Scripture expressly declares otherwise. Someone whose leprosy is cured has the blood of a guilt offering sprinkled upon his ear, thumb, and toe (Lev. 14:14). This is unusual for sacrifices. One might think, therefore, that guilt offerings are no longer subsumed under the *klal* "offerings," so that rules applicable to offerings in general cannot be generalized to guilt offerings in particular. That would be true if not for the express comment by the Torah, "For the sin offering is like the guilt offering" (Lev. 14:13).

[13] *"12. By deducing a word's meaning from context or from subsequent use* [davar

halamed me'inyano v'davar halamed misofo] "A matter in question may be inferred from its context or from what follows it. Context is brought to bear on the Decalogue's injunction "You shall not steal." It is preceded by "You shall not murder" and "You shall not commit adultery." As those injunctions refer to capital crimes, so (in this case) must theft, which is now understood as the capital crime of kidnapping. An example of using a subsequent expression to elucidate an earlier one can be found in the passage we already looked at regarding the accidental ax murder (Deut. 19:5). The killer is permitted to seek safety in a city of refuge "so that the blood avenger may not pursue the manslayer...and kill him. He does not deserve the death penalty" (19:6). To whom does the clause "he does not deserve the death penalty" apply? The manslayer or the avenger? The Rabbis apply it to the manslayer, because Deuteronomy19:6 continues, "since he had never been the other's enemy."

[14] "13. And similarly, by not reconciling two contradictory verses until a third verse reconciles the two [shnei kh'tuvim hamakh'chishim zeh et zeh] "Two contradictory verses may be reconciled by a third. According to Deuteronomy 16:2, "You shall slaughter the Passover sacrifice...from the flock [sheep] and the herd [goats]"—implying that it must come from both. But Exodus 12:5 maintains, "You shall take it from the sheep or from the goats"—implying that it may be either. From a third verse, "Go pick out lambs for your families and slaughter the Passover offering" (Exod. 2:21), the Rabbis conclude that the Passover sacrifice must come the flock and the festival sacrifice (called chagigah) must come from the herd.

◆ ◆ ◆

B. Kaddish D'rabbanan ("Rabbis' Kaddish")

[1] Magnified and sanctified be His great name in the world He created according to His will. [2] May He establish His kingdom in your lifetime and during your days, and in the life of the whole house of Israel, speedily and soon. [3] Say: Amen.

[4] May His great name be blessed forever and for all eternity.

[5] Blessed, praised, glorified, exalted, honored, extolled, lauded, and adored be the name of the Holy One—blessed be He—above all earthly blessings, hymns, praises, and consolations. [6] Say: Amen.

[7] For Israel, for our teachers and for their students, and for all the students of their students, for everyone who studies Torah, whether in this place or in any place: may they and we have abundant peace, grace, love and mercy, long life and ample food, and salvation from their Father in heaven and earth. [8] Say: Amen.

[9] May there be abundant peace from heaven, and good life, for us and for all of Israel. [10] Say: Amen. [11] May the One who brings peace in His heights, in His mercy bring peace for us and for all of Israel. [12] Say: Amen.

[1]יִתְגַּדַּל וְיִתְקַדַּשׁ שְׁמֵהּ רַבָּא בְּעָלְמָא דִי בְרָא כִרְעוּתֵהּ; [2]וְיַמְלִיךְ מַלְכוּתֵהּ בְּחַיֵּיכוֹן וּבְיוֹמֵיכוֹן, וּבְחַיֵּי דְכָל בֵּית יִשְׂרָאֵל, בַּעֲגָלָא וּבִזְמַן קָרִיב, [3]וְאִמְרוּ אָמֵן.

[4]יְהֵא שְׁמֵהּ רַבָּא מְבָרַךְ לְעָלַם וּלְעָלְמֵי עָלְמַיָּא.

[5]יִתְבָּרַךְ וְיִשְׁתַּבַּח, וְיִתְפָּאַר וְיִתְרוֹמַם וְיִתְנַשֵּׂא וְיִתְהַדָּר, וְיִתְעַלֶּה וְיִתְהַלָּל שְׁמֵהּ דְּקֻדְשָׁא, בְּרִיךְ הוּא, לְעֵלָּא מִן כָּל-בִּרְכָתָא וְשִׁירָתָא, תֻּשְׁבְּחָתָא וְנֶחֱמָתָא, דַּאֲמִירָן בְּעָלְמָא, [6]וְאִמְרוּ אָמֵן.

[7]עַל יִשְׂרָאֵל וְעַל רַבָּנָן וְעַל תַּלְמִידֵיהוֹן, וְעַל כָּל תַּלְמִידֵי תַלְמִידֵיהוֹן, וְעַל כָּל מָן דְּעָסְקִין בְּאוֹרַיְתָא, דִּי בְּאַתְרָא הָדֵן וְדִי בְּכָל אֲתַר וַאֲתַר, יְהֵא לְהוֹן וּלְכוֹן שְׁלָמָא רַבָּא, חִנָּא וְחִסְדָּא וְרַחֲמִין, וְחַיִּין אֲרִיכִין, וּמְזוֹנֵי רְוִיחֵי, וּפֻרְקָנָא מִן קֳדָם אֲבוּהוֹן דְּבִשְׁמַיָּא וְאַרְעָא, [8]וְאִמְרוּ אָמֵן.

[9]יְהֵא שְׁלָמָא רַבָּא מִן שְׁמַיָּא, וְחַיִּים טוֹבִים, עָלֵינוּ וְעַל כָּל יִשְׂרָאֵל, [10]וְאִמְרוּ אָמֵן.

[11]עֹשֶׂה שָׁלוֹם בִּמְרוֹמָיו, הוּא בְּרַחֲמָיו יַעֲשֶׂה שָׁלוֹם עָלֵינוּ וְעַל כָּל-יִשְׂרָאֵל, [12]וְאִמְרוּ אָמֵן.

BRETTLER (BIBLE)

[7] *"For Israel"* This prayer for Torah scholars has no biblical precedent, since institutionalized Torah study does not occur in biblical times. Until at least the exilic period, priests were responsible for preserving *torah* (Jer. 18:18; Ezek. 7:26), by which was meant divine instruction, and in the early post-exilic periods, Levites were its teachers (Neh. 8:9). Only with the Rabbis would Torah scholarship break free of these hereditary connections.

FRANKEL (A WOMAN'S VOICE)

[7] *"For Israel, for our teachers"* Even Jews who rarely set foot in synagogue are familiar with the version of this Aramaic prayer known as the Mourner's *Kaddish*. Not so of this particular version known as *Kaddish D'rabbanan*, recited upon concluding study of a Jewish text. Its uniqueness lies in the addition of the paragraph beginning, "For Israel, for our teachers and for their students and for all the students of their students"—a prayer for material well-being and divine grace for all who

B. *KADDISH D'RABBANAN* ("RABBIS' *KADDISH*")

[1] Magnified and sanctified be His great name in the world He created according to His will. [2] May He establish His kingdom in your lifetime and during your days, and in the life of the whole house of Israel, speedily and soon. [3] Say: Amen.

[4] May His great name be blessed forever and for all eternity.

DORFF (THEOLOGY)

[7] *"For Israel, for our teachers and for their students"* This paragraph makes this the *Kaddish D'rabbanan*, the *Kaddish* for rabbis and teachers and their students. In many congregations only mourners recite it here, but one need not be a mourner to recite it. It is said whenever we complete the study of a piece of our tradition, as long as a *minyan* is present. We pray for those who carry on our tradition by studying and teaching it, for as the Jewish traditions understands it, study of Torah is an act that sanctifies God.

study Torah. For centuries this *Kaddish* was recited by and on behalf of men only, for they held the monopoly on Torah study. Teachers and students alike were an exclusively male fraternity. Fortunately, that is no longer the case. Today many Jewish women not only study but teach and interpret Torah—a phenomenon that the late Reform theologian Jakob Petuchowski charmingly called "the ever-widening holiness franchise."

L. HOFFMAN (HISTORY)

Kaddish D'rabbanan

A full discussion of the *Kaddish* is postponed to a subsequent volume on "Concluding Prayers." We should consider the oddity of having two versions of the *Kaddish*—This one and the *Kaddish D'rabbanan* preceding—one after the other with only a psalm intervening. In short, the *Kaddish* is an ancient prayer that followed study and had nothing to do with death or mourning. By the high Middle Ages, however, it was assumed that saying a

The result was twofold. First, the *Kaddish D'rabbanan,* which was still being said by the whole congregation as a concluding prayer to their morning study, was reserved for mourners alone. Second, wherever possible, an additional *Kaddish* was added, but in order to "justify" it liturgically, an additional reading, usually a psalm, was chosen to separate the two recitations of *Kaddish* from each other.

יִתְגַּדֵּל וְיִתְקַדָּשׁ שְׁמֵהּ רַבָּא בְּעָלְמָא דִי בְרָא כִרְעוּתֵהּ;¹

וְיַמְלִיךְ מַלְכוּתֵהּ בְּחַיֵּיכוֹן וּבְיוֹמֵיכוֹן, וּבְחַיֵּי דְכָל בֵּית²

יִשְׂרָאֵל, בַּעֲגָלָא וּבִזְמַן קָרִיב, ³וְאִמְרוּ אָמֵן.

⁴יְהֵא שְׁמֵהּ רַבָּא מְבָרַךְ לְעָלַם וּלְעָלְמֵי עָלְמַיָּא.

⁵יִתְבָּרַךְ וְיִשְׁתַּבַּח, וְיִתְפָּאַר וְיִתְרוֹמַם, וְיִתְנַשֵּׂא וְיִתְהַדָּר,

וְיִתְעַלֶּה וְיִתְהַלָּל שְׁמֵהּ דְּקֻדְשָׁא, בְּרִיךְ הוּא, לְעֵלָּא

J. HOFFMAN (TRANSLATION)

[7]*"For our teachers"* Hebrew, *rabbanan,* translated immediately above as "rabbis." The *rabbanan* refered to a particular kind of teacher, the way the modern "professors" indicates a particular kind of teacher. We have no exact word for *rabbanan* in English; here we emphasize their role as teacher, while in the title we emphasize their role as rabbi.

Kaddish saved the soul of a loved one from punishment after death. Unlike today, however, when mourners say the *Kaddish* in unison, medieval Jews assigned individual recitations of the *Kaddish* to single mourners. As long as mourners were few, there were enough instances of the *Kaddish* to go around. But as Jewish urban populations grew, and as the custom of *yahrzeit* (marking the anniversary of a loved one's death by saying *Kaddish*) caught on, the numbers of mourners began to outstrip the instances of *Kaddish* in the service.

5 Blessed, praised, glorified, exalted, honored, extolled, lauded, and adored be the name of the Holy One—blessed be He—above all earthly blessings, hymns, praises, and consolations. 6 Say: Amen.

7 For Israel, for our teachers and for their students, and for all the students of their students, for everyone who studies Torah, whether in this place or in any place: may they and we have abundant peace, grace, love and mercy, long life and ample food, and salvation from their Father in heaven and earth. 8 Say: Amen.

9 May there be abundant peace from heaven, and good life, for us and for all of Israel. 10 Say: Amen. 11 May the One who brings peace in His heights, in His mercy bring peace for us and for all of Israel. 12 Say: Amen.

מִן כָּל־בִּרְכָתָא וְשִׁירָתָא, תֻּשְׁבְּחָתָא וְנֶחֱמָתָא, דַּאֲמִירָן בְּעָלְמָא, 6 וְאִמְרוּ אָמֵן.

7 עַל יִשְׂרָאֵל וְעַל רַבָּנָן וְעַל תַּלְמִידֵיהוֹן, וְעַל כָּל תַּלְמִידֵי תַלְמִידֵיהוֹן, וְעַל כָּל מָן דְּעָסְקִין בְּאוֹרַיְתָא, דִּי בְּאַתְרָא הָדֵן וְדִי בְּכָל אֲתַר וַאֲתַר, יְהֵא לְהוֹן וּלְכוֹן שְׁלָמָא רַבָּא, חִנָּא וְחִסְדָּא וְרַחֲמִין, וְחַיִּין אֲרִיכִין, וּמְזוֹנֵי רְוִיחֵי, וּפֻרְקָנָא מִן קֳדָם אֲבוּהוֹן דְּבִשְׁמַיָּא וְאַרְעָא, 8 וְאִמְרוּ אָמֵן. 9 יְהֵא שְׁלָמָא רַבָּא מִן שְׁמַיָּא, וְחַיִּים טוֹבִים, עָלֵינוּ וְעַל כָּל יִשְׂרָאֵל, 10 וְאִמְרוּ אָמֵן.

11 עֹשֶׂה שָׁלוֹם בִּמְרוֹמָיו, הוּא בְּרַחֲמָיו יַעֲשֶׂה שָׁלוֹם עָלֵינוּ וְעַל כָּל־יִשְׂרָאֵל, 12 וְאִמְרוּ אָמֵן.

7 *Dividing* Kaddish

A. PSALM 30

David's psalm, a song for the dedication of the house. [2] I will exalt You, Adonai, for You have lifted me up and given my enemies no joy from me. [3] Adonai my God, I cried out to You and You healed me. [4] Adonai, You raised my soul from the grave, gave me life as I was falling into a pit. [5] Sing to Adonai, all His righteous, laud His holiness, for momentary is His anger, lifelong His favor. [6] By night weeping abides, but morning brings joy! [7] When I was well, I said, "Never will I falter." [8] Adonai, in Your favor You made me strong as a mountain. [9] Then You hid Your face and I was terrified. [10] But it was to You, Adonai, that I cried out; to my Lord I pleaded for mercy. [11] What would silencing me serve, sending me to my grave? [12] Can dust laud You, or declare Your faithfulness? [13] Hear me, Adonai, and have mercy on me. [14] Adonai, help me! [15] You turned my suffering into dance, opened my sackcloth and clothed me with joy, that I might sing praise to You. [16] I will not be silent! Adonai my God, I will laud You forever!

[1]מִזְמוֹר שִׁיר חֲנֻכַּת הַבַּיִת לְדָוִד.
[2]אֲרוֹמִמְךָ, יְיָ, כִּי דִלִּיתָנִי, וְלֹא שִׂמַּחְתָּ
אֹיְבַי לִי. [3]יְיָ אֱלֹהָי, שִׁוַּעְתִּי אֵלֶיךָ
וַתִּרְפָּאֵנִי. [4]יְיָ, הֶעֱלִיתָ מִן שְׁאוֹל נַפְשִׁי,
חִיִּיתַנִי מִיָּרְדִי בוֹר. [5]זַמְּרוּ לַיְיָ חֲסִידָיו,
וְהוֹדוּ לְזֵכֶר קָדְשׁוֹ. כִּי רֶגַע בְּאַפּוֹ, חַיִּים
בִּרְצוֹנוֹ; [6]בָּעֶרֶב יָלִין בֶּכִי, וְלַבֹּקֶר רִנָּה.
[7]וַאֲנִי אָמַרְתִּי בְשַׁלְוִי, בַּל אֶמּוֹט לְעוֹלָם.
[8]יְיָ, בִּרְצוֹנְךָ הֶעֱמַדְתָּה לְהַרְרִי עֹז;
[9]הִסְתַּרְתָּ פָנֶיךָ, הָיִיתִי נִבְהָל. [10]אֵלֶיךָ יְיָ
אֶקְרָא, וְאֶל אֲדֹנָי אֶתְחַנָּן. [11]מַה בֶּצַע
בְּדָמִי, בְּרִדְתִּי אֶל שָׁחַת; [12]הֲיוֹדְךָ עָפָר,
הֲיַגִּיד אֲמִתֶּךָ. [13]שְׁמַע יְיָ וְחָנֵּנִי; [14]יְיָ,
הֱיֵה עֹזֵר לִי. [15]הָפַכְתָּ מִסְפְּדִי לְמָחוֹל
לִי; פִּתַּחְתָּ שַׂקִּי וַתְּאַזְּרֵנִי שִׂמְחָה. לְמַעַן
יְזַמֶּרְךָ כָבוֹד, [16]וְלֹא יִדֹּם; יְיָ אֱלֹהָי,
לְעוֹלָם אוֹדֶךָ.

BRETTLER (BIBLE)

[1] *"David's psalm"* The first verse of a psalm, noting how it was recited and who composed it, is called a superscription. Superscriptions are often secondarily added to the psalm. In this case, the odd syntax of the Hebrew words "a song for the dedication of the house" disrupts the phrase "a psalm by David," suggesting that these middle words were a later insertion. They might reflect a reinterpretation of this originally pre-exilic psalm when it was reused during the dedication of the Second Temple after the return from exile, or even in 164 B.C.E., after the Temple was restored by the Hasmoneans (Macc-abees). Originally, the psalm

(p. 194)

DORFF (THEOLOGY)

[4] *"You raised my soul from the grave,gave me life as I was falling into a pit"* Psalm 30, like all of the Bible except the Book of Daniel, does not believe in resurrection of the dead. Hence the verse later on, "What would silencing me serve, sending me to my grave? Can dust laud You?" These introductory verses, then, are metaphors for God's changing our mood from sadness to joy. As the psalmist says toward the end, "You turned my suffering into dance." What a wonderfully hopeful way to end these introductory prayers!

FRANKEL (A WOMAN'S VOICE)

[3] *"I cried out to You and You healed me"* We began our Morning Blessings by thanking God for surviving the night. We end it by again expressing gratitude for God's gift of life: "Adonai my God, I cried out to You and You healed me." Traditionally, this psalm is recited upon recovering from serious illness. Its inclusion here suggests that we are all seriously ill with the affliction of mortality. We remind ourselves that as life is transitory, so too is suffering. We reassure ourselves that though God's

A. PSALM 30

[1] David's psalm, a song for the dedication of the house. [2] I will exalt You, Adonai, for You have lifted me up and given my enemies no joy from me. [3] Adonai my God, I cried out to You and You healed me. [4] Adonai, You raised my soul from the grave, gave me life as I was falling into a pit. [5] Sing to Adonai, all His righteous, laud His holiness, for momentary is His anger, lifelong His favor. [6] By night weeping abides,

anger may momentarily flare up, there is always forgiveness in its wake; that though we lie down at night in tears, we awake with renewed faith. Ministering steadfastly to our ailing spirit, God nurses us back to life, and we repay the debt each morning with *rinah*, "joy."

J. HOFFMAN (TRANSLATION)

[2] *"Lifted"* The Hebrew word here comes from a root meaning "to draw water" and probably originally referred to drawing water up from a well. It may have retained this connotation when this psalm was written: water and well imagery abounds in the Bible, including the famous: "Draw forth water in gladness from the wells of salvation" (Isa. 12:3) though that verse uses a different verb for "draw forth."

[4] *"Grave"* Probably "underworld" is intended.

L. HOFFMAN (HISTORY)

THE KADDISH YATOM *("MOURNER'S* KADDISH*") PRECEDED BY PSALM 30— DIVIDING THE END OF THE* BIRKHOT HASHACHAR *(MORNING BLESSINGS) AND THE NEXT MAJOR SECTION (SEE VOLUME 3—*P'SUKEI D'ZIMRAH *[MORNING* PSALMS]).

[1]מִזְמוֹר שִׁיר חֲנֻכַּת הַבַּיִת לְדָוִד. [2]אֲרוֹמִמְךָ, יְיָ, כִּי דִלִּיתָנִי, וְלֹא שִׂמַּחְתָּ אֹיְבַי לִי. [3]יְיָ אֱלֹהָי, שִׁוַּעְתִּי אֵלֶיךָ וַתִּרְפָּאֵנִי. [4]יְיָ, הֶעֱלִיתָ מִן שְׁאוֹל נַפְשִׁי, חִיִּיתַנִי מִיָּרְדִי בוֹר. [5]זַמְּרוּ לַיְיָ חֲסִידָיו, וְהוֹדוּ לְזֵכֶר קָדְשׁוֹ. כִּי רֶגַע בְּאַפּוֹ, חַיִּים בִּרְצוֹנוֹ; [6]בָּעֶרֶב יָלִין בֶּכִי, וְלַבֹּקֶר רִנָּה. [7]וַאֲנִי אָמַרְתִּי בְשַׁלְוִי, בַּל אֶמּוֹט לְעוֹלָם. [8]יְיָ, בִּרְצוֹנְךָ

[5] *"Laud"* This is the same verb we usually translate as "gratefully acknowledge," but here we feel that poetic impact is more important than literal accuracy, and so we choose a word that we can incorporate into the psalm poetically, here and twice below.

[5] *"Momentary is His anger, lifelong His favor"* Our translation follows one common understanding of the enigmatic Hebrew here, the other being "momentary is His anger; life results from His favor." Yet a third possible reading of the Hebrew is "a   *(p. 195)*

but morning brings joy! [7] When I was well, I said, "Never will I falter." [8] Adonai, in Your favor You made me strong as a mountain. [9] Then You hid Your face and I was terrified. [10] But it was to You, Adonai, that I cried out, to my Lord I pleaded for mercy. [11] What would silencing me serve, sending me to my grave? [12] Can dust laud You, or declare Your faithfulness? [13] Hear me, Adonai, and have mercy on me. [14] Adonai, help me! [15] You turned my suffering into dance, opened my sackcloth and clothed me with joy, that I might sing praise to You. [16] I will not be silent! Adonai my God, I will laud You forever!

הֶעֱמַדְתָּה לְהַרְרִי עֹז; [9] הִסְתַּרְתָּ פָנֶיךָ, הָיִיתִי נִבְהָל. [10] אֵלֶיךָ יְיָ אֶקְרָא, וְאֶל אֲדֹנָי אֶתְחַנָּן. [11] מַה בֶּצַע בְּדָמִי, בְּרִדְתִּי אֶל שָׁחַת; [12] הֲיוֹדְךָ עָפָר, הֲיַגִּיד אֲמִתֶּךָ. [13] שְׁמַע יְיָ וְחָנֵּנִי; [14] יְיָ, הֱיֵה עֹזֵר לִי. [15] הָפַכְתָּ מִסְפְּדִי לְמָחוֹל לִי; פִּתַּחְתָּ שַׂקִּי וַתְּאַזְּרֵנִי שִׂמְחָה. לְמַעַן יְזַמֶּרְךָ כָבוֹד, [16] וְלֹא יִדֹּם; יְיָ אֱלֹהַי, לְעוֹלָם אוֹדֶךָּ.

BRETTLER (BIBLE)

was a thanksgiving psalm, a genre well attested in the Psalter, in which a person thanks God for being saved, usually from illness and/or enemies.

[2] *"I will exalt You"* The psalmist exalts God, who has raised him up from *sh'ol*, the biblical underworld. This should not be taken literally, but symbolically, as being in desperate straits.

[4] *"The grave...a pit"* A typical biblical poetic verse, in synonymous parallelism. *Bor*, literally "pit," is the entrance to the underworld and thus a suitable parallel for *sh'ol* (cf. Isa. 14:15).

[5] *"His righteous"* Either the pious in general or a particular class of Jews, like the later Essenes.

[5] *"His holiness [zekher kodsho]"* Literally, "his holy remembrance." But *zekher*, "remembrance," often parallels *shem*, "name," in the Bible, so it comes to mean "name." Similarly, Psalm 106:47 says, "to acclaim your holy name" (*l'hodot l'shem kodshecha*).

[7] *"When I was well"* The psalmist reflects personally on his once-held but mistaken belief that all would go well no matter what. He now understands that well-being depends on his relationship with God.

[9] *"You hid Your face"* God's presence is very reassuring, while God's absence creates panic. The psalmist shares the biblical idea that God sometimes "hides His face" from us—one reason why innocent people suffer. This hiding of God's face may result from human misbehavior, but equally, God sometimes hides His face for no clear reason at all and needs to be "called back."

[11] *"What would silencing me serve?"* This verse assumes that God enjoys begin praised and that there is no praise of God in *sh'ol*. The psalmist is saying, "If You kill me, you will be praised less, so let me live for Your sake."

[13] *"Hear me, Adonai"* As currently vocalized, this is a continuation of the plea to God. The Septuagint (the early Greek translation) reads it not as an imperative, *sh'ma*, "hear," but as a past tense, *shama,* "He has heard." In this reading, we are about to see that God has heard the plea and answered it.

[15] *"Suffering into dance"* Dancing is typically associated with joy in ancient Israel (cf. Jer. 31:13; Lam. 5:15).

[16] *"I will laud You forever"* Returning to the earlier theme, that only the living praise God. The psalmist ends with the hyperbolic promise that he will acknowledge God "forever." The term "acknowledge" here recalls earlier usage (Ps. 30:5, 10) and ties the psalm together.

———◆———

J. HOFFMAN (TRANSLATION)

moment of His anger, but long life is His will" (that is, "He wants a moment of His anger but long life [for us]").

[6] *"Weeping abides"* Literally, "weeping spends the night," but we don't have a verb for that in English. Another possible reading of the Hebrew is "one spends the night weeping."

[7] *"Well"* Literally, "serene," but it seems to contrast with "ill" here, referring to the time before God healed the author.

[10] *"Pleaded for mercy"* From the root *ch-n-n.* Others translate "appeal." This is the same root used rabbinically for "supplications" (see above, p. 160, 167). But the root recurs both here and immediately below, so we translate "pleaded for mercy" here and "have mercy on me" below.

[11] *"Silencing me"* Literally, "my blood," commonly translated, "What would my death serve?" But again we have a play on words, this time with *d-m.* Here those letters refer to blood; below, to silence.

¹¹ *"Grave"* Literally, "pit," but not the same word used above. Again, this probably refers to the netherworld.

¹³ *"Have mercy"* Usually translated, "be gracious." (See above, "Pleaded for mercy.")

¹⁴ *"Help me"* Others, "be my help," which we feel is too weak.

¹⁵ *"Clothed"* Literally, "girded." (This same verb is used in the blessings—see p. 138.) But we feel that "girded" in modern English is too far removed from the notion of clothes to successfully carry the imagery here.

¹⁶ *"Silent"* A play on words. (See above, "Silencing me.")

♦ ♦ ♦

B. Mourner's *Kaddish*

¹Magnified and sanctified be His great name in the world He created according to His will. ²May He establish His kingdom in your lifetime and during your days, and in the life of the whole house of Israel, speedily and soon. ³Say: Amen.

⁴May His great name be blessed forever and for all eternity.

⁵Blessed, praised, glorified, exalted, honored, extolled, lauded and adored be the name of the Holy One—blessed be He—above all earthly blessings, hymns, praises, and consolations. ⁶Say: Amen.

⁷May there be abundant peace from heaven, and life, for us and for all of Israel. ⁸Say: Amen.

⁹May the One who brings peace in His heights, in His mercy bring peace for us and for all of Israel. ¹⁰Say: Amen.

יִתְגַּדַּל וְיִתְקַדַּשׁ שְׁמֵהּ רַבָּא בְּעָלְמָא דִּי¹ בְרָא כִרְעוּתֵהּ; ²וְיַמְלִיךְ מַלְכוּתֵהּ בְּחַיֵּיכוֹן וּבְיוֹמֵיכוֹן, וּבְחַיֵּי דְכָל בֵּית יִשְׂרָאֵל, בַּעֲגָלָא וּבִזְמַן קָרִיב, ³וְאִמְרוּ אָמֵן.

⁴יְהֵא שְׁמֵהּ רַבָּא מְבָרַךְ לְעָלַם וּלְעָלְמֵי עָלְמַיָּא.

⁵יִתְבָּרַךְ וְיִשְׁתַּבַּח, וְיִתְפָּאַר וְיִתְרוֹמַם, וְיִתְנַשֵּׂא וְיִתְהַדָּר וְיִתְעַלֶּה וְיִתְהַלָּל שְׁמֵהּ דְּקֻדְשָׁא, בְּרִיךְ הוּא, לְעֵלָּא מִן כָּל־בִּרְכָתָא וְשִׁירָתָא, תֻּשְׁבְּחָתָא וְנֶחָמָתָא, דַּאֲמִירָן בְּעָלְמָא, ⁶וְאִמְרוּ אָמֵן.

⁷יְהֵא שְׁלָמָא רַבָּא מִן שְׁמַיָּא, וְחַיִּים, עָלֵינוּ וְעַל כָּל יִשְׂרָאֵל, ⁸וְאִמְרוּ אָמֵן.

⁹עֹשֶׂה שָׁלוֹם בִּמְרוֹמָיו, הוּא יַעֲשֶׂה שָׁלוֹם עָלֵינוּ וְעַל כָּל יִשְׂרָאֵל, ¹⁰וְאִמְרוּ אָמֵן.

Comments on the *Kaddish* can be found in the forthcoming *My People's Prayer Book Vol. 6—Tachnun (Concluding Prayers)*.

About the Contributors

MARC BRETTLER

Marc Brettler, Ph.D., is Dora Goldberg Professor of Biblical Studies and Chair of the Department of Near Eastern and Judaic Studies at Brandeis University. His major areas of research are biblical historical texts, religious metaphors, and gender issues in the Bible. Brettler is author of *God Is King: Understanding an Israelite Metaphor* (Sheffield Academic Press) and *The Creation of History in Ancient Israel* (Routledge) as well as a variety of articles on the Hebrew Bible. He is also associate editor of the new edition of the Oxford Annotated Bible.

ELLIOT N. DORFF

Elliot N. Dorff, Ph.D., is Rector and Distinguished Professor of Philosophy at the University of Judaism in Los Angeles. His book *Knowing God: Jewish Journeys to the Unknowable* (Jason Aronson) includes an extensive analysis of the nature of prayer. Ordained a rabbi by the Jewish Theological Seminary of America, Dorff is a member of the Conservative Movement's Committee on Jewish Law and Standards, its Commission on the Philosophy of the Conservative Movement, and its Commission to write a new Torah commentary for the Conservative Movement. He has written eight books and over 150 articles on Jewish thought, law, and ethics, and he has served on several federal government commissions on issues in bioethics.

DAVID ELLENSON

David Ellenson, Ph.D., is president of Hebrew Union College–Jewish Institute of Religion. He also serves as its I. H. and Anna Grancell Professor of Jewish Religious Thought. Ordained a rabbi by Hebrew Union College–Jewish Institute of Religion, he has served as a visiting professor at Hebrew University in Jerusalem, the Jewish Theological Seminary, and at the University of California at Los Angeles. Ellenson has also taught at the Pardes Institute of Jewish Studies and at the Shalom Hartman Institute in Jerusalem. Ellenson has published and lectured extensively on diverse topics in modern Jewish thought, history, and ethics.

ELLEN FRANKEL

Dr. Ellen Frankel is currently the CEO and Editor-in-Chief of the Jewish Publication Society. A scholar of Jewish folklore, Frankel has published eight books, including *The Classic Tales; The Encyclopedia of Jewish Symbols,* co-authored with artist Betsy Teutsch; *The Five Books of Miriam: A Woman's Commentary on the Torah; The Jewish Spirit;* and *The Illustrated Hebrew Bible.* Frankel travels widely as a storyteller and lecturer, speaking at synagogues, summer study institutes, Hillels, Jewish women's groups, Jewish community centers, museums, schools, retirement communities, and nursing homes, and to radio audiences.

JOEL M. HOFFMAN

Joel M. Hoffman, Ph.D., teaches advanced Hebrew, translation, and the history of Hebrew at Hebrew Union College–Jewish Institute of Religion in New York; he has also taught at Brandeis University, and lectured in America, Europe, and Israel. He has served as Hebrew consultant to Harper San Francisco and Jewish Lights Publishing. Hoffman's research in theoretical linguistics brings him to a new approach to ancient Hebrew, viewing it not merely as a dead language, but as a spoken language of antiquity. In addition to his graduate-level teaching, Hoffman teaches youngsters at various Hebrew schools. He considers teaching his greatest joy.

LAWRENCE A. HOFFMAN

Lawrence A. Hoffman, Ph.D., has served for over two decades as Professor of Liturgy at Hebrew Union College–Jewish Institute of Religion in New York, where he was ordained a rabbi. Widely recognized for his liturgical scholarship, Hoffman has combined research in Jewish ritual, worship, and spirituality with a passion for the spiritual renewal of contemporary Judaism.

He has written and edited numerous books, including *The Art of Public Prayer, 2nd Edition: Not for Clergy Only* (SkyLight Paths)—now used nationally by Jews and Christians as a handbook for liturgical planners in church and synagogue, as well as a revision of *What Is a Jew?,* the best-selling classic that remains the most widely read introduction to Judaism ever written in any language. He is also the author of *Israel— A Spiritual Travel Guide: A Companion for the Modern Jewish Pilgrim* and *The Way Into Jewish Prayer* (both Jewish Lights). Hoffman is currently a developer of Synagogue 2000, a transdenominational project designed to envision and implement the ideal synagogue of the spirit for the twenty-first century.

YOEL H. KAHN

Yoel H. Kahn, Ph.D., is Rabbi/Scholar-in-Residence at Congregation Sherith Israel, San Francisco, California, and Visiting Assistant Professor of Jewish Studies at the Graduate Theological Union, Berkeley, California. He is a member of the Central Conference of American Rabbi's Responsa Committee, and the CCAR Editorial

Committees for the new *Union Prayer Book*, *Clergy Manual*, and *Guide to Officiation at Same-Sex Union Ceremonies*. Kahn has published and lectured extensively on liturgy, sexuality, theology, and liberal Jewish decision making. His forthcoming book is on the creation and maintenance of identities and boundaries in Jewish liturgy.

LAWRENCE KUSHNER

Lawrence Kushner is Rabbi-in-Residence at Hebrew Union College–Jewish Institute of Religion, New York. He served as spiritual leader of Congregation Beth El in Sudbury, Massachusetts, for twenty-eight years and is widely regarded as one of the most creative religious writers in America. Ordained a rabbi by Hebrew Union College–Jewish Institute of Religion, Kushner led his congregants in publishing their own prayer book, *V'taher Libenu (Purify Our Hearts),* the first gender-neutral liturgy ever written. Through his lectures and many books, including *The Way Into Jewish Mystical Tradition; Invisible Lines of Connection: Sacred Stories of the Ordinary; The Book of Letters: A Mystical Hebrew Alphabet; Honey from the Rock: An Introduction to Jewish Mysticism; God Was in This Place and I, i Did Not Know: Finding Self, Spirituality, and Ultimate Meaning; Eyes Remade for Wonder: A Lawrence Kushner Reader* and *Jewish Spirituality: A Brief Introduction for Christians,* all published by Jewish Lights, he has helped shape the Jewish community's present focus on personal and institutional spiritual renewal.

DANIEL LANDES

Daniel Landes is Director and Rosh HaYeshivah of the Pardes Institute of Jewish Studies in Jerusalem and was an adjunct Professor of Jewish Law at Loyola University Law School in Los Angeles. Ordained a rabbi by Rabbi Isaac Elchanan Theological Seminary, Landes was a founding faculty member of the Simon Wiesenthal Center and the Yeshiva of Los Angeles. He has lectured and written various popular and scholarly articles on the subjects of Jewish thought, social ethics, and spirituality.

NEHEMIA POLEN

Nehemia Polen is associate professor of Jewish Thought at Boston's Hebrew College. He is the author of *The Holy Fire: The Teachings of Rabbi Kalonymus Shapira, the Rebbe of the Warsaw Ghetto* (Jason Aronson, 1994, 1999), as well as many academic and popular articles on Hasidism and Jewish spirituality. He received his Ph.D. from Boston University, where he studied with and served as teaching fellow for Nobel laureate Elie Wiesel. In 1994 he was Daniel Jeremy Silver Fellow at Harvard University, and has also been a Visiting Scholar at the Hebrew University in Jerusalem. He was ordained as a rabbi at the Ner Israel Rabbinical College in Baltimore, Maryland, and served as a congregational rabbi for twenty-three years. In 1998–1999 he was a National Endowment for the Humanities Fellow, working on the writings of Malkah Shapiro (1894–1971), the daughter of a noted Hasidic master, whose Hebrew memoirs focus on the spiritual lives of women in the context of pre-war Hasidism in Poland. The book, *The Rebbe's Daughter* (Jewish Publication Society), is scheduled for publication in March 2002.

List of Abbreviations

Artscroll   *Siddur Kol Ya'akov, 1984.*

Birnbaum   *Daily Prayer Book: Hasiddur Hashalem, 1949.*

FOP   *Forms of Prayer, 1997.*

Fox   Everett Fox, *The Five Books of Moses* (New York: Schocken Books, 1995).

GOP   *Gates of Prayer, 1975.*

HS   *Ha'avodah Shebalev, 1982.*

KH   *Kol Haneshamah, 1994.*

JPS   *Jewish Publication Society Bible* (Philadelphia: Jewish Publication Society, 1962).

NRSV   *New Revised Standard Bible, 1989.*

SLC   *Siddur Lev Chadash, 1995.*

SOH   *Service of the Heart, 1967.*

SSS   *Siddur Sim Shalom, 1985; revised, 1998.*

SVT   *Siddur Va'ani T'fillati (1998).*

UPB   *Union Prayer Book, 1894–1895.*

Glossary

The following glossary defines Hebrew words used regularly throughout this volume, and provides the way the words are pronounced. Sometimes two pronunciations are common, in which case the first is the way the word is sounded in proper Hebrew, and the second is the way it is sometimes heard in common speech, under the influence of Yiddish, the folk language of Jews in northern and eastern Europe (it is a combination, mostly, of Hebrew and German). Our goal is to provide the way that many Jews actually use these words, not just the technically correct version.

- The pronunciations are divided into syllables by dashes.
- The accented syllable is written in capital letters.
- "Kh" represents a guttural sound, similar to the German (as in "sprach").
- The most common vowel is "a" as in "father," which appears here as "ah."
- The short "e" (as in "get") is written either "e" (when it is in the middle of a syllable) or "eh" (when it ends a syllable).
- Similarly, the short "i" (as in "tin") is written either "i" (when it is in the middle of a syllable) or "ih" (when it ends a syllable).
- A long "o" (as in "Moses") is written "oe" (as in the English word "toe") or "oh" (as in the English word "Oh!").

Acharonim (pronounced ah-khah-roe-NEEM, or, commonly, ah-khah-ROE-nim): The name given to Jewish legal authorities from roughly the sixteenth century on. The word means, literally, "later ones," as opposed to the "earlier ones," authorities prior to that time who are held in higher regard and are called Rishonim (pronounced ree-shoh-NEEM, or, commonly, ree-SHOH-nim). Singular: Acharon (pronounced ah-khah-RONE) and Rishon (pronounced ree-SHONE).

Adon Olam (pronounced ah-DOHN oh-LAHM): An early morning prayer of unknown authorship, but dating from medieval times, and possibly originally intended as a nighttime prayer, because it praises God for watching over our souls when we sleep. Nowadays, it is used also as a concluding song for which composers have provided a staggering variety of tunes.

Akedah (pronounced ah-kay-DAH): Literally, "binding"; the technical term for the Genesis 22 account of the binding of Isaac on the altar; read liturgically as part of the *Birkhot Hashachar*. By extension, a genre of poem, especially for the High Holy Days, pleading for forgiveness on account of the merit of Isaac's near self-sacrifice.

Alenu (pronounced ah-LAY-noo): The first word and, therefore, the title of a major prayer compiled in the second or third century as part of the New Year (Rosh Hashanah) service, but from about the fourteenth century on, used also as part of the concluding section of every daily service. *Alenu* means "it is incumbent upon us..." and introduces the prayer's theme: our duty to praise God.

Amah (pronounced ah-MAH): A rabbinic measure, amounting, roughly, to a forearm: the distance from the elbow to the tip of the little finger.

Amidah (pronounced either ah-mee-DAH or, commonly, ah-MEE-dah): One of three commonly used titles for the second of two central units in the worship service, the first being The *Sh'ma* and Its Blessings. It is composed of a series of blessings, many of which are petitionary, except on Sabbaths and holidays, when the petitions are removed out of deference to the holiness of the day. Also called *T'fillah* and *Sh'moneh Esreh*. *Amidah* means "standing," and refers to the fact that the prayer is said standing up.

Amora (pronounced ah-MOE-rah): A title for talmudic authorities and, therefore, living roughly from the third to the sixth centuries. Plural: Amoraim (pronounced ah-moe-rah-EEM, or, commonly, ah-moe-RAH-yim). Often used in contrast to a Tanna (pronounced TAH-nah), the title of authorities in the time of the Mishnah, that is, prior to the third century. Plural: Tannaim (pronounced tah-nah-EEM, or, commonly, tah-NAH-yim).

Arvit (pronounced ahr-VEET, or, commonly, AHR-veet): From the Hebrew word *erev* (pronounced EH-rev) meaning "evening." One of two titles used for the evening worship service (also called *Ma'ariv*).

Ashkenazi (pronounced ahsh-k'-nah-ZEE, or, commonly, ahsh-k'-NAH-zee): From the Hebrew word *Ashkenaz*, meaning the geographic area of northern and eastern Europe; Ashkenazi is the adjective, describing the liturgical rituals and customs practiced there, as opposed to Sefardi, meaning the liturgical rituals and customs that are derived from *Sefarad*, Spain (see **Sefardi**).

Ashre (pronounced ahsh-RAY, or, commonly, AHSH-ray): The first word and, therefore, the title of a prayer said three times each day, composed primarily of Psalm 145. *Ashre* means "happy" and introduces the phrase "Happy are they who dwell in Your [God's] house."

Atarah (pronounced ah-tah-RAH): A stole worn by some Reform service leaders (in place of an actual *tallit* with *tsitsit*), prior to the liturgical renewal of the late twentieth century that featured a recovery of tradition and the reuse of the traditional *tallit*. (See *tallit*.)

Av harachamim (pronounced AHV hah-rah-khah-MEEM, or, commonly, ahv hah-RAH-khah-meem): Literally, "Father of mercy,"a prayer composed in the wake of the Crusades to commemorate the death of German Jewish martyrs; now part of the weekly Shabbat service (after reading Torah), and one of the main prayers comprising the Memorial Service *(Yizkor)*.

Avodah (pronounced ah-voe-DAH): Literally, "sacrificial service," a reference to the sacrificial cult practiced in the ancient Temple until its destruction by the Romans in the year 70 C.E.; also the title of the third to last blessing in the *Amidah*, a petition for the restoration of the Temple in messianic times. Many liberal liturgies either omit the blessing or reframe it as a petition for divine acceptance of worship in general.

Avot (pronounced ah-VOTE): Literally, "fathers" or "ancestors," and the title of the first blessing in the *Amidah*. The traditional wording of the blessing recollects the covenantal relationship between God and the patriarchs: Abraham, Isaac, and Jacob. Most   liberal liturgies also include explicit reference to the matriarchs: Sarah, Rebekah, Rachel, and Leah.

[The] Bach (pronounced BAHKH): An acronym for Rabbi Joel Sirkes (Poland, 1561–1640), formed by juxtaposing the two Hebrew initials of his major legal work, *Bayit Chadash* (BaCH).

Bar'khu (pronounced bah-r'-KHOO, or, commonly, BOH-r'khoo): The first word and, therefore, the title of the formal Call to Prayer with which the section called The *Sh'ma* and Its Blessings begins. *Bar'khu* means "praise," and introduces the invitation to the assembled congregation to praise God.

Barukh k'vod (pronounced bah-RUKH k'-VOD): The first two words of a response in the third blessing of the *Amidah* taken from Ezekiel 3:12, meaning "the glory of Adonai is blessed from His place."

Barukh she'amar (pronounced bah-ROOKH sheh-ah-MAHR): Literally, "Blessed is the One by whose speech [the world came to be]," the first words, and, therefore, the title of the blessing that opens the *P'sukei D'zimrah*, the "warm-up" section to the morning service composed mainly of biblical material (chiefly psalms) that were intended to be sung as praise of God.

Benediction (also called a "blessing"): One of two terms used for the Rabbis' favorite prose formula for composing prayers. The worship service is composed of many different literary genres, but most of it is benedictions. Long benedictions end with a summary line that begins *Barukh atah Adonai...* "Blessed are You, Adonai..." Short blessings have the summary line alone.

Ben Sirah (pronounced behn SIH-rah): Author of a book of wisdom similar in style to Proverbs, probably dating to 180 or 200 B.C.E., and containing, among other things, a moving description of the High Priest in the Jerusalem Temple. Though not included in the Jewish Bible, it is known because it became part of Catholic scripture. The book carries the author's name, but is called, by Catholics, Ecclesiasticus. A recently discovered Hebrew edition of Ben Sirah contains a prayer that some identify (probably incorrectly) as an early version of the *Amidah* (see **Amidah**).

Bet Yosef (pronounced bayt yoh-SAYF): Commentary to the *Tur* by Joseph Caro, sixteenth century, Land of Israel; and a precursor to his more popular code, the *Shulchan Arukh*.

Binah (pronounced bee-NAH, or, commonly, BEE-nah): Literally, "knowledge" or "understanding," and the title of the fourth blessing in the daily *Amidah*. It is a petition for human knowledge, particularly insight into the human condition, leading to repentance. In kabbalistic circles, it is one of the uppermost *s'firot*, representing a stage of divine thought prior to creation.

Birkat (pronounced beer-KAHT): Literally, "Blessing of..." The titles of many blessings are known as "Blessing of...," for example, "Blessing of Torah" and "Blessing of Jerusalem." Some titles are commonly shortened so that only the qualifying last words are used (such as "Jerusalem" instead of "Blessing of Jerusalem"), and they are listed in the glossary by the last words, e.g., *Y'rushalayim* instead of *Birkat Y'rushalayim* ("Jerusalem" instead of "Blessing of Jerusalem"). Those blessings that are more generally cited with the full title appear under *Birkat*.

Birkat Hashir (pronounced beer-KAHT hah-SHEER): Literally, "Blessing of song," and the title, therefore, of the final blessing to the *P'sukei D'zimrah*, the "warm-up" section to the morning service composed mainly of biblical material (chiefly psalms) that were intended to be sung as praise of God. Technically, a *Birkat Hashir* concludes any *Hallel* (see **Hallel**), in this case, the Daily *Hallel*, which is the central component of the *P'sukei D'zimrah*.

Birkat Hatorah (pronounced beer-KAHT hah-toe-RAH): Literally, "Blessing of Torah," the title for the second blessing in the liturgical section called The *Sh'ma* and Its Blessings; its theme is the revelation of the Torah to Israel on Mount Sinai.

Birkat Kohanim (pronounced beer-KAHT koe-hah-NEEM): Literally, "Blessing of the Priests," but usually referred to as "the priestly benediction," a reference to Numbers 6:24–26. Also the title of the final blessing of the *Amidah*. See also **Kohanim**.

Birkhot Hashachar (pronounced beer-KHOT hah-SHAH-khar): Literally, "Morning Blessings," the title of the first large section in the morning prayer regimen of Judaism; originally said privately upon arising in the morning, but now customarily recited immediately upon arriving at the synagogue. It is composed primarily of benedictions thanking God for the everyday gifts of health and wholeness, as well as study sections taken from the Bible and rabbinic literature.

Birkhot mitzvah (pronounced beer-KHOT meetz-VAH): Blessings said upon performing a commandment; normally of the form, "Blessed are You, Adonai our God, Ruler of the universe, who sanctified us with commandments and commanded us to...."

Birkhot nehenin (pronounced beer-KHOT neh-heh-NEEN): Blessings said upon enjoyment of God's world (e.g., eating food, seeing rainbows, hearing a thunderstorm, seeing a flower); normally of the form, "Blessed are You, Adonai our God, Ruler of the universe, who...."

B'rakhah (pronounced b'-rah-KHAH): The Hebrew word for "benediction" or "blessing." See *Benediction*. Plural ("benedictions") is *b'rakhot* (pronounced b'-rah-KHOTE).

Chanukah (pronounced KHAH-noo-kah): An eight-day festival beginning on the twenty-fifth day of the Hebrew month of Kislev, corresponding, usually, to some time in December. Chanukah celebrates the miraculous deliverance of the Jews as described in the books known as *Maccabees* (pronounced MA-kah-beez). Although not canonized in the Jewish Bible, Maccabees is carried in Catholic scripture and describes the heroic acts of a priestly family, known also as the Maccabees, or the Hasmoneans (pronounced has-moe-NEE-'ns), in 167 B.C.E.

Chanuki'ah (pronounced khah-noo-kee-YAH, or, commonly, khah-noo-KEE-yah): An eight-branch candelabra for Chanukah candles.

Chasidism (pronounced KHAH-sih-dizm): The doctrine generally traced to an eighteenth-century Polish Jewish mystic and spiritual leader known as the Ba'al Shem Tov (called also the BeSHT, an acronym composed of the initials of his name B, SH, and T). Followers are called Chasidim (pronounced khah-see-DEEM or khah-SIH-dim; singular, Chasid pronounced khah-SEED, or, commonly, KHA-sid) from the Hebrew word *chesed* (pronounced KHEH-sed), meaning "loving-kindness" or "piety."

Chatimah (pronounced khah-tee-MAH): The final summary line of a benediction (see *Benediction*).

Cheshvan (pronounced KHESH-vahn): A Hebrew month corresponding to late October or November.

Chokhmah (pronounced khokh-MAH, or, commonly, KHOKH-mah): Literally, "wisdom," but in kabbalistic circles, one of the uppermost *s'firot,* representing a stage of divine thought prior to creation.

Daily Hallel (pronounced hah-LAYL, or, commonly, HAH-layl): English for *Hallel Sheb'khol Yom.* See ***Hallel***.

David (pronounced dah-VEED): Literally, "David," a reference to the biblical King David, and the title of the fifteenth blessing of the daily *Amidah,* a petition for the appearance of the messianic ruler said by tradition to be a descendent of King David. Some liberal liturgies omit the blessing or reframe it to refer to a messianic age of perfection, but without the arrival of a human messianic ruler.

Doxology: Technical term for a congregational response to an invitation to praise God; generally a single line of prayer affirming praise of God forever and ever. Examples in The *Sh'ma* and Its Blessings are the responses to the Call to Prayer and to the *Sh'ma* itself. From the Greek word *doxa*, meaning "glory."

El Adon (pronounced ayl ah-DOHN): An early medieval (or, perhaps, ancient) poem celebrating God as a king enthroned on high; it is arranged as an acrostic, that is, each line begins with a different letter of the alphabet. Nowadays *El Adon* is a popular Sabbath morning hymn.

Eretz Yisrael (pronounced EH-retz yis-rah-AYL): Hebrew for "the Land of Israel."

Gaon (pronounced gah-OHN; plural: Geonim, pronounced g'-oh-NEEM): Title for the leading rabbis in Babylon (present-day Iraq) from about 750 to 1038. From a biblical word meaning "glory," which is equivalent in the title to saying "Your Excellence."

Gematria (pronounced g'-MAHT-ree-ah): The system of assigning a numerical value to each Hebrew letter according to its sequence in the alphabet; then matching the total represented by a word or phrase to another word or phrase with the same value, thereby applying the meaning implicit in one word or phrase to the other.

Genizah (pronounced g'-NEE-zah): A cache of documents, in particular, the one discovered at the turn of the twentieth century in an old synagogue in Cairo; the source of our knowledge about how Jews prayed in the Land of Israel and vicinity prior to the twelfth century. From a word meaning "to store or hide away," "to archive."

Gra (pronounced GRAH): Elijah of Vilna, known also as the Vilna Gaon, outstanding halakhic authority of Lithuania (1720–1797).

G'ulah (pronounced g'-oo-LAH): Literally, "redemption" or "deliverance," and the title of the seventh blessing of the daily *Amidah*, as well as the third blessing in The *Sh'ma* and Its Blessings; its theme affirms God's redemptive act of delivering the Israelites from Egypt, and promises ultimate deliverance from suffering and want at the end of time.

G'vurot (pronounced g'voo-ROTE): Literally, "strength" or "power," and the title of the second blessing in the *Amidah*. It affirms the power of God to bring annual rain and new growth in nature and, by extension, to resurrect the dead. Some liberal liturgies omit the belief in resurrection or replace it with wording that suggests other concepts of eternal life.

Haftarah (pronounced hahf-tah-RAH, or, commonly, hahf-TOE-rah): The section of Scripture taken from the prophets and read publicly as part of Shabbat and holiday worship services. From a word meaning "to conclude," since it is the "concluding reading," that is, it follows a reading from the Torah (the Five Books of Moses).

Haggadah (pronounced hah-gah-DAH, or, commonly, hah-GAH-dah): The liturgical service for the Passover eve Seder meal. From a Hebrew word meaning "to tell," since the Haggadah is a telling of the Passover narrative.

Hakafah (pronounced hah-kah-FAH): "Going around [the room]," a procession in which the Torah is not only taken from the ark but is carried to the *bimah* during the introductory prayers. As the procession winds its way to the *bimah*, people approach the Torah, even kiss it.

Halakhah (pronounced hah-lah-KHAH, or, commonly, hah-LAH-khah): The Hebrew word for "Jewish law." Used as an anglicized adjective, halakhic (pronounced hah-LAH-khic), meaning "legal." From the Hebrew word meaning "to walk, to go," so denoting the way on which a person should walk through life.

Hallel (pronounced hah-LAYL, or, commonly, HAH-layl): A Hebrew word meaning "praise," and by extension, the name given to sets of psalms that are recited liturgically in praise of God: Psalms 145–150, the Daily *Hallel*, is recited each morning; Psalm 136, the Great *Hallel*, is recited on Shabbat and holidays and is part of the Passover Seder. Psalms 113–118, the best-known *Hallel*, known more fully as the Egyptian *Hallel*, is recited on holidays and gets its name from Psalm 114:1, which celebrates the moment "when Israel left Egypt."

Hallel Sheb'khol Yom (pronounced hah-LAYL [or, commonly, HAH-layl] sheh-b'-khol YOHM): The Hebrew term for "The Daily *Hallel*." See **Hallel**.

Halleluyah (pronounced hah-l'-loo-YAH, but sometimes anglicized as hah-l'-LOO-yah): A common word in psalms, meaning "praise God," and the final word of a congregational response within the third blessing of the *Amidah* (from Ps. 146:10).

Hat'fillah (pronounced hah-t'-fee-LAH): Literally, "the *T'fillah*," another name for the *Amidah*. See *T'fillah*.

Hoda'ah (pronounced hoe-dah-AH): Literally, a combination of the Hebrew words for "gratitude" and "acknowledgment," so translated here as "grateful acknowledgment." The title of the second to last blessing in the *Amidah*, an expression of our grateful acknowledgment to God for the daily wonders that constitute human existence.

Hoeche K'dushah (pronounced HAY-kh' k'DOO-shah): A Yiddish term combining German and Hebrew and meaning, literally, "the High *K'dushah*." Refers to a way to shorten the time it takes to say the *Amidah* by avoiding the necessity of having the prayer leader repeat it all after it is said silently by the congregation.

Inclusio (pronounced in-CLOO-zee-oh): A rhetorical style common to biblical prayer, whereby the end of a composition reiterates the theme or words with which the composition began.

Kabbalah (pronounced kah-bah-LAH, or, commonly, kah-BAH-lah): A general term for Jewish mysticism, but used properly for a specific mystical doctrine that began in western Europe in the eleventh or twelfth centuries; recorded in the Zohar (see **Zohar**) in the thirteenth century, and then was further elaborated, especially in the Land of Israel (in Safed), in the sixteenth century. From a Hebrew word meaning "to receive" or "to welcome," and secondarily, "tradition," implying the receiving of tradition from one's past.

Kabbalat Shabbat (pronounced kah-bah-LAHT shah-BAHT): Literally, "welcoming the Sabbath," and therefore a term for the introductory synagogue prayers that lead up to the arrival of the Sabbath at sundown Friday night.

Kaddish (pronounced kah-DEESH, or, more commonly, KAH-dish): One of several prayers from a Hebrew word meaning "holy," and therefore the name given to a prayer affirming God's holiness. This prayer was composed in the first century but later found its way into the service in several forms, including one known as the Mourners' *Kaddish* and used as a mourning prayer.

Kaddish D'rabbanan (pronounced kah-DEESH d'-rah-bah-NAHN, or, commonly, KAH-dish d'-rah-bah-NAHN): A form of the *Kaddish* (see **Kaddish**) containing a unique paragraph requesting well-being for all who study Torah. It appears liturgically as a conclusion to study passages.

Kaddish Yatom (pronounced kah-DEESH yah-TOHM, or, commonly, KAH-dish yah-TOHM): That version of the *Kaddish* that is said by mourners specifically to memorialize the deceased.

Kavvanah (pronounced kah-vah-NAH): From a word meaning "to direct," and therefore used technically to denote the state of directing one's words and thoughts sincerely to God, as opposed to the rote recitation of prayer.

K'dushah (pronounced k'-doo-SHAH, or, commonly, k'-DOO-shah): From the Hebrew word meaning "holy," and therefore one of several prayers from the first or second century occurring in several places and versions, all of which have in common the citing of Isaiah 6:3: *kadosh, kadosh kadosh...*, "Holy, holy, holy is the Lord of hosts. The whole earth is full of His glory."

K'dushat Hashem (pronounced k'-doo-SHAHT hah-SHEM): Literally, "sanctification of the name [of God]," and the full name for the prayer that is generally called *K'dushah* (see **K'dushah**). Best known as the third blessing in the *Amidah*, but found also prior to the morning *Sh'ma*. Used also in variant form *kiddush hashem* (pronounced kee-DOOSH hah-SHEM) as a term to describe dying for the sanctification of God's name, that is, martyrdom.

Keva (pronounced KEH-vah): A Hebrew word meaning "fixity, stability," and therefore the aspect of a service that is fixed and immutable: the words on the page, perhaps, or the time at which the prayer must be said. In the early years, when prayers were delivered orally and improvised on the spot, *keva* meant the fixed order in which the liturgical themes had to be expressed.

Kibbutz G'luyot (pronounced kee-BOOTS g'-loo-YOTE): Literally, "gathering the exiles," and the title of the tenth blessing of the daily *Amidah*, a petition for Jews outside the Land of Israel to return home to their land as a sign that messianic times are imminent. Some liberal liturgies omit the blessing or interpret it more broadly to imply universal messianic liberation, but without the literal belief that Jews outside the Land of Israel are in "exile," or that they need to or want to "return home."

Kiddush (pronounced kee-DOOSH, or, commonly, KIH-d'sh): Literally, "sanctification," the name given to the prayer recited over wine at the outset of Sabbaths and holy days, declaring the day in question sanctified. A shorter version is recited the next morning after services, at which time worshipers commonly share a meal or light refreshments together. By extension, *Kiddush* is sometimes used to designate that meal as well.

Kohanim (pronounced koe-hah-NEEM): Literally, "priests," plural of *kohen* (pronounced koe-HAYN), "priest," a reference to the priests who offered sacrifices in the ancient temple until its destruction by Rome in the year 70 C.E. Also the name of modern-day Jews who claim priestly descent, and who are customarily given symbolic recognition in various ritual ways—as, for instance, being called first to stand beside the Torah reader and to recite a blessing over the reading. It is also the title of the last blessing in the *Amidah*, which contains the priestly benediction from Numbers 6:24–26. Another more popular name for that blessing is *Shalom* (pronounced shah-LOME), "peace," because the priestly benediction requests peace. See also **Birkat Kohanim**.

Korbanot (pronounced kohr-bah-NOHT; singular: *korban*, pronounced kohr-BAHN): Literally, "sacrifices," but used liturgically to denote passages from Torah and rabbinic literature that explain how sacrifices are to be offered. These are inserted especially in the *Birkhot Hashachar* and the *Musaf* service.

K'riat Hatorah (pronounced k'ree-AHT hah-toe-RAH): The public reading of the Torah.

K'riat Sh'ma (pronounced k'-ree-YAHT sh'-MAH): Literally, "reciting the *Sh'ma*," and therefore a technical term for the liturgical act of reading the prayer known as the *Sh'ma* (See **Sh'ma**).

Liturgy Public worship, from the Greek word *leitourgia*, meaning "public works." Liturgy in ancient Greece was considered a public work, the act of sacrificing or praising the gods, from which benefit would flow to the body politic.

Ma'ariv (pronounced mah-ah-REEV, or, commonly, MAH-ah-reev): From the Hebrew word *erev* (pronounced EH-rev), meaning "evening": one of two titles used for the evening worship service (also called **Arvit**).

Machzor Vitry (commonly pronounced MAKH-zohr VEET-ree): Earliest comprehensive compendium of liturgical custom in France (eleventh to twelfth century).

Mah Tovu (pronounced MAH toh-VOO, or, commonly, mah TOH-voo): Technically, the prayer to be said upon approaching or entering a synagogue; in practice, the first prayer of *Birkhot Hashachar*.

Maimonides, Moses (known also as Rambam, pronounced RAHM-bahm): Most important Jewish philosopher of all time; also a physician and very significant legal authority. Born in Spain, he moved to Egypt, where he lived most of his life (1135–1204).

Massekhet Sofrim (pronounced mah-SEH-khet sohf-REEM): Literally, "Tractate [dealing with issues relevant to] scribes," an eighth-century compilation (with some later interpolations) dealing with such matters as the writing of Torah scrolls, but also including much detail on the early medieval (and possibly ancient) prayer practice of Jews in the Land of Israel.

Menorah (pronounced m'NOH-rah): A candelabra, originally the one in the desert Tabernacle of Exodus, with seven branches. The term was once commonly used also for the eight-branch candelabra for Chanukah, but now the term *chanuki'ah* is preferred for that one.

Mid'ora'ita (pronounced mee-d'-oh-RYE-tah): Strictly speaking, commandments derived directly from Torah, which are of a higher order than those rooted only in rabbinic ordinance (called ***Mid'rabbanan***), but all are binding.

Mid'rabbanan (pronounced mee-d'-rah-bah-NAHN): Commandments rooted only in rabbinic ordinance. See ***Mid'ora'ita***.

Midrash (pronounced meed-RAHSH, or, commonly, MID-rahsh): From a Hebrew word meaning "to ferret out the meaning of a text," and therefore a rabbinic interpretation of a biblical word or verse. By extension, a body of rabbinic literature that offers classical interpretations of the Bible.

Minchah (pronounced meen-KHAH, or, more commonly, MIN-khah): Originally the name of a type of sacrifice, then the word for a sacrifice offered during the afternoon, and now the name for the afternoon synagogue service usually scheduled just before nightfall. *Minchah* means "afternoon."

Minhag (pronounced meen-HAHG, or, commonly, MIN-hahg): The Hebrew word for custom and, therefore, used liturgically to describe the customary way that different groups of Jews pray. By extension, *minhag* means a "rite," as in *Minhag Ashkenaz*, meaning "the rite of prayer, or the customary way of prayer for Jews in *Ashkenaz*"— that is, northern and eastern Europe.

Minim (pronounced mee-NEEM): Literally, "heretics" or "sectarians," and the title of the twelfth blessing of the daily *Amidah*, a petition that heresy be eradicated, and heretics punished. Liberal liturgies frequently omit the blessing, considering it an inappropriate malediction, not a benediction at all, or reframe it as a petition against evil in general.

Minyan (pronounced meen-YAHN, or, commonly, MIN-y'n): A quorum, the minimum number of people required for certain prayers. *Minyan* comes from the word meaning "to count."

Mi sheberakh (pronounced, commonly, MEE sheh-BAY-rakh): A standard blessing beginning, "May the One who blessed [our ancestors]…," which could be adapted for any number of instances. This set of prayers requesting God's blessing on those who receive an *aliyah* or on their family members is perhaps the best known addition to the service.

Mishnah (pronounced meesh-NAH, or, commonly, MISH-nah): The first written summary of Jewish law, compiled in the Land of Israel about the year 200 C.E., and therefore our first overall written evidence for the state of Jewish prayer in the early centuries.

Mishneh Torah (pronounced MISH-n' TOH-rah): Code of Jewish law by Moses Maimonides (composed in 1180), called also the *Yad* (pronounced YAHD), a Hebrew word made of the letters that, together, stand for the number fourteen—a reference to the fact that the code is divided into fourteen books. Unlike other codes, the *Mishneh Torah* sums up every aspect of Jewish law, even hypothetical precepts relevant only in messianic times, as well as philosophical introductions on the nature of God and prayer.

Mishpat (pronounced meesh-PAHT): Literally, "justice," and the title of the eleventh blessing of the daily *Amidah*; a petition for just rulership, a condition associated with the messianic age.

Mitzvah (pronounced meetz-VAH, or, commonly, MITZ-vah; plural: *mitzvot*, pronounced meetz-VOTE): A Hebrew word used commonly to mean "good deed," but in the more technical sense, denoting any commandment from God, and therefore, by extension, what God wants us to do. Reciting the *Sh'ma* morning and evening, for instance, is a *mitzvah*.

Modeh/ah ani (pronounced moh-DEH ah-NEE [for women, moh-DAH ah-NEE]): Literally, "I gratefully acknowledge [...that You have returned my soul to me]"— therefore, the standard prayer to be said upon awakening.

Modim D'rabbanan (pronounced moe-DEEM d'-rah-bah-NAHN): *Modim* is the first word of the second to last blessing of the *Amidah*, and therefore a shorthand way of referring to that prayer. *Modim D'rabbanan* is the name given to the form of the prayer that is reserved for congregational recitation during the repetition of the *Amidah* by the prayer leader. Literally, it means "the *Modim* of our Rabbis," and refers to the fact that the prayer is composed of what were once several alternative responses, each of which was the custom of one of the Rabbis of the Talmud.

Musaf (pronounced moo-SAHF, or, commonly, MOO-sahf): The Hebrew word meaning "extra" or "added," and therefore the title of the additional sacrifice that was offered in the Temple on Shabbat and holy days. It is now the name given to an added service of worship appended to the morning service on those days.

M'zuzah (pronounced m'-zoo-ZAH, or, commonly, m'-ZOO-zah): The Hebrew word in the Bible meaning "doorpost," and by extension, the term now used for a small casement that contains the first two sections of the *Sh'ma* (Deut. 6:4–9; 11:13–21) and is affixed to the doorposts of Jewish homes.

N'filat apa'im (pronounced n'-fee-LAHT ah-PAH-yim): Literally, "falling on one's face," and therefore a technical term for the *Tachanun,* that section of the daily service that features supplications and is said with head resting on forearm, as if "prostrate" before God.

N'illah (pronounced n'-ee-LAH, or, commonly, n'-EE-lah): The concluding service for Yom Kippur.

Nishmat kol cha'i (pronounced nish-MAHT kohl KHA'i): A blessing mentioned in the Talmud as one of two benedictions in use as the *Birkat Hashir* (pronounced beer-KAHT hah-SHEER), the blessing that ends a psalm collection known as *Hallel*. (See ***Hallel***.) Nowadays, we use it 1) as part of a longer **Birkat Hashir** after the Daily *Hallel*, that constitutes the central section of the *P'sukei D'zimrah* for Sabbaths and festivals; and 2) to conclude a similar *Hallel* in the Passover Haggadah.

N'kadesh (pronounced n'kah-DAYSH): The *Amidah* is first recited silently by each worshiper individually and then repeated aloud by the prayer leader, at which time its third blessing appears in extended form. *N'kadesh* (literally, "Let us sanctify…") is the first Hebrew word of that extended blessing and is thus, by extension, a common way to refer to it.

Orach Chayim (pronounced OH-rakh KHA-yim): Abbreviated as O. Ch. Literally, "The Way of Life," one of four sections in the *Tur* and the *Shulchan Arukh*, two of Judaism's major law codes; the section containing the rules of prayer.

Payy'tan (pronounced pah-y'-TAHN; plural: *Payy'tanim*, pronounced pah-y'-tah-NEEM): A poet; the name given particularly to classical and medieval poets whose work is inserted into the standard prayers for special occasions.

Perek (pronounced PEH-rek; plural: *p'rakim*, pronounced p'-rah-KEEM): Literally, a "section" or "chapter" of a written work, and used liturgically to mean the sections of the *Sh'ma*. Each of its three biblical sections is a different *perek*.

Piyyut (pronounced pee-YOOT; plural: *piyyutim*, pronounced pee-yoo-TEEM): Literally, "a poem," but used technically to mean liturgical poems composed in classical and medieval times, and inserted into the standard prayers on special occasions.

P'sukei D'zimrah (pronounced p'-soo-KAY d'-zeem-RAH, or, commonly, p'-SOO-kay d'-ZIM-rah): Literally, "verses of song," and therefore the title of a lengthy set of opening morning prayers that contain psalms and songs, and serve as spiritual preparation prior to the official Call to Prayer.

Purim (pronounced PU-rim, or, pu-REEM): A festival falling on the fourteenth day of the Hebrew month of Adar, generally corresponding to late February or early March. It celebrates the miraculous deliverance referred to in the biblical Book of Esther. Literally, *purim* means "lots," as in the phrase "drawing of lots," because the date on which the Jews were to have been killed was chosen by lot.

Rashba (pronounced rahsh-BAH): Halakhic authority, Shlomo ben Aderet, Barcelona (1235–1310).

Rashi (pronounced RAH-shee): Solomon ben Isaac (1040–1105), most significant Jewish biblical exegete and founder of French Jewry.

R'fuah (pronounced r'-foo-AH, or, commonly, r'-FOO-ah): Literally, "healing," and the title of the eighth blessing of the daily *Amidah*, a petition for healing.

Rosh (pronounced ROHSH): The Rosh (1250–1328), otherwise known as Rabbeinu Asher, or Asher ben Yechiel, was a significant halakhic authrority, first in Germany and later in Spain. His son, Jacob ben Asher, codified many of his father's views alongside his own in his influential law code, the *Tur*.

Rosh Chodesh (pronounced rohsh KHOH-desh): Literally, "the head of the month," and therefore the Hebrew name for the one- or two-day new moon period with which lunar months begin. It is marked as a holiday in Jewish tradition, a period of new beginnings.

Rubric (pronounced ROO-brick): A technical term for any discrete section of liturgy, whether a prayer or a set of prayers. The *Sh'ma* and Its Blessings is one of several large rubrics in the service; within that large rubric, the *Sh'ma* or any one of its accompanying blessings may be called a rubric as well.

Seder (pronounced SEH-der, or, commonly, SAY-der): The Hebrew word meaning "order," and therefore 1) the name given to the ritualized meal eaten on Passover eve, and 2) an early alternative term for the order of prayers in a prayer book. The word Siddur (see ***Siddur***) is now preferred for the latter.

Seder Rav Amram (pronounced SAY-dehr rahv AHM-rahm): First known comprehensive Jewish prayer book, emanating from Rav Amram Gaon, a leading Jewish scholar and head of Sura, a famed academy in Babylonia (modern-day Iraq), c. 860 C.E.

Sefardi (pronounced s'-fahr-DEE, or, commonly s'-FAHR-dee): From the Hebrew word *Sefarad* (pronounced s'-fah-RAHD), meaning the geographic area of modern-day Spain and Portugal. Sefardi is the adjective, describing the liturgical rituals and customs that are derived from *Sefarad* prior to the expulsion of Jews from there at the end of the fifteenth century, as opposed to Ashkenazi (see **Ashkenazi**), meaning the liturgical rituals and customs common to northern and eastern Europe. Nowadays, Sefardi refers also to the customs of Jews from North Africa and Arab lands, whose ancestors came from Spain.

S'firot (pronounced s'-fee-ROTE; singular: *s'firah*, pronounced s'-fee-RAH): According to the Kabbalah (Jewish mysticism, see **Kabbalah**), the universe came into being by a process of divine emanation, whereby the divine light, as it were, expanded into empty space, eventually becoming physical matter. At various intervals, this light was frozen in time, as if captured by containers, each of which is called a *s'firah*. Literally, *s'firah* means "number," because early theory conceptualized the stages of creation as primordial numbers.

S'firotic (pronounced s'fee-RAH-tik): Relating to one or more *s'firot*, or to the system of *s'firot*.

Shabbat (pronounced shah-BAHT): The Hebrew word for "Sabbath," from a word meaning "to rest."

Shacharit (pronounced shah-khah-REET, or, commonly, SHAH-khah-reet): The name given to the morning worship service; from the Hebrew word *shachar* (SHAH-khar), meaning "morning."

Shalom (pronounced shah-LOME): Literally, "peace," and a popular title for the final benediction of the *Amidah*, more properly entitled *Kohanim* (pronounced koe-hah-NEEM), "priests," or, more fully, *Birkat Kohanim* (pronounced beer-KAHT koe-hah-NEEM), "blessing of the priests," "priestly benediction." See also **Birkat Kohanim**, **Kohanim**.

Shanim (pronounced shah-NEEM): Literally, "years," and the title of the ninth blessing of the daily *Amidah*; a petition for a year of agricultural abundance, such as is associated with messianic days.

Shefa (pronounced SHEH-fah): In kabbalistic worship, the plenitude of blessing that flows vertically through the *s'firot* to the world we inhabit.

Shirat Hayam (pronounced shee-RAHT hah-YAHM): Literally, "Song of the Sea," the song of praise and gratitude sung by Israel after the splitting of the Red Sea, and, since the Middle Ages, a prominent constituent of the *P'sukei D'zimrah*, the "warm-up" section to the morning service composed mainly of biblical material (chiefly psalms) that were intended to be sung as praise of God.

Shivah d'n'chemta (pronounced shih-VAH d'-n'-KHEM-tah): "Seven weeks of comfort." The seven Sabbaths following Tisha B'Av, which take us all the way to Rosh Hashanah, call for **Haftarot** that guarantee hope.

Sh'liakh tsibbur (pronounced sh'-LEE-ahkh tsee-BOOR): Literally, the "agent of the congregation," and therefore the name given to the person who leads the prayer service.

Sh'ma (pronounced sh'-MAH): The central prayer in the first of the two main units in the worship service, the second being the *Amidah* (see **Amidah**). The *Sh'ma* comprises three citations from the Bible, and the larger unit in which it is embedded (called The *Sh'ma* and Its Blessings) is composed of a formal Call to Prayer (see *Bar'khu*) and a series of blessings on the theological themes that, together with the *Sh'ma*, constitute a liturgical creed of faith. *Sh'ma*, meaning "hear," is the first word of the first line of the first biblical citation, "Hear O Israel: Adonai is our God; Adonai is One," which is the paradigmatic statement of Jewish faith, the Jews' absolute commitment to the presence of a single and unique God in time and space.

Sh'mini Atseret (pronounced sh'-MEE-nee ah-TSEH-ret): Literally, "the eighth day of solemn assembly," and the name given to the eighth and final day of the autumn festival of Sukkot.

Sh'moneh Esreh (pronounced sh'-MOE-neh ES-ray): A Hebrew word meaning "eighteen," and therefore a name given to the second of the two main units in the worship service that once had eighteen benedictions in it (it now has nineteen), known also as the *Amidah* (see **Amidah**).

Shul (pronounced SHOOL): Yiddish for synagogue.

Shulchan Arukh (pronounced shool-KHAN ah-ROOKH, or, commonly, SHOOL-khan AH-rookh): The name given to the best-known code of Jewish law, compiled by Joseph Caro in the Land of Israel and published in 1565. *Shulchan Arukh* means "The Set Table," and refers to the ease with which the various laws are set forth—like a table prepared with food ready for consumption.

Shulchan Arukh D'rav (pronounced shool-KHAHN ah-ROOKH d'-RAHV, or, popularly, SHOOL-khahn AH-rukh d'-RAHV): Halakhic compendium by R. Shneur Zalman of Liady, eighteenth-century founder of Chabad Chasidism.

Siddur (pronounced see-DOOR, or, commonly, SIH-d'r): From the Hebrew word *seder* (see **Seder**) meaning "order," and therefore, by extension, the name given to the "order of prayers," or prayer book.

S'lichah (pronounced s'lee-KHAH, or, commonly S'LEE-khah): Literally, "pardon" or "forgiveness," and the title of the sixth blessing of the daily *Amidah*, a petition for divine forgiveness of our sins.

Tachanun (pronounced TAH-khah-noon): A Hebrew word meaning "supplications," and therefore, by extension, the title of the large unit of prayer that follows the *Amidah*, and which is largely supplicatory in character.

Tallit (pronounced tah-LEET; plural: *talitot*, pronounced tah-lee-TOTE): The prayer shawl equipped with tassels (see *Tsitsit*) on each corner, and generally worn during the morning *(Shacharit)* and additional *(Musaf)* synagogue services.

Tallit katan (pronounced tah-LEET kah-TAHN): Literally, "a little *tallit*," used originally as an undergarment to allow the wearing of *tsitsit* privately, all day long, in cultures where Jews wanted to look the same as everyone else.

Talmud (pronounced tahl-MOOD, or, more commonly, TAHL-m'd): The name given to each of two great compendia of Jewish law and lore compiled over several centuries, and ever since, the literary core of the rabbinic heritage. The Talmud Yerushalmi (pronounced y'-roo-SHAHL-mee), the "Jerusalem Talmud," is earlier, a product of the Land of Israel generally dated about 400 C.E. The better-known Talmud Bavli (pronounced BAHV-lee), or "Babylonian Talmud," took shape in Babylonia (present-day Iraq), and is traditionally dated about 550 C.E. When people say "the" Talmud without specifying which one they mean, they are referring to the Babylonian version. Talmud means "teaching."

Tetragrammaton The technical term for the four-letter name of God that appears in the Bible. Treating it as sacred, Jews stopped pronouncing it centuries ago, so that the actual pronunciation has been lost; instead of reading it according to its letters, it is replaced in speech by the alternative name of God, Adonai.

T'fillah (pronounced t'-fee-LAH, or, commonly, t'-FEE-lah): A Hebrew word meaning "prayer," but used technically to mean a specific prayer, namely, the second of the two main units in the worship service. It is known also as the *Amidah* or the *Sh'moneh Esreh* (see *Amidah*). Also the title of the sixteenth blessing of the *Amidah*, a petition for God to accept our prayer.

T'fillin (pronounced t'-FIH-lin, or, sometimes, t'-fee-LEEN): Two cube-shaped black boxes containing biblical quotations (Exod. 13:1–10; 13:11–16; Deut. 6:4–9; 11:13–21) and affixed by means of attached leather straps to the forehead and left arm (right arm for left-handed people) during morning prayer.

T'hillah l'David (pronounced t'-hee-LAH l'-dah-VEED): Literally, "A psalm of David," and the first two words of Psalm 145; hence, the rabbinic name for Psalm 145, which eventually became known, more popularly, as *Ashre* (pronounced ahsh-RAY, or, commonly, AHSH-ray). See ***Ashre***.

T'lata d'puranuta (pronounced t'-LAH-tah d'-poo-rah-NOO-tah): "The three readings of retribution." As the Rabbis saw it, God must have allowed, and perhaps even caused, the Temple to fall as punishment for Israel's sins. The three weeks prior to Tisha B'Av, therefore, anticipate the fall, culminating in Shabbat *Chazon* (khah-ZOHN), ("The Sabbath of 'the Vision,'") which features Isaiah's premonitory vision of Jerusalem's fall and the expectation of ultimate recovery (Isa. 1:1–27).

Tsadikim (pronounced tsah-dee-KEEM): Literally, "the righteous," and the title of the thirteenth blessing of the daily *Amidah*, a petition that the righteous be rewarded.

T'shuvah (pronounced t'shoo-VAH, or, commonly t'SHOO-vah): Literally, "repentance," and the title of the fifth blessing in the daily *Amidah*, a petition by worshipers that they successfully turn to God in heartfelt repentance.

Tsitsit (pronounced tsee-TSEET): A Hebrew word meaning "tassels" or "fringes" and used to refer to the tassels affixed to the four corners of the *tallit* (the prayer shawl, see ***Tallit***) as Numbers 15:38 instructs.

Tur (pronounced TOOR): The shorthand title applied to a fourteenth-century code of Jewish law, compiled by Jacob ben Asher in Spain, and the source for much of our knowledge about medieval liturgical practice. *Tur* means "row" or "column." The full name of the code is *Arba'ah Turim* (pronounced ahr-bah-AH too-REEM), "The Four Rows," with each row (or *Tur*) being a separate section of law on a given broad topic.

Un'taneh Tokef (pronounced oo-n'-TAH-neh TOH-kehf): A *piyyut* (liturgical poem) for the High Holy Days emphasizing the awesome nature of these days when we stand before God for judgment. Widely, but incorrectly connected with a legend of Jewish martyrdom in Germany, the poem more likely derives from a Byzantine poet, circa sixth century. It is known for its conclusion: "Penitence, prayer, and charity avert a bad decree."

V'hu rachum (pronounced v'HOO rah-KHOOM): Literally, "He [God] is merciful," and, because of its sentiment, a common introductory line to prayers lauding God's gracious beneficence. The best example is a seven-paragraph penitential prayer that makes up the bulk of the version of *Tachanun* (pronounced TAH-khah-noon) that is said Mondays and Thursdays.

Yahrzeit (pronounced YOHR-tseit): A Yiddish word meaning the practice of marking the anniversary of a loved one's death by saying *Kaddish*. People speak of "having *yahrzeit*" on a given day, at which time the name of the person being memorialized may be mentioned aloud at services prior to the Mourner's *Kaddish* (see ***Kaddish***).

Yichud (pronounced yee-KHOOD): Literally, "unification"; in kabbalistic worship, prayers have esoteric significance, generally the unification of the letters that make up God's name, but standing also for the conjoining the God's masculine and feminine aspects and, deeper still, the coming together of the shattered universe in which we live.

Yigdal (pronounced yig-DAHL): A popular morning hymn that encapsulates the thirteen principles of faith composed by prominent medieval philosopher Moses Maimonides (1135–1204). These thirteen principles were arranged poetically as *Yigdal* in the fourteenth century by Daniel ben Judah Dayan (pronounced dah-YAHN) of Rome.

Yishtabach (pronounced yish-tah-BAKH): The first word, and, therefore, the title of the blessing used as the *Birkat Hashir* for weekdays (see **Birkat Hashir**). On Sabbaths and festivals, it is expanded by the addition of *Nishmat kol cha'i* (pronounced neesh-MAHT kohl KHA'i), a blessing mentioned in the Talmud (see **Nishmat kol cha'i**).

Yizkor (pronounced yeez-KOHR, or, commonly, YIZ-k'r): The Memorial Service, said on Yom Kippur and the three festivals (Passover, Shavuot, and Sh'mini Atseret).

Yotser (pronounced yoe-TSAYR, or, commonly, YOE-tsayr): The Hebrew word meaning "creator," and by extension, the title of the first blessing in The *Sh'ma* and Its Blessings, which is on the theme of God's creation of the universe.

Y'rushalayim (pronounced y'roo-shah-LAH-yeem): Literally, "Jerusalem," and the title of the fourteenth blessing of the daily *Amidah*; a petition for the divine building up of Jerusalem, a condition associated with the imminence of the messianic age. Some liberal liturgies interpret it more broadly to include the restoration of modern-day Jerusalem, currently under way.

Zohar (pronounced ZOE-hahr): A shorthand title for *Sefer Hazohar* (pronounced SAY-fer hah-ZOE-hahr), literally, "The Book of Splendor," which is the primary compendium of mystical thought in Judaism; written mostly by Moses de Leon in Spain near the end of the thirteenth century, and ever since, the chief source for the study of Kabbalah (see **Kabbalah**).

About JEWISH LIGHTS Publishing

People of all faiths and backgrounds yearn for books that attract, engage, educate and spiritually inspire.

Our principal goal is to stimulate thought and help all people learn about who the Jewish People are, where they come from, and what the future can be made to hold. While people of our diverse Jewish heritage are the primary audience, our books speak to people in the Christian world as well and will broaden their understanding of Judaism and the roots of their own faith.

We bring to you authors who are at the forefront of spiritual thought and experience. While each has something different to say, they all say it in a voice that you can hear.

Our books are designed to welcome you and then to engage, stimulate and inspire. We judge our success not only by whether or not our books are beautiful and commercially successful, but by whether or not they make a difference in your life.

We at Jewish Lights take great care to produce beautiful books that present meaningful spiritual content in a form that reflects the art of making high quality books. Therefore, we want to acknowledge those who contributed to the production of this book.

Stuart M. Matlins, Publisher

PRODUCTION
Tim Holtz & Bridgett Taylor

EDITORIAL
Amanda Dupuis, Martha McKinney,
Polly Short Mahoney & Emily Wichland

TEXT DESIGN
Reuben Kantor, QEP Design, Jamaica Plain, Massachusetts

TEXT & HEBREW COMPOSITION
Itzhack Shelomi, New York, New York

JACKET DESIGN
Glenn Suokko

JACKET PRINTING
John P. Pow Company, South Boston, Massachusetts

TEXT PRINTING & BINDING
Hamilton Printing Company, Rensselaer, New York

Spirituality

Does the Soul Survive?
A Jewish Journey to Belief in Afterlife, Past Lives & Living with Purpose
by *Rabbi Elie Kaplan Spitz*; Foreword by *Brian L. Weiss, M.D.*

Spitz relates his own experiences and those shared with him by people he has worked with as a rabbi, and shows us that belief in afterlife and past lives, so often approached with reluctance, is in fact true to Jewish tradition. 6 x 9, 288 pp, HC, ISBN 1-58023-094-6 **$21.95**

The Women's Torah Commentary: *New Insights from Women Rabbis*
on the 54 Weekly Torah Portions Ed. by *Rabbi Elyse Goldstein*

For the first time, women rabbis provide a commentary on the entire Torah. In a week-by-week format; a perfect gift for others, or for yourself.
6 x 9, 496 pp, HC, ISBN 1-58023-076-8 **$34.95**

The Gift of Kabbalah
Discovering the Secrets of Heaven, Renewing Your Life on Earth
by *Tamar Frankiel, Ph.D.*

Makes accessible the mysteries of Kabbalah. Traces Kabbalah's evolution in Judaism and shows us its most important gift: a way of revealing the connection between our "everyday" life and the spiritual oneness of the universe. 6 x 9, 256 pp, HC, ISBN 1-58023-108-X **$21.95**

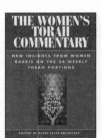 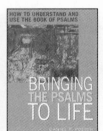   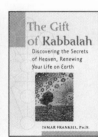

Bringing the Psalms to Life: *How to Understand and Use the Book of Psalms*
by Rabbi Daniel F. Polish 6 x 9, 208 pp, Quality PB, ISBN 1-58023-157-8 **$16.95**;
HC, ISBN 1-58023-077-6 **$21.95**

The Empty Chair: *Finding Hope and Joy—*
Timeless Wisdom from a Hasidic Master, Rebbe Nachman of Breslov AWARD WINNER!
4 x 6, 128 pp, Deluxe PB, 2-color text, ISBN 1-879045-67-2 **$9.95**

The Gentle Weapon: *Prayers for Everyday and Not-So-Everyday Moments*
Adapted from the Wisdom of Rebbe Nachman of Breslov
4 x 6, 144 pp, Deluxe PB, 2-color text, ISBN 1-58023-022-9 **$9.95**

Ancient Secrets: *Using the Stories of the Bible to Improve Our Everyday Lives*
by Rabbi Levi Meier, Ph.D. 5½ x 8½, 288 pp, Quality PB, ISBN 1-58023-064-4 **$16.95**

Or phone, fax, mail or e-mail to: **JEWISH LIGHTS** Publishing
Sunset Farm Offices, Route 4 • P.O. Box 237 • Woodstock, Vermont 05091
Tel: (802) 457-4000 • Fax: (802) 457-4004 • www.jewishlights.com
Credit card orders: (800) 962-4544 (9AM–5PM ET Monday–Friday)
Generous discounts on quantity orders. SATISFACTION GUARANTEED. Prices subject to change.

Spirituality—The Kushner Series
Books by Lawrence Kushner

The Way Into Jewish Mystical Tradition

Explains the principles of Jewish mystical thinking, their religious and spiritual significance, and how they relate to our lives. A book that allows us to experience and understand the Jewish mystical approach to our place in the world. 6 x 9, 224 pp, HC, ISBN 1-58023-029-6 **$21.95**

Eyes Remade for Wonder
The Way of Jewish Mysticism and Sacred Living
A Lawrence Kushner Reader Intro. by *Thomas Moore*

Whether you are new to Kushner or a devoted fan, you'll find inspiration here. With samplings from each of Kushner's works, and a generous amount of new material, this book is to be read and reread, each time discovering deeper layers of meaning in our lives.
6 x 9, 240 pp, Quality PB, ISBN 1-58023-042-3 **$16.95**; HC, ISBN 1-58023-014-8 **$23.95**

Because Nothing Looks Like God

by *Lawrence and Karen Kushner*; Full-color illus. by *Dawn W. Majewski*

What is God like? The first collaborative work by husband-and-wife team Lawrence and Karen Kushner introduces children to the possibilities of spiritual life with three poetic spiritual stories. Real-life examples of happiness and sadness—from goodnight stories, to the hope and fear felt the first time at bat, to the closing moments of life—invite us to explore, together with our children, the questions we all have about God, no matter what our age. **For ages 4 & up**
11 x 8½, 32 pp, HC, Full-color illus., ISBN 1-58023-092-X **$16.95**

 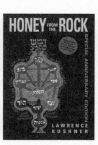   

Invisible Lines of Connection: *Sacred Stories of the Ordinary* **AWARD WINNER!**
6 x 9, 160 pp, Quality PB, ISBN 1-879045-98-2 **$15.95**; HC, ISBN 1-879045-52-4 **$21.95**

Honey from the Rock: *An Introduction to Jewish Mysticism* **SPECIAL ANNIVERSARY EDITION**
6 x 9, 176 pp, Quality PB, ISBN 1-58023-073-3 **$15.95**

The Book of Letters: *A Mystical Hebrew Alphabet* **AWARD WINNER!**
Popular HC Edition, 6 x 9, 80 pp, 2-color text, ISBN 1-879045-00-1 **$24.95**; *Deluxe Gift Edition*, 9 x 12, 80 pp, HC, 2-color text, ornamentation, slipcase, ISBN 1-879045-01-X **$79.95**; *Collector's Limited Edition*, 9 x 12, 80 pp, HC, gold-embossed pages, hand-assembled slipcase. With silkscreened print. Limited to 500 signed and numbered copies, ISBN 1-879045-04-4 **$349.00**

The Book of Words: *Talking Spiritual Life, Living Spiritual Talk* **AWARD WINNER!**
6 x 9, 160 pp, Quality PB, 2-color text, ISBN 1-58023-020-2 **$16.95**;
152 pp, HC, ISBN 1-879045-35-4 **$21.95**

God Was in This Place & I, i Did Not Know
Finding Self, Spirituality and Ultimate Meaning
6 x 9, 192 pp, Quality PB, ISBN 1-879045-33-8 **$16.95**

The River of Light: *Jewish Mystical Awareness* **SPECIAL ANNIVERSARY EDITION**
6 x 9, 192 pp, Quality PB, ISBN 1-58023-096-2 **$16.95**

Life Cycle/Grief

Against the Dying of the Light
A Parent's Story of Love, Loss and Hope
by *Leonard Fein*

The sudden death of a child. A personal tragedy beyond description. Rage and despair deeper than sorrow. What can come from it? Raw wisdom and defiant hope. In this unusual exploration of heartbreak and healing, Fein chronicles the sudden death of his 30-year-old daughter and reveals what the progression of grief can teach each one of us.
5½ x 8½, 176 pp, HC, ISBN 1-58023-110-1 **$19.95**

Mourning & Mitzvah, 2nd Ed.: *A Guided Journal for Walking the Mourner's Path through Grief to Healing* with *Over 60 Guided Exercises*
by *Anne Brener, L.C.S.W.*

For those who mourn a death, for those who would help them, for those who face a loss of any kind, Brener teaches us the power and strength available to us in the fully experienced mourning process. Revised and expanded. 7½ x 9, 304 pp, Quality PB, ISBN 1-58023-113-6 **$19.95**

Grief in Our Seasons: *A Mourner's Kaddish Companion*
by *Rabbi Kerry M. Olitzky*

A wise and inspiring selection of sacred Jewish writings and a simple, powerful ancient ritual for mourners to read each day, to help hold the memory of their loved ones in their hearts. Offers a comforting, step-by-step daily link to saying Kaddish.
4½ x 6½, 448 pp, Quality PB, ISBN 1-879045-55-9 **$15.95**

    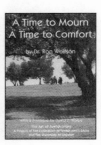

Tears of Sorrow, Seeds of Hope
A Jewish Spiritual Companion for Infertility and Pregnancy Loss
by Rabbi Nina Beth Cardin   6 x 9, 192 pp, HC, ISBN 1-58023-017-2 **$19.95**

A Time to Mourn, A Time to Comfort
A Guide to Jewish Bereavement and Comfort
by Dr. Ron Wolfson 7 x 9, 336 pp, Quality PB, ISBN 1-879045-96-6 **$18.95**

When a Grandparent Dies
A Kid's Own Remembering Workbook for Dealing with Shiva and the Year Beyond
by Nechama Liss-Levinson, Ph.D.
8 x 10, 48 pp, HC, Illus., 2-color text, ISBN 1-879045-44-3 **$15.95**

Healing/Wellness/Recovery

Jewish Paths toward Healing and Wholeness
A Personal Guide to Dealing with Suffering
by *Rabbi Kerry M. Olitzky;* Foreword by *Debbie Friedman*

Why me? Why do we suffer? How can we heal? Grounded in personal experience with illness and Jewish spiritual traditions, this book provides healing rituals, psalms and prayers that help readers initiate a dialogue with God, to guide them along the complicated path of healing and wholeness. 6 x 9, 192 pp, Quality PB, ISBN 1-58023-068-7 **$15.95**

Healing of Soul, Healing of Body
Spiritual Leaders Unfold the Strength & Solace in Psalms
Ed. by *Rabbi Simkha Y. Weintraub, CSW,* for The National Center for Jewish Healing

A source of solace for those who are facing illness, as well as those who care for them. Provides a wellspring of strength with inspiring introductions and commentaries by eminent spiritual leaders reflecting all Jewish movements.
6 x 9, 128 pp, Quality PB, Illus., 2-color text, ISBN 1-879045-31-1 **$14.95**

Jewish Pastoral Care
A Practical Handbook from Traditional and Contemporary Sources
Ed. by *Rabbi Dayle A. Friedman*

Gives today's Jewish pastoral counselors practical guidelines based in the Jewish tradition.
6 x 9, 464 pp, HC, ISBN 1-58023-078-4 **$35.00**

Twelve Jewish Steps to Recovery: *A Personal Guide to Turning from Alcoholism & Other Addictions . . . Drugs, Food, Gambling, Sex . . .* by Rabbi Kerry M. Olitzky & Stuart A. Copans, M.D. Preface by Abraham J. Twerski, M.D.; Intro. by Rabbi Sheldon Zimmerman; "Getting Help" by JACS Foundation 6 x 9, 144 pp, Quality PB, ISBN 1-879045-09-5 **$13.95**

One Hundred Blessings Every Day: *Daily Twelve Step Recovery Affirmations, Exercises for Personal Growth & Renewal Reflecting Seasons of the Jewish Year* by Rabbi Kerry M. Olitzky 4½ x 6½, 432 pp, Quality PB, ISBN 1-879045-30-3 **$14.95**

Recovery from Codependence: *A Jewish Twelve Steps Guide to Healing Your Soul* by Rabbi Kerry M. Olitzky 6 x 9, 160 pp, Quality PB, ISBN 1-879045-32-X **$13.95**; HC, ISBN 1-879045-27-3 **$21.95**

Renewed Each Day: *Daily Twelve Step Recovery Meditations Based on the Bible* by Rabbi Kerry M. Olitzky & Aaron Z. Vol. I: *Genesis & Exodus*; Vol. II: *Leviticus, Numbers and Deuteronomy*
Vol. I: 6 x 9, 224 pp, Quality PB, ISBN 1-879045-12-5 **$14.95**
Vol. II: 6 x 9, 280 pp, Quality PB, ISBN 1-879045-13-3 **$14.95**

Children's Spirituality

Because Nothing Looks Like God

by *Lawrence and Karen Kushner*
Full-color illus. by *Dawn W. Majewski*

For ages 4 & up

MULTICULTURAL, NONDENOMINATIONAL, NONSECTARIAN

What is God like? The first collaborative work by husband-and-wife team Lawrence and Karen Kushner introduces children to the possibilities of spiritual life. Real-life examples of happiness and sadness—from goodnight stories, to the hope and fear felt the first time at bat, to the closing moments of life—invite us to explore, together with our children, the questions we all have about God, no matter what our age.

11 x 8½, 32 pp, HC, Full-color illus., ISBN 1-58023-092-X **$16.95**

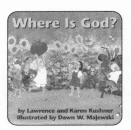

Where Is God?
What Does God Look Like?
How Does God Make Things Happen? (Board Books)

For ages 0–4

by *Lawrence and Karen Kushner*; Full-color illus. by *Dawn W. Majewski*

Gently invites children to become aware of God's presence all around them. Three board books abridged from *Because Nothing Looks Like God* by Lawrence and Karen Kushner.
Each 5 x 5, 24 pp, Board, Full-color illus. **$7.95** SKYLIGHT PATHS Books

Sharing Blessings

For ages 6 & up

Children's Stories for Exploring the Spirit of the Jewish Holidays
by *Rahel Musleah* and *Rabbi Michael Klayman*
Full-color illus. by *Mary O'Keefe Young*

What is the spiritual message of each of the Jewish holidays? How do we teach it to our children? Many books tell children about the historical significance and customs of the holidays. Through stories about one family's preparation, *Sharing Blessings* explores ways to get into the *spirit* of 13 different holidays.
8½ x 11, 64 pp, HC, Full-color illus., ISBN 1-879045-71-0 **$18.95**

The Book of Miracles

For ages 9 & up

A Young Person's Guide to Jewish Spiritual Awareness
by *Lawrence Kushner*

Introduces kids to a way of everyday spiritual thinking to last a lifetime. Kushner, whose award-winning books have brought spirituality to life for countless adults, now shows young people how to use Judaism as a foundation on which to build their lives.
6 x 9, 96 pp, HC, 2-color illus., ISBN 1-879045-78-8 **$16.95**

Life Cycle & Holidays

How to Be a Perfect Stranger, 2nd Ed. In 2 Volumes
A Guide to Etiquette in Other People's Religious Ceremonies

Ed. by *Stuart M. Matlins* & *Arthur J. Magida* AWARD WINNER!

What will happen? What do I do? What do I wear? What do I say? What are their basic beliefs? Should I bring a gift? Explains the rituals and celebrations of North America's major religions/denominations, helping an interested guest to feel comfortable. *Not* presented from the perspective of any particular faith. SKYLIGHT PATHS Books

Vol. 1: *North America's Largest Faiths,* 6 x 9, 432 pp, Quality PB, ISBN 1-893361-01-2 **$19.95**
Vol. 2: *Other Faiths in North America,* 6 x 9, 416 pp, Quality PB, ISBN 1-893361-02-0 **$19.95**

Celebrating Your New Jewish Daughter
Creating Jewish Ways to Welcome Baby Girls into the Covenant— New and Traditional Ceremonies

by *Debra Nussbaum Cohen;* Foreword by *Rabbi Sandy Eisenberg Sasso*

Features everything families need to plan a celebration that reflects Jewish tradition, including a how-to guide to new and traditional ceremonies, and practical guidelines for planning the joyous event. 6 x 9, 272 pp, Quality PB, ISBN 1-58023-090-3 **$18.95**

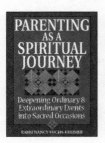    

The New Jewish Baby Book AWARD WINNER!
Names, Ceremonies & Customs—A Guide for Today's Families
by Anita Diamant 6 x 9, 336 pp, Quality PB, ISBN 1-879045-28-1 **$18.95**

Parenting As a Spiritual Journey
Deepening Ordinary & Extraordinary Events into Sacred Occasions
by Rabbi Nancy Fuchs-Kreimer 6 x 9, 224 pp, Quality PB, ISBN 1-58023-016-4 **$16.95**

Putting God on the Guest List, 2nd Ed. AWARD WINNER!
How to Reclaim the Spiritual Meaning of Your Child's Bar or Bat Mitzvah
by Rabbi Jeffrey K. Salkin 6 x 9, 224 pp, Quality PB, ISBN 1-879045-59-1 **$16.95**

For Kids—Putting God on Your Guest List
How to Claim the Spiritual Meaning of Your Bar or Bat Mitzvah
by Rabbi Jeffrey K. Salkin 6 x 9, 144 pp, Quality PB, ISBN 1-58023-015-6 **$14.95**

Bar/Bat Mitzvah Basics, 2nd Ed.: A Practical Family Guide to Coming of Age Together
Ed. by Cantor Helen Leneman 6 x 9, 240 pp, Quality PB, ISBN 1-58023-151-9 **$18.95**

Hanukkah, 2nd Ed.: The Family Guide to Spiritual Celebration
by Dr. Ron Wolfson 7 x 9, 192 pp, Quality PB, Illus., ISBN 1-58023-122-5 **$18.95**

The Shabbat Seder: The Art of Jewish Living
by Dr. Ron Wolfson 7 x 9, 272 pp, Quality PB, Illus., ISBN 1-879045-90-7 **$16.95**

The Passover Seder: The Art of Jewish Living
by Dr. Ron Wolfson 7 x 9, 352 pp, Quality PB, Illus., ISBN 1-879045-93-1 **$16.95**

Women's Spirituality / Ecology

Torah of the Earth: *Exploring 4,000 Years of Ecology in Jewish Thought*
In 2 Volumes Ed. by *Rabbi Arthur Waskow*

Major new resource offering us an invaluable key to understanding the intersection of ecology and Judaism. Leading scholars provide us with a guided tour of ecological thought from four major Jewish viewpoints.
Vol. 1: *Biblical Israel & Rabbinic Judaism,* 6 x 9, 272 pp, Quality PB, ISBN 1-58023-086-5 **$19.95**
Vol. 2: *Zionism & Eco-Judaism,* 6 x 9, 336 pp, Quality PB, ISBN 1-58023-087-3 **$19.95**

Ecology & the Jewish Spirit: *Where Nature & the Sacred Meet* Ed. and with Intros.
by Ellen Bernstein 6 x 9, 288 pp, Quality PB, ISBN 1-58023-082-2 **$16.95**;
HC, ISBN 1-879045-88-5 **$23.95**

The Jewish Gardening Cookbook: *Growing Plants & Cooking for Holidays & Festivals*
by Michael Brown 6 x 9, 224 pp, Illus., Quality PB, ISBN 1-58023-116-0 **$16.95**;
HC, ISBN 1-58023-004-0 **$21.95**

 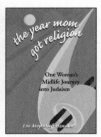  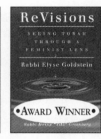 

Moonbeams: *A Hadassah Rosh Hodesh Guide*
Ed. by *Carol Diament, Ph.D.*

This hands-on "idea book" focuses on *Rosh Hodesh*, the festival of the new moon, as a source of spiritual growth for Jewish women. A complete sourcebook that will initiate or rejuvenate women's study groups, it is also perfect for women preparing for *bat mitzvah*, or for anyone interested in learning more about *Rosh Hodesh* observance and what it has to offer. 8½ x 11, 240 pp, Quality PB, ISBN 1-58023-099-7 **$20.00**

The Women's Torah Commentary: *New Insights from Women Rabbis on the 54 Weekly Torah Portions* Ed. by *Rabbi Elyse Goldstein*

For the first time, women rabbis provide a commentary on the entire Five Books of Moses. More than 25 years after the first woman was ordained a rabbi in America, these inspiring teachers bring their rich perspectives to bear on the biblical text. In a week-by-week format; a perfect gift for others, or for yourself. 6 x 9, 496 pp, HC, ISBN 1-58023-076-8 **$34.95**

Lifecycles, in Two Volumes AWARD WINNERS!
V. 1: *Jewish Women on Life Passages & Personal Milestones*
Ed. and with Intros. by Rabbi Debra Orenstein
V. 2: *Jewish Women on Biblical Themes in Contemporary Life*
Ed. and with Intros. by Rabbi Debra Orenstein and Rabbi Jane Rachel Litman
V. 1: 6 x 9, 480 pp, Quality PB, ISBN 1-58023-018-0 **$19.95**; HC, ISBN 1-879045-14-1 **$24.95**
V. 2: 6 x 9, 464 pp, Quality PB, ISBN 1-58023-019-9 **$19.95**

ReVisions: *Seeing Torah through a Feminist Lens* AWARD WINNER!
by Rabbi Elyse Goldstein 5½ x 8½, 224 pp, Quality PB, ISBN 1-58023-117-9 **$16.95**;
208 pp, HC, ISBN 1-58023-047-4 **$19.95**

The Year Mom Got Religion: *One Woman's Midlife Journey into Judaism*
by Lee Meyerhoff Hendler 6 x 9, 208 pp, Quality PB, ISBN 1-58023-070-9 **$15.95**

Spirituality & More

The Jewish Lights Spirituality Handbook
A Guide to Understanding, Exploring & Living a Spiritual Life

Ed. by *Stuart M. Matlins, Editor-in-Chief, Jewish Lights Publishing*

Rich, creative material from over 50 spiritual leaders on every aspect of Jewish spirituality today: prayer, meditation, mysticism, study, rituals, special days, the everyday, and more.
6 x 9, 456 pp, Quality PB, ISBN 1-58023-093-8 **$18.95**; HC, ISBN 1-58023-100-4 **$24.95**

Six Jewish Spiritual Paths: *A Rationalist Looks at Spirituality*

by *Rabbi Rifat Sonsino*

The quest for spirituality is universal, but which path to spirituality is right *for you?* A straight-forward, objective discussion of the many ways—each valid and authentic—for seekers to gain a richer spiritual life within Judaism. 6 x 9, 208 pp, HC, ISBN 1-58023-095-4 **$21.95**

Criminal Kabbalah
An Intriguing Anthology of Jewish Mystery & Detective Fiction

Edited by *Lawrence W. Raphael*; Foreword by *Laurie R. King*

Twelve of today's best known mystery authors provide an intriguing collection of new stories sure to enlighten at the same time they entertain.
6 x 9, 256 pp, Quality PB, ISBN 1-58023-109-8 **$16.95**

 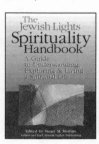 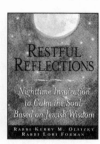 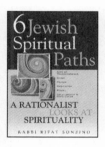 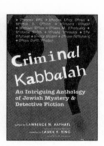

Mystery Midrash: *An Anthology of Jewish Mystery & Detective Fiction*   AWARD WINNER!
Ed. by Lawrence W. Raphael 6 x 9, 304 pp, Quality PB, ISBN 1-58023-055-5 **$16.95**

Sacred Intentions: *Daily Inspiration to Strengthen the Spirit, Based on Jewish Wisdom*
by Rabbi Kerry M. Olitzky & Rabbi Lori Forman
4½ x 6½, 448 pp, Quality PB, ISBN 1-58023-061-X **$15.95**

Restful Reflections: *Nighttime Inspiration to Calm the Soul, Based on Jewish Wisdom*
by Rabbi Kerry M. Olitzky & Rabbi Lori Forman
4½ x 6½, 448 pp, Quality PB, ISBN 1-58023-091-1 **$15.95**

The Enneagram and Kabbalah: *Reading Your Soul*
by Rabbi Howard A. Addison 6 x 9, 176 pp, Quality PB, ISBN 1-58023-001-6 **$15.95**

Embracing the Covenant: *Converts to Judaism Talk About Why & How*
Ed. and with Intros. by Rabbi Allan L. Berkowitz and Patti Moskovitz
6 x 9, 192 pp, Quality PB, ISBN 1-879045-50-8 **$15.95**

Wandering Stars: *An Anthology of Jewish Fantasy & Science Fiction* Ed. by Jack Dann;
Intro. by Isaac Asimov 6 x 9, 272 pp, Quality PB, ISBN 1-58023-005-9 **$16.95**

Israel—A Spiritual Travel Guide AWARD WINNER!
A Companion for the Modern Jewish Pilgrim
by Rabbi Lawrence A. Hoffman 4¾ x 10, 256 pp, Quality PB, ISBN 1-879045-56-7 **$18.95**

Spirituality

My People's Prayer Book: *Traditional Prayers, Modern Commentaries*
Ed. by *Dr. Lawrence A. Hoffman*

Provides a diverse and exciting commentary to the traditional liturgy, helping modern men and women find new wisdom in Jewish prayer, and bring liturgy into their lives. Each book includes Hebrew text, modern translation, and commentaries *from all perspectives* of the Jewish world.

Vol. 1—*The Sh'ma and Its Blessings,* 7 x 10, 168 pp, HC, ISBN 1-879045-79-6 **$23.95**
Vol. 2—*The Amidah,* 7 x 10, 240 pp, HC, ISBN 1-879045-80-X **$23.95**
Vol. 3—*P'sukei D'zimrah* (Morning Psalms), 7 x 10, 240 pp, HC, ISBN 1-879045-81-8 **$24.95**
Vol. 4—*Seder K'riat Hatorah* (The Torah Service), 7 x 10, 264 pp, ISBN 1-879045-82-6 **$23.95**
Vol. 5—*Birkhot Hashachar* (Morning Blessings), 7 x 10, 240 pp, ISBN 1-879045-83-4 **$24.95**

   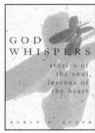 

Becoming a Congregation of Learners
Learning as a Key to Revitalizing Congregational Life by Isa Aron, Ph.D.; Foreword by Rabbi Lawrence A. Hoffman, Co-Developer, Synagogue 2000
6 x 9, 304 pp, Quality PB, ISBN 1-58023-089-X **$19.95**

Self, Struggle & Change
Family Conflict Stories in Genesis and Their Healing Insights for Our Lives by Dr. Norman J. Cohen 6 x 9, 224 pp, Quality PB, ISBN 1-879045-66-4 **$16.95**; HC, ISBN 1-879045-19-2 **$21.95**

Voices from Genesis: *Guiding Us through the Stages of Life*
by Dr. Norman J. Cohen 6 x 9, 192 pp, Quality PB, ISBN 1-58023-118-7 **$16.95**; HC, ISBN 1-879045-75-3 **$21.95**

God Whispers: *Stories of the Soul, Lessons of the Heart*
by Rabbi Karyn D. Kedar 6 x 9, 176 pp, Quality PB, ISBN 1-58023-088-1 **$15.95**

The Business Bible: *10 New Commandments for Bringing Spirituality & Ethical Values into the Workplace*
by Rabbi Wayne Dosick 5½ x 8½, 208 pp, Quality PB, ISBN 1-58023-101-2 **$14.95**

Being God's Partner: *How to Find the Hidden Link Between Spirituality and Your Work*
by Rabbi Jeffrey K. Salkin; Intro. by Norman Lear AWARD WINNER!
6 x 9, 192 pp, Quality PB, ISBN 1-879045-65-6 **$16.95**; HC, ISBN 1-879045-37-0 **$19.95**

God & the Big Bang
Discovering Harmony Between Science & Spirituality AWARD WINNER!
by Daniel C. Matt 6 x 9, 224 pp, Quality PB, ISBN 1-879045-89-3 **$16.95**

Soul Judaism: *Dancing with God into a New Era*
by Rabbi Wayne Dosick 5½ x 8½, 304 pp, Quality PB, ISBN 1-58023-053-9 **$16.95**

Finding Joy: *A Practical Spiritual Guide to Happiness* AWARD WINNER!
by Rabbi Dannel I. Schwartz with Mark Hass
6 x 9, 192 pp, Quality PB, ISBN 1-58023-009-1 **$14.95**; HC, ISBN 1-879045-53-2 **$19.95**

Theology/Philosophy

Love and Terror in the God Encounter: *The Theological Legacy of Rabbi Joseph B. Soloveitchik, Vol. 1* by *Dr. David Hartman*

Renowned scholar David Hartman explores the sometimes surprising intersection of Soloveitchik's rootedness in halakhic tradition with his genuine responsiveness to modern Western theology. An engaging look at one of the most important Jewish thinkers of the twentieth century. 6 x 9, 240 pp, HC, ISBN 1-58023-112-8 **$25.00**

These Are the Words: *A Vocabulary of Jewish Spiritual Life*

by *Arthur Green*

What are the most essential ideas, concepts and terms that an educated person needs to know about Judaism? From *Adonai* (My Lord) to *zekhut* (merit), this enlightening and entertaining journey through Judaism teaches us the 149 core Hebrew words that constitute the basic vocabulary of Jewish spiritual life. 6 x 9, 304 pp, Quality PB, ISBN 1-58023-107-1 **$18.95**

Broken Tablets: *Restoring the Ten Commandments and Ourselves*

Ed. by *Rabbi Rachel S. Mikva*; Intro. by *Rabbi Lawrence Kushner* AWARD WINNER!

Twelve outstanding spiritual leaders each share profound and personal thoughts about these biblical commands and why they have such a special hold on us.
6 x 9, 192 pp, HC, ISBN 1-58023-066-0 **$21.95**

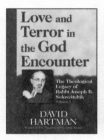  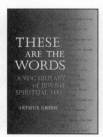  

A Heart of Many Rooms: *Celebrating the Many Voices within Judaism* AWARD WINNER!
by Dr. David Hartman 6 x 9, 352 pp, HC, ISBN 1-58023-048-2 **$24.95**

A Living Covenant: *The Innovative Spirit in Traditional Judaism* AWARD WINNER!
by Dr. David Hartman 6 x 9, 368 pp, Quality PB, ISBN 1-58023-011-3 **$18.95**

Evolving Halakhah: *A Progressive Approach to Traditional Jewish Law*
by Rabbi Dr. Moshe Zemer 6 x 9, 480 pp, HC, ISBN 1-58023-002-4 **$40.00**

The Death of Death: *Resurrection and Immortality in Jewish Thought* AWARD WINNER!
by Dr. Neil Gillman 6 x 9, 336 pp, Quality PB, ISBN 1-58023-081-4 **$18.95**

The Last Trial: *On the Legends and Lore of the Command to Abraham to Offer Isaac as a Sacrifice* by Shalom Spiegel 6 x 9, 208 pp, Quality PB, ISBN 1-879045-29-X **$17.95**

Tormented Master: *The Life and Spiritual Quest of Rabbi Nahman of Bratslav*
by Dr. Arthur Green 6 x 9, 416 pp, Quality PB, ISBN 1-879045-11-7 **$18.95**

The Earth Is the Lord's: *The Inner World of the Jew in Eastern Europe*
by Abraham Joshua Heschel 5½ x 8, 128 pp, Quality PB, ISBN 1-879045-42-7 **$14.95**

A Passion for Truth: *Despair and Hope in Hasidism* by Abraham Joshua Heschel
5½ x 8, 352 pp, Quality PB, ISBN 1-879045-41-9 **$18.95**

Your Word Is Fire: *The Hasidic Masters on Contemplative Prayer* Ed. by Dr. Arthur Green and Dr. Barry W. Holtz 6 x 9, 160 pp, Quality PB, ISBN 1-879045-25-7 **$14.95**

The Way Into... Series

A major 14-volume series to be completed over the next several years, **The Way Into... provides an accessible and usable "guided tour" of the Jewish faith, its people, its history and beliefs—in total, an introduction to Judaism for adults that will enable them to understand and interact with sacred texts.** Each volume is written by a major modern scholar and teacher, and is organized around an important concept of Judaism.

The Way Into... will enable all readers to achieve a real sense of Jewish cultural literacy through guided study. Available volumes include:

 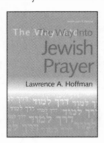 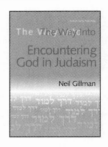 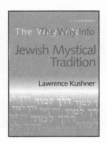

The Way Into Torah

by *Dr. Norman J. Cohen*

What is "Torah"? What are the different approaches to studying Torah? What are the different levels of understanding Torah? For whom is the study intended? Explores the origins and development of Torah, why it should be studied and how to do it.
6 x 9, 176 pp, HC, ISBN 1-58023-028-8 **$21.95**

The Way Into Jewish Prayer

by *Dr. Lawrence A. Hoffman*

Opens the door to 3,000 years of the Jewish way to God by making available all you need to feel at home in Jewish worship. Provides basic definitions of the terms you need to know as well as thoughtful analysis of the depth that lies beneath Jewish prayer.
6 x 9, 224 pp, HC, ISBN 1-58023-027-X **$21.95**

The Way Into Encountering God in Judaism

by *Dr. Neil Gillman*

Explains how Jews have encountered God throughout history—and today—by exploring the many metaphors for God in Jewish tradition. Explores the Jewish tradition's passionate but also conflicting ways of relating to God as Creator, relational partner, and a force in history and nature.
6 x 9, 240 pp, HC, ISBN 1-58023-025-3 **$21.95**

The Way Into Jewish Mystical Tradition

by *Rabbi Lawrence Kushner*

Explains the principles of Jewish mystical thinking, their religious and spiritual significance, and how they relate to our lives. A book that allows us to experience and understand the Jewish mystical approach to our place in the world.
6 x 9, 224 pp, HC, ISBN 1-58023-029-6 **$21.95**

Or phone, fax, mail or e-mail to: **JEWISH LIGHTS Publishing**
Sunset Farm Offices, Route 4 • P.O. Box 237 • Woodstock, Vermont 05091
Tel: (802) 457-4000 • Fax: (802) 457-4004 • www.jewishlights.com
Credit card orders: **(800) 962-4544** (9AM–5PM ET Monday–Friday)
Generous discounts on quantity orders. SATISFACTION GUARANTEED. Prices subject to change.